To Deanna,

American Aria

with best
wishes,

Sherrill
Milnes

American Aria

Encore

∾

Sherrill Milnes

WITH CONTRIBUTIONS BY DENNIS MCGOVERN

AMADEUS
PRESS

AN IMPRINT OF HAL LEONARD CORPORATION
NEW YORK

Unless otherwise noted, all photographs reproduced in this book are from the author's private collection.

Published in 2007 by
Amadeus Press (an imprint of Hal Leonard Corporation)
19 West 21st Street, New York, NY 10010

Printed in the United States of America

Book design by Snow Creative Services

Library of Congress Cataloging-in-Publication Data is available upon request.

ISBN-10: 157-467160-X
ISBN-13: 978-157-467160-5

www.amadeuspress.com

Dedication: In Praise of Teaching

The great majority of singers now studying (and instrumentalists, for that matter) will never have big performing careers. Fortunately, however, their lives will be richer because of their study, as will the lives of those for whom they perform, because music has an intimacy that strikes the heart and bonds people together. Many of these singers and instrumentalists will stop their studies after their final recital at college or university. Once they leave the educational womb, there is often a role reversal, as the former student becomes the teacher and the resource person. The new teacher must then instruct and inspire a new group of students, and the whole process begins all over again. Even if one's job is not specifically teaching, we all teach by example. I believe that the ability and desire to communicate enriches the soul of the giver.

Formal teaching and conducting is certainly what I studied and prepared to do. And I was looking forward to it, not as a fallback in case I didn't have a career, but as my first choice. That attitude and point of view are some of the reasons why I teach and give so many master classes around the world. But the greatest reason is simply that I love it.

A man should hear a little music, read a little poetry, and see a fine picture every day of his life, in order that worldly cares may not obliterate the sense of the beautiful which God has implanted in the human soul.
—Goethe

This book should be required reading for all singers.
—Matthew Epstein

Contents

Foreword

You ARE ABOUT TO READ what took only a few years to conceptualize and write, but a lifetime to create. The meticulous way in which Sherrill writes about his life is the way a quality craftsman builds his own house, brick by brick; every word with careful consideration and every period of his life cared for and communicated with great expression. It's a process that befits him well, because that's how the famous baritone has lived his life. He has conquered all the Verdi baritone roles and virtually every other major tour de force for his voice category. As a singer, teacher, and conductor, he has inspired those with whom he worked and thrilled those for whom he sang, around the globe. One does not say "operatic baritone" without thinking "Sherrill Milnes," the naive midwestern farm boy turned operatic matinee idol. The latter version of this man many have seen on all the major stages of the world. The former version few have known, until now.

The most interesting things happen as you read through the pages of this book. You learn about America and its operatic history while discovering the greatness of other artists that existed in Sherrill's world. You are entertained while you delve into the mind of a singer—his strengths and weaknesses and the inner workings of his subconscious thoughts. He explains how it feels to hit a high on a major operatic stage or to suffer a personal loss while "the show must go on." It's a private journey that lets you in without dramatizing the facts or, as can sometimes happen in operatic biographies, reading as a litany of "and then I sang . . ., and then I sang. . . ."

Like every human drama, this story is filled with love, valor, success, controversy, heartbreak, panic, and hope. It takes you all over the world, makes you laugh and cry, and gives you a real slice of Americana that dates back to the Revolutionary War. It's Norman Rockwell and international jet-setting all rolled into one lifetime.

The most important thing to remember before beginning this story is the humanity of it all. The artist who has lived and written this story reminds us that we are all on an amazing journey, full of beginnings and endings. We never know where we will arrive. As they say, life often happens while you're doing something else, whether it's milking cows on the farm or becoming one of the great singers of the twentieth century. Whatever it is, we never stop being human. We all have amazing stories; these are Sherrill's. The operatic bad guy opens his heart to the world to show who he really is and how he got there. The craftsman and his craft . . . the cows and the curtain calls . . . the American and the aria . . .

Maria Zouves

Acknowledgments

THANKS (in no particular order) to:

All the people mentioned in the book, as well as Arturo Carvallo, Joan Dornemann, Dr. Roger Smyth, Benito Vassura; Herbert Barrett, John Anderson, Alexandra Bacon, Nancy Wellman, Mary Lynn Fixler, and everyone at Barrett Management; Herbert Breslin, Hans Boone, Howard Hartog, David Sigall, Michel Kallipetis, Christopher Lee, Wolfgang Hartl, Wolfgang Stoll, Erich Arthold, Uli Civoj, and John Magro; my devoted Sherrill Milnes Fan Club, founded by Beate Jacobowski and Dorothea Kuehn; Sir John Tooley and others at the Royal Opera House; Robert Gardiner, Edgar Vincent, Cynthia Robbins, Anthony Bliss, Charles Riecker, Orin Brown, William Woodruff, Don Carroll, Alvin Goldfine, Alvin Deutsch, Rona Shays, Dr. Henry Singman, Werner Klemperer, Robert Overman, Jerry Krell, Mike Odze, Orin Brown, Patrick and Claire Shelby, Dieter Peters, Barry Tucker, Roger Hall, Barry Cohen, Ernie Gilbert and Video Arts International, Curtis Page, Jan Holmquist, Violet Peterson, Don and Marianne Recht, Mary Ann Humphreys, Margaret Bollinger, and all the many other hometown friends; and my in-laws, Nick and Angie Zouves, and their whole loving Greek family.

I want to thank my literary agent, Don Gastwirth, without whom there would probably be no book.

I want especially to thank my children for being my children—Eric Knowlton, Erin Michelle, Shawn Edward, and Theophilos Zouves Milnes; my first wife, Charlotte Slack Shnaider; and Nancy Stokes Milnes, who was my supportive wife and partner for twenty-five years and with whom I shared a good part of this story.

There are so many more people who have had a positive influence on my life, I regret I cannot mention them all.

A special thanks and appreciation must go to my wife, Maria, who endured, over the last few years, my often tedious and time-consuming job of writing my life story. Sometimes my obsessive nature about writing and details would try everybody's patience, but with her love, sensitivity, and input, I was able to finish the book and tell my story with our emotions and relationship even stronger.

I would like to include the following letter from a voice student of mine at Northwestern University to whom I gave extra time, work, and TLC, especially at the time of his senior recital. If a teacher receives only one of these in a lifetime or one even close to this, it is reward enough!

Dear Sherrill,

How can I ever thank you for all you've given me? Your support, encouragement, patience, understanding, generosity; your treatment of me as more than a student but a friend. The way you and Maria welcomed me into your home, and I feel, your hearts—the very opening of my throat! The stories, the time, the knowing glances, the handshakes . . . the belief. That itself is an amazing gift. To have someone like you, or rather, you, believe in me. It goes a long way, truly. And then all the extra time and energy you dedicated for the recital! I really could never have asked for anything like it, but you gave it freely. I am forever grateful and, as I told you, in my heart and mind, and hopefully, occasionally in the flesh . . . you will always be my teacher.

Thank you, Sherrill. Those who come after me into your studio don't know yet how lucky they are. But I feel the luckiest of all!

With love and gratitude,
Faithfully, your pupil,
David

Prologue

THE YEAR 1776 IS INDELIBLY STAMPED on the memory of every American: it was the year of the Revolutionary War and the Declaration of Independence, key events in the founding of our country. Yet in that same year, other things were going on all over the world. It was the year the explorer James Cook led his third journey around the world. The German author E. T. A. Hoffmann (the "A" stood for Amadeus)—two of whose works provided the plots for operas—was born; at the same time, a much more famous Amadeus was in Salzburg composing sacred music and other orchestral works. This was some twelve years before he created *Don Giovanni*, which I later sang in that same city and which became a very important opera in my career.

I firmly believe that there are events that are connected in our lives, and though we might not be aware of them at the time they are occurring, they are all linked to who and what we are today.

I am connected to 1776 by my great-great-great-grandfather on my mother's side, Matthew Lyon, who was born in County Wicklow, Ireland, in the late 1740s. His big adventure began when he was about thirteen and stowed away on a ship that brought him to the colonies. Upon arriving here, the ship's captain found that the young stowaway could not pay his passage, so the captain had Master Lyon indentured as a servant for three years in Litchfield, Connecticut. Later he volunteered for Ethan Allen's Green Mountain Boys, and while serving as a lieutenant, he participated in the capture of Fort Ticonderoga, the day the fateful "shot heard round the world" was fired. Part of Lyon's participation in it was recalled by Stewart H. Holbrook in his book *Ethan Allen*:

> By now more than two hundred Americans swarmed in and around
> the fort, and they were joined throughout the day by country folk

An oil painting
of Matthew Lyon,
my great great
great grandfather,
which hangs in
the Vermont state
capitol.

from near-by farms, come to see what was up. Soldiers and farmers
fell downstairs, tumbled off walls, broke jugs, bottles, and windows.
Matthew Lyon, the ebullient Irish-Yankee who later became a national
character, felt that something special was needed to mark the day.
Fetching a bucket of powder from the magazine, he poured it down
the gullet of Old Sow, a thirteen-inch mortar—and let her go. It was
a blast so mighty, legend has it, that the fort fairly rocked.

Lyon was later cashiered out of the service for deserting a post on the
Onion River. He was vindicated and later served as commissary-general
and colonel of the militia. He was deputy secretary in 1778 and became
a clerk in the Court of Confiscation, and he served in the state legislature
in Vermont for four years. During this time he helped draft the constitu-
tion for this new independent and sovereign state.

Matthew Lyon founded the town of Fair Haven, Vermont, in 1783.
He built sawmills, gristmills, and an iron foundry and started the
newspaper called *The Scourge of Aristocracy and Repository of Important
Political Truth*.

Lyon's first wife, Mary Hosford (sometimes written Horsford), Ethan
Allen's favorite niece, died in 1782, leaving an infant daughter, Lorraine.

(This relationship partly explains Lyon's Green Mountain Boys and Revolutionary War involvement, as well as his friendship with Ethan Allen.) The following year, when thirty-three years of age, he married Beulah Chittenden, the daughter of the first governor of Vermont, Thomas Chittenden. Chittenden was elected governor in March 1778 and served for fifteen years in that office. At that time, Vermont was not recognized as a state—it was called the New Hampshire Grants. General George Washington wrote to Chittenden to resolve boundary disputes with New York and New Hampshire. The southern states did not want Vermont admitted, fearing that New England would control Congress. But with the help of General Ethan Allen, it became a state, and Lyon became its first secretary of state. They say that Governor Chittenden could barely write his own name, but that he had uncanny qualities of perception, was very keen, and had a judgment of men and measures that was unerring. He was a large landowner in the Onion River County of Vermont when Matthew Lyon married his daughter.

While reading the recent book *John Adams*, by the Pulitzer Prize–winning author David McCullough, I unexpectedly came across the following:

> [Matthew] Lyon became the U.S. congressman from Vermont (in the new anti-Federalist, Republican Party) and continued to make his own brand of noise. In Europe, French armies had been sweeping across Italy and Austria, in a campaign of French aggrandizement led by young General Napoleon Bonaparte, who appeared invincible. The French had become formidable as never before.
>
> January, 1798, in Congress Hall in Philadelphia, by contrast was marked by a battle royal on the floor of the House. Vicious animosity of a kind previously confined to newspaper attacks broke out in the first physical assault to occur in Congress. In the midst of debate, Federalist Roger Griswold insulted Republican Matthew Lyon of Vermont. Lyon then crossed the chamber and spat on Griswold. Soon after Griswold retaliated with a cane. Lyon grabbed fire tongs from the fireplace, and the two went at each other until, kicking and rolling on the floor, they were pulled apart. To some the scene provided comic relief. To others it was sad testimony to how very far the republican ideal had descended. It was also apt prelude to much that would follow in the country.

That the contest for the presidency in 1800 was to be unlike any of
the three preceding presidential elections was clear at once. For the
first (and last) time in history, the President (John Adams) was running against the Vice President (Thomas Jefferson). The two political
parties had also come into their own with a vitality and vengeance
exceeding anything in the country's experience.

Lyon had been elected to Congress by the new Republican Party on
May 15, 1797, and served until March 3, 1801, during which time the
above physical confrontation took place. In addition, under the newly
passed Alien and Sedition Act, anyone openly criticizing the president
or the government ran the risk of being fined or sent to prison. Matthew
"Spitting" Lyon of Vermont (as he was sometimes called) and eleven
others were charged and convicted under the new law. In the spring
of 1800 Lyon, who had been overtly critical of President John Adams,
spent four months in a foul Vermont jail and was fined $1,000, which
was eventually paid by friends. After his release, he became something
of a national hero and in fact was still a member of Congress, the jail
sentence notwithstanding. Interestingly enough, in 1832 this fine was
repaid to his family by the State of Vermont with interest. Lyon revenged
this perceived wrong done to him by casting the deciding vote that
elected Thomas Jefferson president of the United States, thereby defeat-
ing John Adams.

In a move to leave behind the state and federal governmental problems and certain other events described in the preceding pages, Lyon
and his new bride, Beulah, moved to Eddyville, Kentucky, situated on the
Cumberland River, in what is now known as Lyon County. (It was actually named after Lyon's son, Chittenden, who was six feet six inches tall
and weighed 350 pounds. He, too, became a politician with an impetuous
Irish temper.) Matthew and Beulah had several children and the youngest, Elizabeth Ann Lyon, in later life wrote a book, *Recollections of a
Frontier Life*. It was published in 1885, two years before her death. I have

a copy of the book in which she describes life and its extreme hardships in the nineteenth century.

From his home in Kentucky, Matthew Lyon lost much of his money in an effort to build ships for the U.S. government during the War of 1812, at which time he was supported by his children. In 1820 President James Monroe, having learned of Lyon's financial plight, appointed him United States Factor to the Cherokee Nation in the Arkansas Territory. He became a candidate for the Arkansas Territory's delegate to Congress. He was defeated by sixty-one votes. Then in his seventy-third year, the six-foot-two-inch Lyon took a 3,000-mile round trip down the Mississippi to New Orleans with a large flatboat loaded with Indian commodities, furs, and the like. He successfully exchanged his cargo for trade goods, storekeepers' supplies, ironware, and machinery for a large cotton gin he then had under construction. He returned to Spadra Bluff, Arkansas, his home there, and died on August 1, 1822 at age seventy-six. He was buried there, but in 1833 his sons and old Eddyville friends disinterred his body and brought it back to Eddyville. His final resting place is in the old graveyard close to his sweet young daughter, Lorraine, his baby by his first wife and the cherished great-niece of Ethan Allen. The graveyard is near to the dark waters of Barkley Lake, Kentucky.

In 1827 Matthew's daughter, Elizabeth Ann Lyon, after marrying Dr. John Roe when she was sixteen years of age, moved to Illinois, north of Springfield. Dr. Roe continued his practice and study of medicine in that area. They had several children, one of whom was a son, Franklin Morris Roe, who became a physician in Downers Grove, Illinois. He married Mary Ann Ketcham, and they had several children. One of these was Charles Ketcham Roe, born September 19, 1858. He was my grandfather, the father of Marion Thelma Roe, my mother, who married my father, James Knowlton Milnes, on August 2, 1928. (All of this comes to me from a variety of sources: Scribner's *Dictionary of American Biography*, my mother, various Web sites that mention Matthew Lyon, and my own memories.)

Charles K. Roe embodied the spirit and energy of Matthew Lyon, albeit on a much smaller scale and in a more loving manner. As a community leader, he affected and inspired people around him with his love of singing, positive attitude, and love of the Gospel. It's amazing to me that I knew and spent time with someone who was alive during our Civil War, and that it was my grandfather.

Charlie Roe was a deeply religious man and a fine amateur singer. He was educated at Naperville College and Jennings Seminary in Aurora, Illinois. Dr. Duane E. Chapman of the Community Methodist Church of Westmont, Illinois, was a former student pastor who knew my grandfather in the late 1920s. He described Charlie Roe's love of music and singing in a letter to me:

> Mr. Roe was the song leader at the Community Methodist Church and his daughter, Thelma, (my mother) was the organist. He led the singing both at Sunday school and the Church services. Charlie was a large man, fairly tall with an unusually deep and heavy chest. When he got happy during the Song service his volume was as great as his distinguished grandson's—and the quality was excellent—a deep, rich baritone. Singing was a part of Mr. Roe's Christian witness.

Grandfather Charles Ketchum Roe, 1940, the year before he died.

Charlie Roe loved every church regardless of denomination and even though he was never wealthy, he gave substantial amounts to his own mission church in Westmont, next to Downers Grove. In addition, during the Depression, he and a friend, Irving Heartt, borrowed money to keep the neighboring Downers Grove Methodist Church out of bankruptcy. My grandfather's part of that loan came from a big mortgage on the two small farms he owned. When he died in 1941, our family moved to the smaller of those farms and over the years that mortgage was slowly paid back by my parents.

Charlie Roe had been the township road commissioner in the 1920s and 1930s, and I rode with him many times in my early years as he drove around the township in his 1925 Model T Ford. I remember him well, with his full mane of white hair and white mustache.

Music and a sense of adventure are definitely in my genes: from my third great grandfather, to my grandfather, to my mother, to me. In my own life, there have been personal trials, operatic successes, and formidable people, all of which have had a permanent effect on me. Whether

Dad and Mom with Roe (standing) and me, 1937.

it was record-breaking applause in Vienna, or career-threatening surgery, sets falling down around me in a performance, being kicked out of school, losing my mother to cancer, or the emotions of my unwilling last performance at the Met, all these experiences are part of me.

However, one should always start from the beginning, and my life started with my parents, Marion Thelma Roe Milnes (she used her middle name) and James Knowlton Milnes; my brother, Roe Knowlton Milnes; and me, Sherrill Eustace Milnes—an *atypical* American farm couple and their two farm kids.

American Aria

CHAPTER ONE

Roots on the Farm

FRANKLIN DELANO ROOSEVELT WAS in the middle of his New Deal in 1935, the year I was born. Business wasn't booming, but things were getting better: the country was getting back on its feet after the crash of 1929. Chicago won the National League title in baseball even though they went on to lose the World Series to Detroit. The first Howard Johnson's opened; Ma Barker, Dutch Schultz, and Huey Long were all assassinated; and an American hero, Will Rogers, died in a plane crash.

My brother, Roe, who is three and a half years older, and I were raised in the shadow of the Great Depression. Downers Grove is a suburb thirty miles west of Chicago. We lived on a small dairy farm just outside of that town for some twenty-five years. This was not really farm country, so Roe and I, and perhaps two others, were the only farm kids in a school of about twelve hundred. Because this was real suburbia, my brother and I were thought a little strange. The other kids asked in disbelief: "You milk cows?" "You like classical and sacred music?" Boys who milked cows, shoveled manure, sang in church choir (even if your mother was the conductor)—well, jocks didn't do that. Although I did play freshman football and ran cross-country as a sophomore, I was still a farm boy, with my work and chores devoted to the land.

Our farm was small and, especially by today's standards, quite primitive. From age six, when we moved to the farm, until I was ten, we had no indoor plumbing, only an outhouse, a "one-holer," about seventy-five feet from the house. Come rain, shine, or freezing sleet and snow, when nature called, you traveled. I came to know the Sears, Roebuck and the

Montgomery Ward ("Monkey Ward," as it was called by midwesterners) catalogs very well—thanks to a big shortage of toilet paper!

We also had no central heating. We had a potbellied stove in the middle of the living room with a vent in the floor for the upstairs, where we all slept. It was never able to make things warm enough in the winter. Getting into bed with cold, cold sheets in a cold, cold room was not my favorite sport. I'll never forget when our first furnace and its ductwork were put in by my father and his lifelong friend, John Clifton, who was an engineer by profession as well as a jack of all trades. Finally we had heat all over the house—what a concept, what a luxury! The furnace still had to be filled with coal by hand, which we'd haul in our old 1937 Dodge truck. Every night we would stoke the furnace, which meant banking the coal in a circle so the fire wouldn't go out. We finally got a coal bin with an auger, a mechanism that checked the furnace's thermostat and fed the coal automatically.

My mother, a trained musician, made bread, butter, and cottage cheese for the family, and she sold eggs for ten cents a dozen to the neighbors. Ten cents—remember this was the 1940s. Selling meat to the slaughterhouse and milk to the dairy was our main form of income. During that time, my father later told me, he never paid any income tax at all, because he never made any profit—just enough to slowly pay down my grandfather's leftover mortgage.

Sometimes I milked our twenty cows twice a day before and after school, but usually my dad did the milking in the morning so that Roe and I could more easily go to school. If you had a cold or the flu or your back hurt, you couldn't cancel your chores: the cows wouldn't wait. I suppose that's where I first developed a work ethic in general. Also, running cross-country in high school taught me some things about pain, concentration, and hanging in. Even though the course was just two miles, I thought that was almost impossible to complete. I remember during the last several laps looking down at the grass and thinking how wonderful it would be just to lie down for a moment. My lungs burned and my legs ached and it took all my guts to keep going. I look back on competing in high school and working on the farm and realize I needed the same physical endurance and determination that is necessary for *Rigoletto* or *Falstaff.* The demands it puts on your body and the need to keep going versus the desire to "lie down in the grass" are still part of my work ethic.

When you are milking, one of the most painful sensations you can feel is being hit right across the face by a sudden swish of a cow's tail. The end of the tail, catching you with your eyes open, without giving you time to react, hurts so much that you want to kill the cow—or at least beat on her. Sometimes the cow would also kick at you, and if her hoof was in the gutter with all the manure, it would shower you with that manure. I loved that job!

When we switched to milking machines, the whole process became more complicated. First you had to wash the cow's udders with a chlorine solution and then put on one machine cup for each teat. When the udder was empty, you had to remove the machine quickly or the cups could fall off and the milk would spill in the gutter and be lost. Then you had to strip by hand the remaining milk, which was the creamiest. When each thirty-two-gallon can was full, you had to carry it to the milk house and place it in a cold-water tank to cool. As a result you were always on the run to stay ahead of the machines—and this had to be done twice a day.

With my 4-H prize–winning heifer, Rosie, 1948.

In high school, after I started to study voice, I did more vocalizing and singing in the barn than I did in the house. It seemed a good use of the time and I felt alone and uninhibited with no one around to hear what I considered my vocal squawking. Friends used to make jokes about my singing and its effect on the cow's ability to give more (or less) milk.

I was a member of a 4-H club, and my major project was a purebred Holstein calf whose registered name was Florem Rosalie. In 1948 she won first place in the DuPage County Fair as best heifer in the county. I grew to love her. I even slept with her during the birth of her three calves and helped to deliver them.

As years went on, it became increasingly difficult to maintain a small dairy farm, and we were always small, never milking more than twenty cows. The local dairies were reluctant to pick up our few cans of milk every day, preferring to patronize the large farms. Also, there evolved increasingly strict regulations over cleanliness, storage, and milk temperatures that made sophisticated and expensive equipment necessary. We finally had to give up the dairy.

My parents decided to switch to beef by breeding our dairy herd to a series of Angus bulls and gradually raising beef cattle and selling packaged frozen beef either in quarters or halves. My father and a friend who was a butcher processed, froze, and sold the meat.

Most of our breeding bulls were not aggressive, but I learned that any bull deserves respect—and more than a little distance. Their strength is enormous, and if they decide to use it, they can be very dangerous. Their heads are as hard as rocks. I remember one day watching one of our bulls nosing around behind a big Holstein cow who was either startled or didn't welcome his advances. She kicked him right in the middle of the head with a mighty blow, and he just blinked and looked back at her with a curious expression.

One of our Angus bulls was more dominant and mean than the others. We always showed caution and gave him a wide berth. One summer a calf had been born in the fields and my father went out to pick it up and carry it back to the barn. I tagged along with him but did not go over the fence into the field. The bull was curious about his offspring and was trailing along behind. As my father got close to the calf, the bull began to snort and paw the earth. Dad started to pick up the calf, and the bull lowered his head and charged. To my ten-year-old mind, this was as scary as any bullfight scene in pictures or movies. I yelled with all my might, but the bull kept charging. My dad dropped the calf, ran for the fence, and rolled under it. The bull was right behind him and caught my dad's right foot with his head and drove it into the dirt. It could have smashed his foot totally, but fortunately, it had been raining earlier that day, and the earth was soft. So his foot was just pushed into the mud. My dad finished his escape pulling his injured foot behind him. The bull just stood there showing his frustration and anger by snorting, pawing the earth, and throwing his head around in defiance.

The irony of this is that the fence was just barbed-wire strands, so the bull could easily have pushed his way through it and really hurt my father. But he was used to stopping at fences and did just that. My dad's ankle was swollen and sprained a little, but there was no major damage, and he was able to go about the rest of the day's chores with only a slight limp. We left the calf there in the field until the bull returned to the barn, then went back and gathered up the calf as quickly as possible. After that little adventure, for the rest of my life I treated any bull of any size or age with great respect. There certainly was something there for every Iago to learn about dealing with an Otello gone mad.

In addition to cattle, we always had a few workhorses, just plugs, nothing fancy. Slowly we added some riding horses, and a stable developed. Soon my father and brother started giving riding lessons for children, adults, and private groups. Cub Scouts, Boy Scouts, and Girl Scouts could earn a badge in riding, or in the grooming and care of horses. Everyone used the three-mile perimeter of the farm as the trails on which they rode. At the peak in the 1960s, we had more than forty horses.

Once in a while, the horses would get out and run wild for miles. Our whole family would be out on foot, in cars, and on other horses, trying to round them up. When I tell friends about this I know they picture a John Wayne movie in the old West, with us armed with ropes and lassos racing after herds of horses. But this was suburbia, with houses, grass, and lawns in neighborhoods, not open country. We really went crazy trying to round up the horses and put them back in the barn. Sometimes it took all day. Over the years, there was more than one lawsuit, as well as angry neighbors, due to trampled flowers, gardens, lawns, and broken fences. Sometimes I loved living on a farm and sometimes I hated it.

Every Saturday and Sunday masses of kids arrived at the farm, all wanting to learn to ride, and all of them saying they knew how to ride better than they actually did. This often led to a variety of accidents, most of them minor, like bouncing off the horse or becoming afraid and crying. Once in a while there would be a cut or a bruise that required a doctor or a hospital visit. My father always paid the bills for any treatment without question to reduce the possibility of a lawsuit. We had no accident insurance—the cost was so prohibitive we could not have stayed in business.

Of course my father, my brother, and the trail guards who accompanied every rider employed their own safety measures, as well as taking with a grain of salt the rider's assessment of his or her own horsemanship skills. Usually a gentle, slow horse was given to the beginners. Only those with proven riding skills could try a faster horse.

The addition of these faster horses led to some mischievous pranks. There was a major road near the farm with a ditch that ran alongside it and a small rise of earth behind. Roe and I would ride there with some neighbor boys at Halloween. It was easy to hide the horses behind the small hill and crawl close to the road. Then we would wait for a car or truck to come and would throw some lighted firecrackers in front of it and watch the reaction. Usually the drivers would slam on their brakes and then, if nothing else happened, go on their way. If there were some guys in the car, they would often get out, ready to fight whoever was responsible. Then we would jump on the horses and gallop off. At other times we would throw live firecrackers into rural mailboxes and blow the doors off. I believe that is a federal offense.

Another dumb thing we did in the early years was to shoot at a neighbor's barn a half mile away while out hunting pheasants or rabbits. Of course, we never thought about the serious consequences of hitting the farmer or one of the animals. We were a bunch of kids doing stupid things, and I was in the middle of it. In hindsight, what we did was very foolish, but it was great fun.

As part of the stables activities, we provided hayrack rides with tractors or horses, outdoor wiener roasts, and square dances and parties in the haylofts. On weekend evenings as many as 200 people would come to the farm for hayrack rides. Then we would use all of our eight hayracks and two tractors and the team of horses. We would need the whole family to drive the various rides and organize the wiener roasts and the dances in the hayloft. Even a detail like parking all the cars so they would fit on the farm property took all the family's cooperation and planning.

Many years later, I went home to Downers Grove the day after a very successful Met performance of *Rigoletto*: curtain calls, huge bravos, all the excitement of being an opera star. That next night on the farm, I was helping out by driving a tractor for one of a group of hayrack rides. Near the end of the ride, the people started yelling: "Hey! Hey you, Mr. Driver! How long is this ride? When do we get back?"—a normal situation on a hayrack ride. I guess you could say that for many years, my life was "Bravo!" and applause one night and "Hey, Mr. Driver! When is it over?" the next.

The farm figured in my career in more than one way. When I first started to study opera roles, I found that different kinds of laughs were needed to portray different kinds of characters. There are Iago laughs of a demonic and evil nature; Don Giovanni laughs of sexuality and fulfillment; Hamlet laughs of instability and moral confusion; Scarpia laughs of power and sadistic enjoyment.

I would often practice these laughs while plowing the fields with our old Allis Chalmers tractor. With the roar of the tractor motor it was even better than singing in the shower or—as I found out some years later in New York—singing in the subway. You really feel off in your own world, totally uninhibited. So there I was doing a bunch of different characters and their laughing styles, with facial expressions to match, feeling completely isolated and free. After some time I looked up, and on the road that ran parallel to the field was a parked car with four heads popping out of it, staring at a crazy man driving around on a tractor, laughing uncontrollably. They soon drove off, so I could be mortified all by myself. It was a long while before I practiced on the tractor again.

In those years, as many farmers did, we castrated all the male pigs and bull calves ourselves. My brother and I would hold them down and my father would do the operation, using gasoline for a disinfectant. I'm not sure why we used gasoline except that it had done the job for many years, and even with gas rationing during the war, we had a lot of it because of the necessity of farm work and tractors. One morning after castrating six or eight bull calves the day before, my father came into the house and very seriously said, "We have to go out to the barn." We all did, and there were all the castrated bull calves lying dead. We found out later they died of lead poisoning. I will always remember the sight of these 150- to 200-pound animals, bigger than any huge dog you have seen, lying dead on the floor of the barn. I was nine. Although I was scared as well as fascinated by the sight of these dead animals, it never occurred to me that this was a financial disaster for the family and a huge worry for my parents. Kids, of course, never think about the money problems of the family.

We also had pigs and I suppose over the years I must have seen a thousand of them being born, as well as dozens and dozens of calves. I never cared much for pigs and am amazed at how many people own them now and treat them as house pets. I always thought they were dumb and dirty, and except for the bacon, I didn't have much use for them. But my parents knew that they were a good income source and went together with cattle, so we had over a hundred of them. Farrowing or birthing time was not terribly pretty: there were little blobs of bodies covered with afterbirth all over the place. Then we had to put two-by-fours on edge around the perimeter of the pens, about half a foot high, spaced so that there was enough room for the piglets to avoid being squashed or suffocated against the wall when the sows lay down. Some sows are actually so big and fat that by the time they realize they're lying on their piglets and move, the babies are dead. Now that's basically not very bright.

From time to time, the pigs would escape from their pens and we'd have to chase them back. Tommy, our bull terrier of many years, was a perfect pet: short-haired, no mess indoors, very loving, and equally at home inside or outside. But he was ferocious with animals, especially when they were out of their pens. He would help us round them up. One time, an escaped sow he was chasing back to the pen turned angrily and, with a loud snort, caught Tommy's head in her jaws and cracked it like a wooden box. Anyone who knows pigs knows the enormous power in their jaws. I wanted to shoot her, and I'm sure I kicked at her repeatedly to ease my youthful anger and frustration. I was heartbroken and hated pigs even more. We mourned Tommy for a long time. Many other pet dogs followed him, but none was more loved.

As a kid I had a lot of excitement during silo-filling time in the fall. Guys would come in with several huge machines: the field chopper, wagons, tractors, and the blower. The chopper would make silage out of the green corn in the field by grinding the whole stalks of corn, and the blower would then force it up a round tube about fifty feet in the air into the silo. The noise and the action for a kid of school age were pretty exciting, and I'd hurry home from school each day to help out. That was one time of the year I really enjoyed being on the farm.

However, many jobs I disliked. Every summer we made hay by mowing it, raking it in rows, and, when it was dry, baling it. Baling was the dirtiest job. Each stroke of the plunger of our old two-man Case baler would blow dust in your face. Allergies didn't matter. You'd come off that baler after a day of the hot sun beating down and you'd be covered with dust, hay, weeds, and dirt. With the sweat all over your body, it was as though you had covered yourself with tar.

In any given summer we would bale as many as 5,000 bales, each one weighing forty to sixty pounds. Then we would have to lift and stack them all in the hayloft. For many years, Roe, Dad, and I did it ourselves, but sometimes we'd hire friends to help (for a penny or so a bale). I'm sure that some of those young men worked harder than they had ever worked in their whole lives, especially when you consider that this was a Chicago suburb and most of their fathers were white-collar workers. Some of them have remained our friends to this day, but after all those bales of hay, I'm not quite sure why.

Even with all the hard work, however, for me there was always something attractive and exciting about the power of these machines, plus the internal satisfaction of accomplishing work by your own labor. *And I never had a problem sleeping.*

My Dad, the Hardworking Farmer

The old-fashioned farmer had to set his sights and then just go ahead with the work. I don't think it would be unfair to say that traditionally

Dad riding his horse, General, in a Fourth of July parade in Downers Grove, c. 1958.

speaking, most farmers aren't very artistic. They don't have big emotional highs and lows. Well, my dad had them just like my mother, who was a musician. She always had her music to express her emotions and to rely on. My dad wasn't in the performing arts, although as an untrained singer, he loved to sing in the church choir and the oratorio society. He had only the farm, and I realize that sometimes it was very hard on him. Oh, he learned how to shut off all his psychological needs and just plow through. That in itself was a great gift and accomplishment. If he needed to work the fields for sixteen hours, that's what he did. If he had to keep that tractor going for all those hours because he had eighty acres to plow, he did it because there was no other choice.

Because my dad hadn't been brought up on a farm and had studied to spend his adult life as a minister—as had his father before him—all of this work was new to him. Working on motors and fixing machinery did not come easily. He had to learn all the little commonsense, practical things after the fact. We didn't have the time or money to go the hardware store or the repair shop every time we needed something; we just had to make do. Unfortunately things that were homemade tended to break down sooner, so it seemed the repairs just went on and on. We'd fix something and then a few days later have to fix it again. He was constantly flooded with work, and it must have been incredibly frustrating for him. Looking back, I know that my dad had to shut off a section of his mind to keep from yelling, "I hate it. I just hate it."

The four of us all shared two things as a family. One of them was work, hard work. It's strange, but our dairy farm seemed to have its own unique environment. The bottom line was that the cows all had to be milked

Thelma Roe Milnes conducting, c. 1958.

twice a day, plus the work in the fields—whether we were ready or not, healthy or sick. The world centered on the barn, the fields, and then our little sanctuary, the house.

My mother and music were the second constant elements that bound us together. All year long, every year, my mom had Thursday night church choir rehearsals and Sunday morning services at the First Congregational Church of Downers Grove. In addition, there were the holiday seasons: the extra concerts of *Messiah* or other great oratorios, as well as all the other holiday music. The church is where music became an integral part of my life.

Oddly enough, in my early years my brother, Roe, was the singer. His voice showed itself much more naturally and quickly than mine, and he was encouraged by everyone to study. The three of us—Mom, Roe, and I—would perform many local concerts; Roe would sing some solos, and I would play the "Meditation" from the opera *Thaïs* or some other solo on the violin and sing duets with Roe. Mama would play piano for all of us, including accompanying her own solos. She was a fine soprano with

Roe, *left*, and I sing with Mom, 1951.

a rich warm, sound. My voice was not very developed, and at the time no one thought I was much of a singer. It didn't really grow into a career voice until much later. Although Roe didn't pursue a career, he is still fondly remembered by residents of Downers Grove who attended public school there as the singing bus driver. He drove school and charter buses for many years and would sing to the kids and get them to sing as well.

The Milneses and the Roes had a large extended family. Particularly important in my growing up were the "spinster" aunts, we all called the three older women, related on my mother's side, who lived together. When I was young, our family would have Thanksgiving and other holiday dinners at their house. They always seemed as old as the hills, but I suppose to a grade-schooler all older aunts seem old as the hills. After my career began and I was making recordings, they always wanted me to sing for them. Whenever I would sing in my hometown church, they would always come. They had no record player of any sort with which to listen to me, so I bought them one. One must realize that these women had been born sometime in the 1880s or 1890s and didn't understand any of the principles of sound reproduction. It took some time to teach them how to operate the machine, but once they learned, they somehow thought that every time they played one of my records, I was somewhere singing live and they could hear it in their home. I decided there was no reason to try to explain exactly how it worked. It was lovely that they thought I was always singing personally to them.

CHAPTER TWO

Growing Up in Downers Grove

DURING MY ELEMENTARY SCHOOL YEARS, if we'd lived on the south side instead of the north side of Seventy-fifth Street in Downers Grove, I probably wouldn't be writing this book. I'm sure I wouldn't have had a career about which to write. Seventy-fifth Street was the township boundary line; the south side of the street belonged to the county. Those kids went to a one-room country schoolhouse, with grades one through eight all taught together and, clearly, no music of any kind—not unlike the world depicted in *Little House on the Prairie*. Fortunately, we lived on the north side of the street, which was the southern limit of the Downers Grove Township. It was, at that time, one of the best school systems in the country.

In second grade, with my mother's urging, I started studying piano. I was not a good practicer. I was lucky, however, that Mama was a trained musician. For most of my school years she directed the choirs at the First Congregational Church of Downers Grove, where I grew up musically and spiritually. She taught piano at home, so I heard thousands of piano lessons over the years. Her main goal as a teacher was to engage and interest children in music, not so much to develop concert pianists. She nourished their musical feelings, so naturally those same feelings were always abundant in our house. My own first piano lessons were with her, but that didn't work; lessons from a parent almost always degenerate into discussions of family matters, so you seldom actually work on the music.

My mother suggested I study with Marion Lower, a friend of hers and the organist at the First Methodist Church in Downers Grove, the same church that my grandfather had helped save during the Depression. I continued piano study into high school, but my talent didn't lie there, so I stopped private work. However, the skills that I acquired then, plus mandatory college piano study, have served me over and over again in my career. I'm only sorry I don't play better now. Even so, I did most of my own study of roles and songs at the keyboard.

In those years, my mother used every scare tactic in the book to make me practice, because, like any normal kid, I was loath to do so. I'd work just a bit the day before a lesson to avoid total embarrassment, and that was it. I still think, perhaps facetiously, that one of the key motivations for a child practicing seriously is fear of embarrassment in front of the teacher. However, a few of my instrumentalist friends claim they loved to practice when they were young.

I went to a grade school where there was, as part of the curriculum, an orchestra, a choir, and a band. There was a new teacher for the grade-school orchestra, named Margaret Thompson, who encouraged me to take private lessons on the violin as well as play in the orchestra. For all my years in grade school, I was last chair second violin, and that's as low as you go; the chair below that is out in the hall. The new director was a fine violinist and an inspiring teacher. I think I had a slight crush on her, inasmuch as a grade-schooler can have a crush. Margaret and her husband, Rob Thompson, a well-known actor and acting teacher in the area, have been mainstays of the community artistically for half a century. Margaret and my mother were good friends, and Margaret was the leader of the church *Messiah* orchestra under my mother's direction. Later, when the Downers Grove Oratorio Society (now the Downers Grove Choral Society) was formed, she gave full support by helping to organize and lead the orchestra.

She nursed me along on the violin through the squeak-and-squawk years. Little by little my fear-of-embarrassment practicing paid off, and I slowly moved up from last chair. I suppose my little crush inspired me as well. Encouraged, I practiced more, so that by my senior year in high school I was concertmaster. I was a good leader of the section and had a full, rich sound and good intonation but lacked some technical speed and dexterity. However, my love of the orchestral sonority and sweep inspired me to play in one orchestra or another for seventeen years, from early grade school through my master's degree at Drake University.

Twice a year in grade school, the whole orchestra would go to a matinee performance of the Chicago Symphony in downtown Chicago. I loved it for the bus ride with my friends, getting the day off from school, making paper airplanes out of the programs, being noisy in general—all the regular kid things. Obviously, though, while I was just being a kid, something was speaking to me that would express itself later in my life. I never went away from those concerts thinking, "Oh, that was the greatest thing I ever heard!" But neither did I go away thinking, "Boy, was that a drag, who cares about classical music!" Kids don't usually express profound feelings for the fine arts; it's a rare child who sees or hears a work of art and says "awesome." But if they don't hate it, it is having an effect.

I don't know exactly when or how I learned to sight-read and to sing harmony. Obviously it had a lot to do with the fact that I started studying piano and violin early on, so I learned to sight-read without specifically studying sight-reading; it became second nature. I only remember that I was always good at it and automatically loved to sing harmony parts.

Grade school orchestra, with conductor Margaret Thompson. I am at far right, second row, c. 1947.

In seventh grade at Lincoln School during the Christmas program, I was singing a bass part in "The First Noel" and someone in front of me turned around and said loudly, "That's not the way it goes! What are you singing?" I was mortified and embarrassed to death. I thought I was singing a harmony part, but I wasn't sure they were wrong, so I assumed I was. At that point I didn't understand about the structure of harmony and chords, so I wasn't at all sure what I was singing. I just knew that it sounded good to my ear. I'm a very sensitive person, and while that's a sine qua non for a performer and can be a great strength, it can also sometimes be a weakness. For instance, I don't get angry easily, but when I do, it costs me a lot of bile, a lot of worry, a lot of stomach burn. If I lash out verbally in anger, I analyze the situation for days, wondering if I've done the right thing and chastising myself for possible improper behavior toward another.

I loved singing in the children's choir of the Congregational Church. We usually sang once a month in the service, and I looked forward to that Sunday. I was thrilled when, some years later in the eighth grade, while my voice was in the process of changing, my mother invited me into the adult choir. I sang as sort of a nasal tenor for two years and after that I settled down into a baritone.

The organist for all the services at church was a cousin of ours, Donald Drew. He was a superb service organist and composer and was a constant a source of inspiration for me. Several of his compositions were sung frequently, and I especially love his solo setting of "Bless the Lord, O My Soul," which I have sung on the *Hour of Power* Sunday morning television program from the Crystal Cathedral.

As a sophomore in high school, when my voice had finally settled down, my mother encouraged me to study privately. By this time we had learned our lesson that studying with a parent doesn't work. My mother's good friend Marilyn Bowers, a mezzo-soprano and a soloist at the church, was willing to teach me, and for the first time I worked on my voice as an instrument, with vocalizing and scales. I was lucky that Marilyn had studied with Hermanus Baer of Northwestern University, with whom I later studied. In fact, all my vocal training, though it was from various teachers, followed the same broad vocal technique lines.

I didn't think my voice was very pretty, and as a matter of fact I was right. But some wee small voice inside me said that regular study with a teacher was the way to improve, to find out how much I could grow, how good I could become. I guess this same small voice said to me that to find out what gifts I had, what heredity of music I had in me, it was necessary to study. Even though the vocalizing and scales were a real drag and rather boring, I worked hard on the music and the various pieces I was assigned, especially when I had to sing solos in the church services or other performances.

I was always very nervous in front of an audience and very much preferred to sing in choirs. I never felt I interpreted the music very well in solos and basically didn't like my sound. I was quite inhibited and certainly was not the hot vocal talent or the best singer in high school or in early college. I was, however, a good musician and played many different instruments. But when you're singing, the audience only cares if they like the sound and beauty of your voice, not how many instruments you play.

In fact, I remember many years later, as a graduate student, hearing some recordings of my voice, and only then thinking that the sound wasn't too bad. It is no wonder that contemplating a singing career was never a dream of mine. The phrase "to sing at the Met," for instance, simply did not exist in my vocabulary. Nor did I know what a career meant in terms of traveling, the amount of learning necessary, the amount of music needed to sustain a career, and a multitude of other factors that go into creating a professional singer.

My love of the choral sound and of choral singing has never diminished, however. In the 1970s, 1980s, and 1990s in New York, when I conducted Martin Josman's National Choral Council's annual *Messiah* sing-in at Avery Fisher Hall or at the Riverside Church *Messiah* sing-along, I couldn't wait to join in the choruses.

As I mentioned before, I was very lucky to attend public schools in Downers Grove. In the high school curriculum, for instance, I had band, orchestra, and a cappella choir every day—very unusual for any town. That meant that in seven periods in the school day, I had three music classes and four academic subjects—and I loved it. When I was a freshman, William G. Pohlman, the choral director, invited John Shoemaker—my close friend and the son of the high school band director—and me to join the elite a cappella choir. Mr. Pohlman never used a piano with which to rehearse or perform. He gave us our notes with a pitch pipe and just expected us to sight-read.

My first a cappella choir concert was on a Monday noon in March of 1949 for a Kiwanis club meeting. I was very excited to sing in this concert, and John and I planned to drive to it in my parents' 1946 Ford coupe. On the way we took a shortcut through a wooded area called Denburn Woods. We were going too fast around a corner and skidded off the gravel road into a ditch. As a result, we sweated for an hour trying to get the car out and missed the concert completely. The next day we sheepishly showed up for choir rehearsal and explained what had happened. The director was furious with us, but we were not expelled, and for that we were very grateful.

This choir was the level of most college choirs and laid the foundation for many years of choral singing. It sharpened my sight-singing and introduced me to other repertoires that I had not sung with my mother in church. This experience helped me in later years to be a professional choral "ringer" all around Chicago. (A ringer is a professional singer who fills out any choir that is short of certain voice categories, for any given concert.) It also helped me set up my eventual membership in the Chicago Symphony Chorus, which had a huge influence on my musical life.

After studying violin with Margaret Thompson in grade school, I played under John Svoboda, who had just joined the high school faculty. A Northwestern University graduate and a fine violinist, as well as a good conductor, he was a big inspiration to me. He also allowed me to play on one of his two violins, which was light years better than my own poor instrument. It was in these years that Roe, Mother, and I performed our programs together and I first tasted the "Meditation" from *Thaïs*. I grew to love it and—of course—had no idea of the later importance of that opera in my career. But I did become rather spoiled by the beautiful tone of John Svoboda's violin. When I later went to Drake University and played in the Des Moines Symphony, I had to use my old cheap fiddle, and the sound was just not the same.

As concertmaster of the Downers Grove high school orchestra. John Svoboda is the conductor; John Shoemaker (Shoe) is on trombone; and Charlotte Slack, who became my first wife, is first cellist.

John Svoboda also showed me a quick way to read the alto clef, and with that I learned to play viola almost in a day. My hands were big and my fingers thick, so I fit the viola very well. I was a better musician than the first-chair viola player and was asked to play viola in string quartets. Mr. Svoboda also showed me how to play jazz bass, and with my good sense of harmony I was quickly able to earn money all through high school and college by playing dance jobs. That also led to crooning with bands, which for me was a total change of style and sound. But I enjoyed it very much, and it served me later in radio and television voice-overs. My teachers always instilled in me a desire to make beautiful music, whether in a group or as soloist, never thinking, "Boy, am I great!," but "Boy, what great music we are making." I just loved being a part of that big, beautiful sonority—music.

When I was a junior in high school, Clarence Shoemaker (the band director and father of my lifelong friend John) asked me if I would have any interest in learning to play the tuba. He would teach me over the summer, since the only tuba (really sousaphone) player was graduating and leaving. I thought it would be exciting, so I took a lesson every day in between chores on the farm. The following fall I joined the concert band and played in all the concerts as well as in the state music contest. It was quite exciting to be the harmonic foundation for the whole band.

We lived three and a half miles from high school, and there were no buses. We had to hitchhike, walk, or be driven each day. I remember more than once in severe winters riding a horse to school or occasionally my dad driving my brother and me on our big Allis Chalmers tractor when the snow was too deep for any other vehicle.

In December of 1951 on the day before the school Christmas program, there was a terrible storm, feet and feet of snow. I was going to be very busy the next day—solo and choruses with the a cappella choir, first tuba in the band, concertmaster of the orchestra, with each group performing several pieces—lots of responsibility; and no matter what, I had to be there.

On the morning of the concert, I woke up and it was still storming. The snow was already so high, I knew no cars or trucks were going to make it through. The only way to get there was to plow through the snow, sinking to my knees with every step until I got close to town, where it was a little better. I wore a sweater, a heavy coat, a scarf, and gloves. I put my dress shoes in my pocket, put on big leather boots with thick soles, and started to trudge. As I walked through the snow and through the cold, I could feel something in my big toe, a little like gnawing. My feet were getting colder and colder, and soon the toe just felt slightly uncomfortable, so I forgot it and thought about the music program coming up. In about an hour, I got to school and my feet were totally numb, so I ignored them.

During the band's performance of Bach's "Jesu, Joy of Man's Desiring" (I still love the tuba part that is the foundation upon which this soaring melody rests), I wiggled my toes to help warm them up, and could feel something squishy. "That's weird," I thought. The band went offstage, and I had to change clothes for my next appearance; I had to wear a robe for choir, a uniform for band, and a shirt and tie for orchestra. By this time the dull ache had become a sharp pain. When I took off my shoe, I saw that a nail from my boot had pushed up through the sole, made a hole in my toe, and actually dug the flesh out. The squish was blood. I thought, "I can't believe this, I've dug a hole in my toe, almost without knowing it." So I shoved Kleenex in my shoe and tried to forget what happened; there was nothing to do except go on and perform with that hole in my toe. I guess it was my first experience with living that old cliché "The show must go on!"

Coming of Age the Old-Fashioned Way

As I have said before, John Shoemaker and I were good friends from grade school on. When we were freshmen in high school, we were both still virgins, and the idea of a naked female body lying next to you was very exciting. Somehow we heard about a "house of ill repute" that was not very far away. It was on the old Route 66 south of Downers Grove on the road to Joliet, where the Illinois State Penitentiary is located. Ironically, it was in a tiny town called Godly.

The entire town consisted of a gas station, a tavern, and a few houses. About two hundred feet to the right of the tavern was another building. That was *the place*. We drove down there once, saw it, and went into the tavern. That in itself was very exciting, but they wanted to see our IDs, which we didn't have. So we left. John then got the bright idea that we would take driver's license application forms and fill them out neatly. We did so and gave ourselves birthdates that put us just over the legal limit. Then John went down to his basement and took pictures of the forged applications in a small darkroom his father had. They turned out to look like real driver's licenses. Remember that all of this took place in the late 1940s, long before computers.

First we used the fake IDs to see a burlesque show in downtown Chicago and there was no problem, although we were very nervous. We soon got up our courage and drove down to Godly with our hearts pounding. We were both over six feet tall, and thankfully they didn't bat an eye at the IDs. In the tavern they gave you a number and you sat there. When the bartender called your number, you went out the back door, down the steps, and across the two hundred feet to the other building. You knocked, said your number, and went in. We were pretty scared, but also excited. There were four or five attractive women sitting in the living room. They were wearing robes with little or nothing underneath. You had your pick of whoever was available. You would walk up to a woman and nod, and she would take you upstairs to a small single bedroom. Then she'd ask whether you wanted a five, a ten, or a fifteen. I don't think I ever had the fifteen. That was an "around the world." The prices seem pretty ridiculous by today's standards, but back then it was a lot of money. I never had more than a five. The women were all very polite, and, I thought, beautiful. In hindsight, I don't know if I'd feel the same way now, but at the time, it was an incredible adventure. For a few years we continued to use the same IDs. We thought we were really hot stuff.

Who's She?

All through school I took a minor beating over my first name, with the assumption that it was a girl's name. Of course the spelling isn't that of the girl's version of the name, but it does look and sound like the normal female-gender name. My father was a Methodist minister before I was born and for the first five years of my life. I found out much later that my name came from the Right Reverend Henry Knox Sherrill, a well-known Episcopalian bishop in the Northeast who was very respected and instrumental in modernizing that church. My father didn't know Reverend Sherrill, but he admired his writings and his theology so much he gave me his last name as my first. It was only a few years after I found out the origin of my name that I learned of the death of the widow of Reverend Sherrill, in Brooklyn Heights, New York. I was very saddened to read her obituary in *The New York Times* because I've always felt tied to that family in name.

Among many faux pas related to my name, the first was when I went to Drake University for my freshman year. I went to the men's dormitory and they didn't have my reservation. It turned out that my assigned room was in the girls' dorm! If only I'd been a little older and more sophisticated, I'd have just moved in. But as it was, it scared me to death, because I thought perhaps they wouldn't let me into the university! I still get mail addressed to "Ms. Sherrill Milnes."

People also show their operatic ignorance due to my name. Many people confuse Robert *Merrill* with *Sherrill* Milnes. I have been known on occasion as the great baritone *Sherrill Merrill*. Another funny mis-understanding happened to my wife's sister, Cathy, who is an actor and encounters the usual colleagues who act a bit pompous from time to time. One particular person was driving her crazy discussing how much she knew about music, opera, and the like. Instead of bragging about being related to me, Cathy simply said that she knew Sherrill Milnes and had seen some Met performances. Her snooty friend buried herself abruptly by saying, "Oh, big deal, I've heard all of *her* recordings and I don't think *she's* even very good"!

When I was on tour with the Goldovsky Opera Company, rooming with the now famous bass-baritone Justino Díaz, we'd frequently get invitations to parties addressed to "Miss Sherrill Milnes" and "Miss Justina Díaz." Given our size and looks, I've often wondered what roles in *The Barber of Seville* they thought these two women were performing.

You would think organizations with which I've been associated would get the name and gender right, especially when they're soliciting funds and contributions. In the past I have received solicitations more than once for Ms. Sherrill Milnes, even from my alma mater. Needless to say, these solicitations are not at the top of my contributions list.

To this day, my wife, Maria, is handed my credit card to sign at restaurants—she just smiles, hands it to me, and says to the waiter, "He's Sherrill, not me—it's a long story. . . ."

Most friends sincerely wish the best to a hometown product gone big city and take real pride in it. But not always. Perhaps the unsupportive ones can't truly reconcile themselves to a local boy becoming famous when they didn't or couldn't explore their own dreams and remained local. After I'd come to New York and debuted successfully at both the New York City Opera and the Met, my father told one of our friends (who happened to be a local church soloist) that I was now a leading baritone at the New York City Opera and the Metropolitan Opera. The neighbor said, "Oh, that can't be; I remember Sherrill's singing. I think you've got that wrong, you've misunderstood, maybe he's in the chorus." He was so adamant that I couldn't be a leading singer of these opera houses that he convinced my father that I was indeed in the chorus! I remember explaining to my father how it was our neighbor and not he who was mistaken, and that I was perhaps not a star yet but indeed a leading baritone at these famous theaters. It was not so easy to analyze and explain where I was in my career and all the steps necessary to arrive there. It was easier for my mother to understand because she was a professional, and even though she wasn't famous, she could identify with the small career steps necessary to arrive on a national level. I still have a few hometown friends who start conversations with, "I remember Sherrill when he could barely carry a tune, and had a rather ugly voice." In fairness, I did not have a terrific voice in my public school days.

There are many reasons why the so-called local talent never makes it to the big time. Different and more important priorities; obligations to family and children, which can be far more important than career considerations; lack of money, in the sense that early in a career, one does not make enough to live on; or lack of drive, ambition, or desire specifically for a career. This is not a criticism at all, but a description. A life takes many different turns, and career possibilities often do not present themselves. There is not enough work for everyone as it is, in the operatic world, so it's fortunate that many people who perhaps are talented enough to try for a career choose not to. Living a productive, loving, and satisfying life is far more important than the possibility of a career.

I had studied advanced swimming and lifesaving at North Central College my first year out of high school. As a result, in the summer of 1953 I got a job as a lifeguard at the Hinsdale Golf Club near my home. It was my first job off the farm and the first one for which I was paid. I got a great tan, and it was quite exciting to see all the young, nubile female bodies. However, it was a lot of work and responsibility to watch out for fifty or sixty people in the water, many of whom were little kids. After a couple of months there, John Shoemaker asked me if I wanted to work with him on the night shift at the Conrad Hilton Hotel coffee shop in downtown Chicago, where he was already working. The money was better than at the golf club, and even though the swimming pool view was much nicer than the coffee shop one, I decided to take the job. It was fun working with John, taking the train into Chicago, and for a while it held its big-city fascination—especially the oddity of working from midnight to eight in the morning and then sleeping during the day. Also, I had never had a job where tips were a part of my wages, and that was an interesting study in humanity and generosity.

But by September I was tired of the big city and the midnight shift—and, as it turned out, the lack of tips—and was ready for college. The world of academia won out over my brief working association for Mr. Hilton.

Drake—Out and Back

I think of myself as a moral man, yet practical at the same time. In school, I wasn't a member of the jock group. I was an athletic farm boy who sang. Aside from the occasional firecracker in the mailbox, I knew how to get along with people pretty well, and I'd never call myself a thief. It never would have occurred to me to take anything from someone's person or home. Stealing a car or a radio or anything like that was something I just wouldn't do; the thought would never occur to me. But I guess I never felt that an occasional lift from a supermarket, or some other petty theft, would hurt anyone.

In high school, John Shoemaker and I were involved in a small insurance fraud when we filed a claim for a stolen radio in my car. We had heard about the scheme, which sounded so easy. We hoped to get forty or fifty dollars out of it. We got caught, however, maybe because my car had never had a radio in it. Not very smart. We were hauled into the local police station, where they knew all about the fraud. We admitted it to Chief Springborn and to John's father, my father, and George Bunge, the father of a close school friend, Bill Bunge, who were all there. George Bunge was a local lawyer and county judge. We were let off with a stern warning, embarrassed to death knowing that we caused our parents to go through this ordeal. Pretty thoughtless!

But it seemed that I hadn't learned my lesson. Some years later at Drake University, I developed a scheme to get an almost-new tuxedo. I looked in the paper and saw ads for used tuxes on sale for ten or fifteen dollars, and I bought one. Then I rented a tux from a rental place that looked something like the cheap one. I cleverly returned the cheap, used one, so that I got a tux that was worth maybe a hundred dollars or more for one that cost ten or fifteen.

Soon after, John and I were called separately into the dean's office without knowing the other was being questioned. As we were known to be very close friends, the administration thought anything one of us would do automatically involved the other. The dean asked me about the tux and I admitted the scheme. The rental place in Des Moines had traced me from the label inside the tux in my dorm room. At the same time, John had taken some music from an attic in an old storeroom in the music school, which he admitted. There had also been a number of auto and auto parts thefts around the university and they asked us about that. Even though neither of us had anything to do with those auto thefts, I don't think they believed us at all, and we were both suspended.

That was a huge blow, but we really had no recourse because we were guilty of those petty tux and music thefts. The school sent us both home. An interesting sidelight to this was that we were kept around long enough to play the spring band concert, possibly because John was the first trombone player and I was the first tuba.

At this point, I personally decided never to do anything like that again, because I knew how much I had hurt the people that I loved the most. I'm sure John felt the same way. Our parents were devastated when they were told. We had to pack our meager belongings and take what had suddenly become a very, very long drive from Des Moines to Downers Grove (some 330 miles). We thought the punishment was severe, but I'm sure the school authorities were convinced that we were involved in the whole car theft ring and were letting us off easy by not bringing in the police. John and I returned home with our tails between our legs.

After a short time at home trying to cope with our embarrassment and shame, we realized that we had to find work. John had always been savvy about finding jobs and earning money. After several interviews, we both got jobs at Foote Brothers Gear, a local machine shop, and worked there for a few months. The previous summer, John had played trombone for the Barnes and Carruthers Theatrical Agency in the pit band of their state fair tours. He had the job coming up again that current summer, 1955. At the last minute the tuba player got sick and canceled and someone was needed immediately. So with John's recommendation, and without an audition, I was hired. I was lucky, because I was only an OK tuba player. I don't think I would have gotten the job if I had had to audition, but they were stuck. Fortunately, I owned my own tuba and was ready to go.

The shows toured out of Chicago, and that summer there were four separate companies going on the road. We did four weeks playing in state fairs, with different acts each week. There was a chorus line of girls, and Rex Allen, the old Texas singer and movie cowboy, was one of the headliners. The pay was $125 a week, plus transportation and room. I thought that was a fortune. You played two shows a day and the rest of the time you had nothing to do. I saw Yellowstone National Park, Old Faithful, the Rocky Mountains, and other natural wonders of the country, and I loved it. It was at this time that I began writing to the university and found that they were willing to take me back the following semester. I went back in the fall and reentered school. Having been expelled and knowing that everyone knew that, it was embarrassing to return as though nothing had happened. It took some emotional adjustment on my part. In hindsight, it was interesting to note who of the student body and faculty were supportive and who were cold and judgmental. However, I went on to earn both my bachelor's and master's degrees and years later was awarded a Distinguished Alumnus Award and an honorary doctorate.

The Little House on the Farm

During the period of my suspension, when I was home and out of school, I was very down and depressed. Disappointing my loved ones by my attitude and performance weighed heavily on me. It was at this point that my relationship with Charlotte Slack began to blossom.

In 1952, my senior year in high school, I was the concertmaster of the orchestra, and Charlotte was the first chair cello and also a singer.

Music was a strong common bond and we dated a bit at that time, although nothing too serious. We continued a relationship when I went to Drake, while she was still in high school. Then, after her high school graduation, she also attended Drake in order to study with the fine cello teacher there, John Ehrlich. When I was suspended, our relationship continued through telephoning and writing. Charlotte remained friendly, nonjudgmental, and supportive. Over the next months and through many affectionate conversations, we began falling in love. I proposed during the winter-spring of 1955–56, and we were married that June in the Congregational Church where I grew up. My dad and the regular minister, Reverend Edgar Cook, officiated.

That fall I was reinstated in school, and for the next two years Charlotte and I lived as a married couple off campus. The Selective Service System was still in force and I was called for my physical, which made it likely that I would be drafted during my master's study. Then, after two years of military service, I would have had to try to get back into the swing of school life, which I thought would be the worst thing that could happen.

With my first wife, Charlotte, 1960.

I calculated that I could get my master's of music education in two summer sessions and two semesters, a total of twelve months. So I wrote my draft board explaining that I was married and wanted to stay in school to finish my degree, and after that I would happily be drafted. I had already decided that after boot camp I would try out for the marching band, concert band, and some dance band work. I was allowed to finish my degree, which I did in the twelve months. During that period, ironically, the government abolished the Selective Service System, so I was never drafted.

After graduation Charlotte and I came home from Drake and moved into another house on the farm. This house had an interesting history. After World War II, my folks were taking part in the Displaced Persons Program, which the president and Congress had established to help the war-torn European population. The DPs were allowed to enter the country if they had work and a suitable place to live. Although ours wasn't a large farm, there was always a need for extra help. So we built a small house from scratch with very little money. We built it with picks and shovels, a manure loader on the front of a tractor, a lot of backbreaking work, and a lot of ingenuity on the part of my dad. He would drive to the gravel pit in our old 1937 Dodge truck and get all the materials we needed. We mixed and poured all our own cement and built the rest of the house as safely and cheaply as possible. It took a lot of work and cooperation from the whole family. It wasn't very big, but it was livable.

Through the government program we found a Latvian family, a man, his wife, and their son, who wanted to come over to live here. It was the start of a new life for them, and the two families got on very well. The man tried hard on the farm, but he was an accountant by training, and the manual labor was finally too much for him. Eventually, with my parents' blessing, they left for something more suitable to his talents.

Thus we had this additional house, now empty, into which Charlotte and I moved. I had my master's and she had her bachelor's degree. We were living on the farm and happy to be there. I started to hustle like crazy to make a living and start building a career in Chicago. Any singing job within reason that came along I took, and as a result I was making pretty good money. Our son, Eric, was born in 1959 and our daughter, Erin, in 1965. As our family grew, so did our little house. We added to it until it was almost three times the original size. All in all we lived

My favorite photo of my daughter, Erin. She is a freedom fighter who has worked for Amnesty International.

there for seven or eight years. During this time, I began singing with the Chicago Symphony Chorus and various regional opera companies and touring with the Goldovsky Company. Sometimes Charlotte would go out on the road with me, but usually she was home with the family.

It was a good place to live and a good place to raise a family. I think if I had taken a high school job or university position teaching music, we might still be married; who knows? It was a good life, and Charlotte was a good wife and mother. The children were a joy. But slowly our lives went in different directions. My passion and desire for music were growing by leaps and bounds, yet hers seemed to be staying at a constant level. There was nothing wrong with that, but we were growing apart.

I had known Nancy Stokes as a freshman at Drake, when I was a graduate student. She sang in Douglas Moore's *The Devil and Daniel Webster* with me in Drake's "Night of Opera" production. Then I graduated, and Charlotte and I moved to the farm. We heard that Nancy had received a Fulbright scholarship and had gone to Italy. Some of the stories about her studies and performances drifted back to the United States. None of my classmates had ever been to Europe, and it was exciting to hear all about it, even if some of the stories were probably exaggerated. A couple of years later I ran into Nancy at a college choir reunion. We enjoyed talking about living and working in Italy, experiences that were still in my future.

Soon after this I signed a contract with the Met and realized that the time had come in my career when it was necessary to live closer to New York. So Charlotte, the children, and I left the house on the farm for the first time in our marriage and bought a house in Cresskill, New Jersey, just over the George Washington Bridge. The kids were enrolled in school there, and my life as a full-time singer began to grow.

I would see Nancy from time to time because she was singing for the Goldovsky Company, with which I was still singing. Then she auditioned for and was hired by the new Metropolitan Opera National Company. It had been formed by Rudolph Bing and was run by one of the best-known singers in America, Risë Stevens. In that season with them, Nancy sang over sixty performances as both Mimi and Musetta in *La Bohème*, the Countess in *Le nozze di Figaro*, and Violetta in *La traviata*.

It was at this time that my marriage to Charlotte really started to unravel. I was working in Manhattan and part of my social life was there, while Charlotte was often rooted to the house and children. It just didn't look as if it was going to work. We were drifting apart, and finally I asked for a separation. It was hard on the children, especially Eric, who was older—but it was as amicable as a separation and eventual divorce can be.

Among the painful memories connected with my family and my music, one of the most vivid moments dealt with Eric. Charlotte and I had recently separated, and Eric was living in New Jersey with her and his sister Erin. Fortunately, she was really too young to fully understand the changes going on in her life and the lives of her parents. During this separation period, I was singing in a benefit performance of *Elijah* in Englewood, New Jersey. Eric's grandmother brought him to hear me sing. The music is exciting, and my son was so swept up by it that afterward he kept saying to me, "Dad, why can't you come home? Come on

With my second wife, Nancy Stokes, and our son, Shawn, in happier times in front of the Sydney Opera House, 1979.

home, Dad." Well, I couldn't go home with him, and I couldn't really explain why. But I can still hear him pleading with me.

During the two years that it took for our divorce to become final, I moved around a lot in New York City and finally found my own place on the Upper West Side. I was seeing Nancy more and more, and, I suppose partly because our life goals were so similar, we fell in love. In time we married, and Manhattan became our home.

Nancy continued singing and had a good career going. However, she wanted a child and basically gave her career up when our son, Shawn, was born. She's now a respected voice teacher in New York with her own studio.

With my sons
Eric and Shawn at
home, 1988.

It's hard to say why, after twenty-five years of marriage to Nancy and the birth of our son, the relationship slowly broke down. Some of it was my being away so much. On the one hand, I wanted her to have her teaching studio and that sense of her own skills, her own worth and ability. On the other hand, I came to hate the fact that her new career sometimes didn't allow her to go certain places with me. All the years Shawn was in school, it was harder for both of them to leave. We would arrange it when possible, but usually not during the school year. Over time, however, Shawn saw many new productions and performances all over Europe, which I think was an education for him.

I suppose I just got used to being alone and having that sense of freedom. When I was at home, however, I did everything I could at Shawn's school, at home, at sport groups, at PTA meetings, and so on. I tried everything in my power to avoid taking anything away from the family. Once again, this marriage of many years ended. It was much more difficult than the first. More children, more invested time, more life used up, less energy, older all around.

Charlotte and Nancy were important parts of my life. I don't maintain close personal relationships with them, but we are friendly. They are the mothers of my children, and I remember all the good times. Eric, Erin, and Shawn are grown and I love them. The farm and the small house we built on the property have been torn down. The trees are gone. The area is totally changed. It is a subdivision of fine homes, but there is no longer any physical trace of my farm life. Things change, and life moves forward.

CHAPTER THREE

On the Road: From Chicago to Santa Fe, to Tanglewood and Goldovsky

IN THE FALL OF 1958 FRITZ REINER and the Chicago Symphony asked Margaret Hillis to form a new chorus for them. I knew her from Drake University, where she had been invited by the then dean of the College of Fine Arts, Frank Jordan, to be a guest conductor for our choirs. During her two weeks on campus in the spring of 1958, she told me about the new chorus she was forming in Chicago and asked me to audition for her. So, the following autumn, I did and was accepted into the Chicago Symphony Orchestra Chorus in its inaugural year as one of the few union members who were paid—not much, but paid. For five years I sang in every concert of the Chicago Symphony that required a chorus. Fritz Reiner knew and loved all of the major choral works, so we performed a wide variety of music. Reiner was one of our great conductors and brought the orchestra to new artistic heights, but he was a taskmaster, and we in the chorus were greatly in awe as well as a little afraid of him. But with Margaret preparing us, as well as conducting her own concerts, it was a thrilling experience, and my musical skills, knowledge, and inspiration grew by leaps and bounds.

Margaret Hillis was an American original. Born in Kokomo, Indiana, in 1921, she was first introduced to music at home and at school, like me. She was taught piano at home but took up tuba and string bass in order to play with the school bands. She also was a talented amateur golfer, winning many junior tournaments, and during World War II she enlisted in the Navy and became a distinguished flying instructor. After the war she studied music at Indiana University and Juilliard, where she became a protégée of Robert Shaw. In 1952 she was invited to become the choral conductor for the American Opera Society, a position she held for sixteen years, and in the mid-1950s she was briefly chorus master at the New York City Opera. She went on to become the foremost female choral director in the country.

During my first year in the CSC, Margaret asked me, along with several other chorus members, to be part of the chorus in Santa Fe that summer. I was quite excited, because it was my first professional experience outside Chicago. The pay was rather poor, $50 a week, but I didn't care about that. Margaret was to prepare all the opera choruses, and the chorus was to present a series of its own concerts on Sunday afternoons, including Igor Stravinsky's *Threni: Lamentations of the Prophet Jeremiah*, to be conducted by the composer. Also there would be some small roles given out after we arrived. For me it seemed a golden opportunity. I decided to drive my old Rambler on the long trip to Santa Fe.

I have had a lifelong affair with automobiles, starting with my grandfather Charlie Roe's 1925 Ford Model T coupe. Charlie Roe, who was the township road commissioner, would drive around inspecting the mostly dirt and gravel roads in the area. When I was small I went with him and watched him take notes about the roads. With great admiration, I would see him greet most people on the street, because he knew everyone in town—and everyone knew him. (Downers Grove, at that time, had a population of only a few thousand people.) After his death, unbeknownst to me, his Model T was stored in a shed on the farm. Years later I discovered it and asked my dad if it could be my first car, and eventually he gave it to me. After a lot of work to put it in running order, I drove it with great pride. It was equipped with one seat, a crank start, two forward speeds, a spark advance and throttle on the steering column, a magneto (no generator), two-wheel brakes, a rumble seat, a thermometer outside on top of the grill where you added water, and skinny balloon tires. It rode like a tractor—not tops on the list of auto comforts—but I loved it.

I drove that car around town without insurance and without a driver's license. Every time I would see a police car, I would quickly drive around the corner, pull the car to the curb, get out, and nonchalantly walk down the street. Thankfully, I never was caught—the police were not so interested in car registration and insurance in the 1940s as they are now.

A multitude of cars followed, but the first really long trip I made was this drive out to Santa Fe. I was concerned about my beat-up old Rambler's ability to keep going nonstop from Chicago to Santa Fe. It took about thirty hours of driving, and I have a tendency to fall asleep at the wheel even on short distances, especially when alone. So I drank gallons of coffee, chewed wads of gum, sang at the top of my voice, kept the windows open, and slapped my face; in short, I did everything I could think of to stay awake. By traveling on the slow side, the old car made it, and I didn't doze off. After the drive back home at the end of that summer, it did die, and I traded it in on a 1956 Olds, which I drove to Tanglewood the next year.

That summer in Santa Fe, the chorus stayed at the (no longer existing) Montezuma Hotel. The aptly named hotel was somewhat less than luxurious, but the hotel cost was part of the contract. In the first week of rehearsals, I was given the part of the commissioner in *Madama Butterfly*, a spoken part in *Die Fledermaus*, and various guards and waiters in other operas. I determined that my job in *Butterfly* was to sing louder, longer, more beautifully, and more impressively than the baritone singing Sharpless! Although, of course, that is overstated, I did approach the role with the idea of wringing every nuance possible out of it and impressing the management.

The principals were all the best young American singers of the time. In Santa Fe I met Charlie Anthony and Nico Castel, with whom I have sung many, many times since at the Met and other theaters. Charlie has the world record of the most performances at the Met of any singer ever, and Nico has become, after a distinguished singing career, the acknowledged language guru of the world. He also has published many volumes of opera translations, much valued in the industry.

The apprentices were given makeup classes, movement classes, and aria concerts of our own. The Sunday afternoon concert with Stravinsky conducting his own oratorio was a highlight of the summer. *Threni: Lamentations of the Prophet Jeremiah* is a twelve-tone work and very dissonant; in fact, I did not enjoy the music very much. But it was a challenge just to sing the right notes! Stravinsky was quite old at the time, but to be led by one of the musical giants of this century was a thrill. I benefited a lot from that whole summer and am very grateful for the experience.

John Crosby, the director and founder of the festival, was complimentary to me and said he would like me to audition for him in subsequent seasons for the possibility of returning as a leading artist. I was anxious to return, so I auditioned with regularity for several years. Each time John was very cordial and complimentary, thanked me for singing, and said that as soon as there was a spot on the roster, he would be in touch. After a few years of auditioning to compliments but no callbacks, I became frustrated and finally gave up.

Young singers approach me all the time with questions about how I hit it big and if I ever suffered disappointments. They don't believe me when I tell them of the many competition losses and audition failures. Sometimes young artists lose faith due to a particular defeat. A career takes time to build, and new artists should expect to endure certain failures before the possibility of successes. The point is to keep working and improving.

When one starts a career, it is necessary to use every scrap of newspaper reviews you have. My bio from the Herbert Barrett Management, after the Santa Fe experience, credited me with having sung at the Santa Fe Opera. After a few years, Barrett's publicist decided that "leading artist at Santa Fe" sounded better than the old phrase. At some point I saw that exaggeration in my bio and was temporarily embarrassed, but I soon accepted it as a normal publicity hyperbole. A year later Joseph Lippman, the vice president at Barrett's, received a call from the Santa Fe management, saying that they had seen my bio and—because I had never been a leading artist at Santa Fe—they would appreciate it if that part were deleted. Joe, rather annoyed, replied that he would certainly remove it from my bio and would never use it again. When this was related to me, I had to smile, even though I certainly would not have responded in that manner, given my appreciation for all that I learned there. I guess one reason a manager is there is to be the bad guy while the artist can be the good guy.

Interestingly enough, at a New Year's Eve party some fifteen years later, I ran across John Crosby. I had already become a leading singer at the Met and other world theaters and had attained some success. This party was well into the evening and everyone had been drinking, including me. John saw me and said, "Hello, Dick, how's Doris?" I knew instantly that he had momentarily mistaken me for Dick Cross (Doris was Doris Yarick Cross). I said to John, "Doris is fine, but I'm not who you think I am." (I had seen Dick and Doris recently, because I was part-time faculty at Yale, where Doris is the head of the opera school.) John immediately said, "Oh, God, I'm sorry, I know it's you, Sherrill, and how are you?" A friendly party conversation ensued. At some point John suggested to me that I should come back to Santa Fe. He described the beauty of the area, the family vacation qualities, and the artistic values there. He also mentioned that the fees were still quite low, but that he thought that I should do it "for old times' sake." At that time in my career, dates were plentiful, and of course I hadn't forgotten that Santa Fe, other than that one summer, had never played a part in my career. Plus, I still remembered that they had contacted my press agent to have my bio changed. The fact was, when I needed them and could have used the engagements, they weren't there for me. Probably because I had been drinking, I said I really didn't think that a whole summer with low pay would fit in with my plans and besides, given their past track record, there was no "old times' sake."

Having said all this, it certainly doesn't negate at all what John Crosby and his festival have done for opera in the United States and for many, many American singers. It remains a major force in the operatic world.

I remember two highlights from the early 1960s in the Chicago Symphony Chorus: recordings of Beethoven's Ninth Symphony and Prokofiev's *Alexander Nevsky*. They were both recorded by RCA, and the producer was Richard Mohr, with whom, later in my career, I would make more than twenty-five recordings. That first recording session was the Beethoven, and it is very clear in my mind. The entire chorus, about 250, was standing on tiers in Orchestra Hall, with microphones all over the place. My heart was pounding just as much as when I was a soloist years later. (When I saw the movie *Dead Poets Society* with Robin Williams, I was totally blown away by the power of that film and Williams's performance was awesome. Beethoven's Ninth Symphony was featured prominently in the film's sound track. Just out of curiosity, I waited to the very end of the credits to see which recording was used. There are of course upward of a hundred different Beethoven's Ninths on the market. It turned out to be the Reiner recording from Chicago. Not a big contribution on my part, but I loved knowing that my voice was in that chorus and part of the movie.)

Margaret Hillis conducted her own programs in Orchestra Hall every year, and she asked me to be the soloist in the *Elijah* and in another concert, *Die erste Walpurgisnacht*, both by Mendelssohn. I also had the opportunity of performing the Bach *Magnificat* with the Chicago Symphony and Frank Miller, one of the world's great cellists. In the bass aria, "Quia fecit mihi magna," the cello performs the melody and the bass repeats it as call-and-response. When I heard Mr. Miller begin playing at the first rehearsal, my jaw dropped. His phrasing was so musical and fluid that I thought if I could do half as well with my voice as he did with his cello, I would be twice as good as I would have been otherwise. I have never forgotten his playing.

I also had a number of church and synagogue jobs, one of which was with the University of Chicago's Rockefeller Chapel Choir. It was probably the best-paying church job there was, but more important than the money was the opportunity to be a soloist in that fine choir. Four or five times a year Richard Vickstrom, its well-known director, and the choir would present major oratorios with members of the Chicago Symphony. To sing solos with Adolf Herseth, Ray Still, Clark Brody, Phillip Farkas, Frank Miller, and other world-class players was an opportunity I would have paid to have. But to be paid well for singing these works *and* with these players was mind-blowing and immensely inspiring.

I had learned to sing a little Hebrew in college with the Bloch *Sacred Service*. This skill allowed me to audition for the eminent composer of Jewish music Max Janowski. He was the choir director at KAM Isaiah Israel Temple on the South Side of Chicago. My sight-reading skills were of prime importance because the choir sang only Janowski compositions and he hated wrong notes. Max liked me and I sang with him for several years, which of course taught me the flavor of Jewish music and cantorial style. My favorite composition of his is *Avinu Malkeinu*, which I have sung many times over the years and have recorded on an RCA album of sacred music. Many years later this piece became a common thread to my new wife, Maria, because she had sung the same piece for several years as a temple soloist and loved it as much as I did. Even Barbra Streisand has gotten into the act: she recorded the song as the last track on her 1997 album *Higher Ground*.

Boris Goldovsky

In 1960 I was studying voice with Hermanus Baer at Northwestern University and working with the new opera man there, Robert Gay, who had been an associate of Boris Goldovsky. Goldovsky was a name I knew only from the Metropolitan Opera radio broadcasts, because he did many intermission features in his memorable Russian accent. Mr. Gay told me that the following fall the Goldovsky Company would be touring with *Don Giovanni* and suggested that perhaps I should audition.

Boris Goldovsky was one of the most important popularizers of opera in our time. Born in 1908 in Russia, he originally studied piano at the Moscow Conservatory; he then moved to Berlin and finally immigrated to the United States in 1930. After coming to this country, he became an ardent opera fan and supporter, heading the opera department at the New England Conservatory of Music and Tanglewood's opera workshop from the mid-1940s through the mid-1960s. In 1946 he founded the New England Opera Theater, which presented the North American premiere of Berlioz's *Les Troyens*. But perhaps Goldovsky's most important work was founding the Goldovsky Opera Theater, a touring company that performed operas in the smaller American cities. It was for this company that I was auditioning.

I flew to Cleveland, where Mr. Goldovsky was holding auditions, and sang for him. His auditions were easier than many, because he played for you himself, and you felt he was part of your audition. Instead of offering me a contract for the touring company, however, Goldovsky asked me if I could come to his workshop at Tanglewood. I had no idea what Tanglewood was but was smart enough not to let him know that, so I agreed. I went away from the audition thinking, however, that I'd failed it. Because he'd said nothing about a job, I went back to Chicago rather depressed. What I didn't know, but would soon find out, was that Tanglewood was the summer home of the Boston Symphony and a paradise of learning for anyone in music, instrumental or vocal. Charles Munch was the music director of the orchestra, and you heard all the concerts of that great symphony all summer long.

I decided to drive to Tanglewood, which is in western Massachusetts. It was the first time I had driven a long distance since Santa Fe the year before in the old Rambler. I had the 1956 Olds 98 with everything on it. I had bought it used, and it was a hot car, bright red, massive chrome, and those huge bumpers that most cars had in the 1950s. It burned some oil, but I loved it. The trip was about 1,200 miles long and took twenty-four hours. During the trip, I noticed I was adding more and more oil at each gas stop, and I could see smoke from the burning oil in the exhaust. By the time I arrived, the Olds was burning about a quart of oil every tank of gas and beginning to make strange grinding noises. I thought perhaps the piston bearings or main bearings were starting to go. I was almost afraid to drive it even around the grounds where we stayed. It also seemed that the longer it ran, the more noise it made, so I determined to find another car in the Pittsfield area. After looking around at various car dealers, I found a Dodge that was affordable. When I brought the Olds in for them to look at, I prayed that it would run well enough to get a decent trade-in. Fortunately, they only drove it around the block, and it ran just fine. So they gave me a good trade-in, and I bought my first new car. I was both proud of the new car and grateful that the Olds held together long enough to dump it.

Five years later I bought my next new car, a 1966 Chrysler Imperial with everything on it. That was a beautiful automobile. However, my ultimate pride and joy was a 1976 Cadillac Eldorado convertible. It was loaded with everything you can imagine and was the last of the gunboat-size cars. You could sit three in front and three in back almost without anyone touching. My son Eric still has this impressive car—a long way from my grandfather's 1925 Model T Ford.

At Tanglewood, I found I was in a group of forty of the hottest young talents in America, including George Shirley, Spiro Malas, Justino Díaz, and Jeanette Scovotti. In Goldovsky's workshop, as fast as you could memorize and stage a scene, you'd perform it. This group of singers was musically quicker than any I had ever experienced. Boris had stagings that followed and used the energy of the music and made believable drama out of it. He was very specific about what he wanted us to do, and his instructions always made musical and emotional sense. I must have sung more than a dozen different scenes, as well as *Il tabarro* by Puccini and a world premiere of a modern opera, *Port Town*, by Jan Meyerwitz.

When I received the manuscript for *Port Town*, I found that I had been assigned the part of the "Gop." At least I thought it was the "Gop." I wondered for many weeks before arriving what this strange character was with such a name. I felt very foolish when I was told that my part

As the Cop in the world premiere of *Port Town* by Jan Meyerwitz, Tanglewood, 1960.

As Masetto in *Don Giovanni* with Boris Goldovsky, Tanglewood, 1960.

was the town "Cop" in this port town on the coast. The composer, Jan Meyerwitz, sure suffered from poor penmanship.

This was a new speed of learning and performing for me, and at the end of the summer, having seen me work and perform, Boris offered me Masetto in the *Giovanni* production. And so that fall, I went on my first truck-and-bus tour. Six or seven performances a week with a double cast—you simply sang every other performance with everything in English. It was this fall of 1960 that I consider the beginning of my career: I was finally able to earn a living from singing.

Actually, the early 1960s were a wonderful time to be young and on tour. Kennedy had been elected president, and the torch was passed to a younger generation of leaders. The popular movies were classics such as *Psycho* and *The Apartment*, from the theater; the title song in *Camelot* and "Try to Remember" from *The Fantastiks* had captured the hearts of Americans.

When you toured, your whole world became the performance. Your only responsibility was to be in good voice and deliver the goods onstage.

Your whole schedule—your whole life—was arranged. You had to try to stay in good health, and your time onstage was your existence.

Every day we would start off as early as six. The earliness of the hour could be rough, but you could always sleep on the bus. After some time on tour, you tended to lose a sense of reality about the rest of the world. You cared only about the three or four performances a week, keeping in good voice, and being paid. You worked hard for those evenings, but the rest of the time you had nothing to do, no responsibilities.

That was a big trap. You could easily become lazy. You didn't do anything physical other than the performance. If you weren't singing, you sat on the bus, slept, rested, went out to eat, went to a movie, went to bed, and then got back on the bus. Those tours lasted anywhere from four to sixteen weeks, and that was a lot of sitting.

After some lazy weeks, I decided to find a YMCA in each town and go there and work out to get some muscle tone back. Once I got into that routine, I really felt better physically and mentally. As a teenager I had been rather thin, and I had never liked the size of my chest. I thought it was semi-concave, with no pecs, as we call them now. That's what I worked to get, and eventually I added some bulk and some much-needed definition.

It was the first time I had been paid a large sum of money for a prolonged period for doing what I loved the most, singing. We got our transportation along with our salary but had to pay for our own room and board. Needless to say, we didn't stay at Hiltons. Generally, we would choose a small motel where we stayed alone or shared a room that ranged in price from $8 to $20. If you had a roommate, that was cut in half. To save extra money, some of the company would "ghost." That meant that two of them would take a room for the night, pull the mattress off the bed, and put it on the floor. Then two more people would join them and sleep on the box spring, and in the morning they'd divide the bill by four. I don't know how much sleep they got, but it lowered the overhead.

Once in a while there was a problem with Boris's system of double casting. Both names were always listed in all the programs so that a specific version for each evening was not needed. Then an announcement was made as to which of the singers would appear.

In 1964 another baritone and I were splitting several weeks as Giovanni in *Don Giovanni* in the northwestern United States. Quite a few years later Glenn Ross hired me for a production of *Il trovatore* with the Seattle Opera. Glenn had brought Seattle from a nice little company into a major operation before turning over the reigns to Speight Jenkins, who has made it one of our most important companies. During my stay Glenn and I became quite friendly, and something came up in conversation one day about the fact that it had taken him a while to hire me.

He had waited until he heard that I was in good shape vocally and was singing well. It seems that he had read a bad review I got for the *Giovanni* back during the Goldovsky tour and remembered it. He didn't think he could gamble on someone who had gotten such a terrible review from one of the major Seattle papers. It wasn't all that many years after the tour, so I was able to remember that I hadn't sung that performance. Either the announcement was wrong or the critic had misread the program or something, but I had gotten the bad review for a performance my colleague had sung, and because of it I wasn't hired for years. It gave me a certain amount of pleasure to verify that it hadn't been my performance that the critic disliked.

When one starts a career, one needs any good reviews that are printed. Singing Masetto in *Don Giovanni* with Boris's company in those early years, it was difficult to find reviews, and when you did find them, Masetto was often unmentioned. I paid bellhops to look for reviews in the following days and then mail it to some town well ahead on our tour. Usually they didn't do it at all and you wasted your money, but once a bellhop came through, and I got a paper with a good review for me. It said something like "Sherrill Milnes was luxury casting as Masetto, strong and good as the country bumpkin."

I was elated. This paper was from Cleveland, Tennessee, a tiny little town. I used it in my subsequent publicity material—I just left out the word "Tennessee." You work with what you have!

In five years, in many more cities and with many more reviews, I traveled more than 100,000 miles and sang more than 300 performances of about a dozen operas, including *Don Giovanni*, *La traviata*, *Tosca*, *Rigoletto*, *La Bohème*, *Carmen*, *The Barber of Seville*, and even Rossini's *Il turco in Italia* and the American premiere of Paisiello's *King Theodore in Venice*. I have often said that the Goldovsky tours were my Fulbright scholarships and gave me the same opportunities as other singers had gotten singing in smaller German theaters. Those tours taught me about stamina, how to deal with fatigue, how ill you can be, how bad a cold you can have, or how tired you can be—and still be able to go on. They helped me develop important parts of my technique that have served me well for my entire career.

↷

Voice-Overs

In my student years and early career, I'd do anything and everything to get a music job. During college at Drake University, I was asked to help the state celebrate some anniversary by wearing a corncob costume and singing the Iowa state song at one of the best hotels downtown. I was running around this hotel ballroom in my silly costume singing at the top of my lungs, "Ioway, Ioway, that's where the tall corn grows." I looked a lot like the Fruit of the Loom commercial (probably like the banana) we have seen on television.

In 1958, after returning to the farm, I even entered amateur contests that paid as little as ten bucks. I'd continued playing in dance bands and had learned to croon. I could sight-read the jazz idiom. The Four Freshmen, the HiLos, Stan Kenton, Les Brown—that was all music I loved.

One day I was working in the barn in my overalls when the phone rang. It was a voice-over job for a demo (demonstration tape), but it required that I join the union, AFTRA (American Federation of Television and Radio Artists), which would cost $300—a fortune to me. But after talking to the secretary on the phone about the possible money that you could earn from voice-overs (I had never heard of this before), I decided to give it a try. I went to Universal Studios on East Walton Street on the near North Side of Chicago and made the demo. There were three other guys singing on the commercial, and they soon found out I could sight-read, sing the rhythms, and adopt a ballsy barroom sound or the lightest crooning sound. Their group was called the Jays with Jamie (three guys and a girl), and they started to use me for all the commercials where they wanted a four-guy sound; Marlboro cigarettes, International Harvester and John Deere farm machinery, Schlitz, Budweiser, Miller, Old Milwaukee, and, ironically, Falstaff beer. I couldn't believe that for a few hours a week, without having to worry about my voice or vocal technique, I could make so much money. I remember getting an $18,000 residual check once; it sent me into shock. I bought new robes for my mother's church choir, a team of Belgian horses for our farm's hayrides, and lots of things for my family and me, including increasing the size of our house.

One day in 1962 I got a call to do another Marlboro commercial while I was on tour singing *The Barber of Seville* with Goldovsky in Phoenix, Arizona. Boris was a genius in music, but he was at the same time very pragmatic in all other matters. I explained the situation to him, and he recommended I make an offer to my double-cast partner, John Robert Dunlop. This had never occurred to me, and so I offered him an extra week's salary if he would sing one extra performance, which was all the time I needed to fly to Chicago, make the commercial, and fly back. He agreed, and so after singing a performance of *Barber*, I flew off to Chicago on a red-eye flight. I arrived in the early morning, showered at a friend's apartment, went to the recording studio, and made the spots. After finishing the session, I flew back to join the Goldovsky Company in Phoenix and continued singing on the tour as though there had been no interruption, except that I knew the commercial would continue to pay over a long period of time. However, for all the apparent ease of voice-over work, it could be very spotty and infrequent, and sometimes there was no work at all. There seemed to be no guarantee and no way to plan on income.

During one of the many Marlboro commercial sessions, we four guys were told that the Oscar Peterson trio was in the next studio recording the *My Fair Lady* album. We were excited to check out the session, so during the first break we went into the engineer's booth to watch and listen. Ray Brown was the bassist and the drummer was Gene Gammage. They were fabulous, and we stayed there as long as we could. That was real swinging jazz. When that album came out, I bought it immediately and took extra pleasure because I had watched those guys record it.

In my early years at the Met, I continued doing radio and television voice-overs, which were all still done in Chicago with the same vocal group. It always seemed to work time-wise with my rehearsals and performances to fly to Chicago and back. One rather dicey experience, however, happened near the end of my first year at the Met.

I was the first cover (by contract, if there was a problem I had to be ready to go on) for the role of Carlo Gerard, the leading baritone in *Andrea Chénier*. There was a dress rehearsal in which Anselmo Colzani was singing Gerard and I was supposed to be in the house. I had had a call from Chicago asking me to be available for a Marlboro recording session on the same day of the *Chénier* dress rehearsal. I had already made all of the voice-over spots for the cigarette commercials and I knew that this could continue to pay as the others had.

But how could I be in Chicago singing "You get a lot to like with a Marlboro, filter, flavor, pack or box," and at the same time still cover the rehearsal at the Met? I decided that I couldn't miss the recording session, no matter what, so I took an early plane to Chicago and called in sick to the Met from a pay phone. I told an assistant in the rehearsal department that a friend I knew from college, Pat Shelby, was picking me up from my hotel. I would be staying at his house, because I was alone in New York and didn't want to be sick by myself. I did not give the rehearsal department a telephone number where I could be reached, because, of course, I was not going to be there. I said I would call later and give them a number.

In the meantime, I arrived at Universal Studios in Chicago and sang the sessions with the same group and with the arranger and composer of the Marlboro jingle. Incidentally, that was Dick Marx, the father of the now famous Richard Marx of pop/rock fame. I sang many different commercials with Dick in my Chicago years.

We finished the sessions, and in the late afternoon I flew back to New York and went back to the hotel. I was nervous about returning and making up excuses not so much for my illness, but for my lack of communication. There was a stack of messages when I returned, all from Frank Paola, the then head of the rehearsal department, saying, "Call the Met immediately; where are you?" It turned out that Colzani had become hoarse during the rehearsal, and Mr. Bing had told him to go home and rest for the opening night. Colzani's cover was me, and I was not there. Even though I had called in sick, they didn't know where I was. For some reason, Mr. Bing had not been told that I was not available, so when he asked for the cover to continue the rehearsal, he was told only then that I was ill. He was not pleased.

The next day I nervously called Frank Paola. He said that he and Mr. Bing were quite upset about my misconduct, and that, at the least, I owed Mr. Bing an apology as to why I had been out of touch for a whole day. So I went to Mr. Bing's office and made up my story about being sick and visiting a friend in New Jersey to recover. The story was a little thin, but it was the only one I had. I apologized and said something about not being clear as to a cover's responsibility because it was my debut year, but that I now understood everything. He chastised me mildly in his austere Austrian manner and I left thinking, that's one little trick I'll never do again.

Coincidentally, that was about the end of commercials in Chicago for me. The whole jingle business drifted away to New York, Nashville, and Los Angeles. Subsequently I did try to pick up some voice-over sessions in New York, but to no avail. It's a very closed shop. However, the Marlboro money continued to come in for quite some time.

The only foray into the New York commercial scene came when someone from the William Morris Agency asked me about doing a Toyota spot, singing a sound track to the tune of "Funiculì, funiculà" with Toyota words. Half the New York Philharmonic was on the session, as well as a jazz rhythm section and a chorus. My part ended on a high A-flat, a note I liked in my throat. When the track was finished, we were flown to the Pacific coast in Oregon for the filming. To my own sound track, I lip-synched the famous Toyota line, "Ho, ho, ho, ho, what a feeling, Toyota." Everything was first class, with a lot of work, and a lot of repetitions, but because my vocals were prerecorded, I was always in perfect voice! One interesting film trick was the famous Toyota jump that we all remember. I jumped normally about a dozen times and they filmed it at twenty times the normal speed and then slowed it down for the commercial, so it looked like I jumped in slow motion. It was great fun and perhaps the biggest thrill was when my oldest son, Eric, saw it on a fully loaded 747 on the way to Miami and said loudly to me, so everyone heard it, "Hey, that's you, Dad."

CHAPTER FOUR

Regional Companies: An Appreciation

WITHOUT A DOUBT, THE REGIONAL COMPANIES in the United States have saved opera from becoming a totally elitist art relegated to two or three major cities. Although grand opera can hardly be compared to the latest Tom Cruise or Steven Spielberg movie, there is a large and appreciative audience out there.

One of the operatic forces I worked with early in my career was Tony Stivenello. Born in Venice, Italy, of a family involved in opera production, Tony came to the United States with a big music tradition behind him. He was someone who could provide a total production for an opera company and was what I call the perfect traffic cop. He spoke Italian, French, and some German, and knew his entire repertoire from memory. He could tell you, in his heavy Italian accent, exactly what you needed to know to be able to stage a scene in the shortest possible time. He could produce almost any opera in a day or two, plus one or two rehearsals onstage. The last rehearsal onstage was facetiously referred to as a "dress rehearsal." Tony wasn't facetious and he knew this type of scheduling was serious and assumed that the singers knew their parts very well when they arrived.

In the early years of the regional companies, their budgets rarely allowed rehearsals for more than a few days. Tony was not the only director out there who could do the job fast, but he was perhaps the best and the one I worked with the most in those early years. I would have to say that all my prior experience and study with the Goldovsky stage methods and the many performances on the road with his company served me well in this new-to-me, instant type of opera.

Stivenello furnished all the costumes, the sets, props, the staging savvy, and anything else needed for a production. The costumes were pretty much one size fits all, with a drawstring at the back to make them fit and the excess material covered by some kind of cape, jacket, or cloak. You furnished your own shoes and if you needed boots, Tony provided leg pieces that simulated them. Often the only chorus rehearsal was the one onstage with orchestra, the day before the performance.

In the performance Tony would sometimes don a costume and sing and move around in the chorus, telling them where to move when they needed help. It was your responsibility to remember all the details without making Tony repeat himself. He'd give you the necessary dimensions of the role and the entrance and exit routes. Bottom line, he gave you the basic international staging with few psychological insights into the characters. If there was time, however, he could tell you much more.

His sets were mostly hung from the stage fly; there was very little that was solid. Sometimes hung marble columns would have wrinkles in them because the set needed to be ironed, and you quickly learned not to lean on the sets. But the opera companies were getting whole productions for very little money, certainly for far less than now. There were obvious downsides, but performances went on with a minimal production staff and little office help. Without Tony's budget-sized productions, many of our regional companies wouldn't exist today, or at least not in their present size and excellence.

The lack of rehearsal time sometimes led to funny things. The third act of *Carmen* with the smugglers in the mountain featured a budget version of Carmen's fire: a few sticks bound up around a red light bulb and the electrical cord running offstage and plugged into an outlet. During one performance, as the chorus exited before Micaela's entrance, one of the choristers hoisted up the bales of contraband and got his foot caught in the cord. He dragged the "fire" offstage with him in rhythm to the music. It was a funny sight watching the fire disappear step by step.

Depending on the cast and how good the singers were, you could have some terrific performances. One city in which I worked with Tony was San Antonio, Texas, where the symphony used to present two weekends of opera each season, all conducted by Victor Alessandro. That was the first time I had done that kind of limited rehearsal. One of the memorable productions was a *Traviata* with Anna Moffo in her prime. She was one of the best Violettas of our time. Barry Morell, an undervalued tenor at the Met with a brilliant voice, was the Alfredo. Things went very well. It was a really hot performance, mostly due to Anna. Subsequently with that company, I sang *Faust*, *Traviata*, one of the relatives in *Gianni Schicchi*, *Pagliacci*, *Butterfly*, and *Lohengrin*, all with Tony Stivenello and Victor Alessandro.

Interestingly enough, with this very short rehearsal period, you could have a fine performance if it was just one, as in the case of *Traviata* in San Antonio. If you had more than one, the other performances could sometimes be terrible. I think that occurred because nothing you did in the first performance was really fixed or set. You were winging it, totally playing off the other person. In the second or later performances you would never remember exactly what you did the first time around.

I would be remiss in any discussion of my career if I failed to talk about the European influence on operatic life in the United States. Before, during, and after World War II, many fine musicians emigrated to the United States, including pianists, conductors, coaches, and instrumentalists of all kinds. They used their talent and their passion to establish and nurture opera companies all over this country.

Among the first and most important names here would have to be Gaetano Merola, who was born in Naples in 1882 and moved to the United States after studying at the Naples Conservatory. He was an assistant conductor at the Met and worked for various smaller companies. He founded the San Francisco Opera in 1923 and ran the company until his death thirty years later. He rarely abandoned the standard repertory he knew and loved, but he built a loyal audience there. His successor, Kurt Herbert Adler, turned the San Francisco Opera into one of the foremost opera companies in the world, as it still is today.

When I debuted in New York, many of the conductors and coaches were European: Kurt Adler, Jan Behr, Julius Berger, Fausto Cleva (who was a mainstay in the Italian wing at the Met), Otto Guth, John Gutman, Felix Popper, Fred Popper, Julius Rudel (who was the boss of the New York City Opera), George Schick, Ignace Strasfogel, Walter Taussig, and John White. There were a host of others who took university positions and helped train our American performers. The pioneers of our regional opera companies included Paul Csonka, Walter Herbert, Herman Herz, Richard Karp, and Rudolph Kruger. There was also an Italian group, which included Victor Alessandro (American born), Arthur Cosenza (American born), Arturo di Filippi, Aurelio Fabiani, and Frank Pandolfi.

I sang performances with many of these people and their regional companies. They operated on a shoestring with a very small budget and almost no one on the staff. Their productions would cost in the tens of thousands, as compared to hundreds of thousands or more now. All of these people worked their tails off for very little salary.

I don't know if historians would agree with me, but it seems that these people who worked for opera unselfishly out of their passion and knowledge allowed the regional companies to survive a time when the national love of opera was not as great as it is today and financial support was even harder to find. They allowed their new creations to function and stay in business for enough decades to reach a time when they could grow into the many well-established companies that we have now. Financial support has never been easy, but the companies now have public relations people, subscription departments, and other support staffs with far more outreach power. The production values now are reflected onstage, and in general the level is quite high. But we are where we are today because of these pioneers.

In 1962 I auditioned for and won one of the Ford Foundation prizes. It was a very unusual contest. They picked thirty winners, several from each voice category. There was a cash award, and, more important, they paid the fee of each of the winners for the next two years with any of the regional opera companies in the United States. Only the Met, New York City Opera, Chicago Lyric, and San Francisco were excluded. It was the Ford Foundation's aim to help these singers and at the same time help the regional companies by underwriting the fees of those who won. My career picked up quickly, for several companies jumped at the opportunity to have, in essence, a free singer. In those two years of underwriting I added to my credits Baltimore; Central City, Colorado; Cincinnati; Houston; Pittsburgh; San Antonio; and a few others.

Cincinnati Zoo

The old Cincinnati Summer Opera had its performances out of doors at the zoo. There was a theater with a normal, albeit small, stage and a covered auditorium with open sides leading out to all the animal areas and cages. The dressing rooms were in the back, unconnected to the stage. Only one had an air conditioner, which made it the prize room. All the rest were sweatboxes, because Cincinnati in the summer is very hot and humid. Usually your makeup had sweated off by the second act and you had to forget about it for the rest of the opera.

The performances normally began at eight-thirty in the evening. Even at that hour it was too bright for the lights to have much effect. Also, while it was still light, the animals were wide awake, so that when the opera began the elephants would trumpet, the lions would roar, the monkeys would scream, and the birds would sing or chirp. It was quite disconcerting to sing with the animals echoing all your phrases. Finally, when the sun set, a half hour or so later, the noise would cease and you could settle down to a normal performance. The audiences were very appreciative and often came with the whole family, using the zoo for a picnic and family outing and the music as the evening's dessert. While there were many downsides to this setting, it was on balance a very simpatico environment in which to sing.

Outdoor concerts present their own kinds of problems. If it's cold you can see your breath and have to worry about the cold air rushing over your throat, irritating it and causing a cough. I've been onstage with heaters clustered around the conductor and soloists to keep us semi-comfortable. And conversely, I've been in ninety-plus-degree weather at night where everyone was really sweating. On a few occasions I removed my white dinner jacket while singing because even late in the evening the temperature was still very high.

Sometimes you encounter bugs and insects. They are drawn to the lights, so when you inhale to begin singing, you could breathe one in. I suppose the protein is good for you if you can swallow it, but to spit it out is usually preferred, assuming that you haven't already choked on the darn thing.

There can also be problems with colds and allergies. Years ago, in Santa Fe, I was in that chorus for a production of Donizetti's *Anna*

Bolena. Santa Fe had an open stage and the bass, singing the role of Henry VIII in this opera, had had a bad cold with no cover or substitute to take his place. So he had been singing several performances while sick. During one of these, when his cold was the worst, he sneezed onstage between phrases, and out of his nose flew a huge, long line of, well, there's no other way to say it, *snot!* It was at least a foot long and hung out of his nose. I was onstage playing one of the guards and saw this. The Henry didn't know what to do. I have no idea why he didn't just wipe his nose and be rid of it, but, I guess out of frustration, the only thing that occurred to him was to snuff the whole long strand of snot back into his nose and go on singing. I was grossed out and couldn't imagine how all that stuff went back into his head.

Once in a while Mother Nature adds to the drama of a musical work. I have had storms raging outside during Mendelssohn's *Elijah*, at the moment when there was a storm in the music. The audience reacted emotionally to the weather as well as to the music. Personally, I have to admit that singing stormy music during a real electrical storm is quite exciting.

More than once a dog, which was probably lost, has wandered onstage during the program and evoked much laughter from the audience. Or a baby has started crying and won't stop. It's always a question whether to acknowledge the presence of an outside intrusion or the sounds of the audience while you are singing. I guess the only answer is to try to maintain the mood of the music at all costs.

Microphones at outdoor concerts can present their own problems. Feedback and other electronic difficulties sometimes defy you to give a serious performance. You need to learn to use the mike as a friend. Leaning in on the lows and laying back slightly on the highs generally give better ambience for the voice.

There is an odd sensation outdoors using a microphone: I feel more removed from the audience and therefore less nervous. Plus the knowledge that just by leaning into the mike all sounds can be as loud as you want them. What a concept! Of course, soundmen and mike technique are what the whole pop field is based on. It has almost nothing to do with personal vocal technique, and that is a strange concept for a classically trained singer. In a theater, you use the acoustics to gauge your singing, but outdoors it is the audio man who makes your sound, and one has to give in to that fact. So we quickly become used to microphones and how to use them.

In a park, seeing the audience move around in the distance is also something you have to get used to. People coming and going, children running around, in general picnicking, talking, paying more attention to their friends than to the music is the norm. But I know a setting of that kind can often give the listener more enjoyment, because of that same informality.

I sang many of my first operas, in the original language, out of doors at the Cincinnati Zoo—*Trovatore, Traviata, Forza, Butterfly, Pagliacci, Carmen, Tosca,* and *Aida*—mostly with the team of the Italian conductor Anton Guadagno and the Argentine-born stage director Tito Capobianco. These two men really introduced me to Italian opera in Italian and using that language as a normal working tool. Theretofore all my experience had been with English as the normal working language. My debut there in 1963 was in *Il trovatore,* and I was very nervous—almost afraid to go to the first rehearsal. Although Anton and Tito were very cordial and eventually became my close friends, at that time I didn't know them or they me, and I felt quite inadequate. The rest of the cast all spoke Italian easily and were experienced in the bigger opera companies.

To add to my insecurity, I had learned *Trovatore* at home on the farm with my mother playing piano, plus listening to a few recordings, so I really didn't know how well I knew it or how good my Italian diction and style were. Also the whole area of marking (singing half-voice or in general saving the voice in staging rehearsals) was brand new to me. All those things combined to make me feel like a fish out of water or a step-child in a situation where I didn't belong. I did know enough to refrain from letting on how insecure I felt. Fortunately, my vocal technique and all the Goldovsky training and experience served me well, and I had a good success in my debut.

Being out of doors, however, did lead to some mistakes onstage. Sometimes the cast was too relaxed, which led to some strange events. There was a *Traviata* with the well-known and beautiful American soprano Mary Costa as Violetta and bass-baritone Eugene Green as the Barone. Gene and I were talking together in the wings while Mary was singing the verses of the famous aria "Ah! Fors'è lui" and cabaletta "Sempre libera." My character, Giorgio Germont, does not appear in the first act, so I was just chumming and not paying much attention to curtain calls. There is a pause between verses that sounds almost the same as the end of the act. Gene was telling me a story, as he often did, and all of a sudden in a pause in his story, he heard silence onstage and assumed it was the end of the act. He said, "Excuse me, I have to take my bow," and ran out onstage without thinking or looking. The curtain was open as Gene looked out and saw the audience. He immediately realized that he had run out in the middle of the aria. Mary looked askance and started to panic, but as Gene slowly backed offstage, she regained her composure and continued the scene. He was dying of embarrassment as he exited and didn't say another word until the end of the act, when he took his appropriate bows. I doubt that he ever made that mistake again. I don't have any idea what the audience thought, but I have never let Gene forget that moment.

In *La forza del destino* there is an outdoor scene where the monk, Melitone, is serving soup from a kettle. A small piece of plywood on the stage painted to look like bushes and small trees fell over, and Andrew Foldi as Fra Melitone just reached over and picked it up. The set piece had a mind of its own and wouldn't stay put. So Andy stood there with his leg holding up the stage piece while he continued serving soup to the masses.

My first *Tosca* in Italian was at the Cincinnati Zoo. I had already sung it forty or fifty times in English with the Goldovsky Company. In a translation many things change. The nuances and the dimensions of each character are affected; obviously, the relation of lyric to music is changed, and the flow of the material different. You cannot know what the composer really had in mind without knowing the opera in the original language. I was both lucky and honored to have had as my Tosca the beautiful Dorothy Kirsten. The American public had grown to love her not only for her concert and operatic appearances, but also thanks to her performances on radio and television and in movies. I had sung with her in a production of *Madama Butterfly* in San Antonio, where she taught me a great deal and was a wonderful colleague.

However, Sharpless in *Butterfly* is a very different part from that of Scarpia and not to be compared. Scarpia and Tosca have a special relationship; much of how the baritone plays his role is determined by how the soprano plays her part. Dorothy was a very feminine and refined Tosca and knew every detail of the words and music, and she provided a study in stagecraft and believable operatic portrayal. It was from Dorothy that I learned the famous hand kiss near the end of the first act when Tosca exits. Scarpia tries to kiss her hand and she pulls it away in disgust and anger. Scarpia then savors her violent reaction, enjoying it more than the kiss. Many famous sopranos know this bit of staging, but my first exposure to it was from Dorothy, and I have used it in all my performances of *Tosca*.

This was in the mid-1960s, before there were any TV monitors backstage. All choral directors since the beginning of opera have had to look through some kind of peephole in the curtain whenever there was a backstage or offstage cue that required conducting. It was particularly difficult when the curtain was open and hanging in folds on each side of the stage. The choral director had to push aside those folds and find the little peephole with one hand, conduct with the other hand behind him, and hope that the chorus could follow.

The chorus conductor that summer was Robert Evans, a very fine coach, accompanist, and linguist at the Conservatory of Music, University of Cincinnati. Robert's special gifts were not so much in the choral field, and I don't think he was very happy conducting backstage and preparing the operatic choruses for the summer season. I had worked with Robert at Tanglewood several years before and knew him as a brilliant language coach and pianist. He was also rather high-strung as well as a perfectionist.

Tosca has several offstage cues. In the second act, there is a cantata in which the soprano sings with the chorus, and the choral director has to push aside the little flap in the opened curtain to follow the beat. In the dress rehearsal, with Guadagno leading the orchestra, Robert missed the tempo, and the cantata was not with the orchestra at all. Guadagno stopped the orchestra and started yelling "Maestro Evans!" in his heavily accented and rather staccato English. This is always an embarrassing moment for all the people involved, but for Robert, with his perfectionist nature, it was a disaster. Red-faced, he came out onstage and exclaimed in a loud, tremulous voice, *"Somebody closed my hole."* The whole place went up for grabs. Dorothy came out onstage laughing hysterically, and even Guadagno had to laugh. It took five to ten minutes for everything to settle down. Often in a very dramatic opera in high-tension moments, when something funny or silly happens, it's like poking a hole in a dam. With all that pressure behind it, the tension and laughter just pour out.

Grant Park and New York City Opera

In Chicago, in the 1950s and1960s, the Grant Park concerts in the summer were a wonderful outdoor series featuring orchestra, chorus, and well-known conductors performing many works, pop and classical, most familiar to the public. In my post-college years living on the farm, I learned that sometimes they hired local singers for solo parts. So in 1962 I auditioned for Edward Gordon, the assistant manager of the concerts, and he hired me to sing *Carmina Burana*, by Carl Orff, that next summer. Gordon was a great friend of young, undiscovered talent all through his tenure at Grant Park. Later, as the manager of the famous Ravinia Festival, he always tried to encourage and use fine new talent for his concerts.

Carmina Burana was to be conducted by Julius Rudel, the head of the New York City Opera (NYCO) and a well-known and important name among conductors. Fortunately, the tessitura of the *Carmina Burana* was perfect for my voice, and I think Rudel was impressed, because he asked me to audition for the NYCO. I can't say I remember the audition, but I know he offered me a bevy of small parts. At the time I was flattered, but as I thought about it, I decided to decline the offer. In the early and middle 1960s, I was touring with Goldovsky singing leading roles, albeit on a small scale. My reasoning was that singing major parts like Scarpia, Rigoletto, Figaro, Marcello, Germont, and Escamillo, even in smaller venues, was far more valuable than singing small parts, even in a New York venue. Some people thought I should go to New York because that was where all the musical ears and all the action were. But, I thought, if I am singing tiny roles, my exposure and growth would be limited anyway.

I should add that in 1960, after my first Tanglewood experience, I auditioned for and subsequently went with Herbert Barrett Management, with which I have remained for my whole career. That is where I met Joseph Lippman, vice president of the management. He worked for his artists with a fury and always said to them, "Reengagement is the name of the game." He had all sorts of ideas about how to present yourself in a better light. He knew the opera repertoire like almost no one else and he certainly made me a better performer.

My refusal of the NYCO offer paid off, because Goldovsky continued to ask me to tour with his company in other major roles. So I went on living in Chicago, still in the little house on the farm, and traveled from there to my next engagement. I guess I thought that you could fly from O'Hare just as easily as from LaGuardia. Only the auditions were difficult, because they were usually in New York, so I would fly there when absolutely necessary. During this period I was married to Charlotte and my two older children, Eric and Erin, were born. Expanding my career meant, unfortunately, that I was often away from home. This is a big downside of career singing and certainly was a factor in our eventual divorce.

For the 1964–65 season, Herbert Barrett decided that a mixed quartet could be a successful and bookable group, so he formed a quartet called, playfully, "442 Nite." The soprano was Joan Gavoorian, the mezzo-soprano was Lillian Garabedian, the tenor was Jerold Siena, and the baritone was me. We made up a beautiful program of various operatic and Broadway pieces and rehearsed them well. Our first date was a few months hence at Bob Jones University in Greenville, South Carolina. Because we all had other engagements to sing, we planned to fly separately and meet there. It turned out that Joan, Lillian, and I would be in New York before the concert and would fly together, and Jerry Siena would come from another part of the country and would fly by himself.

We were booked on Eastern Airlines flight 663, a DC-7 that was to take off from Kennedy Airport in the afternoon of the day before the performance. However, some personal business came up for me at the last minute, and I switched to a later flight—fate, God, who knows what protected me. With the women onboard, their afternoon flight took off in clear weather, and for no apparent reason exploded and immediately crashed into the Atlantic Ocean. All the passengers were killed, and many bodies were never recovered. It was a terrible tragedy, and we all suffered at the loss of these lovely and talented young women, as well as the many others on the plane. I thank God that my plans changed at the last moment; fate can twist and turn in all of our lives.

After a couple of years with the Barrett management and a good beginning to my career, the New York City Opera wanted to hear me again. I was now armed with many more performances under my belt than at the first audition. So in the spring of 1964 I auditioned in the old theater on Fifty-fifth Street (the Masonic Temple), which was at that time the home to the NYCO. This time they offered a per-performance contract (poor money, but normal for them) of Germont, *Traviata*; Valentin, *Faust*; Tonio, *Pagliacci*; Figaro, *The Barber of Seville*; and a staged version of *Carmina Burana*. There was a guarantee of a certain number of performances and some covers, plus two more years of major parts. I accepted the offer.

My debut at the New York City Opera in the fall of 1964 was as Valentin in Gounod's *Faust*. I did not sing the first performance of that season and so did not have any stage rehearsal, only room rehearsals with the cast. The Méphistophélès was Norman Treigle, whom I knew from Central City, and the conductor was Franco Patane, the father of the now deceased Giuseppe Patane.

Norman was perhaps the most powerful stage personality of any singer out there. He almost never sang out in rehearsals, sometimes singing even the low notes down an octave. He had those notes to burn, even low Cs and low B-flats. All new singers at the City Opera had heard of Norman and were quite in awe of him. Part of this came from the fact that he did so many evil-villain parts with such intensity that it was hard to divorce him from his roles. Though he seemed a rather closed and unapproachable human being, this was not the real Norman. He was a supportive colleague who was always ready with ideas and suggestions and certainly made me feel welcome. I appreciated this especially, because Patane, while a real veteran and a knowledgeable musician, was very dour and not very inspirational, plus he smoked incessantly. Norman had an undeniable energy and ever present underlying power. Slight of build and of average height, he gave no outward sign of the power of his personality and his voice.

In the relatively short rehearsal time, I never heard Norman sing out. In the opera, the baritone is killed in a duel with Faust with the help of the devil. In the following scene, Valentin's dead body is laid out on a funeral bier. Once my character was "killed," I had to lie very still. I did this in the rehearsals and with Norman never singing out, I had no idea of the effect his voice would have on my ears when he in fact finally did sing out.

Earlier in performance, lying still with my eyes closed, I couldn't see where he was. When the moment arrived, Méphistophélès—Norman— appeared just above me onstage and sang a phrase starting on the written note D above middle C. This wide-open note in any baritone or bass voice is a big, fat sound, but in Norman's voice it was a veritable cannon. I was sure that my whole body jumped at the explosion of his sound, and I remained embarrassed through the rest of the scene. Dead bodies don't jump.

Earlier in the same performance, after my aria, "Avant de quitter ces lieux," the conductor did not stop to allow for any applause. I was too nervous to really know that he could have helped my debut by giving the audience a chance to show their appreciation. Some days later I found out that Norman had gone back to the conductor's room in the intermission after my aria and chewed Patane out for stepping on my applause. Norman never told me about the incident; he just went to bat for me because he thought it was right. We went on to perform many times together, and my respect for him only grew.

In Santiago, Chile, in 1968 at the Teatro Municipal, Norman and Beverly Sills were singing *Tales of Hoffmann*, staged by Tito and Gigi Capobianco. I remember that the costume of Dr. Miracle was a black body stocking and demonic face makeup, all black and white. On the back of the costume was a fluorescent painted skeleton that showed only when a certain spotlight hit it. So when Norman turned around fast, he effectively disappeared and the skeleton instantly appeared. It was a startling and stunning effect. There were no bows between the acts because of the big makeup changes and to keep the drama more alive by shorter intermissions. Beverly was singing gloriously, and because this was the beginning of her enormous fame, the audience was well aware of her. Norman was not as well-known by this audience, but his performance was so powerful that after one of the acts the audience started clapping in rhythm and chanting "TREI-GLE, TREI-GLE, TREI-GLE," until he came out in front of the curtain.

It's a terrible shame there is not more video evidence of the power of Norman's performing. I saw him or performed with him in *Boris Godunov*, as Escamillo in *Carmen*, as the four villains in *Tales of Hoffmann*, as Reverend Blitch in *Susanna*, and in *Faust*, Boito's *Mefistofele*, *Don Giovanni*, *Julius Caesar*, and *The Love for Three Oranges*. Many of these productions were put together by the team of Tito and Gigi Capobianco. On his own Norman was a giant and never less than riveting; in Capobianco productions he was unforgettable.

Central City, Colorado, was a wonderful experience in the summer of 1964. It lies in the Rocky Mountains outside of Denver and sits about 7,500 feet above sea level amid a host of ghost towns, mostly from burned-out silver mines. The opera *The Ballad of Baby Doe*, by Douglas Moore, was written about the silver mines in this area. The panorama was simply stunning, and to sing opera in this setting was a thrill. We performed *Il trovatore* and *Don Giovanni*, in which I was one of the Masettos. Because of the double casting there was a huge array of American talent there that summer. Norman Treigle was probably the best-known singer, and he was the Don in my cast. I watched him like a hawk, because his manner onstage and the power of his body and hands were a marvel. His energy and movement seemed to motivate the music, and I learned much by watching and imitating him.

There were also Richard Cross, Richard Cassilly, Spiro Malas, Herb Beattie, John Craig, John Fiorito, Tom Paul, Justino Díaz, Charles Anthony, Ben Rayson, Chester Ludgin, Beverly Bower, Lucine Amara,

Maria Ferriero, Margaret Willougher, Mary Ellen Pracht, and a few others. In American talent in 1964, that was a very heavy list. Nat Merrill staged both operas, and Emerson Buckley conducted. It was a great experience for me, particularly, because I still lived on the farm. And although I had been touring with Goldovsky before, my experience with New York–based singers was very limited. There was also an unknown bass in the chorus by the name of Samuel Ramey, who was rarely, if ever, to sing in choruses again!

Tito Capobianco continued to play a very important part in my operatic life. Tito was born in Argentina in 1933 and studied law and philosophy before turning to music. His first production was of *Pagliacci* in his native country in 1953; its acclaim led to his appointment as technical director of the Teatro Colón in Buenos Aires, followed by the general directorship of the Teatro Argentino in the late 1950s. In the early 1960s, he came to the United States to be the artistic director of the Cincinnati Opera, but he first came to notice in the mid-1960s with his stunning stagings for the New York City Opera, which led to worldwide engagements.

In 1982, as the head of the San Diego Opera, Tito invited me to sing *Henry VIII* by Camille Saint-Saëns, a real tour de force for the baritone. This very powerful opera takes place during the time Henry breaks with the Catholic Church, leading to the establishment of the Church of England. This was the first time I had sung a real and important histori-cal character, and there was something very strong and meaningful about those performances, as though I were really a part of that history.

Even before that, in 1978, Tito had sold me on the idea of learning the opera *Hamlet*, by Ambroise Thomas. This opera became rather a calling card for me for quite a few years, and I sang it with many differ-ent companies in both English and French. This identification with the part of Hamlet also led to the Decca recording with Joan Sutherland and Richard Bonynge that for many years was the only modern version avail-able. I believe that I have sung it more often than any living baritone, and it is a part I love very much.

In English, it is much more Shakespearean and intimate. In French it is grander, more operatic, less Shakespearean, but powerful. Audiences tended to like it more in French than in English even though they understood less—I suppose some kind of snobbery was part of the reason. (Now, with supertitles, there is less and less a case for presenting opera in an English translation.) For me, they were simply different operas, each with its own set of problems and satisfactions.

Ambroise Thomas left the world a big problem in that he wrote the opera with Hamlet alive at the end. At the English debut of the opera, Thomas was told that this was not Shakespeare, that Hamlet must die at the end as in the play. Thomas wrote a brief new ending in which Hamlet dies, but he did not go back far enough in the opera to prepare a workable, definitive version that can be accepted by everyone. Also, the opera has no major tenor role. Combined with other difficulties, this means that *Hamlet* is generally undervalued and done less often than it deserves, for within its covers it has some of the most beautiful music ever composed.

Once in San Diego, when I came to rehearsal, I saw a man seated in the corner with a baseball cap pulled down so far I couldn't see his face. Eventually Tito called me over and introduced him: "Sherrill, I'd like you to meet Burt Lancaster." He lifted his cap, and I saw it was him. I made some inane noise while I shook his hand. Tito had asked him to stage an opera, and Burt wanted to watch a whole rehearsal period, from beginning to performance, before giving an answer. I suppose he chose *Hamlet* because it was a piece from the theater, a world he knew.

It was inhibiting for all of us to have someone of such enormous fame sitting off in a corner just watching us work. It turned out that Burt loved opera and was very knowledgeable about it. That was the beginning of our long-term friendship as he sat through weeks of rehearsals and watched this *Hamlet* "take life." We were reticent to ask any advice because he was a guest, but there were some troubling phrases in the translation. So we finally did ask him, and he had some very good input about the Shakespearean English.

During the room rehearsals, he mentioned that I should lose ten to fifteen pounds to be an ideal weight for the role, because he knew that on film, you look ten to fifteen pounds heavier. Sometime later, when we moved from room rehearsals to stage rehearsals and anyone who was not in the cast was seated in the auditorium, he asked me how I had lost that weight. Of course, I hadn't lost any at all. Because of the distance and the different perspective, weight reads in a different way. I'm also tall enough to carry some weight. I think if one is too thin you can lose power and support in singing, something most singers know. At the same time, too much weight is never good.

In 1976 Burt was filming in Munich and came to a *Tosca* performance I was singing at the National Theater. Subsequently he and I did several gala events together, and he appears in a video with me, *All Star Gala: Sherrill Milnes and Friends*.

I think the whole world feels about movie stars the same way I do. Their strengths, talents, and looks are frozen in time, and they never age. So we think of them as they were in the last film in which we saw them. They are always remembered as a favorite character in a certain movie that you love and identify with. That certainly was the way it was with Burt Lancaster.

After the San Diego *Hamlet* and *Henry VIII*, Tito and my publicity agent at the time, Edgar Vincent, almost insisted on my singing *Thaïs*, by Jules Massenet. They all but guaranteed that it would be a big success for me and very satisfying to sing. It turned out that they were right. I was to be co-starred with Beverly Sills and perform in San Francisco. I didn't know the opera at all, except for the famous "Meditation," which was my big violin solo in high school. It is really a two-singer opera with the courtesan Thaïs wearing sequins, and the baritone, a third-century cenobite named Athanaël, wearing burlap robes. But even with this discrepancy in costuming, this work turned out to be a big tour de force for the baritone. The production at the San Francisco Opera was a critical and audience success. I had to be in pretty good physical shape, because I had to carry Beverly across the Egyptian desert about forty times. Of course that was really about thirty-five feet across the stage, but nonetheless it took some strength. It was later performed at the Met and on the Met tour, where, mostly because of Beverly's fame, we were selling out various municipal auditoriums of 10,000 to 15,000 seats, no small feat.

As an aside, some years later, Beverly Sills was honored as a Kennedy Center honoree. I was asked to help make the presentation along with Carol Burnett. It was great fun, and I sang a spoof duet with Carol, praising and joking about Beverly's talents as part of the ceremony.

In addition, the following remarks were part of my tribute. "What do the cities of Detroit, Cleveland, Washington, New York, Boston, San Francisco, Memphis, Dallas, and Atlanta have in common? Give up? Those are the very cities where I carried Beverly Sills across the Egyptian desert—now that's real dedication to one's art as well as to one artist. But besides giving me strong arms, I remember especially that Beverly always smelled good, which in our sometimes sweaty world of opera is very unusual and very nice."

Beverly, of course, knows this story very well. Besides the happy memories of times I shared with her onstage, Beverly's Farewell Gala at the New York State Theater gave me an opportunity to sing the beautiful Bernstein/Sondheim song "Maria," from *West Side Story*. Audiences always react strongly to this song, and it took on a special meaning for me many years later when I met and eventually married my present wife, Maria Zouves.

At the first performance of *Thaïs* in San Francisco, Kirk Douglas came backstage to congratulate me. Needless to say, I was thrilled to meet him and told him that I had learned how to carry Beverly across the stage and how to wear my loincloth and burlap robe by watching his movie *Spartacus*. It was rather an inane thing to say, but I couldn't think of anything else. Fans tell me that they are sometimes tongue-tied backstage when they are trying to talk to me, and I am exactly the same way.

At a later performance in San Francisco, a dapper, elegant gentleman came backstage and congratulated me on a fine job and said that fifty years before he had made his Paris Opera debut as Athanaël in *Thaïs*. His name was Martial Singher, probably the most famous French baritone of the past. His words and compliments to me were especially meaningful, and I was quite moved by his enthusiasm. Coincidentally, on the Herbert Barrett Management list of singers in 1959–60 was Martial Singher, who then retired, and the next year, 1960–61, appeared the name of Sherrill Milnes. I knew that it was purely coincidental, but I have always considered it good luck and with great pride.

Leonard Warren

When I began my career, I was often compared with the great operatic baritone Leonard Warren. Warren belonged to a category of singers called "the American Verdi baritone." Other names often on that list are Lawrence Tibbett, John Charles Thomas, Robert Weede, Richard Bonelli, Robert Merrill, Cornell MacNeil—and I guess I have to be put on the list as well. If I have left anyone out, I apologize, but for some, this whole category is somewhat arbitrary and has to do with relative fame as much as voice quality.

My voice teacher at Drake University during my bachelor's and master's degree years was Andrew White. During the late 1930s and early 1940s he had lived in New York and studied with Sidney Dietch, who was also Warren's voice teacher. Warren and White were contemporaries, and Andy's baritone was similar in timbre and range to Warren's. My own opinion is that had family responsibilities not come along and World War II not interrupted the entire life of the United States, Andy White would have had a major world career. He was a featured soloist with Fred Waring and the Pennsylvanians and sang many concerts with them. He subsequently sang with our regional opera companies as well as the New York City Opera, where he debuted as Escamillo in *Carmen*. In addition to a fine oratorio and concert career, he had a long, distinguished teaching career. Partly because of my study with Andy White, my voice color and general timbre are quite similar to his, and more to the point, similar to Leonard Warren's. This has to be part of the reason that in my early career people would say things like, "You will be Warren's successor."

Born in New York City on April 21, 1911, of Russian parents, Leonard Warrenoff became one of the most famous and beloved operatic baritones in the world. As Leonard Warren, he sang in the Radio City Music Hall chorus and from there moved on to the Met. His remarkable voice had a dramatic intensity that did not come naturally to him. As with everything else in his life, he worked at that until he got it right. Fortunately, his incomparable voice and dramatic power are still available to us on recordings of some of his most famous roles.

In 1939 Warren entered the Metropolitan Opera Auditions of the Air, which were broadcast live on the radio. One of the judges that year was the noted conductor Wilfred Pelletier, who led the Met Orchestra for twenty-eight seasons and had the good fortune to marry the beloved American singer Rose Bampton. Bampton sang leading soprano and mezzo roles in operas all over the world and went on to equally great heights as a teacher. Pelletier later told my friend Jon Spong that he was listening to the contestants from behind a screen and so could not see them. When he heard Warren he thought someone was pulling a fast one and playing a recording of an established singer, because the quality was of such a high caliber. Pelletier was prepared to be angry at what he thought had been a joke when he found out that it really was one of the contestants. Warren obviously won the auditions and was awarded a contract. His stage debut was as Paolo in *Simon Boccanegra*, with Tibbett in the title role; Pinza, Martinelli, and Rethberg were also in the cast. Warren's vocal excellence ensured that in subsequent seasons, he moved into all the major Italian roles.

Through the next two decades Warren, along with Robert Merrill, dominated the Italian wing of the Metropolitan Opera. Warren's flawless technique, seamless flow of sound, and brilliant top voice were his vocal trademarks, and these qualities became the standard by which others would be measured, including me.

There is a story that Lawrence Tibbett once protested Warren's singing the part of Ford in *Falstaff*, saying, "I don't want him [Warren] doing to me what I did to Antonio Scotti when I sang Ford to his Falstaff." Apparently, Tibbett had stolen the show from Scotti, and, recognizing Warren's greatness, Tibbett didn't want Warren doing the same thing to him! In his time, Tibbett owned such roles as Rigoletto, Don Carlo, Germont, Iago, Count di Luna, Falstaff, Scarpia, and Tonio, which he performed in all the world theaters. Leonard Warren died on March 4, 1960, during a performance of *La forza del destino* onstage at the Metropolitan Opera. In that scene, a doctor, examining the wounded tenor, sings, "E' salvo" (he's saved). Warren, the baritone, exclaims "E' salvo, e' salvo, o gioia" (he's saved, he's saved, oh joy) because he wants to kill the tenor himself to avenge his father's death. Just after Warren had sung "O gioia," he had a massive cerebral hemorrhage, and people who saw it say he fell like a statue. Doctors have speculated that he was probably dead before he hit the stage. The curtain came down and Richard Tucker, the tenor in that performance, ran out and grabbed his friend. Osie Hawkins, the stage manager and a former singer at the Met, tried to give Warren mouth-to-mouth resuscitation. There was blood oozing from Warren's nose and many thought he had fainted and broken it in the fall. Rudolf Bing was in the audience. Thirty to forty minutes after rushing backstage, he came out in front of the curtain and announced, "Ladies and gentlemen, the great baritone Leonard Warren has just died, and so we will terminate the performance out of respect for this great artist." Mrs. Warren was also in the audience. Can you imagine a wife watching her husband collapse and die onstage?

After spending many hours sorting out arrangements in the theater that night, Osie Hawkins eventually went home. After getting ready to go to bed, he went into the bathroom, looked in the mirror, and saw a streak of dried blood on the side of his face—Warren's blood—and, as he told me, "That's an image indelibly imprinted on my mind, forever."

Oddly enough, I never heard Warren sing live. I played in dance bands all through my college years in order to earn money, and, I suppose because of the farm work ethic, when I committed to something, come hell or high water, I followed through, with few exceptions. Leonard Warren was presenting a recital in Des Moines and it fell on a night when I had a dance job. At that time in my musical and vocal development, I didn't know too much about opera and the famous singers of the world. And so while I wanted to hear his recital, I didn't think about it as a once-in-a-lifetime opportunity. I played my dance job and made my paltry $15. Only in subsequent years did I realize that I was never to have that opportunity again. So that decision not to call in sick prevented me from ever seeing Warren perform. I have regretted it ever since.

When Warren died in 1960, I was still living in Downers Grove and was just starting to tour with the Goldovsky Opera Company. By the time of my Met debut in 1965, I had sung with many regional companies and had debuted with the New York City Opera. This was the time when people began comparing me to Warren, saying, "You may be the next Verdi baritone," and so on. I really didn't know what that meant, or how to think about it in those terms. When you are a young singer, you don't think about your own possible place in history. You are too busy preparing and performing and just getting through the day. The whole business of having a title or inheriting a mantle seemed a little too mystical for me.

In 1968 I was invited to a cocktail party after singing in the world premiere of Marvin David Levy's opera of the O'Neill play *Mourning Becomes Electra*. Henry Butler, the librettist, introduced me to the lady he was with. "Sherrill Milnes, I'd like you to meet Mrs. Leonard Warren, Agatha." I was a little stunned. She looked at me eye to eye, as though she were seeing inside me, and said nothing for a few seconds; I felt the room was completely empty save for the two of us. Finally she said, "So you're the one." Fortunately, I was old enough not to be totally embarrassed, but still, I was young enough not to know what to do. Then after some moments of looking at each other, we embraced for what seemed like an eternity. I'm sure it was just a few seconds, but I was nonetheless extremely moved by this very emotional encounter.

I was told that after her husband's death, Agatha Warren never went to an opera that he had performed. She'd seen me in Tchaikovsky's *Pique dame* (*Pikovaya dama*) and Verdi's *Luisa Miller* because he'd never sung them. In fact, *Luisa* was probably the only Verdi opera she ever heard me sing. Subsequently, I became friendly with Leonard Warren's sister, Vivian, and Agatha's brother, Roy.

Some years later, after Agatha's death, Vivian and Roy decided to give me all of Warren's recital music, as well as his monogrammed briefcase—the one he had with him the night he died. I have kept that briefcase by my piano for over twenty years and always assumed it was empty. Recently I took it out just to look at it, touch it, and contemplate its history. While looking inside, I saw something stuck to an inside flap, and my heart jumped as I looked further. It was the *Forza* program for the night he died, opened to the cast list. I'm sure he was the last person to touch it, having put it in his case before he went onstage, just as I did for every performance I sang. Finding it was a chilling experience, but at the same time an emotional one. Since then, I guess I have believed a little more in fate or destiny.

In the years following Leonard Warren's death, and well before my debut there, the Met needed and was looking for a new Verdi baritone. They brought in many baritones from around the world, but none seemed to fit the bill. Robert Merrill and Cornell MacNeil were already in full international careers, so they were not available to sing more performances than were already scheduled at the Met. Any theater that puts on more than 250 performances a year needs many singers—-especially for the heavier baritone parts. And so, to that extent, they were looking for me, but I knew only this in hindsight, certainly not at the time. I suppose this was another reason the older veteran singers would use phrases such as "You're Warren's successor." This phenomenon of comparison comes up even now, although I am basically retired.

I suppose it remains to be seen whether the statement of the esteemed Pulitzer Prize–winning music critic of the *Los Angeles Times*, Martin Bernheimer, comes true: "It appears that Sherrill Milnes may be the last singer to be a part of the unbroken line of American Verdi baritones dating back to the Tibbett-Thomas era." I hope he's wrong, for Verdi's sake and for the sake of the memory of the great men who preceded me.

CHAPTER FIVE

Met Audition
and Mr. Bing

NINETEEN SIXTY-FIVE WAS A YEAR of great diversity. Lyndon Johnson sent the first ground troops into Vietnam and also signed the Voting Rights Act. Winston Churchill died and Malcolm X was assassinated. The top films were *The Sound of Music* and *Dr. Zhivago*, and Americans were singing "The Shadow of Your Smile" and cheering for the World Champion Baltimore Orioles.

In the spring of 1965, John Gutman of the Met—one of Bing's assistants and close friends—still looking for a Verdi baritone, called Joe Lippman at the Barrett office to ask if I would audition for them. Joe, of course, said yes, but that I couldn't audition at the time they wanted to hear me because I was in Phoenix, Arizona, singing the role of Sharpless in *Madama Butterfly*. Instead of letting it go, Joe looked at my schedule, found a date when I could audition, and asked where the company would be at that time. In Atlanta, Georgia, on tour, Gutman said. So Joe suggested that the Met pay for me to fly down to Atlanta to sing for them. He knew that the old Fox Theater in Atlanta was not unlike the old Met, and he pointed that out to Gutman. Gutman agreed, and three weeks later, having told no one of the audition, I flew to Atlanta.

I went to the Fox Theater the next afternoon having no idea of the circumstances of the audition. The *Samson et Dalila* set was already up onstage, and Osie Hawkins was in the wings organizing the audition. Richard Woitach was there to play for me. At the time I didn't know any of these people, of course. I walked onstage with heart pounding and saw Mr. Bing, John Gutman, Robert Herman, Paul Jaretski, and

George Schick sitting in the house. They asked what I wanted to sing and I replied, "Avant de quitter ces lieux," from *Faust*, and "Eri tu" from Verdi's *Un ballo in maschera*. I think perhaps it was a little easier being in a set than on an empty stage, as I felt a part of a bigger piece. Because I was so nervous, I don't remember the audition very well, but it must have been good, because after the second aria, Bing asked me to come into the house and speak with them. When he said, "I would like to have you with us," my heart leaped. He mentioned *Faust*, *Queen of Spades*, and possibly *Aida* and *Samson et Dalila*. These were all very exciting to me and I said so. The only request I made was, "Please, no more Masettos." I had done the role sixty times in my life and I really didn't want to do it ever again. Mr. Bing said he did not think that would be a problem—there were plenty of other things to sing.

After a little more conversation during which I was introduced to the other administrators, I went back to the hotel feeling like I was on cloud nine. Only then did I make some phone calls to other people to share my elation and excitement. Within a week, Joe Lippman had worked out the details for the first year of a three-year contract. On December 22, 1965, I would debut as Valentin in Gounod's *Faust*, with a second performance to follow; then would come two performances of *Queen of Spades* and one performance of *Aida* in January of 1966—five performances in all over a period of fourteen weeks, with covers of about four other operas that I already knew.

I was singing at the same time at the New York City Opera and several other regional opera houses, so it was a full schedule. At that time Lincoln Center did not exist, so I had the privilege of singing one season at the historic old Met. A host of other singers also debuted during the 1965–66 season, including Mirella Freni, Reri Grist, Pilar Lorengar, Renata Scotto, James King, Alfredo Kraus, John Reardon, and Tom Stewart. By any standards, it was an exciting season.

My debut was in a new production of the Gounod opera, designed by Jacques Dupont and staged by the French filmmaker and actor Jean-Louis Barrault. The cast included Justino Díaz as Méphistophélès, John Alexander as Faust, and Montserrat Caballé as Marguerite in her first performance at the Met, all conducted by Georges Prêtre. Montserrat's and my roles had been sung earlier in the season by Gabriella Tucci and Robert Merrill. Debuting with Caballé was a big gamble for me, because she was the big European star and I was the new American kid. It would have been very easy to be run over by the audience's and critics' rush to applaud and praise her and forget about my debut and me. The upside of my gamble was that because Montserrat was debuting in this production, it rather guaranteed that every critic would attend. At that time, New York had about seven daily newspapers and five weeklies. I ended up not being overshadowed at all and garnered around a dozen good reviews from that one performance.

Because this was my Met debut, these reviews were extremely important. Naturally, I was thrilled when Douglas Watt in the *New York Daily News* enthused: "Sherrill Milnes . . . made a fine appearance and sang his big first-act aria flawlessly and with a sensitive grasp of the French style." Similarly, Alan Rich in the *Herald-Tribune* noted "another major debut of high quality. Sherrill Milnes . . . sang an excellent Valentin, clean, robust, and dramatically sound." Even the critic from the *New York Times* singled me out, saying: "The twenty-nine-year-old baritone handled himself with aplomb . . . the rich, fresh sound of his voice . . . rang out reassuringly in his aria in the Kermesse Scene." Quite an impressive set of clippings for a relative newcomer!

One particular prescient critic, Miles Kastendieck, writing in the *World Telegram*, gave me perhaps the nicest compliment, forecasting my future career:

> Mr. Milnes almost stopped the show after "Avant de quitter," and his dying scene achieved distinction. Here is an exceptionally fine baritone, full resonant, and communicative.
>
> He reminded me of a young Merrill and could become as vital a member of the company.
>
> He moved easily on stage, portraying the soldier as well as the brother knowingly. With this ability and a voice like his, he should go far in the younger generation of singing actors.

The baritone part of Valentin is beautiful; he has the famous aria "Avant de quitter ces lieux" and some other scenes, but he does not control the opera. The role is often either the biggest part for a secondary baritone or the smallest part for a first baritone. It can, however, give the management a sense of your immediate or eventual value to that particular opera house. My debut performance was the sixth or seventh in a run, so I had no stage or orchestra rehearsal. My staging was in a room with the cast and the director with the proverbial stagebook, complete with photos of the set, a very normal situation in the world of opera. Nonetheless it was a little scary for me, never having been on the stage at the "Old Met." I hadn't even auditioned there, having sung for the administration on the stage of the old Fox Theater in Atlanta.

In the only musical rehearsal, Maestro Prêtre said that he started the aria "Avant de quitter ces lieux" without the traditional extra measure of introduction. I, of course, understood what that meant and in the rehearsal sang it easily without the first bar of E-flat-major chords. The problem was that I had sung the part of Valentin many, many times in other theaters, as well as in concert, and had always sung the aria with that first bar of E-flat-major chords. My mind would probably have fed me the right information, but it was my Met debut, and I was very nervous, so past habits took over.

I started the recitative "O sainte médaille, qui me vien de ma soeur" and continued with the short dialogue with Wagner (a smaller baritone part), and then the ascending melodic line before the aria proper began. My mind and my voice were ready to sing at the point that was normal for me, one bar later. Then at the last split second, I remembered that I had to start singing right on the first downbeat. So with no breath in my lungs, I threw what air I had at my vocal cords and hoped I had enough breath to finish the phrase. I sang the whole first line of my famous aria in my debut at the Metropolitan Opera on air fumes (which is my way of saying that I just squeezed out the notes).

Naturally, I was positive that everyone in the public knew exactly what I had done and I was embarrassed to death. I remember thinking, "This is it; it's over; I've failed onstage at the Met; I might just as well stop singing and leave; everyone knows what a stupid thing I've just done." My knees continued to shake badly for the rest of the scene.

Of course, as almost always happens, no one in the audience knew that anything was amiss. Singers always think the listener sees into our minds and into our insecurities, and so we assume the worst. Even after the performance, I asked colleagues and friends, as subtly as possible, whether they had noticed anything awry at the beginning. No one had. Even the critics failed to pick up on my panic. But the memory of that moment lingered on.

Since then, Montserrat and I have sung together dozens of times all over the world and, partly because of that Met debut, we have stayed close friends. Perhaps another reason for our continuing relationship was that I sang several times with her husband, Bernabé Martí. He was a fine spinto tenor and very likely abandoned his career on the early side. I'm sure he saw that because of Montserrat's very special timbre and beauty of voice, she would naturally assume a prestigious place in the world of singers. Many times in performance with Montserrat, Bernabé was backstage in the wings, supporting her and offering his advice.

Two weeks after my debut, Mr. Bing called me into his office and asked if I had ever sung Don Fernando in Beethoven's *Fidelio*. I said no, but I looked at the part in his office and saw that although it was a bit low, it was doable; short, but important. He explained that in Europe many first singers sing this part and he wanted as fine a singer as possible to do it. It occurred to me that singing this role would cast me with a different group of singers and conductors from my more usual Italianate colleagues, so I agreed. There were eight performances, and as a result I sang in James King's debut, and with Birgit Nilsson, Sándor Kónya, Walter Berry, Jess Thomas, William Dooley, Ingrid Bjoner, Joseph Rosenstock, Erich Leinsdorf, and Karl Böhm, as well as performing the work on a radio broadcast in my first season.

A few weeks after that Mr. Bing asked me if I could learn and sing Jack Rance in Puccini's *La fanciulla del West* for some student matinee performances. Again I said yes. This was my first taste of this part, which years later became an important role for me. In 1991 I did a new production of the opera directed by Giancarlo del Monaco that turned out to be a great success for everyone and was later filmed for worldwide viewing.

One morning, about a month after my first *Fanciulla*, the phone rang and woke me up. The rehearsal department asked me if I could sing Jack Rance in an hour and a half for a student performance. The scheduled baritone was ill and they couldn't find the cover, and because I had sung it before, I was the only one they could find who could do it. I felt I had to say yes and raced through a shower, grabbed some breakfast, and tried to vocalize. I arrived about twenty minutes before curtain with pounding heart and sweaty body. I went through my makeup and quickly reviewed the staging and the music and went on. By that time I was less nervous, maybe because it was a student audience who didn't know the Italian so well or the story of the opera. Students almost always boo the bad guy, and because the baritone is most often the bad guy, I was soundly booed. I guess that meant I was good.

A cancellation by Tito Gobbi gave me my first *Andrea Chénier* at the old Met in February 1966. I was lucky to have performed the opera a few years before with the then Baltimore Civic Opera and had studied the part with the legendary Rosa Ponselle, so I had many ideas about the role. With more than a week in which to rehearse, I was well prepared for this performance with Renata Tebaldi and Carlo Bergonzi. Even so, it was pretty heavy sledding and a little scary for this young American kid, especially with these big guns of the time, plus Lamberto Gardelli as conductor. After the third act, which has the big aria "Nemico della patria," and the big duet with Maddalena, Renata and I went out in front of the curtain together hand in hand to take bows. After a few moments Renata gently removed her hand from mine and gestured toward me and left the stage to let me take a solo bow, which was very gracious and unusual. We ended up doing many performances together, and I'm grateful for those times onstage. She's a lovely, lovely lady.

Incidentally, I am on the old Decca recording of *Un ballo in maschera*, which was one of Tebaldi's last, and coincidentally, one of Luciano Pavarotti's first recordings. Also in the cast were Regina Resnik and Helen Donath, with Bruno Bartoletti conducting the Santa Cecilia Academy Orchestra in Rome.

Next in my first-season saga, the Greek baritone, Kostas Paskalis, had to cancel all his performances because of illness. George Schick, the music director, asked me if I knew *Un ballo in maschera* or could learn it quickly. I would have four weeks to prepare it and would sing two performances, one with Tucker and Crespin and the other with Bergonzi, both conducted by Francesco Molinari-Pradelli. This was a stretch, because I scarcely knew the opera at all.

I called Mr. Goldovsky, who knew my learning skills as well as anyone. I described my performing schedule outside the Met and the other works I was memorizing at the same time. We determined that I could do it. I was coached every day that I was in town at the Met and wore earphones with a study cassette of my part playing constantly. Even when going to sleep or waking up, I listened. The work was staged by Nathaniel Merrill using what Goldovsky called "artificial insemination." That is when the stage director plays everyone's part and you have to remember whom the director is portraying at any given moment. I still have all my marks in the score with little maps indicating my movements. I remember the music rehearsals well, partly because Maestro Molinari-Pradelli was a very serious and rather dour person. As an old Italian conductor who rarely smiled, for this freshman singer he was quite scary. But I had worked hard, and the opera was in good shape vocally. In fact, he said nothing negative and two or three times looked over the top of his glasses after certain musical phrases, which I took as a compliment, probably erroneously. The performances went very well and got good reviews, and the following season I sang *Ballo* on the Met tour with Leontyne Price and Bruno Prevedi, an underrated Italian tenor. This time I was the scheduled baritone, which is definitely better than being a substitute.

Little by little and one step at a time, albeit quickly, I was finding a place for myself.

After these successful additions to my schedule, Mr. Bing once again called me on the phone, and this time he said, "Sherrill, I don't think we're paying you enough, and I want to give you a $200-a-week raise, retroactive to your debut." I almost dropped the phone. He certainly didn't have to do that, because I was already pleased with my old contract; but I was even more pleased after the raise. And well before that new contract expired, he rewrote and improved it again. Obviously, my efforts and successes were not going unnoticed.

The story of Rudolf Bing is well-known. Born in Vienna in 1902 of British parentage, Bing first worked in a bookshop before becoming involved in producing theatrical events. After working for operas in Darmstadt and Berlin, in 1936 he became general manager of the Glyndebourne Opera, where he stayed through 1949; after World War II, he was one of the founders of the Edinburgh Festival. However, Bing's career took off when, in 1950, he was hired to become general manager of the Metropolitan Opera, a position he held for twenty-two years.

Although somewhat autocratic in his management style, he improved the quality of productions both in performance and settings; he brought black singers and dancers to the Met's stage for the first time, and he took the company into its new headquarters at Lincoln Center in the mid-1960s. His reign as general manager was the second longest of anyone in the company's history.

Mr. Bing was not always liked, especially by some critics and certain singers, but you always knew where you stood with him, unfortunately a trait not often enough imitated by his successors. The buck stopped with him, and he never ducked responsibility by saying he didn't know, or that he did not operate autonomously and couldn't give you an answer because there were other people involved in that decision. He took responsibility. He never said, "I'll have to get back to you on that," which can mean you don't know or you don't care. He also loved and respected the art form in which we exist. I considered him a great general manager and was always treated more than fairly by him.

During performances he would sometimes fetch a stool from backstage and sit close in the wings, hidden by the curtains, and listen to favorite singers or favorite scenes.

Jon Vickers was one of those favorite singers. During a *Fidelio* in which I was singing the part of the minister, Don Fernando, Mr. Bing said to me, while Jon was singing, "He really separates the men from the boys, doesn't he." I felt privileged to have been able to share Mr. Bing's obvious thrill of a demanding score sung in a magnificent style by a great singer. It bothered me a lot when people who never met him or only had negative relationships with him dismissed him as a tyrant or a dictator. I couldn't have disagreed more.

I sang many performances with Jon Vickers over the years—*Pagliacci*, *Queen of Spades*, and *Fidelio*, but *Otello* especially. As Otello, Jon was not as vulnerable as Plácido, but with clearly defined character flaws that the audience could see and feel. Iago chopped away at Vickers's Otello, and when Jon finally collapsed at the end, he seemed an oak tree felled by Iago's ax. Jon was very balletic in his movements and grand as a warrior and leader, probably the best Otello of this century for his physical and vocal style. Although many others contributed to my Iago, Jon, by his nature and our many performances together, helped it to grow into the powerful character Iago is. No normal human being could say the things Iago says. The terrible thing (but great for acting the part) is that he's an enormously intelligent psychotic, and that makes him even more dangerous. It's sort of like Anthony Hopkins in *The Silence of the Lambs*. He is just driven and dominated by evil.

I am grateful to have spent so much time onstage with Jon. He was one of the most compelling, riveting, and intense performers of any time.

In modern times, Jon was the best Peter Grimes in the world, and everyone tried to imitate him. But he told me that when he first performed it, he was consistently panned because he was so different from Peter Pears, who was the first Grimes. Benjamin Britten wrote it for Peter Pears and had certain characteristics in mind, which I'm sure Pears did well. Many people have told me that Pears was convincing in his way. But the voice was not as powerful or as colorful as Vickers, nor was Pears as versatile a performer. Jon said to me that for years, however, he was very frustrated because he was so different from Pears, couldn't sing the part as Pears sang it, and didn't want to because he had his own feelings about it. But he loved it and persevered and continued to get bad reviews. Only when the memory of Peter Pears faded did Jon become the standard for the part and ultimately receive the rave reviews and worldwide respect for the role of Peter Grimes that he deserved.

For years there was a rumor that Jon had approached Mr. Bing about his desire to sing the evil witch in Humperdinck's *Hansel und Gretel*. The idea would not have been that far-fetched. At the Met, the role, though usually given to a mezzo or contralto, has also been sung by tenors, among them Paul Franke and Andrea Velis. With due respect to all the great female artists who have terrified young children in the role, I feel Jon Vickers would have been the scariest Witch of all!

I have already mentioned that Osie Hawkins was on duty the night Leonard Warren died. That took place during his tenure as executive stage manager. Osie also had the task of announcing various cast changes and notices of illness among the cast, sometimes incurring the wrath of the audience. He did all this in his big, stentorian, booming voice, which left little room for argument. He was always very serious, and he took himself very seriously. In 1978 there was a new production of Donizetti's *La favorita* with Shirley Verrett, Luciano Pavarotti, Bonaldo Giaiotti, and me. One evening Bonaldo was a little ill. He had the flu or something, but his doctors didn't actually say he shouldn't perform. So he agreed to sing, but he wanted an announcement made. So Osie went out in front of the curtain and in his very serious voice, said: "Ladies and gentlemen"—there was a big gasp from the audience, who always feared the worst—"our bass this evening, Bonaldo Giaiotti, is somewhat indisposed, but out of respect for the music and for you the public, he has agreed to expose himself." (This was during the time of mooning, streaking, and other such antics.) The audience went berserk with laughter. As soon as he heard the sound of his own voice and the words he had just uttered, Osie turned bright red, and there was maybe five minutes of pandemonium; even the normally very serious Bonaldo was laughing.

George London

In 1972–73 there was to be a new *Don Giovanni* production at the Met, and Mr. Bing asked me to do it. I was very much looking forward to it. Unfortunately, as it turned out, there was a serious financial problem that year, so they had to remount the old production rather than build and stage an entirely new one. I was, of course, very disappointed.

That year Schuyler Chapin was acting director of the Met. Mr. Bing had retired, and his Swedish successor, Goran Gentele had been killed in a tragic car accident before he could take over. I told Schuyler that I really didn't think I could do the old production with just room rehearsals and the stage director reading from the stagebook for my first *Giovanni* in Italian. (Old productions don't receive as much rehearsal or care as new ones.) I felt I needed some outside help. Also, my colleagues were veterans in the various parts: Leontyne Price, Walter Berry, Teresa Stratas, Teresa Zylis-Gara, and others.

We sat down in Schuyler's office to discuss the various possibilities of which singer knew *Don Giovanni* well and who really had a lot to give and, even more important, would be willing to give it. Schuyler had a brainstorm and came up with the name of George London. George was the first American opera singer to have had a *Newsweek* cover; it depicted his legendary *Don Giovanni* in postwar Vienna. George was actually Canadian by birth, but worldwide he was considered American. He sang a wide range of roles within the bass-baritone repertory and was noted for his good looks and dramatic intensity, both of which he used to great advantage in such parts as the Don, Boris, Onegin, Escamillo, Méphistophélès, Amfortas, and the Dutchman.

My first glimpse of George London had been at the old KRNT theater in Des Moines when I was a student. For many years the Metropolitan Opera toured all over the United States, and I sang many of those tours in later years. At Drake in those years a small group of music students had an "in" at the KRNT theater and would work the various shows when they came to town. Union-scale pay was so much more than a local church job or any other work you could find in Des Moines that it made the theater job very desirable. Plus, of course, there was the thrill of seeing the stars of Broadway and opera.

I worked many of these road shows, and in 1955 the Met came to town with *Lucia di Lammermoor* and *Tosca*. *Lucia* starred Roberta Peters, Jan Peerce, and Robert Merrill. I was awed to see these stars arrive for the performance as I worked backstage. I remember loving the vocal opulence even from backstage, where you can't hear too well. The next night was *Tosca* with Licia Albanese, Daniel Barioni (a new Italian tenor at the Met), and George London. I did not see these singers arrive at the theater that night, so my first glimpse of London was as he was walking backstage to his entrance in his Baron Scarpia makeup. That sight just blew me away. Anyone who has seen London as Scarpia will know what I mean. His facial structure with the white powdered wig and his demonic bearing were very impressive and a little scary looking. I suppose that was a moment that helped propel me toward opera and a singing career.

An interesting side story about that *Tosca* in Des Moines was related to me by my pianist, Jon Spong. Jon was born and raised in Des Moines and knew many of the local people involved in the musical decision making. It seemed that when the Met offered *Tosca* to Des Moines that season they offered a choice between Licia Albanese and a young soprano who was new to America. Most of the music committee were older and had never heard of the young soprano and so opted for Albanese, the more famous and beloved diva at that time. What they didn't know was that the Met would soon discontinue touring to Des Moines and other smaller cities. As a result they lost the opportunity to hear the young Renata Tebaldi sing her famous role in their city.

The whole idea of studying Don Giovanni with London, whom I had never met, was thrilling to me. So Schuyler contacted George, presented his idea, and suggested to George how he could help the Met and me. George graciously agreed to offer his knowledge and time, and I went down to Chevy Chase, Maryland, where he and his wife, Nora, lived. We worked together for many hours over several days. Anyone especially interested in George London should read Nora's *An Aria for George*, a very moving book, which fully discusses his life and career, including his tragic stroke. My thoughts about the role of Giovanni have been molded to a large degree by his ideas. He even went so far as to come to stage rehearsals at the Met and make copious notes for each scene, with constant discussions between us to carefully construct and improve the part.

One scene in a run-through rehearsal onstage was lit quite darkly, and I had only a weak follow spot focused on me. George went to the stage director, yelling, "Sherrill's not lit enough! You've got to have more light on him!" The stage director yelled back, "But, George, this is the same lighting you had when you did this production in the 1950s!" And George yelled back again, "That may very well be, but I didn't have some son-of-a-bitch like me sitting out in the house seeing that *that is not enough light!*" He really put himself on the line for my benefit, making himself, at the moment, somewhat unpopular with the stage staff. They increased the spotlight!

I'm often asked if there was a moment when I thought I'd made it. I don't usually think in those terms, being pragmatic and methodical, but if I had to give an answer, I suppose it would be right after I hit that "high A-flat."

Verdi's *Luisa Miller* was a sleeper opera. Most people weren't familiar with the music at all because in 1968 it had not been done in New York for over fifty years. In that year's beautiful new production at the Met by Nat Merrill and Attilio Colonello, the stars were Montserrat Caballé, Richard Tucker, George Tozzi, and Ezio Flagello, with Thomas Schippers conducting. As Miller, the father of Luisa, I was the kid in the cast, the new boy on the block, having been at the Met for only two and a half seasons and not yet having started a European career. In the opening performance I remember at the end of the difficult aria and cabaletta ("Sacra la scelta" and "Ah! fu giusto il mio sospetto"), I took a high A-flat and held it until I thought the top of my head was going to blow off. The audience exploded and, after that huge applause, I realized that I could hold my own with these great singers, my colleagues, the big vocal guns of the day.

Luisa Miller is a work with which I have spent many hours and sung many times. Some of those have been with Renata Scotto, one of my favorite ladies and a great performer. Early in her career there had been friction between her fans and the fans of Maria Callas. One *Luisa Miller* Renata and I did together was televised. Just as she was opening her mouth to sing the first line (during the silence of a half-note rest), someone yelled out loudly and clearly, "Brava Callas!" The moment is sadly captured on videotape for all to hear. Obviously it was an old Callas fan with a long memory, because at that time Callas was long retired. I was holding Renata, as her loving father, and could see her eyes roll back just a bit and feel her body sag slightly. I pulled her up tightly; she got a grip on herself, took a deep breath, and went on to sing very beautifully. This incident has made us very affectionate colleagues ever since in other operas such as *Don Carlo, Otello, Andrea Chénier, Tosca,* and *Macbeth.*

Renata has the most remarkable ability to caress the words and treat them as a special part of the music. She was the first person with whom I sang who could change the flow from performance to performance. I never knew there were so many word colors possible—especially in *Tosca,* which is where I first experienced it. If my reading of a line changed, she would immediately come back with a change of her own. That quality resulted in a different nuance and extra excitement every time.

One of the first *Aida*s of my life was in March of 1966 at the old Met, with Leontyne Price, Franco Corelli, Irene Dallas, John Macurdy, and Thomas Schippers conducting. I didn't rehearse with the cast but with the covers, and so I had never met Leontyne. In the second act when she sees me, she sings, "My father!" I sing, "My daughter!" Others sing, "He's her father!" This continues with all of us repeating these lines. After the act, I went up to Leontyne, offered my hand, and said, "Hello, Ms. Price, I'm Sherrill Milnes, your father." Probably a first—a father meeting his daughter onstage in front of an audience, before having met her personally and privately.

Over the years, I continued to be her father or brother or other relative for quite a few performances of *Aida*, *Un ballo in maschera*, and *La forza del destino*. Perhaps the first moment I cracked through her exterior—a bit of a professional curtain that she puts up—was in *Forza*, in the last scene. I'd been wounded by her lover (the tenor, Don Alvaro) and was dying. Leontyne was my sister in the opera, and she came up to me, her brother, and saw that I had been stabbed. With her back to the audience, she said, out of character, sotto voce, and with a smile, "You sound like a million bucks," and with that, I shoved a knife in her gut to claim vengeance for the murder of our father by her lover.

The tenor in that *Forza* was Richard Tucker. During those rehearsals, the stage director was working out the movements for the famous duet "Solenne in quest'ora," in which the tenor has been wounded and subsequently recovers. The director went away to allow us to run through the duet, and Richard said, "Listen, kid, don't pay any attention to the stage director. Let me show you what Lenny and I used to do." It took me a while to realize he meant Leonard Warren—one of my idols, and a man whom I could never in my wildest dreams think of as Lenny. I was of course very flattered that Richard brought me into that kind of exalted territory, and with such familiarity.

Richard Tucker was the tenor in the much-heralded *Luisa Miller*. In 1968 Montserrat Caballé did not speak English and Richard's Italian was somewhat limited, so he spoke Yiddish to her and she spoke German to him—and they got on like a house afire.

In December 1965 I went to a few performances at the Met before my actual debut. One of these was *Don Carlo*, an opera I had never seen. In the performance were the tenor Bruno Prevedi and the baritone Ettore Bastianini. I knew Bastianini by reputation and recordings, but at the time knew nothing of the tumor that eventually took his life at age forty-five. Prevedi, with whom I sang many times subsequently, told me that he knew Bastianini was dying at the time of the performance, as did Bastianini. I can't imagine how difficult it must have been for him to sing the famous aria "Io morro" (I will die) knowing that his own life was soon to be over. Bruno had tears in his eyes during the whole of the aria, and it was a struggle for both of them to finish the scene. I was totally unaware of any of this until many years later.

That first season I sang and rehearsed with a soprano whom I knew from Central City, Lucine Amara. One of her greatest Metropolitan triumphs was as Ellen Orford in *Peter Grimes*, playing opposite Jon Vickers. In addition to her own performances, she covered almost every famous-name soprano during her long tenure. She was often and rather unfairly referred to as "just a cover artist." "Just" is the wrong word to describe any artist with the talent and the vocal security to cover a multitude of roles. The Met really did not have a singer of her quality very often as the so-called second soprano. She never missed a note or a phrase, and she had a long list of roles under her belt. We sang together in many productions.

Unfortunately Lucine gained her greatest amount of fame (or notoriety) when she sued the Met for releasing her from their employ because of age discrimination. And she won! She came back in 1981 as Amelia in *Ballo* in a cast with Carlo Bergonzi, Lili Chookasian, Judith Blegen, and Louis Quilico. It was a success, but unfortunately, some years later, she agreed to sing one performance as Madelon in *Andrea Chénier*. It was a mistake. The part was totally wrong for her voice and range. I'm sure she felt she had to take the offer so the Met couldn't say they offered her roles and she refused to sing them.

She had only room rehearsals because it was nearly the last performance of *Chénier* that year, and she hadn't properly gotten the music into her voice. It is really a contralto part and too low for her. As a result she rather lost both her place and her pitch sense and became totally confused. Julius Rudel, the conductor, appeared to be having a fit trying to get her back in the right spot in the music, and the prompter was practically crawling on the stage to give her the right notes. Onstage we were all humming her notes, but somehow she was too much in shock about the terrible mistakes she was making to hear us. It was something to which she was very unaccustomed. She was all over the place and couldn't get her concentration back.

As a greater irony, the character of Madelon is blind and unable to see anything, which was of course what her singing sounded like. After what seemed like an eternity, she finished the part, and, in the staging, the baritone—me, Carlo Gerard—helps her off the stage. I felt dreadful. She was an established and valued colleague, and I'd wanted her to do well. I took her arm and was leading her off when she looked at me and said very quietly, "*Ssssshhhhhiiiittt!*" and then exited the stage. Unfortunately some people remember this performance rather than the many, many years of leading soprano roles in which she always gave 100 percent.

CHAPTER SIX

A Life Ends—
A New Life Begins

AT THE END OF THE 1968–69 SEASON at the Metropolitan Opera, there was no signed contract for the next season with the American Guild of Musical Artists, the union for all singers—chorus and soloists—and all the dancers. In the preceding years, AGMA, as a union, had been a little passive in their contract negotiations, tending to follow the leadership of the much more aggressive and powerful American Federation of Musicians, the orchestra union. The current negotiations were far more angry and emotional than earlier contract talks because AGMA thought the Met management had been untruthful about budgets and fund-raising. Most of the union membership felt that the already-expired contract had been a bad deal, and meetings through the final months of the season and the summer had netted nothing but anger. I attended some of those meetings, and there was an emotionally charged, "get even" attitude on the part of the union. They felt they had been betrayed by management in past years and seemed not to care whether there was a season or not. I'm sure that some of their feelings were justified.

There were meetings after meetings, with the membership at large and the majority expressing anger at the Met. Some quieter voices tried to reason with them, but to no avail. George London, Cornell MacNeil, and other well-known names spoke on behalf of a more moderate approach, but still to no avail. I heard more than once "Let's get Bing" and "Burn the place down."

At the same time I was facing a family crisis. My mother had been fighting cancer ever since she was first diagnosed back in 1951. Numerous surgeries to remove the cancerous tissue kept her going. Through the 1960s she was losing her battle, but with occasional blood transfusions she was able to continue her church choir and oratorio society rehearsals and performances, albeit on a reduced schedule. The cancer had invaded her bone marrow and no white corpuscles were being produced. Thanks to the transfusions, her energy would temporarily return. Each time, however, her strength was reduced.

She had planned Mendelssohn's *Elijah* for a December concert in 1969. Elijah is a baritone and a role I have always loved and have sung many times. I wanted to sing in what looked like the last concert my mother would ever conduct, and so we agreed that I would. Even with performances at the Met I was sure that I could fly in for enough rehearsals and sing the concert on December 7. But as we came into the late summer and fall of 1969, it looked as though she would be too weak to conduct even if she were still alive.

By this time, given the apparent impasse at the Met, it was clear that the season was going to be delayed or canceled altogether. We decided that I would conduct the concert, and we asked Andy White, my voice teacher of many years; Jon Spong, who was also a fine tenor; Teresa Orantes, a well-known Chicago soprano; and Margaret Bollinger, a mezzo-soprano and my mother's assistant, to be the soloists.

In 1969 another important change occurred in my life; I married Nancy Stokes, my second wife. That fall she had a contract to sing Violetta in *La traviata* with Goldovsky, and with no dates in my calendar because of the strike, I was free to tour with her. I was also able to spend some time in the little house on the farm to be near my mother and start to organize and rehearse the *Elijah* concert. However, with no dates, my income was reduced to nothing, and I wasn't sure how to deal with that.

One afternoon in September the phone rang in the farmhouse. It was Bob Herman on the line. (Mr. Bing's number-two man and a main negotiator in the contract talks, he later was the very successful manager of the Miami Opera.) He told me that the Met season was canceled indefinitely *and* they would like to keep me under contract for the length of the strike (or the lockout, as the union called it) at my normal weekly salary.

I couldn't believe my ears and almost dropped the phone. All the money that I was to be paid had I been singing would keep coming in. I had to do nothing but refrain from booking other dates so that at such a time as the strike or lockout was over, I would be available to start rehearsing immediately.

Wow! What a deal, I thought. I was a newlywed, my mother was dying, and I could take care of both those responsibilities and be paid at the same time. I wasn't sure how other union members would feel about that if they knew. But I was not going to say no!

I spent the fall on the farm or on tour with Nancy, plus a few visits to New York, where we lived. At the union meetings I attended, I felt somewhat embarrassed, but in my life at the time, this situation was a godsend. I have always thought that a strike should be absolutely a last resort, and this was probably a last resort. Even so, lost salary is rarely made back, even with a good raise. I hoped and prayed for a contract that was fair for everyone.

Finally, after much strife and many angry meetings, there was a settlement in early December. I started rehearsals soon after in New York, and the Met opened on December 9, 1969, with a performance of *Aida.* I was working on a new *Pagliacci*, also starring Lucine Amara, Richard Tucker, and Dominic Cossa, and we labored long and hard to debut it on January 8, 1970.

In the rest of the country, 1969 had been a year of massive unrest. The former President Eisenhower, a symbol of gentler days, died at age seventy-eight. He was joined by other almost mythic figures such as Judy Garland. My mother was dying, and eras she had lived through and been a part of seemed to be dying with her. There was a sense of depression in the air. Only the Woodstock Festival brought some glimmer of hope, and that was also a far-from-perfect experience.

Before that contract settlement, during October and November, my mother's health deteriorated, and our family doctor told Dad, Roe, and me that to continue the blood transfusions was now of little value. We should let her go when God so willed. We all agreed that to discontinue the transfusions was probably the right thing to do and that we would just let God and nature have their way. Returning to the farm in early December for the last set of rehearsals and concert, I called my dad from the airport. When he answered, his voice was tremulous and I knew something had happened. He simply said, "Our princess is gone."

That was like being hit by a two-by-four over my head. I drove the rest of the way to the farm in a daze. This was on a Friday afternoon. A rehearsal was scheduled for that night and the following night, with the concert on Sunday. Those were perhaps the most difficult days of my life. I had to rehearse the chorus and orchestra and conduct a dress rehearsal, and at the same time, with the family, organize all the funeral details. In some ways it was probably good that there was so much to do, because it kept my mind occupied and my body busy. The concert is a bit hazy in my mind, but I know to this day, when I sing *Elijah*, I have to keep some control over my emotions or I can tear up at almost any moment, unable to sing.

Nancy was a champion at this very difficult time. We were newly married, and she was rather unknown in my hometown. It was necessary for her to be a model of discretion and a model at dealing with a myriad of people at a very difficult time in their and our lives. It was not easy to be appropriately sympathetic and loving to people you don't know.

Death affects different people in different ways. I am emotional and rather a romantic, but at the same time can often be stoic and closed. So while I felt huge sorrow and grief, my outer shell betrayed little of what I was feeling internally. However, I could sense myself aging in that time of great stress. As you age you feel more vulnerable as a human being, and in your mind mortality looms larger and larger. My father passed away in 1979, ten years after my mother died. When parents are gone, you begin to realize that there is no more "buffer" generation—that you are now the last, meaning, of course, that you will probably be the next to die. It's a sobering thought, and it makes you mature in a hurry. It can even mean that you begin to take better care of yourself, partly because of that memory of death and suffering and because the sense of your own mortality becomes more vivid in your mind and stays with you for the rest of your life.

Anatole France said: "To accomplish great things, we must not only act but also dream; not only plan but also believe." My mother did all of that and more. On May 27, 1997, I was very proud to make my conducting debut in Carnegie Hall with her most beloved oratorio, Mendelssohn's *Elijah*. It seemed fitting.

⟡

John Dexter

John Dexter was at one time a manager of the Metropolitan Opera as well as a well-known theater director. My own favorite Broadway production of his was Peter Schaffer's *Equus*, the premiere of which I had the pleasure of attending in New York. Coincidentally, Peter Schaffer used to be my upstairs neighbor in New York. I saw him one day in front of our building during the filming of his big hit play *Amadeus*. He had just returned from Prague, where Milos Forman was filming the Mozart movie. I asked Peter how it was going. He said that in fact he had to leave, because his play was being changed as they filmed it. He was smart enough to trust Forman totally and knew that films are not the same as plays and must have different contours. At the same time, he was becoming upset and knew the only thing to do to avoid further frustration was to leave. Ultimately, he was very pleased with the final result.

I saw a John Dexter staging of a wonderful play at London's National Theater called *Saturday, Sunday, Monday*, in which Laurence Olivier had a cameo role. After the performance, John invited me to go backstage. He led me into Olivier's dressing room and said, "Larry, I'd like you to meet the world's greatest *singing* Iago." What an intro! That's enough to intimidate anyone regardless of reputation or fame. Olivier knew Verdi's *Otello* well and what that introduction meant; he was very cordial and polite and made me feel quite at home.

John was a very interesting man. I worked with him in quite a few productions over the years and learned many personal disciplines from him. In Verdi's *I vespri siciliani* (*Les vêpres siciliennes*), the baritone, Monforte, is the ruler of Sicily. In a complicated plot, he discovers his illegitimate son and tries to reestablish a relationship with him. John taught me how to portray Monforte through one phrase, "isolation by power," which I had never heard before. It made perfect sense—all great leaders are isolated by virtue of their power—and I could relate this directly to many of my roles. Of the many things I learned from John, I remember that single phrase the best. It's amazing how one idea can affect so many roles and give a subtext for many different situations. This is called a "transfer of learning." I am grateful to John Dexter, and I am sorry he passed away so prematurely, for we are all poorer for it.

Robert Merrill

There are many generous people in the opera world, and I was very lucky, as the new kid on the block, to be surrounded by some of them. Robert Merrill, for example, said to me during my first days at the Met: "Welcome, it's a pleasure to meet you—good luck—there's always room at the top for the best." Here was the most famous American baritone of the time, extending his hand, smiling, and welcoming me to this mecca of opera, almost as an equal. Years later, Bob told me that after hearing me sing for the first time, he went home and said to his wife, "Marion, I've heard a new baritone; we better start saving our money." Bob had a wonderful and unique way of giving compliments.

A few years ago I was honored by the Players Club in New York with an evening of friends in a "Pipe Night," a sort of roast like the kind that Dean Martin used to have on TV. I telephoned Bob at home to invite him to speak at this roast. He was just going out the door to sing the national anthem at a Yankees game. When he was a kid, he had wanted to be a professional baseball player. He made up for that by singing the anthem at games more often than anyone in history, and has been made an honorary member of the New York Yankees. Bob told me immediately that he would be thrilled to be a part of the evening. "After all," he said, "I was brought up listening to your records." He made up this little turnaround of timing and relative ages right on the spot without missing a beat. I was blown away by his wit and humor and have repeated that story many times around the world. Needless to say, with his wit Bob was a big success at the roast. In fact, that night he was preceded by a very long monologue from a wordy friend of mine. When it was finally his turn, Bob stood up and said, "I thought I was hearing a Wagner opera and would never have the chance to say my own thing." Robert has just passed away, and I want to say he was an icon of our industry, a great artist, and I'm proud to have called him a good friend.

James McCracken

If I am frequently referred to as "an American baritone," James McCracken was definitely "an American tenor." Jim was a hell of a guy and one of the world's major singers. In his early years, as a *comprimario* at the Met, he was frustrated because it seemed they were not going to allow him to move into bigger roles. So he and his wife, the fine mezzo-soprano Sandra Warfield, moved to Europe. Jim started with smaller parts there and worked his way up into such leading roles as Samson, Otello, Canio, Don Alvaro, Florestan, and Radames. In 1972 we sang together in a new production of *Otello* at the Met, staged by Franco Zeffirelli. Jim was a bull of a singer and always caught the audience up in his enthusiasm and vocal energy.

On the Met tour in the same year, we were singing that production in Cleveland at the old Municipal Auditorium. Jim had been suffering from kidney stones, and I am told that there is no pain as great as that for a man. He had sung the other performances before Cleveland in pain, but as he said, "tolerable pain." I had heard the afternoon of the performance that he had been suffering a great deal but would sing anyway. When I arrived at the theater, Jim was already in makeup, but he was hurting badly. I asked if there was anything I could do. He smiled weakly and said, "Only if you can take away the pain." I assured him if there were any small changes in the staging or other musical matters that would help him, I would adjust to whatever he needed. Often certain long phrases or high notes can be shortened to help an ailing colleague. So we started the performance and Jim sang well. He made it through the first act, but after the curtain fell, he limped painfully back to the dressing rooms. During the intermission, the pain became intolerable, and Jim doubled up on the floor.

The cover for Otello was Robert Nagy, and of course he was in the theater, for by that time Jim's distress was common knowledge throughout the company. With a doctor in attendance, Jim finally decided the pain was so extreme there was no way he could go on. An ambulance was called, and he was taken to the hospital. Bob Nagy was backstage and knew that he had to go on. Victor Callegari, the makeup man, hurried to prepare Bob for the second act, knowing that an Otello makeup is not a simple thing. Bob and the management were so eager to get on with the show that he went onstage before the makeup and beard were totally ready. As a result, he did not look like a finished Otello, and even though he sang well, it affected the performance. I remember thinking, if I ever have to jump into a performance already under way, I will take the time to be fully ready. You must look in the mirror and see the real operatic character before you go onstage.

Over the next few days, Jim passed the stones and recovered enough to return to the tour without missing any more performances, an amazing display of courage.

CHAPTER SEVEN

Opera Can Be Dangerous

SINGING OPERA CAN BE DANGEROUS. Perhaps that is a strange thing to say, because singing does not seem to be physically punishing. But when you participate in sword fights, especially when your partner is not so skillful in the art of fencing, it can be very dangerous. I am right-handed and as a result have many scars on my right hand from Jon Vickers, Luciano Pavarotti, Richard Cassilly, Nicola Martinucci, Plácido Domingo, Gianni Raimondi, Michael Molese, and a host of lesser-known tenors. Many mishaps, mostly minor, have occurred over the years, but none more than in the opera *Faust*, where there is a duel between Valentin, the baritone, and Faust, the tenor. Valentin is the better swordsman, but the devil, Méphistophélès, who has made a contract for the tenor's soul, intervenes and allows Faust to win by bewitching Valentin.

One run of performances with the Italian tenor Gianni Raimondi stretched my abilities to memorize. He was not very skilled in fencing, and after many vain attempts to complete the right patterns of swordplay, I determined that I had to call out all the sword movements, his and mine, in order to be effective as well as safe. However, it soon became clear that that was not enough, because when I called out my movements as well as his, he became confused. So I memorized his movements only and called them out in a loud stage whisper at the moment he needed to do them. This may not sound so difficult until you realize that all the directions were exactly the opposite of what I was doing! All the rights became left and all the lefts became right; if I lunged forward, he fell back; and so forth. And even with all my help, a few mishaps occurred and a little blood was spilled.

In *Pagliacci*, the baritone is a fascinating role and comparable to one of the great Verdi roles. Tonio is similar to Lenny in *Of Mice and Men*. He is a big hulking creature filled with what is probably sexual frustration. He desires Nedda, sees her fooling around with another man, and knows he's not "getting any." She leads him on a bit, and his anger in the fight scene just explodes.

At the Met in 1969, the cast for *Pagliacci* was Richard Tucker, Teresa Stratas, Andrea Velis, Dominic Cossa, and me, conducted by Fausto Cleva in a new Zeffirelli production (the one staged immediately after the strike and my mother's death). During rehearsals, Franco never seemed to want to stage this fight in the first act. Every time we came close to that scene, he took a break or skipped it for some other part of the opera. Eventually Teresa and I became tired of avoiding that scene, and finally we went out in the hall and started to stage it. We both wanted to have a strong, muscular fight, so we worked it out in a couple of days, then showed it to Zeffirelli. He bought it as we did it, complete with a whipping, chasing her up a ramp, throwing her in the back of a wagon, and trying to rape her. And then Teresa sticking her fingers in my eyes, scratching my face and—with some preset blood looking as though she had opened my skin—fighting me off, me rolling down the ramp spitting blood, and she chasing me offstage with the whip. It was quite realistic. I had to wear some padding, but even so, I would still often bang my elbows hard enough so that the next day they were sore. One performance, Teresa forgot to close her hand when she poked my eyes and her nails drew blood as they raked down my face. I was a little angry, but since the staging was partly my doing, I chalked it up to Teresa being a great stage player. Fortunately no scar remained.

Not all operas with Teresa were dangerous, however. As Zerlina in *Don Giovanni*, she had the ability to make the Giovanni think he was the handsomest, sexiest man who ever existed. Most Zerlinas do that to a point, but Teresa could really make you feel like a million bucks. When you believed that, the whole opera was easier to perform and came off better.

Unlike most other sopranos (Callas and Scotto excepted), Teresa subordinated her voice to the words and to her own body image. I think she went too far in the direction of physicalizing everything and perhaps did her voice a disservice. She would do whatever she thought the character might do at that moment but then might pay for it in vocal fatigue for several days. There seemed to be a fragility about her voice, so that sometimes when she sang a full-voice dress rehearsal, she had to cancel the opening. In any case, Teresa was a great stage animal with wonderful instincts, who created her own special magic onstage.

In the opera *Tosca*, Scarpia, the baritone, chief of the Roman police, is stabbed by the soprano. In the ensuing fight and the character's subsequent death, I usually stumble onto one of the stage chairs and then fall over backward in the chair before dying. The fall is a little tricky, and it takes good concentration on my part so I don't bang up my elbows or hit my head. Sometimes, of course, I have bruised my elbows or at the least knocked the wind out of myself. I have done this staging all over the world and have escaped any serious injury. I believe that the effect on the audience is worth the risk.

In one production, Scarpia's bed was directly behind the desk where he has his meals and does his writing. In the rehearsals the bed was well away from the desk, and I knew that I could fall back safely. However, in the performance the bed was much closer, and although I was aware of it, it did not occur to me that it would cause a problem in the death scene. Also, this bed was more of a cot than a traditional bed, and its bare steel legs were totally exposed. At the end of the scene, when Tosca stabbed me, I fell into the chair, which unfortunately was a smaller version of what I was used to, and with no high back. The combination of these circumstances fouled up my normal precaution and timing in the fall. So as I went over backward, my head struck one of the steel legs of the cot, and the blow made me see stars. It did not quite knock me out, but fortunately, Scarpia is dying anyway. It was easy to convey the pain and die convincingly.

After the curtain fell, I got up somewhat unsteadily. My legs were wobbly and my head throbbed painfully, but otherwise I knew that I would survive. Charlie Anthony, playing Spoletta (Scarpia's right-hand man), said, "My God, your head is bleeding." "Don't be silly," I said, and put my hand up to my head. My hand came away red with blood, and I said, "Shit, you're right; I've cut open my head." With my hand wiping away the blood, I took all the curtain calls, and bowed in the most normal way I could. But after the curtain calls, they called the house doctor, who looked at the cut and said that he might have to stitch it. I asked if there was a way we could treat it without stitches; just butterfly-tape it. I didn't want any scars from the stitches, so I was very careful and kept the tape on for a week and had no side effects or scars.

A production of *Simon Boccanegra* in Catania, Sicily, staged by Giancarlo del Monaco, brought me an accident. In the first scene, the young Simone is elected by the populace as the doge of Genoa. Near the end of the scene, his pals Pietro and Paulo lift him up on a high pedestal as the crowd cheers him. (There actually was a historical Simon Boccanegra; he was the first doge of Genoa ever to be elected from the working class.)

This pedestal/platform was quite high, and in the rehearsals my henchmen would give me a big lift up. I would step into their clasped hands and jump up onto the pedestal. It took all my strength and agility to land on my feet and maintain my balance. I decided that a built-in step would be necessary to guarantee my arrival on top of the pedestal. I asked if this would be possible and was assured that it would be. Each day at rehearsal I saw that the step was not in place. I was always told that the following day it would be done, but it was never there.

A further complication came when I found that I had to wear a long cape, which tended to wrap itself around me as I jumped up on the pedestal, sometimes tripping me or at least making me look quite clumsy. This went on for many days. Finally the dress rehearsal came; there was still no step, but there was a row of nails where the step was to be. Somewhat encouraged, I was again assured that for the performance there would be a step and that the nails were at the right level for the step. Opening night came and wonder of wonders, there was no step, though the nails were still there. At that point there was nothing more to do; I just concentrated on the performance.

Everything started well, and as I arrived at the jump for the pedestal, I put my foot in Paolo's and Pietro's clasped hands and jumped. I felt a stab of pain in my right hand as I jumped, but I continued to sing. Sometimes during a performance, your adrenaline will numb a certain amount of pain. So I really only sensed a twinge and was very surprised when a bar or two later I looked at my right hand and saw blood all over it. I had ripped open the top of my second finger on the nails, and there I was in the middle of a performance with blood dripping on the stage. I clamped my thumb and third finger over my second finger, trying to stop the bleeding. Fortunately there were only a few minutes left in the act, but I was extremely pissed off. Would I be able to continue the performance? How much damage had I done to my finger?

After the act I screamed my head off in my best swearing Italian and tried to find the Italian equivalent of Band-Aids. I had in fact ripped open about an inch and a half on the top of my right index finger. With it securely wrapped in Band-Aids and hurting a lot, I continued the performance. Maybe the pain and frustration added to the characterization; I don't know. But I have a long scar on the top of my right index finger. The step never appeared in the rest of the seven performances, and certainly there was no apology.

Sometimes problems are not so serious. Simon has a fast makeup change in the first act. The prologue takes place twenty-five years before the rest of the opera. The aging process—the makeup change—is done during Amelia's aria and the following duet between the soprano and tenor, allowing only the bare minimum of time. At the Royal Opera House in London, I was singing a long run of this opera. The makeup man of many years, Ron Freeman, and I had plenty of rehearsals to find the fastest way to age from twenty to fifty. The change of makeup eventually became rather routine. I would change costume first and then go to the makeup room. Ron would always put Kleenex around my neck to protect the collar of the costume and proceed with the aging makeup. A few times we joked about the likelihood of forgetting to remove the Kleenex and going onstage with this ring of white around my collar.

In any run of performances, you become more and more relaxed about everything offstage. I have no idea how it happened or how we forgot, but one evening after the makeup change, I walked onstage as the dignified older Simone and started the scene with Amelia, my long-lost daughter. At one point my eye caught a white reflection on my collar and, sure enough, there was this whole ring of Kleenex around my neck.

Talk about "ring around the collar." I wondered what in the world I could do to fix it without looking foolish. I decided to walk upstage, and with great style and verve, sweep the Kleenex off my costume. I did just that and wadded it up in my hand and stuffed it in a pocket, hoping the audience would think that it was part of the character and the staging.

Stages often have bent nails and other kinds of tacks lying on the stage floor. If one is wearing thin slippers as part of the costume, these can present problems other than vocal. In *Rigoletto*, I normally wore ballet slippers with his acts 2 and 4 costume. In a performance at the Metropolitan Opera in the 1980s, just before returning to the stage at the end of act 2 (the scene with Marullo, the courtiers, and the key), I was about to sing the line "Riedo! perche?" At the very instant of singing, I stepped on a small tack lying head down and point up. It went right through my thin ballet slipper sole and instead of singing the words, I sang, "Aaaahhoouu," or something like that. Not knowing whether the audience had heard anything, I grabbed my foot, saw the tack, and pulled it out. Then I made my reentrance cue, because I had to sing another phrase onstage immediately. Because I was offstage during the accident, I don't think anyone was the wiser. But the tack had made a neat little hole in the bottom of my foot.

In 1978 I was singing *Don Giovanni* on the annual Met tour, on which the last city was Detroit, Michigan. I flew there on a Monday afternoon for a performance the following day. On the flight I had a couple of drinks, looking forward to the free evening. I arrived in the hotel and had just unpacked and settled down when the telephone rang. It was Arge Keller, the senior member of the rehearsal department at the time, asking me how I felt. I said OK but immediately knew something was amiss. Arge explained that Marilyn Horne was ill and hadn't traveled to Detroit, and her cover, Nedda Casei, was also very ill, so they couldn't put on that night's scheduled performance, Rossini's *L'italiana in Algeri*.

With, *left to right*, Loretta Lynn, President George Bush, Barbara Bush, and Dennis Weaver in Washington, c. 1989.

With Burt Lancaster, *center*, and Plácido Domingo, *right*, 1977, in Munich, where Plácido and I were appearing in Götz Friedrich's new production of *Tosca*.

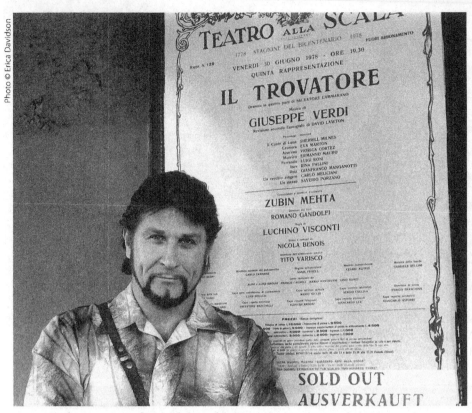

At La Scala in 1978 in front of the sold-out announcement of *Il Trovatore*.
A very proud moment.

With Mom and
Rudolph Bing,
1968, on the
Metropolitan
Opera tour in
Detroit.

As Jack Rance in the 1991 Metropolitan Opera
production of *Fanciulla del West.*

With Tito Capobianco on the occasion
of receiving the Italian Order of Merit,
presented by Italian Consul General Guilio
Cesare di Lorenzo at the Italian consulate in
New York, December 1983.

In the title role of *Henry VIII* by
Camille Saint-Säens, San Diego, 1983.

As Don Giovanni, Salzburg Opera, 1977, with Walter Berry, *foreground*.

With President Clinton at the White House on the occasion of the 1997 Kennedy Center Honors. In the background, *left to right*, Ron Silver, Hillary Rodham Clinton, and Maria.

Backstage at *Otello*, cutting a birthday cake, 1985. *Left to right:* Tony Randall, me, Margaret Price, James Levine, and Plácido Domingo.

The moment of truth: *Macbeth* at the Metropolitan Opera, 1972.

On the set of the Metropolitan Opera production of *Fanciulla*, 1991. *Left to right:* Leonard Slatkin, me, Barbara Daniels, Giancarlo de Monaco.

"Ho, ho, ho, what a feeling, Toyota!" 1989.

This is Maria's favorite photograph of me (as Hamlet).

With Ethel Merman in New York City, c. 1980.

With First Lady Betty Ford on my first visit to the White House, 1976.

In recital with Jon Spong in Carnegie Hall, c. 1990.

With President Ronald Reagan and First Lady Nancy Reagan, 1984.

With José Ferrer, mid-1980s, after a performance in Miami.

He said that he had already contacted the rest of the *Giovanni* cast and they were willing to sing that night, substituting for the Rossini opera, and then sing again the next night in the scheduled performance of *Giovanni*. He wanted to know if I could do it. I took a deep breath and thought, "Oh boy, two performances in a row," and "I just had two drinks!" Fortunately, *Giovanni* is not vocally difficult for me. There is a lot to sing and it is very high energy, but is not high tessitura. Also, I knew that the finances of these tour performances were very complex, with big bucks riding on each show. So I felt a certain fiscal responsibility to the Met and to the presenting auspices in Detroit, whom I knew from other tours. So there was really very little choice but to help out, and I said OK.

There were still four hours to curtain time, so I did a few calisthenics, ordered room service, and took a long hot shower and tried to sweat a bit. By the time I left for the theater, I felt rather normal and ready to sing. The voice perhaps was a little low, but for Giovanni, that is not bad. The performance went quite well. I should add that the same cast had been doing the same production for several weeks and so it was ready to go with no surprises. At the end, I went right home and tried to sleep immediately. I stayed in bed late into the morning and lazed around all day trying to keep my energy low until the performance. All was normal and I felt quite relaxed.

The performances were in the old Masonic Temple in Detroit. The dressing rooms were upstairs, small, tawdry, and ill equipped—usual for old theaters. Late in the opera, during the second-act sextet, I have about twenty minutes to wait for my next entrance. With loudspeakers in the rooms, I could hear exactly where everyone was. I went to the bathroom and closed the door behind me. When I went to open the door, the knob just spun in my hand, and the door would not open. I pushed and wiggled the door with all my force, but nothing happened. I called out and banged on the door and still nothing happened. Then I realized that all my colleagues were onstage and my dressing room was located off in a corner, so no one was close enough to hear. I could hear my entrance music coming closer, and there seemed to be nothing I could do. I don't think I had ever been in that situation before. I yelled and banged on the door some more, but to no avail. The entrance cue was coming closer.

I saw that the center of the door was made of thinner plywood than the outside portion. Giovanni wears boots with heavy soles and heels, so I used them to try to kick out the plywood section of the door. Even though it was thinner, it still took some doing, but finally I splintered enough wood to make an opening. I continued to kick and smash the wood until I made a big enough hole to push myself through and clear the door. As I ran to the stage, I looked back to see the mess I had made of the door, chuckled to myself, and arrived just in time to sing my first recitative lines of the graveyard scene. Fortunately, Giovanni is supposed to be out of breath and excited when he enters, and I certainly was. Maybe my bathroom escape added some extra dimension to the scene, I didn't know, and at that moment, I didn't care. The audience was none the wiser.

Jean-Pierre Ponnelle was one of our greatest and most talented stage directors. He produced a very compelling version of *Don Giovanni* in Salzburg in 1978 conducted by Karl Böhm. In that production, the "Finch'han dal vino" (Champagne Aria) scene had five supers, all so-called whores, as the Don's companions. In the recitative before the aria they were all over me, playing, embracing, and in general being very sexy. It was interesting that in street clothes they were all rather attractive, but once in costume and makeup they lost all their sex appeal. Part of the reason was that Ponnelle wanted them in a rather grotesque makeup, so they looked like witches.

But there is another reason they lost their sexiness onstage. Often when a woman wears a costume and stage makeup, she is less attractive up close than in street clothes with normal makeup. Also the vocal, musical, and stage demands on a singer are enough that during a performance, beauty and sexual overtones become meaningless to your colleagues. It goes without saying, of course, that an attractive female onstage is more fun than an ugly one. I'm sure it's the same for a woman when she's performing opposite a good-looking man. But the actual beauty of the person is about how she sings and plays the part, rather than her physical appearance.

A slight accident occurred in this production of *Don Giovanni*. During the Champagne Aria, I use these so-called whores by playing with them throughout the whole scene. At one point one of the girls kneels in front of me with her face pressed against my crotch. At the dress rehearsal, all went normally. What I didn't know was that after that rehearsal, Jean-Pierre changed the makeup for the whores, deciding to use a real clown white on their faces. So in the opening performance, after that scene, I looked down at my pants and saw a ring of clown white makeup right around the area where she had just been. Which means that I sang most of the aria with an outline of white on the front of my black pants right at the fly. Now that's embarrassing!

In Dallas, Texas, I was singing the Don with the late and wonderfully gifted Donald Gramm as Leporello and John Macurdy as the Commendatore. The old Music Hall had a big, wide-open stage, and much of the set was hung from long pipes in the fly (the overhead space above the stage). All went well in the performance until the graveyard scene, where Giovanni meets Leporello and they both encounter the grave and ghost of the Commendatore. This set had the Commendatore standing in a doorway of a kind of mausoleum.

Early in the recitative I heard some rumbling and noise up in the fly and instinctively moved downstage onto the apron. The whole set, complete with its support pipes attached, came crashing down onto the stage. There was a huge gasp from the audience and I could see Donald Gramm downstage opposite me, so I knew he was safe. While the audience was still reacting, I turned to see John Macurdy standing calmly in his doorway with the pipes and yards of canvas all around him. Oddly, for some reason, as I heard the rumble and noise, I pulled out my sword and brandished it in some kind of defense movement, as though the sword would protect me from falling debris.

John Pritchard was conducting and playing the harpsichord at the same time. He, of course, stopped playing as soon as he heard and saw what was happening. Fortunately, the accident happened in the recitative, so that the harpsichord was the only instrument involved. After the audience and all of us onstage saw that everyone was safe, Maestro Pritchard played the next chord. At the moment, I didn't think what my next line meant: "Sarà qualcun di fuori che si burla di noi" (Someone is outside who is laughing at us). I started to laugh as I realized what I had just said.

We were all very lucky that this was not a big choral scene, as that type of accident could have injured or even killed several people and could have been a terrible disaster. Instead, in my memory, it was only funny, especially to remember John Macurdy standing in the middle of complete chaos, totally unflappable.

On the same tour in Cleveland there was another performance of *Don Giovanni*. In that massive municipal auditorium was an old elevator with crisscross metal doors that worked like an accordion, as well as an antiquated electrical system. It always moved slowly, and even with an operator you had to anticipate all musical entrances by several minutes. Otherwise you could be late to the stage or never make it at all. In the trio with Don Ottavio, Donna Anna, and Donna Elvira near the finale of act 1, the worst happened. The Elvira was new to the Met tour and unused to that theater and elevator. Obviously, either she didn't leave enough time to get to the stage or she didn't hear the musical cue. (The speaker system back stage was poor as well.) Whatever it was, she was still in the elevator when she should have been onstage. So it was a lovely *duet* for about half of the trio, until Elvira finally arrived at the stage, ran on, and started singing in the middle of the music.

That same elevator in Cleveland became infamous in a much more serious accident some years later. It was a tour that I did not sing, but I was told about it. I think the opera was *Boris Godunov*. During the performance, a member of the chorus got on the elevator when it was so crowded that the operator was shoved into the corner. All the choristers' costumes were large Russian robes with long veils and headgear that hung down almost to the floor. Apparently the veil and headgear of the last chorister on the elevator got caught in the metal doors and were hanging outside. As the elevator moved up, her head and neck were pulled down. People screamed and panicked, and the operator tried to stop the elevator. But being jammed in the corner, he couldn't get to the controls quickly, and the elevator continued up. In a few seconds it stopped, but the upward movement had already strangled the chorister and broken her neck. She was rushed to a hospital, but died what must have been a most horrible death. A terrible, tragic accident, and I'm sure unforgotten by the members of the chorus who were present.

"*They've Killed the Dwarf!*"

Some years ago I performed the title role of *Nabucco* in Paris with Grace Bumbry, Ruggero Raimondi, Viorica Cortez, and Carlo Cossutta, with Nello Santi conducting. These performances were easily the most catastrophic production in which I've ever been involved in my entire life. They may even hold some kind of opera record. Why all these things happened in Paris I don't know (maybe because this is the opera house where the story of the Phantom of the Opera originated?), though at the time the Paris Opera House had a reputation for being a bit disorganized. But these problems went beyond disorganization, as you'll soon see.

Nabucco is based on the biblical story of Nebuchadnezzar, the king of Babylon. At one point in the story, Nabucco, a powerful warrior, has conquered all the neighboring tribes and feels himself invincible. He has such a power rush that he announces, "I am no longer a king, I am God!" Well, God decides he doesn't like that and sends a bolt of lightning to strike the king down. As a result Nabucco is crippled, and after much soul-searching because of this dramatic sign from heaven, he becomes a God-fearing man.

For the lightning strike, the director decided to have me enter standing on a shield six feet above the ground, held on the shoulders of four men who, with perfect timing, would drop to their knees, quickly lowering the shield so I could tumble off, as if struck by lightning. The shield was very shaky, so they rehearsed it with a stand-in many times to get it right. Finally we felt it was safe enough for me to try. I don't know if I was heavier or taller or whatever than my stand-in, but when the cue came to drop the shield, one corner guy fell too fast, and the shield tipped, swinging sideways. It turned perpendicular to the floor instead of parallel, and I landed on top of it, with my feet on the floor on each side of the shield and the edge of it between my legs.

If that shield had been a half-inch higher or my legs had been a half-inch shorter, I might not be writing this book today. Or at least, I'd be writing as a soprano or a castrato. The shield hit my genitals and a pain I couldn't describe in words, at least not in printable words, shot through my body, and I rolled to the floor in agony. I thought this was the end of my career . . . and of other things!

I stayed curled up on the floor. The pain started to ebb a little after ten minutes so that I was able to get up and limp around. The next day I was very sore, but with some difficulty I could walk, so obviously nothing was broken. Within two days my entire crotch and most of my thighs were covered in an ugly deep purple bruise. The purple color remained for several weeks, but then, oddly enough, it slowly traveled down my right leg before, in a matter of speaking, it disappeared from my foot. I suppose there is a medical explanation for this phenomenon, but it was very strange to me. There was quite a bit of pain, and of course, a lot of worry, but no permanent damage. Once again, I'll bet most people don't think of opera as being filled with this kind of danger. And this was not the last catastrophe to befall this production.

Opening night, first scene: Nabucco and his armies attack the Israelites and burn their temples to the ground. Before this attack Ruggero Raimondi, the high priest, is standing in the temple. Behind him is the lit menorah with its flames floating in the air. Somehow the menorah caught on fire, and Ruggero had to keep singing while watching it become engulfed in flames. People were trying to beat out the fire with their coats and jackets. The audience, while at first shocked and worried, soon started laughing hysterically. The music was still going on. None of the performers stopped, they just kept on singing, looking horrified out of the corners of their eyes at the fire. Finally, someone in costume came out with a fire extinguisher and spritzed it out. Not a good beginning, to say the least.

Nabucco then made his entrance on a big "war machine"—a cross between the Trojan Horse and a catapult—fifteen feet off the ground, with twenty men pushing it from behind. The floor of the set was raised on platforms, and those platforms had slightly separated, so there was a small gap between two of them. As the stagehands pushed this "war machine," the front wheels fell in the gap, and they couldn't get it moving again. I was weaving back and forth on top, trying to keep my balance, and trying to look like the mighty, undefeatable king. All the while, I was thinking, "This is opening night in Paris, this is a disaster! This whole performance is falling apart before my eyes."

The stage designers also misjudged the distance between the columns of the door through which this "war machine" was supposed to roll. Finally my retinue got the whole thing moving, but then it bumped into a column, preventing it from entering the stage. I pushed the column aside with all my might so we could get through, and we finally started moving in the right direction. But then this huge contraption wouldn't stop. As Ruggero, his back to the audience, watched it come closer, his eyes grew wider and wider, and he started backing up to get out of the way, heading right for the pit. They couldn't seem to stop it, and I could just see Ruggero falling into the pit, with this machine on top of him, and me on top of that.

Again, the music never stopped, and the performance never faltered. With the stagehands going berserk, the contraption did finally stop, just short of everything falling into the pit. But the story is not over yet!

In the third act, Nabucco is in prison, which in this production was a huge stone wall. Like most stage walls, it was made of wood and fiber and hung from the ceiling. I was tied to it with a heavy rope and irons on one ankle. There's a long introduction in which I'm asleep. Then I wake up with a start, as if from a nightmare; and run until the ankle rope becomes taut, jerking me to the ground. During the performance, the huge stonewall wasn't lowered all the way to the floor, which I didn't know. When I ran and jerked the rope, it broke, so I had to stop myself. Then I looked back and saw this two-ton wall swinging back and forth, back and forth, from the rope's pull.

In this scene, my jailer was a dwarf, and as the director had staged it, the dwarf had a whole piece of business bringing out some bread and water, kicking at me, and in general taunting me. During the rehearsals I knew that Maestro Santi did not care for this dwarf business, but it seemed to work out OK through the dress rehearsal and no one objected to it. On opening night, I awoke with a start, did my run, broke the rope, saw the two-ton wall swinging back and forth, fell to the floor, and waited, expecting the dwarf . . . and waited, and waited, and waited. No one had bothered telling me that they'd killed the whole dwarf bit after the dress rehearsal. So I lay there onstage with huge egg on my face, already mortified by what had just happened, with minutes of orchestral playing remaining. There was nothing to do but eat my anger and frustration. At moments like this you can only grit your teeth and pretend that's the way it's supposed to be. I don't even remember what I did to fill the time, but it seemed like an eternity. I was really pissed off. Now I always ask after a dress rehearsal if anything's been changed, that is, "Did they kill the dwarf?"

In the last scene, Baal, the idol, appears. I make a big symbolic gesture to it, and it disintegrates. Through Nabucco, God's power destroys this false god. After my gesture, Baal's head was supposed to fly up into the wings, the legs fall below the platforms, and the arms and torso fly apart and be pulled offstage—with the right lighting, a very effective piece of stagecraft. But something went wrong mechanically. I made the gesture, there was a flash of lightning and a noise, and the head and legs disappeared as they were supposed to. But the torso and arms swung offstage, then swung back on, then swung off again, then swung back on, then swung off. . . . The audience again went bananas. We didn't know whether to laugh or pretend to ignore it.

When everything worked well, the production had the potential to be very impressive. It just didn't work with any regularity.

The theater wanted to film this production for television, and of the eight performances, opening night was a disaster, two weren't so good, two were OK, and three were very good. They were filming one of the not-so-good performances. There is a scene in the second act where Nabucco's daughter, Abigaille, sung by Grace Bumbry, comes racing in and sings. The maestro gave the cue, but there was nobody there. Grace was sitting in her dressing room. After enormous confusion the curtain came down, and the audience was booing and hissing and carrying on. After quite a few minutes, it was announced that Grace was indisposed, but would go on anyway. I think that she didn't feel she was in her top form and she didn't want the performance televised. Perhaps she broke this taping deliberately so they would have to film another one, thereby giving her another shot at it. Also, I'd heard that when Grace had sung the title role of *Salome* in Paris some seasons before, there had been some sort of problem and the audience had it in for her, so she was giving it back a bit. Actually the later filming was a very fine performance, and a video of it is available on the market.

It's too bad they didn't film everything opening night; it would have made the greatest opera bloopers show of all time. I don't know how we got through those performances. Maybe the audience's ultimate applause was for our nerves and chutzpah in continuing to perform through all those disasters!

In 1975 I sang *Otello* in Hamburg with Plácido Domingo in his debut in the title role. Shawn, my youngest son at the time, was two and a half, and he and my wife, Nancy, were in Germany with me. Plácido and I were rehearsing in a room in the opera house in street clothes, with Shawn and Nancy watching. We were in the second act where Otello attacks Iago because he suspects Iago has been lying. We didn't think of what this might look like to a child, to whom this was Uncle Placie and Daddy. At a certain point in this scene Plácido started to strangle me, and Shawn became absolutely hysterical. We had to stop; Shawn was inconsolable because he thought it was all real. Nancy had to take him out in his stroller and it took him hours to calm down. He finally said, "I never want to go back to that yucky place where Daddy works."

In the 1970s in Philadelphia, Plácido and I were appearing in both operas of a double bill of *Il tabarro* and *Pagliacci*. In the commedia dell'arte scene in the second act of *Pagliacci*, there was a piece of upright scenery forming the small back wall of the little stage. Plácido, as Canio, sings the very dramatic aria "No, Pagliaccio non son" and during it becomes appropriately violent. As part of the action, he threw a chair, which hit the upright scenery. This fifteen-foot-high, twenty-foot-wide piece of scenery started falling forward in the middle of his aria. I grabbed it and held it until he finished, and then forced it back into place, so the opera could continue. I guess you could say I held up the show!

Giancarlo del Monaco is the son of the very famous tenor Mario del Monaco. For years he was the intendant (head) of the opera house in Bonn, Germany, as well as a very talented and well-known stage director. He has had many successes in opera houses around the world and in recent years has done some brilliant productions at the Metropolitan. In 1991, in *La fanciulla del West*, he created a particularly beautiful and muscular production. There is a scene where Jack Rance, the sheriff—me—has shot Dick Johnson, the tenor (Plácido). In Minnie's (Barbara

Daniels) cabin in the mountains, Johnson is bleeding and very close to fainting. I grab Johnson by the shirtfront and stick the barrel of my .45 caliber pistol in his face and threaten him. Because of the emotion of the moment and constant urging by Giancarlo to make the scene more dramatic, there was one performance in which I was especially charged. I poked the barrel of the pistol into Plácido's face with such force that I struck him in the mouth. I felt terrible and embarrassed and wondered if I had really hurt him.

I saw a bit of spittle on his lips with something in it that looked like a piece of tooth. My heart really jumped. I said under my breath several times, "Va bene, va bene?" (Are you OK?) He said nothing, and I didn't know whether he had fainted or was just staying in character. Barbara said she was so worried about Plácido that she sang nonsense syllables for a whole page of music, thinking, "My God, we've killed him." She also had seen the spittle on Plácido's mouth with the piece of tooth in it. Somehow we finished the scene and the very dramatic card game without knowing how Plácido was, because the staging called for him to lie on the floor in a semi-faint.

As soon as the curtain fell, we ran to Plácido. He was, in fact, OK, slightly dazed, but not seriously hurt. However, I had broken part of his tooth with the barrel of the gun. It turned out that it had been an old break and so was a fairly easy repair job for a dentist. But accidents do happen, and in the heat of a performance there are no rules on how to respond. It certainly makes you feel foolish, as well as terribly worried about your bruised colleague.

CHAPTER EIGHT

The Audience—
Pleased and Displeased

IN MY OPINION, WE ALL HAVE A BIT of the fan in us. It seems perfectly natural to me for a person to look up to and respect another human being who does something we can't really do, or who does it better. This is not worship. It's just a healthy respect for the unique talents possessed by another human being.

A singer's fans come in all shapes and sizes. Some are quiet and others are very vocal, sometimes even during performances, and occasionally to the detriment of the performance as a whole. Others express themselves quite profoundly through letters and gifts, occasionally going "over the top" with their emotions and their adoration. But in general they do care and are passionate about their feelings. We rely on them, and without our dedicated audience, we performers would have no careers.

There have been moments in my musical life that will remain with me forever. Those moments make the world of singing unique. Sometimes after certain concerts, emotional and meaningful events occur for which there seems to be no particular reason, and there certainly seems to be no way to prepare for them.

The Tivoli Gardens in Copenhagen, Denmark, is kind of a Coney Island amusement park with a recital hall in the center of it. Many orchestra concerts, as well as instrumental and vocal recitals, are presented in this lovely auditorium. I have been there several times performing opera highlights and arias with orchestra, as well as recitals.

After these performances, people always come backstage for photos and autographs and to greet the artist.

After one particular performance, I noticed a small woman waiting in the backstage crowd who looked very pale, unhealthy, and thin-haired. After patiently waiting her turn, she was finally next. She came closer and rather hesitantly looked up at me. After what seemed like an eternity, there was some rush of emotion inside her, and she flung her arms around me. Her head came about even with my stomach, with her arms around my waist. She started to sob uncontrollably, yet said nothing. Eventually between the sobs, she offered an apology and explained that she had just been released from the hospital. It was the first concert she had heard in many years and the first concert of mine she had ever heard. She had been a fan for a long time and didn't want to die before hearing me. When she learned I was coming to Copenhagen, she was afraid she wouldn't be released from the hospital in time to hear me perform, or perhaps not be allowed to leave the hospital at all. She was suffering from cancer and wasn't cured; she didn't know what her future was in terms of life or death; she just wanted to hear me sing, to hear my concert. While she spoke, she continued to sob, her body wracked, shaking with a kind of violence.

An artist does not always know how to react in a situation like that. There is a small part of your psyche that is embarrassed, partly because of so many people standing around not understanding the situation. But it's a very soul-wrenching and emotional experience for the performer, and words sometimes fail you. (I had lived through my mother's cancer struggle, which I'm sure made me more sensitive to this woman's suffering.)

As a result, I was understanding and mature enough to try to comfort her and I continued to hug and hold her. At some point she released her embrace and extracted herself from me, apologized for her behavior, although none was necessary, and thanked me for my art, my singing, and the concert. I slowly took my hands away from hers and she turned and reluctantly left the room.

I was rather stunned and still deep in thought about what had just happened, and of course everyone else around me also felt the emotion and power of those moments. Fortunately, nobody jumped in with some stupid comment or remark, as sometimes happens when people are embarrassed and don't know how to respond. They were appropriately and thankfully hushed by the moment.

This was the singular most powerful moment of many backstage events in my career, because it was a life-and-death situation. The woman's pain and her love for music were so evident. If she was going to die, and she very well may have died since, she wanted to see that concert. This woman had an unbelievable hunger for music and love for an artist. That evening remains a very special moment in my career and one in my life that I cherish deeply.

Not understanding certain customs of a country can embarrass you. Once while singing *Il trovatore* at La Scala in Milan, someone came up to me in the dressing room opening night, and stuck out his hand, and said "Sono da claque" (I'm from the claque). But I thought his name was Da Claque. I didn't know about the history of the artist paying the claque for extra-loud applauding, so I stuck out my hand to shake his and said, "Piacere" (a pleasure). He must have thought, what a jerk. After talking to Ivo Vinco, the husband of Fiorenza Cossotto, who was singing the Azucena that night, I understood who Mr. Da Claque was. Eventually I did pay a nominal amount, but it was the first and last time.

I do not understand the whole principle of paying a group to applaud you more than you perhaps deserve. They say that they lead the applause in order to guide the rest of the audience, who they maintain do not know the particular opera very well. So they claim to perform a positive function. Weak reasoning, it seems to me.

Sometimes we get to see an entire audience react as one. Now, this can be frightening and intimidating, but it can also be fascinating. During an early Met tour, again in Detroit, there was a performance of *Faust*. I wasn't singing and decided to go just to hear the opera, which had a cast headed by Jean Fenn, Nicolai Gedda, Mario Sereni, and the American mezzo Marcia Baldwin as Siebel. The conductor was Georges Prêtre, the same gentleman who conducted my debut at the Met. I was sitting in the fourth row, and the first act went off without a hitch.

At the beginning of the second act, Siebel has her beautiful serenade, "Faites-lui mes aveux." Prêtre gave the downbeat, and maybe twenty or thirty bars into the piece someone in the audience yelled, "Fire!" There was the slightest smell of smoke in the air at that moment. It was very faint, but still there. There were about three thousand people in the house that night, and the entire place exploded. Most of them were dressed to the nines, not exactly sprinting-to-the-nearest-exit clothes, but that's what this audience did.

I remember watching and hearing the confusion all around me, and then I looked up at Marcia. She had a terrified look on her face, and I'm sure that neither she nor Maestro Prêtre had heard the man yell "Fire!" The orchestra just sort of bumped to a stop one section at a time. As the curtain closed, the last thing I remember was that look of panic and confusion on Marcia's face. I wasn't worried for me, because—worst-case scenario—I could jump over the few rows of seats, climb into the orchestra pit, and get out of the theater the back way. But there was pandemonium everywhere else.

Fortunately, one of the sponsors was able to make himself heard by standing on the arms of his seat and yelling repeatedly that there was no fire and the audience shouldn't panic. They calmed down a little, and he told them that some outside smoke had gotten into the air condition-ing duct, which had fanned it through the house, and that's what they smelled. After some ten or fifteen minutes, the audience finally quieted down and took their seats. The orchestra filed back in, and Prêtre started the second act again, and Marcia began her aria for a second time. But her eyes were still darting about, and I'm sure she was more than a little spooked. The performance, as it turned out, was quite good, although I remember thinking it was the only time in my life I had ever seen an audience panic as one and create a real stampede.

It is always heartening to find that the younger generation is affected by the sometimes sophisticated world of opera. As Art Linkletter used to say, "Kids say the darnedest things." On one particular visit of an elementary school class to an *Aida* dress rehearsal at the Met, the teacher decided to have the children write letters to me describing what they liked about the opera. Their words were candid, as are most children's, and filled with cute expressions of enjoyment. It was encouraging to know that even in this modern "pop" culture we live in, opera continues to have a profound effect on young minds.

One student wrote:

> You sang beautifully and acted good. You were great for Radames. Were you shy? Did you like your role? My favorite part was near the Nile River. Can you send me a picture autographed?

And this informal letter really tickled me:

> Hi Sherrill, how are you doing? I know I'm fine. I loved the opera *Aida*. It was one of the best operas I have ever seen. You were great. You sing so nice. I wanted to see the opera again just to see you act.

When onstage in a recital performance, I like to be almost blinded by appropriate lighting, including a small spot on the stage floor in front of me. This light opens the face by showing the eyes, no matter how you are turned, and besides, I have found that I concentrate better when I see less of the audience. Of course, they must be able to read program notes and translations, but the hall should be as dark as possible. Another more selfish reason for wanting to be partially blinded is that I am easily distracted by seeing the audience too clearly. People's faces while they are listening to music so often read so differently that you never know what's on their minds. Sometimes they look bored or even angry, especially when you can see them shift around in their seats or yawn. Perhaps worst of all is seeing people checking their watches, trying to find enough light by which to see the time. That always looks like they're thinking, "My God, when will this be over?"—even if there is a perfectly legitimate reason that doesn't occur to you.

Such was the case in Palm Beach, Florida, where I was performing in a tiny auditorium in which the lights were rather bright. I could see an elderly gentleman in the first row constantly checking his watch, making the kind of faces we make when we are trying to thread a needle. I found myself wondering all sorts of things, none of them having to do with the music. I, of course, thought this poor soul was bored out of his gourd, but I was also angry that he was able to distract me from the business of making music. I was grateful when the concert was over. However, to my great surprise, the front-row gentleman was the first in line to congratulate me on the concert and to say how much he enjoyed it. Hey, you never know!

The great Austrian conductor Karl Böhm asked me to appear in a new production of Verdi's *Macbeth* in Vienna in 1970. He had heard me in his production of Beethoven's *Fidelio* at the Met in the role of Don Fernando and as the Herald in Wagner's *Lohengrin*. It was my European debut and obviously a very important milestone in my career. Otto Schenk was the stage director, with Christa Ludwig as the Lady, Carlo Cossutta, and Karl Ridderbusch heading the rest of the cast.

I was treated with great respect in Vienna and assumed that that was the way it always was. In hindsight, it was probably Böhm's doing. I knew that he liked me and there always seemed to be some kind of familial affection, which continued to show itself throughout these performances and later in Salzburg in a new production of *Don Giovanni*. In Vienna I was "Böhm's boy."

This could have been one of the reasons I did not often work with Herbert von Karajan. It was common knowledge that these two conductors each considered himself the best. I had sung Donner in *Das Rheingold* with von Karajan in a successful production, but after my continuing work with Böhm, even though von Karajan was always friendly, he never used me for other operas.

This 1970 *Macbeth* was a very imaginative production: the procession of kings' ghosts (all in Macbeth's mind, of course) was done on film. They really looked as though they were coming to destroy me, moving from way upstage and slowly traveling down toward me and the audience, becoming larger and larger—you really believed they were there. At the end, when Macduff challenges Macbeth, there was a lengthy two-handed broadsword fight that was beautifully rehearsed and worked out. Macbeth then was run through, and as he died, he sang the seldom-performed "Mal per me," the aria Verdi wrote originally and then discarded in a later version. Both Maestro Böhm and I wanted this very effective finale to the opera.

On opening night, the audience started a little cool; they weren't that familiar with the music, and they'd never heard it before in Italian. Böhm had always conducted the opera before in German, and the flavor of an opera does change with the language. Also, it was a departure for Christa Ludwig, both as a mezzo-soprano singing a soprano part (although there is some precedent for this) and as a Verdi heroine. So we weren't sure if people were enjoying it or not.

We eventually found out. Late in the opera, after I finished the baritone aria "Pietà, rispetto, amore," there were two solid minutes of applause. If you think that fifteen to twenty seconds of applause is good response, then multiplied by five or ten, it's unbelievable, an eternity. My arms even got tired just standing there.

(In regard to acknowledging applause, my feeling is that during applause, singers should hold the position in which they finish singing. In terms of plot or story, applause is a time freeze, so one should "hold" the position and attitude. Once in a while, this is not possible. If your colleagues are the bowing, all-this-applause-just-for-me? false-modesty types, you have to respond in like manner.)

In Vienna, every aspect of the production was as big a success as the cast was. That was the beginning of my European career. It seemed that after that success, all the other major European theaters opened up.

That night, at a party afterward, Otto Schenk, who in Vienna is a well-known actor, director, and comedian, said in a moment of unguarded but black humor that my Macbeth was the "greatest personal triumph in Vienna since Hitler." The newspapers unfortunately picked it up, and he took a lot of flack for it.

There was a performance of Verdi's *Don Carlo* at the Hamburg State Opera in 1978, with Ruggero Raimondi as King Philip, making his debut in that theater, Harold Stamm (a noted Hamburg basso) as the Grand Inquisitor, Katia Ricciarelli as Elisabeth, Cornelius Murgu as Don Carlo, and me as Rodrigo. Giuseppe Patane was conducting, and we had only one rehearsal, the day before the performance.

That evening, I arrived at the theater an hour and a half early only to find Ruggero overwhelmed with laryngitis and totally out of voice. He had had to cancel and was very upset, especially as it was to have been his debut in Hamburg. The management asked Harold to sing Ruggero's part, King Philip, and a famous German bass who lived in Hamburg, Hans Sotin, was asked if he would sing Harold's part, the Grand Inquisitor. It's a big sing, but a short role, therefore not so much to review—and he agreed.

At this time, the stage director August Everding was head of the theater and had just announced he was leaving for a new post in Munich. The Hamburgers didn't like that, thinking he'd used their opera house just as a stepping-stone for his own career (he had been there for only two years). They thought he had sold them short, and, in addition, they didn't like some of Everding's productions. So when the cast changes were announced, not only did they boo loud and hard over losing Raimondi, they booed for all these bad feelings about Everding as well.

The performance started, everything was fine, and we reached the second act. Katia had the difficult but beautiful aria "Non piangere," which is written with two verses. Even though in many productions only one verse is used—followed by a cut to the ensemble, which finishes the aria—she wanted to do both verses as printed because she had sung them in the rehearsal. In the performance, Katia sang the first verse and was getting ready to do the second when the orchestra made the traditional cut. Patane put up his hand to stop her, but she wasn't having any of this; she wanted to do both verses. She made some kind of gesture and wouldn't sing the replacement lines, bringing the orchestra to a halt. Katia committed the almost cardinal sin for any performer by speaking out of character, directly to the audience. In English, to a German-speaking audience, with her heavy Italian accent, she said, "Thank you very much, the musical direction of the theater," and walked off the stage.

Emotionally I could understand it—Patane was a very knowledgeable conductor, but he could be less than supportive, and she probably felt she was being cheated. But we were aghast. The curtain closed and the audience went berserk, dividing into two camps: one group thought she should sing both verses if she wanted to, while the other felt that she was being completely unprofessional in walking offstage. And added to all this was the anti-Everding sentiment.

It was chaos backstage; Patane and Katia were having at it. The famous tenor José Carreras, a friend of Katia's, was in the audience and was verbally attacking both Patane and the theater, and everyone in the whole audience was fighting among themselves. In Hamburg the theater offices are across the street, and it turned out that Everding was in his office listening to this melee on his speaker system. So he ran across the street and into the theater and came out in front of the curtain. The audience again went berserk, spoiling for a fight. If they'd had guns, I'm sure they would have shot him. He managed to announce, "This is a change, usually I'm booed only after a performance and here we are in the middle of it." He went on to explain that there had been a misunderstanding with the orchestral parts, that it was no one's fault, and that they would continue after things had settled down. Very diplomatic!

This was my first experience with a performance that broke down completely, and I was rather in shock. (This was before the ill-fated *Nabucco* in Paris.) They finally decided to start with Katia's aria again. We went into our positions, frozen in place, the curtain rose, the music started, and we went back into action. Katia sang both verses very well and got a big ovation from the audience. In fact, the whole evening ended up being a big success: Harold Stamm, Hans Sotin, yours truly, and all the rest were given huge ovations with lots of bravos. This was the closest I'd ever been in a performance when tomatoes or whatever might have been thrown by the audience. To this day I have still escaped that dubious honor.

In June 1989 the Vienna State Opera had an *Otello* scheduled for the last performance of the season. It was also the last night that the Opera was under the aegis of the intendant Claus Helmut Dreser, who was quite respected and beloved there. It was an important evening and an impressive group of singers: the other principals were Plácido, Katia, and the best of the other regulars of the Vienna State Opera, and the conductor was Michael Schoenwandt.

Because it was an old production, only a day and a half were scheduled for rehearsals. Plácido and I had done this production many times before, both in Vienna and in other venues around the world. Plácido is, of course, the most experienced and the best Otello in the world today. Katia and I had also done other productions together, although Iago and Desdemona don't have much to do together.

There are many mysteries about why certain performances are good and others are not. It is impossible to analyze or predict. That is part of the magic of music. When it's very special, everyone knows it, but not always why, and when it's bad, everyone knows it, but again not always why. A bad cast is of course one of the reasons it's bad, but even a good cast is not always a guarantee of a good evening. It turned out that this night was a particularly hot performance, and the audience felt it and knew it. The chemistry between Plácido and me has usually been pretty potent, and it was that night too. Good applause was somewhat expected; however, what then happened was a unique experience in my life.

First, one must realize that normal applause for a well-sung aria can last from ten to twenty seconds. Once in a great while, under unusual circumstances, it can last up to a minute. At the end of a well-sung opera, applause can last up to twenty minutes, which is considered very long and is certainly very satisfying. (It does, of course, vary from opera house to opera house, audience to audience, country to country, and sometimes only a few minutes of applause are normal.)

The normal international bows are: first tutti bows—the whole cast takes a bow. Then solo bows continue—each singer takes a bow alone in the order of size and importance of the role, with the singer in the title row taking the last bow. And at some point the conductor is slotted in, often last. Then the pattern is repeated as long as there is an audience and applause out front, and as long as our stamina holds up. That night we took the normal bows for what seemed forever.

Very few of the audience left to go home, they just continued to yell and applaud. Then we added Herr Dreser, the outgoing intendant, to the curtain calls. Slowly the number of bows grew and I remember counting *eighty* of them, something I had never experienced before. Finally some of the audience started to go home, but there were still many people applauding and standing.

Finally, one hour and forty-five minutes and 101 curtain calls later—an unbelievable amount of time!—we called it a night. I'm not sure whether I became more fatigued from the singing or from the bows. Any of you who have stood in a wedding reception line can remember that your smile muscles eventually become tired and numb and finally you just can't smile anymore. Well, this was exactly the same thing. I don't expect that this record for a performance in which I sang will ever be matched or bettered.

The Printed Word

Theodore Roosevelt once wrote:

> It is not the critic who counts, not the man who points out how the strong man stumbled or where the doers of deeds could have done them better. The credit belongs to the man who is actually in the arena; whose face is marred by dust and sweat and blood; who strives valiantly, who errs and comes up short again and again; who knows the great enthusiasms, the great devotions, and spends himself in a worthy cause; who at the best knows in the end the triumphs of high achievements; and who at the worst, if he fails, at least fails while daring greatly; so that his place shall never be with those cold and timid souls who know neither defeat nor victory.

To try to take on critics is a fruitless endeavor. The printed word has its own power. Whether it accurately portrays what went on in that particular performance is another question. But once it is printed and read, it is permanently in the reader's mind, accurate or not, even if by chance it is retracted or negated in some future publication. It is true, of course, that music is by its nature subjective, which complicates any reviewing of it, but there are many objective aspects to any performance, which should be much less subject to a critic's emotions or personal preferences.

Most performers are much harder on themselves, and more realistic about a given performance, than the audience or the critics. I always pour out my physical human best, as much as the flesh will allow. I never felt I sang a performance without giving all that I could or all that was appropriate for the musical moment. I guess that's what a career is: many, many performances, each as good as one can do at the moment. I'm as fallible as anyone. I can be tired or rested, worried or inspired, sick or well—just like everybody else. If I feel I've given my utmost, I don't deserve a bad review, or least of all to be crucified by a critic.

We artists are all sensitive, and it seems that we are much more affected by a bad review than we are by a good one. We remember the bad ones for years, while the good ones tend to fade fast. I guess that is human.

Some of my colleagues say they never read reviews. More power to them. I want to know what was said, if only to know what my friends and enemies have read about me. Fortunately, bad reviews in the opera world cannot close the show, as on Broadway, but a series of bad reviews over a period of time can affect a career.

Occasionally there can be something to learn. But what to learn is almost never that which the critic states as fact, but something much less obvious. If you try to analyze what it was the critic liked or disliked and why, you can sometimes improve your performance. The only value of the review to the reviewed is to try to find that point, *if there is one*, analyze it, and use it.

There is some truth to what Joseph Lippman, my late manager at Herbert Barrett Management and a major power in the industry in his time, used to say: "Critics are to music as pigeons are to statues."

Many newspapers have headline writers, which means that a different person from the critic, someone who never saw your performance and has no awareness of the actual content of the evening, writes a headline. I resent this, because the headline often doesn't reflect at all the content of the review. Many readers just glance at a headline and draw conclusions from it. It can be misleading in a positive or negative way.

In 1994 my career was given a near death knell when a critic for the *New York Times* wrote a feature story on me. The critic claimed to be a fan and assured me that he was sensitive to some health problems I had had (described in the chapter "A Decade of Panic"). He wanted to talk about those years as well as my career in general. He was quite friendly, and I was fairly open with him. The article subsequently appeared with the headline "As the Limelight Fades, a Star Lowers His Sights." That was bad enough, but then there were two more sub-headlines: "For Milnes, the Limelight Fades," and "Once Sherrill Milnes seemed all but indestructible. Now he is sixty, and years of vocal problems have eroded the promise."

I broke out in a cold sweat when I saw it. What was really hurtful and infuriating was that the headline did not represent the article at all. I'm sure the headline writer thought it was very dramatic—and he was right. But many people read only the headline and judged accordingly. The writer offered me an apology for the headline, but there was nothing to do after the fact. A few friends told me they thought it was a beautiful and revealing article, but the headlines were undeniable in their effect. Dates started to dry up, and it took many fine performances on my part to counter that effect.

In addition, I have to think that the article was a culprit, two years later, in the Met's decision to let my contract expire and not invite me back after a thirty-two-year career there. (That is also discussed in more detail in the chapter "Life after the Met.")

Critics, of course, are entitled to be subjective as well as objective. But it always bothers me when the audience reaction to a performance differs from that of the critic, positive or negative, and the writer fails to report that difference. Without that report, the reader assumes that the audience agreed with the critic. I feel it is a critic's responsibility to report the evening as an entity, not just that critic's personal reaction. A review is not an editorial.

I'm not sure if this is especially typical of the English press, but I have seen reviews in London, not necessarily about me, where the critic will focus on an inappropriate or poorly executed gesture, without discussing the quality of the singing at all. If you don't sing with the appropriate colors and warmth of sound, it doesn't matter how you put your hand on someone's shoulder or how you take off your gloves. Of course, the mood one creates is paramount, but that mood is created mainly by the body energy, the singing, and the word colors.

There is at least one book published in which the author has compared reviews from different newspapers for the same performance, side by side. It is quite revealing. It makes you wonder if the critics attended the same event. There were diametrically opposed views in some cases.

Even given that the same performances can affect people differently, wrong notes are wrong notes, right notes are right notes, and good performances cannot be bad ones at the same time.

There is a story attributed to Vladimir Horowitz. He had just received a bad review, and he wrote the critic saying, "I am sitting in the smallest room in my house reading your review and I am about to put it behind me." Jokes are of course easy to make and not necessarily to anyone's credit.

I have one other thought about newspapers as well as TV stations. I feel that while papers must publish the news that's fit to print, they should support local arts organizations.

All arts organizations are cliff-hangers, because raising money is always tough. I can't tell you how many times I have sung in a city where there was very little or no space in the paper and no interest from television for the local event. No interviews, TV, or newspapers, and no sense of support and loyalty for the struggling group. The irony is that the lack of local coverage did not affect my career in an international sense, but for the local presenter it had a big effect. The lack of cooperation from local papers and local TV stations I find unconscionable. A report of the event or a feature story or thirty seconds or so on the local news is not a lot to ask.

There's another irony. However meaningless many reviews are, they are still necessary for one's career. Brochures and flyers need good reviews. The managers of companies know the pitfalls and fallacies of reviews, but they still hire singers on the basis of good ones.

CHAPTER NINE

The Recital and the Accompanist

Jon Spong

I FIRST MET MY ACCOMPANIST of thirty-three years, Jon Curtis Spong, at Drake University in 1953. It was an odd coincidence that we would spend so much musical time together, because he was a voice major, not a piano major. He loved to sing, and at Drake we performed together the triumphal scene from *Aida* and the midwestern premiere of Douglas Moore's opera *The Devil and Daniel Webster.* I was Webster and Jon was the Devil. And as I've said, many years later he was the tenor soloist at the *Elijah* performance two days after my mother died.

At school, attending recitals was part of the curriculum. I noticed that some of the voice faculty used Jon as the accompanist for their recitals. His talent was unique. He obviously had studied piano when he was younger, but I don't remember him studying piano at Drake. He just always played well, and that talent at some point led him into organ study as well. Frank Jordan was the dean of Drake's College of Fine Arts during its peak days of enrollment and a great organ teacher. Under his tutelage Jon developed into a fine service player and organ recitalist.

He was also gifted in improvisation. During our many years together doing recitals, we developed a special trick. At the end of a program, in those auditoriums where there was an organ, I would tell the audience that Jon would improvise on some tune that they, the audience, would give him. I would then ask them to call out five or six different numbers. Jon would use those numbers as scale degrees and make a five- or six-note melody out of them. Then he would play that tune a few times and begin to improvise on it. With his imagination and great knowledge of the organ, Jon would play for five to ten minutes using fugues, counterpoint, interesting registrations, and other compositional devices. It was an amazing thing to hear, and the audience was always astonished as I was.

He also kept up his singing. We have for thirty-some years done a switch in the encores of our recitals, where I announce as my next number "a beautiful folksong arranged by Benjamin Britten, 'Oliver Cromwell.'" Jon wrote an article about our "switch" called "Oliver Is Alive and Well," and with his kind permission I'm using parts of it to explain:

> During our many years together as a team, Sherrill has played the accompaniment for my vocal rendition of Benjamin Britten's arrangement of "Oliver Cromwell," a traditional English folk song for children, probably not less than two hundred times. When Sherrill gave his first New York recital in Avery Fisher Hall, in 1973, the audience went wild even though we had been advised against doing it.
>
> On a European recital tour, which began in Vienna, we went to rehearse and check the lighting in the Mozartsaal where we were appearing. Sherrill asked the gentleman in charge for his opinion about the switch encore. He replied, "To my knowledge, that sort of thing has never been done at a vocal recital in Vienna. Perhaps you will just have to take a chance and see what happens."
>
> On our way back to the Sacher Hotel after the rehearsal, Sherrill said, "Oh, let's do it. If they like it in Vienna, they'll go crazy about it every other place in Europe." That night after completing the printed program, we walked offstage and went back to perform the first encore, the Champagne Aria from *Don Giovanni.* The listeners loved it. We walked off again and immediately returned to the stage.
>
> "We took our usual places, and Sherrill announced the Britten piece. We looked at each other and the joke began. Sherrill moved toward the keyboard as I made my way to the curve of the piano. Unlike the titters and applause we were accustomed to from American audiences, there was dead silence in Vienna. Sherrill played the introduction and then I uttered my first vocal sound of the evening. The lights in the Mozartsaal were not low so even without my glasses, I could make out what was going on in the hall.
>
> At first, the listeners looked stunned. Gradually a change came over their faces and by the end of the song, the audience had completely fallen apart in laughter. I took a big soloist bow, "à la the super-

star," and when I motioned to Sherrill, he took a delightful "self-effac-ing, behind the potted palm" accompanist's bow. I walked off briskly with my head held high, and Sherrill followed along meekly, "à la the dutiful accompanist." As Sherrill went back to take a solo bow, he then motioned for me to come onstage with the next encore. Sherrill then said, "You had to know that I was going to sing another piece because there is no way I would let Jon end the recital!" More laughter.

After Vienna, we had no qualms about using our little routine in Germany and France. The audiences always went wild as the Viennese had. Earlier in our "team life," Sherrill and I would sometimes get killed in the press for "Cromwell" with the "how dare they do that at a formal recital!" attitude, or on occasion it would be completely ignored.

Time has a way of giving an "accepted tradition" status to some-thing that has really worked for many years, and most critics nowadays have fun with the switch like everyone else.

I have to say, that the only way it worked is that both Jon and I had to perform with accuracy and aplomb. If it were only a joke and we did not have the necessary techniques to sing and play, it would not work. But we did and it did.

Jon played everything with "fingers to burn" and with sensitivity. It was the highest level of piano playing around and in a league with the best-known accompanists of the world.

In 1987 Jon and I made a recital tour of several large European cities and some small festivals. It was during this tour that the Chernobyl atomic accident occurred, and one of our concerts was to be in Warsaw, Poland. Of course, I was very concerned about the fallout and other dangers about which we constantly read. I asked various U.S. embassies what they thought of going to Poland at that time but could not get a clear answer from anyone. I asked my colleagues from that part of the world what they thought, and they discouraged me from going there, even if we didn't know exactly what the dangers were. But safety was the major factor, and so I canceled the concert in Warsaw. As fate would have it, I have never again had the opportunity to travel to Poland.

One of the concerts on that tour was in West Berlin at the Deutsche Oper. I had sung there often in opera, but never in recital. That evening we started the program with an early French group and I was in normal voice, although I felt a little dust in the air onstage. Then I went off before starting the five Strauss songs. In the wings, I felt something in my throat like a bit of pepper, burning on the side. (In opera they almost always spray the stage with water before each act. The water in the air not only humidifies it, but also forces particles of dust to fall on the floor. In this recital I was singing in front of the closed curtain, so it was impossible to spray.)

I cleared my throat, hummed, vocalized, and tried to knock it out, but it wouldn't move. I swallowed some water and it still wouldn't move. By this time I had been offstage for several minutes, the maximum that I felt I could stay off without the audience becoming restless. So I returned to the piano with Jon and prepared to start the Strauss group. I could still feel the piece of dust or whatever it was and kept trying to clear it with short, quiet coughs. The first piece was "Allerseelen," and during the long introduction I kept thinking, if I try to sing this piece, all that will come out will be a hoarse croak. So before my cue arrived, I put my hand up and said to the audience, "Entschuldigung, bitte" (excuse me, please), and sure enough, only a croak came out. The audience gasped and I looked at Jon and walked off the stage. I was a little panicked at that point and immediately found some more water and gargled, trying to push the little piece of something out of there. It wouldn't budge. I "meeped" around (my word, meaning vocalizing and humming, sliding up and down the scales), making strange nasal sounds. To no avail! I coughed, spit, hacked, blew my nose, swallowed, pushed air while closing my nose, and sang all sorts of musical phrases. My speaking voice improved, but was still not clear, and I realized that I would have to do something soon. This had never happened to me in a concert.

I decided I had to return to the public because I could hear them becoming restless. Without really knowing if I was back to normal, we went back to the stage. I said "Entschuldigung, es tut mir leid" (excuse me, I'm sorry!). To my relief the speaking voice worked and to my surprise, the audience applauded, which made me feel more relaxed. But I must say that I was shaken and, even though my voice worked normally, it took all my concentration and experience to ignore what had just happened. In fact it was many songs later before my metabolism settled down to normal.

The late Thomas Schippers, from Kalamazoo, Michigan, who died much too early at the age of forty-four, was a world-class conductor with a warm sense of humor. I had the pleasure of working with him many times in opera and concert. Some years ago I was offered a recital at the Plum Street Temple in Cincinnati, and they were eager to have Schippers, who was then the director of the Cincinnati Symphony, accompany me at the piano. The maestro had agreed to do so, and I was very flattered. However, I ultimately decided against it because there was just not enough rehearsal time in my schedule to work with a new accompanist, no matter how fine. Jon and I had spent so much time working together that I felt uncomfortable about having a different kind of musical energy at the piano. The phrasings, the breaths, the myriad of details from the pianist in a concert—these were almost an automatic thing with Jon and me.

To Schippers's credit, when Jon and I went to the Temple to rehearse and check out the piano and other things, the presenter showed me a card Schippers had sent in which he expressed his best wishes for our concert and lamented that he wasn't accompanying me.

After Jon joined the faculty of the University of Cincinnati's College Conservatory of Music, he was invited by the well-known philanthropists J. Ralph Corbett and his wife, Patricia, to join them in their box at Music Hall. They enjoyed the concert performed by the symphony with Schippers conducting, and afterward Mrs. Corbett took Jon backstage to meet the maestro. Schippers looked at Jon and said, "Oh yes, you're the one who took the Milnes recital away from me." Jon replied, "No, Mr. Schippers, you're the one who nearly took it away from me!"

Page Turners, Pianos, Misprints, Lost Music . . .

In my recital career, I have always felt that the presence of a page turner can be a hindrance to the vocal and musical communication. Jon and I feel the presence of a third, nonmusical participant rising slightly (sometimes not so slightly) to turn the page can, for many listeners, disrupt the mood we have established. (Using a page turner in the recording studio where an audience is not present is another matter. Also, in an instrumental recital, where there is no text involved, having a page turner can be justified.)

More than once, when arriving for a recital, we have been asked if we needed a page turner. I'm sure we have disappointed more than one budding musician by saying "No, we don't use page turners, but thank you anyway!" If they knew how much I dislike having that third person sitting onstage with us, I don't think they would ask. However, I know that it is quite normal for many of my colleagues to have one.

There are ways to avoid the page-turning problem all together. Jon and I use a large notebook, such as an artist's sketchbook with sturdy paper, and transparent tape. Using a copier, we cut out the music and arrange it in the notebook in such a way that the pages can be turned in a rest or where the music is easier. One could also memorize certain spots that present a difficulty and wait to turn at a more convenient time.

Or an accompanist can play entirely from memory, such as the late Frank LaForge and the late Edwin McArthur did. The danger in that is you might become hopelessly lost and give the singer a real jolt. For example, Edwin McArthur played from memory for Kirsten Flagstad at all her concerts. McArthur told Jon, "I had never forgotten a note of the 'Liebestod' [from Wagner's *Tristan und Isolde*] in public before, but that time I found myself unmercifully lost at one point and just couldn't get back on track. After I brought the utter chaos to a halt right in the middle of the piece, Kirsten turned to me and said in anything but hushed tones, 'Well, what do we do now?'"

Edwin suggested that they start again. He said that all went well the second time and that Flagstad got quite a kick out of telling the story for years afterward. He went on to say that he continued to accompany her recitals from memory, but that each time the Wagner excerpt was featured, Flagstad, with a smile and a twinkle in her eye, would ask him, "Do we know the 'Liebestod' tonight?"

Even if Jon wanted to memorize a program, it would make me too nervous to think that no one onstage had the music. If I needed words or cues, there would be no source from which to draw. I imagine many singers feel as I do. Partly because of this worry, misplacing or losing your concert and recital music is a recurrent nightmare. So Jon always carries our recital music in a briefcase, and we never check it as luggage for fear of losing it.

Once, when taking a taxi to the airport, we left the music briefcase on the curb in front of our hotel. We only noticed it was missing as we approached the airport. So we returned to the hotel, slightly panicked, but found the briefcase patiently waiting on the curb like an old friend, and were still able to make the flight and subsequent concert.

However, that was nothing compared to another experience. We had just given a recital at the Masonic Temple in San Francisco in a series called Today's Artists Today presented by W. Hazaiah Williams. We then were to fly to Atlanta to perform the same concert under the auspices of the Atlanta Opera in the Fox Theater, where coincidentally I had auditioned for the Metropolitan Opera many years before. We arrived a little early at the airport and checked in our luggage, with our music briefcase well in hand. We then went to the cocktail lounge near the departure gate and sat down, put the case on an adjoining stool, and ordered beers. It was warm in the lounge, so we took our jackets off. Other people came and went, and one fellow sat down next to us. He likewise took his jacket off and put it on the back of his chair. Soon our flight time was nearing, so we finished our beers and left for the departure gate. On the way, I asked Jon if he had the music. With a start and a horrified look, he said no! We raced back to the cocktail lounge and looked everywhere. No case! We asked the waiter if he remembered us and did he remember the briefcase? He remembered us, but had no idea about the case. We started to panic . . . no music . . . no concert! All we could think of was that someone had seen us leave without the case, picked it up, and taken off with it, thinking it contained something of value. To us, of course, it was very valuable, but to anyone else it was meaningless.

Because our flight was on Delta, we ran to their office and asked whether, just by chance, someone had turned it in. No luck! What should we do? What could we do? Book a later flight and call the Atlanta auspices to tell them of our later arrival and see how much of the missing music might be available there, perhaps from a music store or local voice teachers? Or locate a baritone aria anthology and sing as many arias as I could remember, anything to put together a program?

We made the call but found that there was very little usable music available in Atlanta. More panic! Jon and I discussed how much of the music he could do from memory and decided that we might have half an evening's worth. Not enough! We then began darting around looking through all the waste containers in case the thief, after discovering the case only had music in it, had dumped it in a wastebasket and kept the case. We even went through all the men's and women's bathrooms looking through the trash. What a wonderful job! One of us would keep watch at the door while the other looked through everything. What a sight we must have been, running around from one restroom to another, from one trash can to another—even looking on top of and behind all the lockers in the hall. Several people from Delta joined the search, as one of their employees had been at the concert the night before and therefore appreciated our dilemma . . . but no luck!

By now, it was almost time for the later flight to leave, which was the last possible flight out of San Francisco for Atlanta. We started to the gate to take the plane to Atlanta; we had decided to try to fake some kind of program for the next evening, not really knowing what we would do. To stay in San Francisco, of course, served no purpose. Then, just at the last moment, I saw one of the Delta agents running down the concourse with something in his arms, a little like the Delta TV ad we have all seen with the agent racing down the concourse leaping chairs and benches, having retrieved someone's belongings. I ran up to him and jokingly fell on my knees with my arms held out. It was no joke that finding the music saved our musical life, at least in Atlanta.

The attendant said that the bartender had found it. Apparently, the guy who sat on the stool next to us put his coat over the back of the chair, effectively covering the briefcase. Then he sat down, not feeling the bump (the briefcase) in his back. He sat there about an hour, all the time we were searching for the music. Eventually he left, and the bartender saw the case sitting on the stool. The music had never been lost—it had just been serving as a backrest for this stranger! How he didn't feel it, I don't know, although the bartender said he was pretty well in his cups. Needless to say, we profusely thanked the Delta agent and all those who helped with our search.

With a little running, we did make the flight and sang the concert the next night, telling the lost-music story to the audience, which they enjoyed immensely. We now guard the music with our lives!

Performing halls and stages and their pianos are often fine and very satisfying. But sometimes they are terrible. Bad pianos and bad stages appeared much more often in the early part of my career when the fee structure was low; conditions improved as the fees improved.

In the late 1950s after graduation from college, when I returned to the farm, I often encountered these poor concert conditions. To earn a living from teaching privately and singing professionally took much running around and performing in a variety of different musical venues. One such venue was to present programs for the many women's clubs in the Chicago area. Every year there was an audition for all the music representatives of these clubs. You would sing and leave them sample programs and your phone number, and if they were interested they would call. My programs were always slanted toward the lighter vein and the more classical pieces selected from among the most well-known. I had two programs of different lengths; thirty minutes for $45 and forty-five minutes for $75. Inevitably they would ask for the cheaper program and request that I do extra encores. They were very tight with the bucks. My prices, even for the 1960s, weren't very high, but it was about all the traffic would bear. And if you sang often enough, it added up.

The places where the clubs held their meetings often presented a problem. If the club had its own building, it usually had some sort of a stage, and that was fine. But the local golf or country club dining room was the most frequent meeting place. There would be a short business meeting, and then lunch would be served. During dessert and coffee, I would be announced, and my accompanist and I would walk out to mild applause. I soon found out that these ladies were more interested in the social aspect of the event than in the cultural or even the entertainment aspect, so I was part of the dessert. In fairness to them, however, I was totally unknown.

When meals are served in any organized affair, it is normal for the waiters to go about their business of serving and clearing the dishes without any regard for what else might be happening. So my accompanist and I had to become used to the sound of clattering dishes and the squeaking swinging door of the kitchen. It took extra concentration and a different attitude toward the program just to keep the music and the voice going during all the hustle and bustle of clearing the tables and serving more coffee. It also seemed inevitable that some of the women would continue to talk throughout. We did realize, however, that there were a few women out there who did in fact enjoy the music and our artistic efforts.

For many of these programs, my accompanist was the now well-known basso Richard Best. Richard is a fine piano player and teaches voice at Southern Illinois University in Carbondale. At one of these "noisy dates" in a country club setting, we had done an up-tempo Italian song and had started the very familiar "Widmung" of Schumann. After a few measures of music, a little old blue-haired lady walked right in front of me, so close I could have reached out and touched her. Obviously my music wasn't touching her because she was on her way to the bathroom. I'm not sure why it shocked me so much. Maybe I was totally into the music and, because I had my eyes closed, didn't see her approaching. I just know that all of a sudden she was right in front of me, paying no attention whatsoever to my singing, and I was dumbfounded and offended.

Without knowing why or having time to think, I stopped singing and turned into the crook of the piano, head down. Richard was also shocked and stopped playing. I remember a slight gasp from some members of the audience in some kind of sympathy. It was the first time in my life that I didn't know what to do in a performance. One instinct said, "Leave the stage and don't finish the concert; they don't deserve it." But another instinct said, "There are people out there who are enjoying it and who are also embarrassed for me and for their unthinking fellow member." I don't know how long I stood there, probably only a minute or so. I remember asking Dick what we should do. Just then the little old blue-haired lady returned, adjusting her dress and her hair, and crossed in front of us just as close as before. With some kind of "musical getting even" Dick started to play the familiar theme from the *William Tell* overture (the *Lone Ranger* theme for you older radio fans—*da da pum, da da pum, da da pum pum pum*) in time to her walking. She still was completely unaware of anything out of the ordinary and returned to her seat. There was some supportive laughter at the musical joke from some members of the club, which I suppose gave us a little more courage.

We waited a few more seconds and I said I would try the Schumann piece again and continue the program. We finally finished, and afterward some women came up and apologized profusely for their colleague's behavior. I guess I ultimately felt some sense of satisfaction for finishing the program.

At another such recital there was a parrot out in the lobby of the country club constantly squawking all through my singing. That was a real joy; I wanted to kill him.

Often the pianos at these engagements were not the best either. Many were terribly out of tune or had a squeaky pedal, or one note had a buzz or thonk, or sometimes a certain note didn't work at all—all these problems were often awaiting you. One extreme example was when the middle F (on the bottom space of the treble clef) on one piano did not sound at all—it just made a thud. That is a very common note in almost any piece and hard to live without. I was singing the familiar old-time song "A Little Brown Bird Singing," and every time Dick had to play the F (the piece was in the key of F), he had to play it an octave higher, which gave the melody a very strange flow indeed. If he had not changed the octave, we would have had a thud every time that first-space F occurred. (We discovered later that a beer bottle had been stuck in the piano.) The whole affair was enough to turn me off concert singing forever. A sense of humor and the drive to make a living was necessary at all times.

Jon Spong and I did a recital in Miami in the late 1960s. This concert series had been in existence for a long time and was run by a very serious elderly gentleman. When we arrived at the airport, there was no one to meet us, and we had to take a taxi to the hotel. Then we had to find our own way to the rehearsal at Dade County Auditorium, because the assistant said they were too busy to pick us up. I was annoyed, but there was nothing to do.

At the auditorium that night, we dressed and prepared ourselves. At eight o'clock a stagehand said everything was ready, and Jon and I walked out onstage to the piano. I bowed to the audience, but then heard and felt some stirring at the piano. I looked over at Jon, who was fumbling with the music, and I saw that there was no music rack at all on the piano. They had forgotten to put it on. I said something silly to the public and we marched offstage. The same stagehand was in the wings, oblivious to what was happening. I told him we didn't have the music rack and he would have to find it before we could go on. He mumbled something about having seen it somewhere and looked around. It was leaning against the wall in a corner, and he retrieved it and walked out onstage, wearing his smart bib overalls, with the rack in his hand. The audience laughed and gave him a good round of applause after he had replaced the rack on the piano. Then Jon and I returned to the stage and started the concert.

Everything ultimately went well, and during the afterglow, when we greeted people backstage, the elderly presenter came up to us with his assistant and stuck out his hand. He said in a rather growly voice, "When Joe [Joseph Lippman] told me your fee, I thought it was too high, but it's not! Thank you and good night." And with that he and his assistant turned tail and left—not another word. What a pleasant fellow!

It took a minute or so to realize that he had just paid me a compliment—understated and obtuse, but a compliment. For him, that was probably the most vocal he could be. After a few more minutes, it occurred to me that his departure meant that we did not have a ride back to the hotel. Dade County Auditorium is very far away from the hotel area, and it is difficult to find taxis. Fortunately, there were still a few fans remaining in the hall, and so we hitched a ride with two of them. Years later Jon and I found out that these two fans were the now career singers, Marvis Martin and Curtis Rayam. At least the elderly gentleman's check didn't bounce!

The worst story I've ever heard concerning a piano is one Jon told me. On a 1970 goodwill tour of Southeast Asia, Andrew White, my college voice teacher, about whom I have spoken, and Jon, as his accompanist, performed a group of recitals.

On the day of an evening concert in Kwangju, South Korea, they stopped by the local music store to inspect the piano that had been made available to them for the recital. It was an upright instrument built by an unfamiliar manufacturer and not very good, but it was the best there was.

That evening, getting to the hall (an unheated theater in the dead of winter) was a slow and frustrating experience because of very heavy traffic. As Andy, his wife, LaRue, and Jon inched their way forward through the mass of vehicles, they saw, out of the window of their taxi, a rickety old truck with a rickety old piano strapped on it, unwrapped and unprotected from the cold, and going in another direction. Even though the piano they had seen earlier was no great shakes, this one was on its last legs. LaRue jokingly said, "Jon, there goes your piano!" They all laughed loudly.

Upon arriving at the theater, they made their way inside with great difficulty pushing through the large, noisy crowd that had gathered outside, seemingly in no hurry to get into the freezing cold theater. Only people who have visited Asia can picture the density of a large crowd and the impossibility of trying to move within the mass of people.

Finally arriving backstage in their tiny dressing room, Andy and Jon prepared for the concert. Soon the crowd filled the hall to overflowing, and a few minutes later Andy and Jon, wearing scarves, overcoats, and gloves, strode onstage to begin. Jon did take the gloves off before starting to play, although I don't think it would have made any difference in the sound. Their first sight was this rickety old piano from the rickety old truck sitting on the stage in front of them. (It seemed that the original piano had become unavailable and the store had found the next best.) It was just awful, but the audience didn't seem to notice, and as the phrase goes, "A good time was had by all"—except for the soloists.

Sometimes cancellations and emergencies come up and you need to be ready with a recital program. Once I substituted at the last minute at Wheaton College, in Wheaton, Illinois, near my hometown, for one of our most popular mezzos, Frederica von Stade, who was ill. After the recital we went out for a bite to eat with some friends and acquaintances from Downers Grove, including Marge Lukes, who was to write the review for the local paper. She was the mother of a high school classmate of mine, so I knew the whole family. Jon and I asked Marge Lukes to send us a copy of the review. She did so, but was very apologetic in her note. It explained that although she had given the newspaper a correct version of the review, a new member of the editorial staff, thinking an error had been made in one place, did a little "correcting" on his own. The following sentence came out in print: "DuPage County residents were pleased to hear the young mezzo, Sherrill Milnes, since she had been the toast of Chicago Lyric Opera, starring in the opera *Hamlet*, a work new to the Lyric." Once again, I suffered a sex change at the hands of a zealous editor!

However, that's better than a mention I once got in an article in my hometown paper, reporting of my success in Vienna. They printed that Sherrill Milnes, a hometown boy, enjoyed a huge ovation at the Vienna State Opera for his role in Verdi's *A Mashed Ball*. Ouch. (Of course, they meant *A Masked Ball*.)

Recitals

Recital programming is a very specific endeavor and needs musical knowledge and sensitivity and often some outside help. We singers must remember that every song, sacred or secular, has a point of view and is sung by someone with a point of view, whether that person is named or unnamed, mythical or real. I had a choral director once who felt that sacred music should not be interpreted because we mortals are not worthy to interpret the word of God, the Bible, or other important religious writings. Of course the big and obvious mistake there was that the very act of not interpreting a piece of music is in and of itself an interpretation. A boring and uninteresting interpretation to be sure, but an interpretation. Fortunately for me, my mother believed that one had to communicate with, and send a message to, the listeners, whether one was singing in church, school, or at home.

Singing full operas is very different from singing a recital of art songs. In opera, generally you have to sing louder and higher and hold notes longer. You are physically farther from the audience than in any recital situation, and you have to sing over an orchestra. Also, except in rare cases, you can't alter keys to suit your vocal needs. Opera does not usu-ally deal with profound emotional issues to the degree and extent that recital repertoire does. I'm certainly not saying that you don't have to look into your guts as Rigoletto, but few operatic situations plumb the spiritual depths and profundity of, let us say, Brahms's *Four Serious Songs* or Schubert's *Winterreise.*

One thing that is easier about opera is that it is not always "your turn." During part of any performance you can rest in your dressing room while a colleague sings another scene. In a song recital, it is always "your turn." Then there is the shifting of stylistic gears. In opera, you are the same character from one end of the work to the other; you are singing in one language and developing a character with a specific perspective. In a recital, you are dealing with different languages, different musical styles, different points of view. Also, in most opera houses, you have a prompter to ease worries about memory slips, and of course you don't have that prompter in recitals.

Mainly because of my mother's musical taste and background, recitals have always been a part of my life—part of my musical foundation, not an add-on. Opera was my add-on. Recitals force you to explore many more colors in your voice, more legato line, and certainly more dynamics. In the roles of my career, I really couldn't sing very softly with the orchestra between the audience and me, or it could become a pantomime. Soft in opera is really more like *mezzo-piano* or *mezzo-forte.* A song recital allows you to use every color, every dynamic that your voice is capable of, and, as an artist, I find that enormously satisfying. Yes, in opera it's great when you are feeling especially hot to wail a long high note, but that is partly a physical feat, not just a musical and vocal feat. Perfectly placed singing is less important in the context of a song recital. The exploration of varying emotions and the use of a myriad of colors are of prime importance. Recitals are a small painting with detailed strokes using a smaller brush. An opera is a big canvas with much bigger strokes. In this real sense, a recital offers a far greater artistic challenge. I also felt that in opera, I was singing to the whole audience as a mass all the time (and naturally, you are singing and relating to your colleagues onstage), whereas in recital I felt that I was singing to each person in the audience one on one, all the time, even when I couldn't see them. It's a different kind of focus and concentration.

The following are just some thoughts about organizing and putting a program together. My ideas have always been rather traditional, and these are some of my methods that have evolved over the years. Certainly I am not pretending to offer a comprehensive plan; there are some fine books out there which have much more information. But I hope that this will be helpful.

When I put a recital program together, I first decide on the German group, or at least the composer, and then build around that. It is the meat to which I add the rest of the meal. I plan a program somewhat chrono-logically. Early baroque or classical-period pieces first, then German lieder, and just before intermission I sing some opera. After the break, I program French lieder or similar period music, and then I finish with an English-language mix of songs from this century. Encores are usu-ally lighter fare with familiar arias and sometimes Broadway tunes, and I often tell the audience some opera stories.

I begin rehearsing with more music than I need and slowly eliminate some of it to make a program of acceptable length. In general, I plan for about sixty minutes of actual music, plus encores, which makes an eve-ning of about two hours. Too much more than that can be too long for an audience, even if the concert is stunning. Better to leave them wanting more than grateful it's over.

Key relationships, meter, tempos, mood changes, and flow from one song to another are major factors in determining the order of the music. In general, too many minor keys and dark, moody texts do not make an interesting evening. Unless you are singing a song cycle, variety is the key. I also always choose music that says something special to me. There is so much music in the world that it is silly to sing pieces that do not speak to you, that you do not love.

In a program you need music and composers that look interesting on paper and at the same time translate to an exciting performance. An interesting program helps bring the audience and the critics to the con-cert in the first place because it looks good. Yet sometimes what looks good on paper is not always as satisfying in sound; therefore, once the audience is in the hall, your performance must appeal to them. Your program should be elevating, thought provoking, and inspiring, but, at the same time, it must be entertaining. You never know when you are singing to a first timer and it is our responsibility to turn on that member of the audience. That way we are doing a service to the presenter, the music, and our industry.

Fame

Tony Randall

IN THE FAMOUS MET PRODUCTION of *Luisa Miller* in 1968, the stage was set up with boxes on the side for a stage audience. It looked like an Italian baroque theater from the viewpoint of the real audience in the theater. Tony Randall, whose love for opera is well-known, had been invited by the management to be a member of the audience onstage, and so he heard me very close up. He came back that first night to congratulate me. I was quite excited to meet this famous actor, and without my knowing it, he was as excited to meet me, and we remained very good friends until his death in May of 2004.

It often happens that stars from different fields are thrilled to meet each other. Of course, the whole world of stardom is somewhat relative. Opera is probably lower on the list than other fields like movies, sports, pop and rock, and television, so I am always excited to meet people that I think of as really big stars.

Tony, as well as having been a famous TV and movie actor and the founder of the National Actor's Theater, was an ardent classical music and opera buff. He was extremely knowledgeable in many areas, and opinionated. He was proud of those opinions; it was part of his charm.

Tony once invited me to be a guest on his very popular television show *The Odd Couple*, in which he costarred with Jack Klugman. His agent, the well-known Abby Greshler, from Hollywood, was to represent me for the project. There is a major difference in the booking schedules for a movie or television series and the one required for an operatic career.

I had been specific with Abby when talking about my availability to do the show. I could not automatically be available to film if I had other dates that were already signed. And I certainly couldn't automatically cancel those dates because there was a last-minute TV possibility.

With no warning, as I was about to leave for performances at the Vienna State Opera, Abby called to say I was expected in Los Angeles the next week to film the show! The set had already been built and the script was written. I tried, as diplomatically as possible, to explain that my contract with Vienna had been signed a year or more before and that it was impossible to cancel at this short notice. I was upset, because I had been clear about this from the beginning.

He argued that this appearance was important to me and to them. Finally, no matter how I reasoned with him, he thought that I had an easy choice to make and should cancel the opera contract. But we in the opera world know that Vienna is a very important theater and certainly had an important place in my career. I'm sure I made him angry by not canceling, but I didn't know what else to do. I called Tony in Los Angeles, and he had thought I was available and was helpless to change it because the set and script had been finished, even though he understood my dilemma. I reluctantly abandoned the show. I understood that for an opera singer to appear on almost any network TV program is a huge plus. But at the same time, to cancel a series of performances at the Vienna State Opera, for this reason and at the last moment, was unthinkable. Then it turned out that this was *The Odd Couple*'s last season. So I never got the chance to appear on that classic show, which still lives on and thrives in reruns.

Some years later, Tony asked me to star on his critically acclaimed series *Love, Sydney*. This time, I could make the date, and so I flew to Los Angeles. The plot had me playing string bass in a jazz band and then being recognized as an opera star from the opera *I Pagliacci*. In an informal conversation with Sydney and his adopted family, I was asked if I ever sang at parties. I said, "Of course," and was then invited to sing at the little girl's birthday celebration. Jon Spong was also on the program and played for me. I sang the famous prologue from *Pagliacci* in English, and then Tony and I sang a duet that we have often sung together at other occasions, "Cecilia." It's a fun piece where Tony sings rather classically and I sing very pop. Our two voices come together very cleverly. Another special memory of that show is that my son Shawn was included as one of the guests at the birthday party, which was his television debut.

Tony was kind enough to write several liner notes for recordings of mine. He was also one of the few individuals to whom I confided all of the vocal and surgical difficulties I was to encounter later in my career.

Some years ago, I met the actor and the then president of Actor's Equity Association, Ron Silver, through mutual friends. He told me that we had in fact met in 1971, at the Vienna State Opera where I was singing *Pagliacci.* He and some friends had met some girls, and they attended the performance. Right after it was over, the girls were ready to go to somewhere more intimate. Ron had a tough choice: if he went backstage, he might lose the opportunity to go with the girls. According to him, he chose to come backstage to meet me. He probably made the wrong choice, although he never told me whether he lost the heat of the moment or ever saw those girls again.

The White House

One of the advantages of being an opera star is the opportunity to meet important people outside of the arts, including presidents and other political figures. My first appearance at the White House was July 27, 1976, at a state dinner for the Prime Minister of Australia, Malcolm Frasier, hosted by President and Mrs. Gerald Ford, who were in their last months in their Washington home. *Charlie's Angels* was the top-rated TV show, and movie theaters were pulling people in to see movies as diverse as *Rocky, Taxi Driver,* and *Network.* It was the end of an era when Chicago's legendary mayor Richard Daley, the father of the present mayor, died. He had always seemed to be a part of the local political scene in Chicago as I was growing up, and now this Illinois farm boy was singing in the White House.

This has to be the ultimate thrill for every American performer. All formal concerts are given in the East Room and are accompanied on a vintage, historic Steinway. That afternoon Jon and I went to rehearse. We were puzzled to find that the damper pedal was not functioning properly; it was sticking periodically, causing notes to smear together. One of the men on the ushering staff said that the piano technician had been there just a short time before and that everything was in working order when he left. We went back to our hotel not knowing in what condition we would find the piano that evening.

When we arrived back at the White House for dinner, the same usher rushed up and with a most relieved expression on his face said that the problem had been solved. A very small piece of wood from one of the ornate and famous eagles on the right front leg of the piano had fallen off and had been found by one of the cleaning men. He didn't know what to do with it, so he decided to place it in the pedal mechanism, directly behind the damper pedal! A logical place in which to put an extra piece of wood? We didn't rat on him.

Even though I was very nervous, the concert was received with great enthusiasm by everyone present, including President and Mrs. Ford, Prime Minister Frasier, Henry Kissinger, Shirley Temple Black, and other distinguished guests.

At the reception following the concert, Mrs. Ford introduced me to Gregory Peck. I was actually talking to Atticus Finch in my all-time favorite movie, *To Kill a Mockingbird*! But as is sometimes the case, he didn't want to talk about himself and instead told me how much he had loved the concert, especially the *Faust* aria "Avant de quitter ces lieux."

I had introduced the aria by saying that for many years an instrumental version of it had been the theme song for the TV show *Lassie*, and I was sure they would recognize it. Mr. Peck said that he was moved to tears by the *Faust* aria, partly because he was a big fan of *Lassie*. He remembered watching a rerun in which the dog helps rescue a wounded fawn, and he was tearing up all through and really cried at the end, just as he did during my performance. My mind flashed back to *The Yearling*, another great Peck film in which he and Jane Wyman are a farm couple whose young son adopts an fawn whose mother has been shot by Peck. A little like my farm background.

Subsequently, Mr. Peck and I met on several occasions, most frequently at the Crystal Cathedral in Orange County, California. I have appeared several times there as soloist on Robert Schuller's *The Hour of Power*. I have been there when Mr. Peck, as a good friend of the cathedral, narrated many special programs as well as recorded readings of the Bible for Dr. Schuller. My favorite story about Dr. Schuller is from my first visit to the Crystal Cathedral. He usually does a short interview with his guests. I spoke of my mother and my music, but also of my father, who, though a hardworking farmer, loved music and singing as much as anyone could. After my solos, Dr. Schuller used a wonderful midwestern expression, saying, "I know there is a farmer in heaven just bursting his buttons." This was well after both my parents had passed away, and I was quite moved.

Within a year I was back in Washington. President Carter had asked me to sing at the Inauguration Day prayer service, to be televised from the steps of the Lincoln Memorial. There was to be a portable organ, and I asked Jon to play for me. I chose the very stirring "The Lord Is My Light" by Frances Allitsen. Because it was January, I knew that it would be cold—the forecast said in the twenties—so I bought some long underwear, the kind my dad wore full-time from October to April. We were supposed to rehearse the day before, but the organ was locked and no one knew where the key was. So we got up early the morning of the service to rehearse, but the car was late. As a result, we arrived just in time to hear the massed choirs rehearse a beautiful spiritual, leaving Jon only a few minutes to practice on an electronic organ that he had never seen or heard. In addition, we never thought about the temperature outside and how that might affect the instrument. You could, of course, see your breath, and even with an electric heater nearby, it was very cold. The keys and some of the stops began to stick, and we wondered if we would be able to get the organ to work at all. The situation was becoming desperate, but as luck would have it, the fellow who had installed the electronic organ agreed to lift up all the sticking keys as soon as Jon had finished playing them.

Then, in the middle of this "rehearsal," a reporter came up, shoved a microphone in our faces, and wanted to ask some questions. We were three minutes from live broadcast—not a good time for an interview! The actual performance must have been a sight, with me singing next to the organ and a man underneath the keyboard pushing the keys up as fast as Jon was pushing them down. Add to that, seeing my breath with every phrase and feeling the burning in my lungs from the very cold air, it was hard to look sincere while singing. But somehow the whole event turned out to be quite beautiful, in no small part due to the participation of Leontyne Price, Ruth Carter (the president's sister), and Martin Luther King, Sr., who were all part of the service.

A few years later I was asked by the Reagan White House to sing in the East Room for a state dinner for the president of Germany. Jon again played for me, and we arranged a mixed program of arias and American music. I decided to perform the "Evening Star" aria from Wagner's *Tannhäuser*, in honor of the guest of honor, and announced it in German. The evening went well, but the most memorable part was talking to the president after the concert. He obviously had done his homework, because after the encores he came up to the platform and put his arm around my shoulders and proceeded to talk about me as though I were his long-lost nephew. The president had had a job in Des Moines as a disk jockey on a radio station and, of course, Drake University in Des Moines is my alma mater. He talked about many details of my college life, playing sousaphone in the marching band, jazz bass in dance bands, and so on. The president never referred to any notes and could not have been more sincere. Several other times I was at the Reagan White House, and every time he was quite affectionate and seemed to remember all the details of our other meetings. This talent was one of his major strengths, and I will always remember my visits during his administration.

Not all of my experiences in Washington have been so satisfying. On July 4, 1992, in an outdoor celebration, I had programmed "It's a Grand Night for Singing," by Rodgers and Hammerstein; a beautiful musical setting of the Gettysburg Address composed by William Stearns Walker; a setting of "America the Beautiful"; one or two other patriotic songs; and the very popular "Ol' Man River," from Kern and Hammerstein's *Show Boat*. "Ol' Man River" has become an American classic loved by everyone. Even with the original words, which some consider politically incorrect, it is still a classic. Ordinarily most singers now slightly alter the text to take out the most potentially offensive sounding phrases without losing any of the original flavor. For me the beauty of the words and the music transcend any racial overtones, and the singing of the piece can reflect the character of Joe in the original show even with some changes.

I had rehearsed all the music with Mstislav Rostropovich, then the music director of the National Symphony, and all was ready. The audience of a half a million to three-quarters of a million people was gathering outside on the National Mall in front of the Capitol. Then, thirty minutes before the beginning, I received word that "Ol' Man River" could not be sung because the lyrics were politically incorrect. I argued with them about the words, the classic nature of the piece, the beauty of the music, and its huge fame and familiarity, but to no avail. Someone from Congress had decided that it was too controversial. We were not allowed to perform it! That was a couple of years before the three-year run of *Show Boat* on Broadway. I wonder if their attitudes would be the same now.

Tenors and Other Stories

Franco Bonisolli was an Italian tenor well-known for his fine voice as well as his huge ego and sometimes strange behavior onstage. Some years ago in Carnegie Hall, when I was in the audience, he was performing Rossini's *William Tell*, with Eve Queller conducting. He kept looking at one particular air conditioning duct on the right side of the stage high up on the wall. Each time he looked, he obviously became more and more annoyed. We all know Italian singers' aversion to air conditioning in general, but the weather in New York at the time was quite warm, and air conditioning was necessary. And, of course, the air conditioning had been on during the dress rehearsal, so it could not have been a surprise. After about an hour and a half into the opera, in the middle of an ensemble in which he was singing, Bonisolli made a rude gesture toward that air duct and strode offstage.

Poor Eve Queller stared after him in disbelief, but she had no choice but to continue to lead the ensemble without the tenor. Fortunately for her, there was an intermission soon; the whole audience was agog and talking among themselves, hardly believing what they had just seen, and wondering if Bonisolli would return to sing.

He did return after the intermission, but the story was not over. Piero Cappuccilli was the baritone, and in the next act he sang the beautiful aria "Resta immobile." The audience loved it and gave him a huge ovation, and in the old-fashioned style of encore, Cappuccilli sang the aria again. While this is bad taste for modern performances, everyone loved it. This whole process was not lost on Bonisolli.

Later, when he sang his famous aria and cabaletta "O muto asil" and "Corriam, corriam," the applause was polite, but not nearly as enthusiastic as Cappuccilli had received. However, Bonisolli had decided that no matter how good or bad it was, he would encore his aria, because his colleague had and he wouldn't be outdone. And so he practically forced Eve Queller to play it again. He did sing it somewhat better the second time, but it didn't matter, because the audience was ready to kill him for his earlier terrible behavior and his obvious disregard for them and for the music.

In my career I have sung quite a few performances with Franco, but one that sticks out in my memory even more than the Carnegie Hall performance was a pair of *Otello*s in Hamburg. During the rehearsal days, Franco told me that he had worked with a doctor on portraying the fainting spell at the end of the third act. He explained in great detail how an epileptic reacts while having a seizure, and that he would be able to reproduce this behavior accurately onstage. He told me I shouldn't worry and should just sing Iago's lines as usual. (It was a production that I had done some years before with Plácido and Jim Levine, and I knew it very well.)

Since I had sung Iago to many famous Otellos, I was very interested to see what Franco would do with the part. He was in fact pretty good in the characterization, but a little light of voice. As we arrived to the end of the third act, he started his epileptic fit while singing the words "Il fazzoletto, il fazzoletto, ah, ah!!" At that moment most Otellos suffer a rather normal fainting spell, fall, and lie still while Iago sings the final sarcastic lines, including "Ecco il leone." Franco, however, after he fell, continued to twitch in convulsions and somehow was able to push some spittle out of his mouth, drooling and making guttural noises all the way to the end of the act. The audience, seeing this so-called realism so overdone, began to laugh and kept laughing until the curtain came down. As Iago, I was shocked; as Sherrill Milnes I was annoyed by his inability to realize how bad his choice of reactions was. There was also another voice in me that wanted to laugh with the audience and say, "What in the hell are you doing, Franco?"

I think we all know that opera is a bigger-than-life art form, and one accepts the phrase "willing suspension of disbelief" when attending a performance. However, to see a fellow singer using some misguided medical facts to enhance a performance was disconcerting at best. The real punch line to this story is that I assumed Franco would have noted the audience's reaction and as a result change his fainting spell for the next performance. But he didn't. It was even more exaggerated, as was the audience reaction. I could not understand this total lack of stage savvy and common sense. He even seemed proud of his medical research and homework and completely ignored the reaction of the audience and his colleagues.

I have previously mentioned Daniele Barioni, the tenor who was part of the Met tour performance of *Tosca* in Des Moines in 1955 with George London and Licia Albanese. He had a wonderful voice, but he himself was a little ditzy. In performance he would often, after singing a glorious high note, kiss his hand and put it to his throat several times. Once, in a performance of *Turandot* in Dayton, Ohio, Barioni was the unknown prince, Calaf. The whole story hinges on three riddles posed by Turandot to all suitors who have asked for her hand in marriage. If they miss any one of the riddles, they are immediately killed. The story requires that all suitors before Calaf, of course, fail to solve one of the riddles and be executed. The first question is: "It soars and spreads its wings . . . and every night it is born anew and every day it dies." The answer is hope (*speranza*)! The second is: "It is fever, force, passion . . . if you lose heart or die it grows cold, but dream of conquest and it flares up. It glows like the setting sun"! The answer is blood (*sangue*)! The third is: "Ice which gives you fire . . . lily white and dark . . . if it allows you your freedom, it makes you a slave; if it accepts you as a slave, it makes you a king!" The answer is Turandot! Only Calaf is able to answer all the questions and is allowed to marry the Chinese princess.

Barioni, Italian born and singing in his native language, obviously wasn't paying any attention to the questions and answered "speranza" twice, thereby missing one of the riddles. He was not killed, of course, but one of the critics picked it up, and wrote, "By rights, Mr. Barioni should have been killed, because he totally missed a question."

There was a *Carmen* in Philadelphia with Regina Resnik and Franco Corelli, with Anton Guadagno conducting. Corelli came to rehearse only for the dress rehearsal, and even then he didn't concentrate very much. The Micaela was my wife at the time, Nancy Stokes, who had rehearsed for the preceding days without a Don José. The first-act duet was staged with Micaela sitting on a bench downstage right and José sitting at the other end of the bench while singing the very melodic "Parle moi de ma mère." At one point, Micaela was supposed to stand up and move away. Because Franco had not really rehearsed, when Micaela stood, the bench tipped up and Franco fell off right on his bottom—a lovely sight.

Before the performance, there was an announcement that out of respect for the Italian ambassador, who was present, Mr. Corelli would sing the famous "Flower Song" in Italian instead of French. (Could it have been that he didn't know it in French?) In the second act, I saw Corelli leave the stage at a moment when he had nothing to sing. I assumed he wanted some water. We often would like some water onstage, but we don't ordinarily leave the stage to get it. A few moments later, he returned to the stage with the glass of water in his hand, looking as though he didn't realize he still had it. After a few moments, I saw him do a double take when he realized he was still holding the glass and make a quick exit offstage and return quickly with no glass in time to sing his next cue. Sometimes rehearsals do pay off. Even if you know what to do for yourself, you can't know the set and what your colleagues are doing.

At a performance of *Macbeth* in Hamburg, there was another unusual happening onstage that I have heard about, but did not see myself. The production starred Piero Cappuccilli and Grace Bumbry. Near the end of the opera in the famous sleepwalking scene, Lady Macbeth expires prostrate on the floor. The applause was quite strong for Grace, who is a great stage personality, and I'm sure she was very good. That production required that the lady remain face down on the stage during the following scene.

Then with no curtain, the next scene, which contains Macbeth's famous aria "Pietà, rispetto, amore," started immediately, and Cappuccilli strode onstage. He was a great favorite all over Europe and sang the aria brilliantly, and the applause was deafening. The audience went berserk, and the applause kept peaking again and again. Piero started to bow, and the applause peaked yet again. This happened several times as Piero continued to bow. At some point, or so I've been told, Grace rose up from her prostrate position on the floor and started to applaud Piero—and then fell back on the floor dead again. It seemed she thought he was getting too much applause and wanted to get in on it. A dead person's applause?

I don't know why Hamburg is the source of several stories, but in 1973 while singing *Un ballo in maschera* there with Luciano Pavarotti, my family and I went out to dine one evening with him. At dinner he was holding Shawn, who was ten months old and in diapers at the time. Luciano looked down and saw that his whole arm was wet; Shawn had just peed on him. Luciano remembers that to this day, even though now both he and I have to look up to my six-foot-three-inch son, who I know looks upon the event with affection and humor.

One famous story at La Scala in Italy is about a tenor whose voice cracked during "Di quella pira," the big *Trovatore* aria with high Cs. The next day he was leaving the city and approached a porter at the airport to help carry his bags. The porter replied, "Aren't you the tenor who cracked last night?" "Well, yes I am," said the tenor. The porter immediately snapped, "You can carry your own bags!

My daughter, Erin, when she was seven or eight, attended a concert I was singing with the New York Philharmonic. Andre Kostelanetz, the longtime husband of Lily Pons, was conducting an all-Russian program. I was to sing two arias in the middle of the program as part of an orchestral suite. Kostelanetz wanted me to sit onstage during the first section of this orchestral portion and then do the two arias. It meant that I was seated for about fifteen minutes before singing. Erin had heard me in very few concerts at that age and was too young to understand the formality of a program. And so, after I had sat there for about ten minutes without doing anything, she became anxious about my inactivity and asked, "When are they going to give Daddy something to play?"

People ask me often who is better or what is the difference between Plácido and Luciano. One difference is that the public can usually pronounce Domingo with no trouble. However, once when I was buying something at Sears, I struck up a conversation with the salesperson, and said that I was an opera singer. She said to me: "You're an opera singer? Did you ever sing with that Italian, uh, what's his name, uh, Paparazzi?"

I Stabbed Her in the Score!

At London's Royal Opera House, known as Covent Garden, I sang Verdi's *La forza del destino* some years ago. The cast was Martina Arroyo; Charles Craig, a well-known English tenor of the time; David Ward, a world-class English bass; Renato Capecchi, the famous Italian buffo; and conductor Edward (Ted) Downes, one of the best English conductors of Verdi. That winter there was a coal strike all over England, and everyone was struggling to stay warm and conserve coal wherever and whenever possible. There was heat in the opera house only during the evening performances. During the day there was none, and we rehearsed in coats, scarves, and gloves. Various colds and flu made the rounds of all of us during the rehearsal period, but we managed to keep everything going, and no one canceled.

Arriving at the theater for the fifth performance of the run, I saw a sign on the backstage board that said Martina had canceled and another soprano would sing the part of Leonora, my sister. It was not a name I knew at the time, and for the purpose of this story, I will leave it out. Martina had become sick suddenly and had canceled only that afternoon. It was impossible to find anyone in one of the major European houses and fly them to London at that late hour. I thought it would be a little tough going, but we would persevere. I went to the soprano's dressing room and introduced myself. She seemed simpatica enough, and we talked through some details. It was then I discovered that she did not know the part from memory and would be using the score onstage. I remember thinking, "Wow, that's a little bottom line for a house of this level; however, we'll make the best of it!" The rest of the cast were pros and troupers and rallied behind her.

From the wings, I must say, it looked strange seeing a singer in costume onstage with a music score in her hands, trying to act and react. Even in the famous soprano aria "Pace, pace, mio Dio," she used the score. If she had had a beautiful voice, you could have more easily accepted the performance, but alas, she didn't. At the end of the opera, when I stab her to avenge our father's death, I had to stab her through the score, which she was holding in front of her. Throughout the evening the English audience had been quite tolerant of the goings-on, and they seemed appreciative of her efforts. During the bows, which at Covent Garden are between paged (held-back) curtains, you walk out into a ten-foot opening at the center of the stage and take the solo bow. When the soprano walked out into the spotlight at center stage, she did a deep curtsy and the audience started with very polite applause. All would have been well except that during the curtsy she fell right on her bottom in front of everybody. In the thick costume and being a little heavy, she struggled in vain for many seconds to get up. She finally succeeded, but only after looking like a complete fool. At those moments a colleague is torn between being realistic about poor vocal quality, visual image, and a poor performance, and trying to be supportive of your cast and partners, knowing and respecting the energy and the guts it takes to get out there. I really don't know what the normally stoic English audience thought. As soon as I removed my makeup, I left without talking to anyone.

My first job working with the Austrian conductor Erich Leinsdorf was in the 1969 recording of Strauss's *Salome* with Montserrat Caballé, James King, and Regina Resnik for RCA in London. At that time, John the Baptist was a part I'd never done before. I had to learn it from scratch, without any stage memories to help with the interpretation, and when we started the recording, I was more than a little nervous.

Maestro Leinsdorf was an imposing, old-world European—a very formidable human being. One day he and I were riding back from the recording studio to our hotel, the Carlton Tower, and, in a very serious tone, he asked me to come to see him in his suite. I didn't know him well at all at the time, and I could only think this must be bad news: he doesn't think I know the part well enough; I don't have the right read on the character; I'm not doing a good job. The way he said it was so serious that I was convinced he was going to fire me. My heart was pounding the rest of the way to the hotel.

Leinsdorf was in his sixties and had a commanding presence, while I was in my thirties. We went up to his suite and he started hemming and hawing. I just wanted him to get it over with, to come out and tell me the bad news. Finally, in his deep Austrian voice, he said, "Sherrill, you know, ah, when you're traveling around the world, and, uh, you check into a European hotel, uh, uh, and you have to give them your passport—and you're traveling, that is, with someone, uh, someone, uh, who's not your wife, and you, you have to give them her passport, I mean, uh, how do you do that?"

Well, I could barely keep myself from laughing, mostly from relief at not being fired. He was in the process of a divorce (I found out later) and was with the woman who would soon become the next Mrs. Leinsdorf. Nowadays, no one would even blink an eye, but at that time, and because Leinsdorf was very old-fashioned in his way, this bothered him a lot. He probably asked me because my wife-to-be and I were in the same boat; traveling together, soon to be married, with different last names on the passports, so I had had to do the same thing. I finally said, "Well maestro, there isn't any technique, you just grit your teeth, smile, and push the two passports across the desk."

There is a scene in *Salome* in which John the Baptist is in the cistern. While making this recording, we couldn't find a place to give my voice the proper echo to make it sound as though St. John were actually deep in the well. We were recording at the Walthamstow Town Hall outside London, where many RCA recordings were then made. The producer was Richard Mohr, a very inventive gentleman, the same one who had produced the Beethoven Ninth recording in Chicago when I was in the chorus those many years before.

He had the idea of having me sing in the kitchen of this town hall. After experimenting with various sounds there, I ended up with my head inside the huge stove ventilator hood; it had just the right reverberation. So I sang that whole section bending over that stove while watching the conductor in another room on a TV monitor. I think RCA should have included a picture of me leaning over the stove in the record package, just to show the things we do for art.

I worked with Maestro Leinsdorf many times after that, especially in the recording studio. Some of my most interesting projects were his idea: Mozart's *Così fan tutte*, Verdi's *Aida*, Puccini's *Il tabarro*, the Brahms *Requiem* with the Boston Symphony, Brahms's *Four Serious Songs* with Leinsdorf at the piano, and Schoenberg's *A Survivor from Warsaw*.

In Boston, an odd thing happened during a performance of the Schoenberg piece, which was coupled with the Beethoven Ninth. The Schoenberg uses a *Sprechstimme* voice (spoken in rhythm with intonation). It is a twelve-tone piece, very modern in its style, with male chorus ending in the "Shema Yisroel," very dramatic and interesting. It is about Jews during the war in a ghetto in Warsaw.

At this particular performance, the Schoenberg was the first half of the program, with the Beethoven as the second half. This meant that the first half was only about eighteen minutes long. We did the Schoenberg, and during the bows Maestro Leinsdorf said to me under his breath, "Shall we do it again?" I was surprised, but as it is rather short for a first half, I said, "Why not?" So we did it again to about the same audience response and then came the intermission.

I was told later that one of the regular matinee attendees, a little old blue-haired lady, arrived a little late that day. She heard the applause for the Schoenberg and sat down for the rest of the concert. After looking at the program, she saw that the Beethoven Ninth was the second piece. She of course could not know that we were doing the Schoenberg again. And so, she dutifully listened to what she thought was the Ninth Symphony and left when it was over, never hearing the second half. She was heard muttering something about that performance being the strangest Beethoven she had ever heard. Leinsdorf got a big kick out of this story. One did not often think of Maestro Leinsdorf as having a good sense of humor, but I was lucky to have known the human side of him as well as the musical side.

There is a fine recording of *Lucia di Lammermoor* on the Decca label with Sutherland, Pavarotti, Ghiaurov, and me. One day before Joan and I were to record the big duet in *Lucia* in Kingsway Hall in London, Richard Bonynge, the conductor, called me at my hotel and asked me if I could sing the duet a whole tone higher. Maestro Bonynge is Joan's husband and a noted musicologist, and he had found an original autograph from Donizetti in which the first page had a modulation that set the rest of the duet a whole step higher. On the phone, I took a deep breath and said if Joan can sing it, so can I. So the next day we recorded it up, and those of you who care to read the score carefully can see where the change is and hear the only recording as Donizetti intended, according to Bonynge. That means at the end I sing an E, and Joan sings a high E on the dominant chord, and then we both sing a long high A-natural together. Whew!

During this same recording of *Lucia*, Luciano became ill for a few days, and because of the shortness of time for the whole recording, we had to sing the famous *Lucia* Sextet without the tenor. As a result, we taped the only version of the *Lucia* Quintet! Luciano added his voice to the track later. The same was true in the baritone-tenor duet often called the Wolf's Crag Scene. I recorded the whole thing with the orchestra and Maestro Bonynge without Luciano. It was very difficult to make harmony without the other voice and to keep some sense of the dramatic flow. But we made it work. I suppose just to keep Luciano on his toes, I sang a high B-flat in a cadenza to force him to sing something yet higher in his cadenza. He did, and it's great. Anyone with a good ear who cares to listen can hear the slight difference in color of his voice in these two sections of the opera. Luciano has a small edge on volume over the rest of us. Sometimes laying down a track and recording it later has an advantage for the other singer, but it is extra hard on the singers who record it the first time.

The following story may sound somewhat critical of Joan, but her vocal artistry in this century is so monumental and so beloved by all of us that I feel she would forgive me.

There was a run of *Rigoletto*s at the Met in a June festival in the 1970s. The cast was Joan, Luciano, Ruggero Raimondi, and me, with Bonynge conducting. In the fourth act the bass, Sparafucile, is supposed to carry the mortally wounded Gilda in a sack out the door of his tavern according to his bargain with Rigoletto. Rigoletto thinks it is the duke who had been stabbed. Joan would never be considered fat, but she is a tall woman with a strong and dramatic bone structure. There was no way that Ruggero could carry her out the door by himself. Gildas are often sung by tiny coloraturas, who are no problem in terms of staging this scene. In this case, I had to help Ruggero by joining him in the tavern so that both of us could grab the sack and carry her outside. I suppose that in some ways it made it more believable, because the weight of the sack was more appropriate to a man.

In my career, I performed with Leonard Bernstein quite a number of times at various galas in New York, as well as performances at the Met. He also hired me for Beethoven's *Missa Solemnis* with both the Boston Symphony and the Cincinnati Orchestras. In oratorio and symphonic works, you are standing in front of the orchestra next to the conductor, and because of the proximity you can really feel and taste his or her energy and musical power at work. Orchestral works are a different experience from opera, and I'm very grateful that I worked in both musical forms with Bernstein.

In Prague, at its spring festival in May 1990, I was singing performances of *Don Giovanni* and *Tosca*. Lenny (although I called him Leonard or mostly, of course, Maestro) was supposed to do a concert with the Czech Philharmonic, one of the great orchestras of the world. At that time, he was increasingly ill and more and more often had been canceling performances. They were all afraid he wasn't going to appear. I had heard these rumors, but one day in the lobby of the Intercontinental Hotel I saw Harry Kraut, Leonard's manager, and he said that Leonard was in fact in the hotel and resting upstairs. He was there to do the Beethoven Ninth, so I asked Harry when and where the rehearsals were.

He said the next rehearsal was the following day, from eleven to two. That day I had a *Tosca* performance, and normally on such a day I don't go out. But something spoke to me. I really wanted to see Lenny working, because it had been a long time since I had experienced his level of musicality and inspiration.

The next day, I went to the rehearsal. It was in an empty hall, and they were playing the second and third movements. Bernstein's rehearsal technique was awesome; he didn't bother with the few wrong notes from the orchestra, or with little ensemble problems; he knew they would fix themselves automatically the next time through, especially with as fine an orchestra as this one. He was concerned with the bigger flow, the bigger line, the bigger swirls of sound. The music that he made with that orchestra—the phrases, the arc of the drama, the intensity of tone colors—was of such a high order that it was mind-boggling, and it moved me to tears. I sat, awed, through the whole rehearsal.

He came back after it was over and greeted and hugged me. I couldn't help but see that he was terribly weak and sick looking. We talked for a few minutes, and then he apologized (if you can imagine) for not being able to come to my *Tosca* performance that night. But he wished me well and we said goodbye. I didn't know, of course, that I'd never see him again, because he died the following October. What a loss! I'm extremely grateful that something moved me to go to this rehearsal, which gave me yet another insight into the great music-making capacity of this man—one of the true geniuses of our time.

CHAPTER ELEVEN

Performance

When It's Your Turn, You Have to Be There

ABOUT THE ONLY RULE THAT EXISTS for stage entrances is when it's your turn, you have to be there. It doesn't matter about backstage speakers or assistant stage managers or being called late for the cue. Bottom line: it only matters that you're onstage at the right time. Some years ago I sang Rigoletto in Caracas, Venezuela. There was very little rehearsal time, but I had brought my own costumes and knew the part very well, so I was not overly concerned.

Sometimes in order to make a bigger fee, the bass, Sparafucile, will also sing the role of Monterone. It can be done because they never appear in the same scene. So with some fancy footwork in the makeup department (changing back and forth) and fast costume changing, that singer can earn extra money. It also makes it cheaper for the company to hire one singer instead of two.

In Caracas we had one day to stage the opera. The next day was the orchestra rehearsal, and the following day was the performance. There was no time to work with makeup and costumes. The performance was in an old school auditorium with the dressing rooms on the lower floors and of course no backstage speakers or public-address system. Michael Burt, the bass singing both roles, was two floors down, and he had to change costumes and makeup between every scene and move very fast between dressing room and stage.

At the performance the opening scene went perfectly well, and Michael was fine as Monterone. Then there was the normal short break for the scene change. No one thought to check with the bass to see if he was ready to start. The orchestra began the theme of the duet between Rigoletto and Sparafucile, and I made my entrance. I approached the door to my house and expected the bass to interrupt me with the line "Signor," followed by my response, "Va, non ho niente." But there was no sound and no body; he was not there. I looked at the conductor in panic and he just shrugged as if to say, "What's to do?," and stopped the orchestra and said, "Maestros, otra vez" (again). So I exited the stage and the orchestra started again. Offstage, I yelled for the Sparafucile. The Marullo, another baritone in the opera, who was standing there, said to me, "I know the part, I used to be a bass and I've sung it." So I said, "You're on," threw him the Sparafucile sword from the prop table, and reentered the stage from up center. The Marullo followed me onstage and as the cue approached he prepared to sing. At the very same moment, the other bass, Michael Burt, having finished his makeup, and having no idea he was late, entered from down left and sang the correct cue at the same time. What a surprise. First there was no Sparafucile and then we had—stereophonic Sparafuciles. I looked helplessly at the Marullo and he shrugged his shoulders and left the stage and Michael and I continued the scene. I have no idea what the audience thought of all this confusion and repetition.

Arriving late onstage for an entrance is a fear I think all singers share and have nightmares about. I have had dreams where I am running toward the stage but never get any closer, and the faster I run, the farther away the stage is. Another version is that I can hear my musical cue coming up, but I can't find the stage.

In the late 1980s many stars, including Helen Hayes, Lorne Greene, Michael Moriarty, James Earl Jones, Joseph Wiseman, Elie Wiesel, and the National Symphony Orchestra (with Julius Rudel conducting), took part in a prestigious concert at the Kennedy Center to raise money for the Holocaust Center. I was to sing several arias as well as "A Survivor from Warsaw," the same work I had sung with Erich Leinsdorf in Boston.

The program was a mixture of many narrated pieces, recited poetry, and music. Because we had very little rehearsal, things backstage were a little disorganized, and there was no one to call us onstage. However, the program was going well, and after I had sung two of my arias, with the

Schoenberg piece to come later, I wandered around backstage waiting, certain that I would know about when to go back to the stage.

At some point in the green room, I saw Ted Koppel talking to some other famous newspeople, so I walked closer to them to hear what they were saying. I should say that in any performance, when backstage between musical pieces, my normal habit is to chew gum to keep my mouth and throat moist. So I was chewing my habitual gum, and being fascinated with the group of famous newspeople talking about the latest national and international news, I forgot about the time.

All of a sudden, I realized that I had not been paying attention to the program and didn't know where they were at that moment, so I ran madly for the stage. As I arrived in the wings, I heard the very modern chords of the Schoenberg piece and I panicked thinking that I was already late for the musical cue. I raced to the door, flung it open, slowed immediately to a walk, and put a performer's smile on my face. Fortunately, I had my copy of the music in hand and stylishly walked to the podium as though all were well with the world. Of course, inside I was dying of embarrassment. I saw Julius Rudel looking wild-eyed at me, but somehow in his glance, I knew that my musical entrance was yet to come.

All of a sudden before my first cue, I realized that I was still chewing my habitual gum. What an embarrassment it was, especially in front of this very heavyweight audience, which included the Secretary of State and several Supreme Court justices. I had to decide whether to perform the role with gum in my mouth and, if not, what to do with the gum in front of an audience! The first cue was close, so in desperation, I pretended to rub my chin with my right hand, took the gum from my mouth, and palmed it for the remainder of the piece. It took all my performance savvy to bring this off. To pretend that the late arrival onstage and the mouth wiping were both part of the interpretation took no small amount of skill. To this day I have no idea what the audience thought of my stage manner, and I didn't ask. I'm only grateful that no one wanted to shake my hand. When it's your turn, you have to be there!

Technique and Confidence

José Ferrer was quoted as saying, "Techniques are methods of producing automatic results . . . which therefore liberate your intuition and your inspiration." I'm sure he was applying this to acting, but as a big opera fan and part-time singer, he knew that it also has a perfect application to singing. (He had performed the role of Gianni Schicchi and had studied Scarpia and Amonasro.)

Inside all of us, we have more than one person lurking; in fact, we are several different people. Our parents, background, religion, even our place in the birth order of the family, as well as other factors, make us what we are as human beings. This means each person's ego and sense of confidence is different in size, use, and availability. No artist can perform without ego. We must feel as though we deserve to be out there.

Some performers love being in front of an audience, while many others are more like me, a little insecure, introverted, and rather shy. Not possible, you say—how can you be a performer and be shy? Many performers are shy in private. If you are one of those, you have to do what is necessary to find your confidence, your ego, and when needed, learn to add to it, to layer it with some artificial security that will function for the moment. At the same time, all of this must be balanced with reality and common sense and *never* with any arrogance.

It is absolutely necessary to have a vocal technique that serves you most of the time, giving you a real sense of security. In addition, if you aren't really prepared, if you haven't spent enough time studying and making the aria, song, or role your own, it will be much harder to get out there onstage. But sometimes, even when you are prepared, you still can have terrible self-doubts.

Singing is the most personal of all the musical art forms, more so than playing cello, piano, violin, or any other musical instrument. Because of this, it requires the strongest sense of self. Everything is built around that strong but at the same time fragile tissue of the larynx. Also, the instrument of our performing is the same instrument of our talking. It is affected by the stress and emotions of our everyday life. As a result, there are performances when you feel especially vulnerable. That's when you need that strong sense of self to keep going and refrain from beating yourself up. It is also vital for us performers to constantly think ahead and never dwell on some mistake or less-than-perfect note that we just sang—at least until after the performance.

When I first performed the role of Falstaff, in some ways I had to subordinate my normal performing ego to get through the role. Gone was the standard "Verdi baritone" *bella figura* part, which usually implies wearing tights and being noble and handsome. Falstaff isn't a Don Giovanni, a sexy guy in beautiful clothes, although he pictures himself that way. In Falstaff, I moved to the baggy pants and pie in the face. Well, maybe not that extreme, but there are many shticky things he does that are appropriate to the opera and character but are certainly not what I had been used to doing in most of my career.

Some years ago I did my first *Gianni Schicchi* by Puccini, another comic role. I enjoyed playing this clever man, who imitates the dead Buoso Donati. There are similarities to Falstaff in the comedy, but humanly they are very different. I have tried to bring a greater element of dignity and vocal line where appropriate to both parts; these are sometimes missing when done by the more traditional comic bass.

At a performance one hears frequently from managers and friends, "Just go out and have fun." I have a problem with the word "fun." Some of that is just a pet peeve of mine, but "fun" is used so often, and it has little to do with a performance. When an activity is hard and demands energy, fun is not an applicable word. Even when you're singing "fun" songs, it's often work to make it look as though you're having fun. The phrase "Go out and have fun!" leaves out so many important ingredients, such as concentration, focus, music making, dramatics, enjoyment, and satisfaction!

It is normal that people want to think you are having a good time, that God gave you a gift and that it just pours out of your mouth. They don't want to see the effort or the technique singing demands. And they certainly do not want to see the private person's insecurities at work. So a major part of any performer's job is not to let that effort show in order to allow the audience to have fun or feel the appropriate emotion.

Having said all that, however, there are, of course, times when you are having fun. When singing in one of the great ensembles in opera, it can be very thrilling. Obviously, when you are singing well, you enjoy it far more than when you are having a tough time. There is no worse suffering than when the voice is not responding well.

Every once in a while in a performance you think, "I couldn't do that any better," but that doesn't happen as often as you'd like. It's far more often that you think, "I can do better than that."

As I mentioned before, we all have different personas within us. If you're standing around with friends on the corner or having a beer and talking, you're one person. You're someone else when you're with a stranger or a business associate. Party behavior is yet another person. They are all related, of course. Goldovsky used to call them your primary and secondary characteristics. He was referring to the stage, but it's just as true in normal social interaction.

Your primaries can't change: height, weight (at least not for that performance), bone structure, general features. Your secondary characteristics can change, and we all do it. The color of voice, the volume, whether it's friendly or angry, the contours of the face, the body language, the intensity of the eyes, and so forth, can all be changed. At a singles party, if you are looking for a date, you are different from the person you are when you're sitting in front of the TV watching *Monday Night Football* with your feet up. If you're chairing a meeting, even in your own home, you become yet another person. And of course, in an auditorium, making a speech or singing a program, you are yet another person.

By its very nature, singing has a formal quality to it. The minute you appear in front of an audience, you become the performer and the private person disappears. There's a line of attention and tension that keeps people at a distance when they're listening to you. At the same time you must pull them into your music by your strength, warmth, and charm.

It may seem strange, but for me the closer the audience was, the harder it was for me to concentrate on what I was doing and the harder I had to work at it. When I was young, for example, I never liked performing in a small, intimate setting, as when my mother wanted my brother and me to perform at home for friends. We did it, of course, but not easily or voluntarily.

Small fundraisers were the same way, because they were often in someone's living room with the audience only a few feet away, where I could see the faces clearly. You often cannot tell from people's expressions whether they are enjoying your singing or not. For this reason, I usually find it easier to create a mood and an aura when I am in a larger theater or auditorium.

Also we performers mustn't forget that backstage or at a reception after a concert, you're still on. Signing pictures and saying "Thank you" over a hundred times and trying to give it a little different color each time is still part of the performance.

When a singer is having vocal difficulty or is singing a performance while ill, the rest of the cast should always try to help them. You often know beforehand if it's going to be a bumpy night. When someone is having vocal problems, rhythms generally go out the window, and if the singer is struggling for the notes, you're not going to get any kind of dramatic play. You just steel yourself beforehand and try not to listen to the difficulties.

Sylvia Sass, a Hungarian soprano who had a brilliant career for a short time, unfortunately had a rough time at the end of it. She had always been a powerful performer, and I was lucky enough to sing in some of her great performances. However, near the end of her career, we sang a series of *Tosca*s in Vienna together. In the famous aria "Vissi d'arte," Sylvia had a lot of trouble, and the audience booed her unmercifully. My character, Scarpia, is onstage standing at the window with his back to the audience, so I heard every nuance of the aria.

Any artist is of two minds when a colleague is having trouble. You obviously sympathize with your partners and have a basic respect for them and their career. On the other hand, you hear their singing and if it's really bad, you can't ignore that fact. You also think that at another time it could be you having a problem or two. If you like your colleagues as people, you sympathize with them more and wish better for them than if they are troublemakers. There is a saying in the industry that if you are singing great, people will tolerate a lot of misbehavior, but if you are having trouble vocally and misbehave, everyone will grease the way on your slide down.

On balance, in a bad performance I wish the audience would just be quiet. Don't applaud, but don't boo. Silence can be devastating.

Unfortunately, singing is a solo art—you are all by yourself. No husband, wife, lover, teacher, or coach can help you when you are onstage. Even the conductor, if he or she is sympathetic, can only help a little. It's a hard, cruel fact, but there it is. Even when you're singing a duet, the two people are singing by themselves and pretending to have a relationship.

In *Tosca*, that night in Vienna, the audience was just tearing the place apart, giving no thought to what Sass had once been. It was terrible, and of course there's not a whole hell of a lot you can do. The tenor, Peter Dvorsky, and I tried to protect Sylvia by taking only tutti bows, meaning we went out in front of the curtain all together every time. That way they would have had to boo Peter and me, and they didn't want to do that. So we minimized the yelling and from our point of view helped her. But at the end of the day, there's little you can do to help an ailing colleague, no matter how much you would like to.

I was always the most nervous at the beginning of a rehearsal period. Maybe abnormally so, but I worried about all the things I had to do: words, movements, vocal demands, timings, whether my acting was up to making the role come alive. Then as the rehearsals progressed and I approached the actual performances, especially as I sang with the orchestra onstage, I settled down. But I could never say that I was totally relaxed. Some of my colleagues say they're not nervous before a performance. I don't understand that and suspect maybe they're not telling the truth.

Performances on radio and especially live television were the worst. The mind seems to send out more nervous signals when the stakes are high. No matter how well rehearsed you are or how many performances you have under your belt before that particular broadcast, your mind is racing and your heart is pounding. Probably seeing the television cameras and knowing that millions of people would see and hear you at that very moment, however good or bad you were, are the main reasons for the extra nerves. My metabolism was so high on some occasions that after certain long high notes my head was spinning enough that I thought I might faint!

The mind knows when your most difficult singing is coming up. Just as you are getting comfortable during a performance, here comes the finale with the big aria, and your mind always kicks up: "This is it! The one they're all waiting for. You had better be good!"

For example, Figaro's aria from *The Barber of Seville*, "Largo al factotum," is the first thing in the opera for Figaro. It is a high-flying, show-biz aria in which I had to really be hot, with the voice very well warmed up in order to sustain the tessitura and high notes. In certain other operas, the big aria or arias happen later. *Macbeth*, for instance, has the beautiful, but difficult, "Pietà, rispetto, amore" at the very end. As a result I would start the opera quite relaxed, but as the aria approached, I could feel my metabolism increasing, reaching its highest pitch. Those are the moments when you ask yourself if this is really what you want to do for a living—somewhat facetiously, of course, but also seriously. This kind of worry is certainly not a reason one performs for a living.

You must keep in mind that the character in an opera never has vocal difficulties with the singing. You must show only the appropriate emotions. Figaro as a character has no problem singing the "Largo" and must have fun with it. So the singer singing the aria has to convey that, even if he's full of vocal insecurities. You must give the audience the feeling of the character while he is singing, not the feeling of the private person.

I think of nervousness as an occupational hazard, so if you can't get used to it, don't sing for a living. One way to think of it is that you are paid for being nervous and you sing for fun. Spending time trying to devise ways not to be nervous is a waste of time. A more meaningful use of the time is learning to channel and control that nervousness in order to have more energy and excitement in your performance.

You can minimize those nerves by being well prepared, well rehearsed, and well coached. Then you know at least that your instincts and your training are the best they can be. Even if you blank out momentarily, your "muscle memory" will carry you though. I tell my master classes that contests are the worst places to try out new arias or pieces. You need all the mileage on those pieces your experience will allow. I was always more nervous in contests than in complete performances, so I would sing only the arias I knew best. If my mind went blank, muscle memory would serve me until I got back on track.

No matter how much I got into a part, whether it was a new one or an old friend, no matter how much study, how much input from the stage director, how many weeks of rehearsal there were, I never felt totally in character until I put on the costume, the makeup, the beard, and the wig and picked up my whip, cane, orb, mace, or what have you. When I can look into a mirror and see another person, then I can become that person. Even when it was a part I hade done before, when doing rehearsals in street clothes, there always seemed to be a number of small pieces of the character missing. When I put on the costume and makeup, certain nuances and other qualities from previous performances came back. It always seemed to trigger memories and new ideas. I could always tell when the rehearsals were starting to take: in the drowsy hours before sleeping and waking, in my subconscious mind I saw myself in the role, and I analyzed and identified many details that I wanted to remember in the performances.

The stage director, of course, has some input into the characterization and certainly guides all the movements and timings of reactions between the principals. But most of the details of the humanity of the role were my own work and my own feelings. In my dressing room, just before a performance, I really had to be all alone, with no one there. I needed the privacy to go into my psyche enough to become Sherrill Milnes, the singer, and then deeper, to become Scarpia, Giovanni, Rigoletto, Boccanegra, or whomever. At that point, I pulled it all together. Some of the nervousness ebbed, and a certain calm entered.

It may seem a silly and small detail, but I always walked from the dressing room to the stage in the mood, style, and age of the character. That small transition seemed to stamp on me the mood for the night. I'm not one of those people who can joke around in the dressing room or stand in the wings chatting away about unrelated things and then say, "Excuse me, I have to make an entrance."

Costumes can often present their own special problems. Rigoletto's costume is one of those because of the hump. I have rehearsed for weeks being told that the hump is on the right side, and then the costume arrives and I discover that the hump is on the left. This changes almost every position in the staging when you hold or embrace the Gilda or when you sing with anyone else. These may seem like simple changes, but I can assure you they're not. Your singing partners must change all their movements: rights become lefts and vice versa through the whole opera. You cannot embrace or even sing to anyone on the hump side.

All of this trouble is created because some designer didn't think it was important to inform the singer or the stage director about the costume design or didn't know the problem existed. Now, of course, I ask immediately which side it's on, or bring my own costume, which has a left-hand hump. It's a little like Marty Feldman in the film *Young Frankenstein* saying, "Hump, what hump?"

Another problem can be in not knowing whether the hump is sewn in the jacket or in the undergarment, which is never removed. In Vienna some years ago, there was a performance of *Rigoletto* where I was in the audience. The Greek baritone Kostas Paskalis as Rigoletto was about to sing the famous aria "Cortigiani, vil razza dannata," in which he curses the courtiers. In most productions, a normal stage direction is to take off the jester's jacket and throw it forcefully on the floor in defiance. Obviously Kostas had no idea that the hump was sewn into the jacket. As a result, when he removed the jacket and threw it on the floor, he threw his hump on the floor as well and had to sing the rest of the act humpless. In this case the audience could see what had happened and snickered throughout the rest of the act.

Makeup can also present problems, often because of a horrible liquid called spirit gum. It is very sticky, dries like Superglue, and is used to attach wigs, beards, mustaches, and false noses. However, sometimes because of sweat, body oil, or other things, it can gradually loosen. Also, while singing, the movement of the jaw or wrinkling the forehead or the nose in normal reactions can loosen the beard, the wig, or the nosepiece.

In Vienna again, while I was singing *Rigoletto*, my beard loosened on my chin during the third act. There is nothing to do while you are onstage to fix this problem, except hope it doesn't fall off. But during the "Cortigiani, vil razza dannata," when I attacked the courtiers (in the same place where Paskalis threw off his jacket) the beard came off entirely. I grabbed it in my hand and kept it palmed during the rest of the act. You're embarrassed, but there's nothing to do.

I always wear a putty nosepiece as Scarpia, mostly to give an aquiline (eagle-like) profile. Scarpia should have the mean look of a predator. But that small piece of putty has to fit on the narrow bridge of the nose with the treacherous spirit gum the only thing holding it in place. Once in a performance in St. Gall, Switzerland, the makeup man used a watered-down version of spirit gum. I asked if it would hold well, and he said it would, absolutely, no problem.

However, in the first act, I felt the nosepiece loosen and saw it fall to the floor. I was angry, because there is nothing comical or funny about the character of Scarpia and his nose falling off rather negates his authority. In the break we glued it on again, but during the second act, I felt it loosen again and start to fall. I caught it in my hand and threw it with great disgust and anger into the wings. Not an ideal thing to happen when Scarpia is threatening Cavaradossi and Tosca with death. Fortunately, as usual, the audience was not so aware of anything going amiss, but I was livid, which in hindsight—who knows?—may have actually enhanced the characterization!

Adding insult to injury, spirit gum is very difficult to remove. You must use acetone or an alcohol-based compound to dissolve it, and you still have to rub very hard. I never learned how not to rub off at least one layer of skin while removing spirit gum and makeup after a performance. When performances were close together, my skin was constantly red and irritated. There's a strong argument for growing your own beard and mustache. Not exactly the life of a star!

My philosophy about auditions is, when possible, tell no one, family and management excluded. If you get nothing you say nothing, and no one is the wiser. If no one knows, no one asks you how you did and you are spared from saying, "Well, I thought I sang OK, but they didn't offer anything, or I didn't win any money," or whatever it is. I always found that to be embarrassing. Those few times when something good happens and you get a job or win some money or recognition, then you can shout it from the housetops. After the fact is best, but it can be difficult to keep your mouth shut.

Early in your career, you want to tell friends everything that is happening, usually because there isn't very much going on, and so each little career step is very exciting. I remember those years in my career very well and the telling of every detail to about twenty close friends (new engagements, famous singers with whom I was to sing, new roles, new recordings, etc.). I even sent to those same people copies of my first twenty or so operatic albums just to keep them up on what was happening and to share my excitement and pride in my career growth. Eventually I found that I just didn't have enough hours in the day to relate everything to everybody. Also, as you become more successful, smaller details of the career become less newsworthy.

Anyone who has ever auditioned dreams of having a snappy comeback to sarcastic or negative remarks from the auditioner. My favorite true story is about Randall Reid Smith, a tenor, who was my son Shawn's babysitter for a number of years. He later went to Germany and got a job in a small opera house. After two years there, he auditioned for a slightly bigger theater. After the audition, the intendant expressed interest but asked Randy if in fact he had noted some slight strain in the high notes. Randy said quite indignantly, "Well, of course, if I had no vocal problems at all, I would be auditioning for the Vienna State Opera or one of the big German theaters, not this small theater!" He got the job.

Like all singers, I've given many performances in my life when I've been sick: cold, flu, infection, or just not feeling up to par. On the day of a performance, if I'm not feeling vocally normal, I'm as nervous as a cat, plus I have to decide whether I am healthy enough to go on. The decision is easy if you have all-out laryngitis and you can't sing. It's difficult when you're 10 or 15 percent off your game: your throat's only a little uncomfortable, or you have no discomfort, just less than your normal response.

When you're in the heat of singing onstage, because of the adrenaline, hoarseness or cold discomfort can diminish. Then when you go offstage and wait for your next entrance, it can all come back, often even worse. If you finish the performance with your voice ragged and worn, singing the next performance could be a problem, depending on how soon it is. These are decisions with which every singer is faced.

If you are in a major city, normally you will see an ear, nose, and throat doctor (a laryngologist or otolaryngologist), who can examine you and offer advice, or, in many cases, tell you to cancel or not. It's much easier for the singer when the doctor takes the responsibility. It's also more readily accepted by the presenting auspices, who will have fewer hard feelings when you have to cancel if a doctor has said you mustn't sing. It's much more difficult when you're in a smaller town where there's no laryngologist. Then you must make the decision to cancel by yourself. It becomes especially problematic when you are the only soloist with an orchestra, even more so when you are a big star, and canceling a concert makes a huge financial problem for the local auspices and disappointment for the audience.

Sometimes if you tell the local sponsors that you're not feeling up to par, they may reply, "We need you to sing anyway and it's OK if you give a little less voice." If you don't sing they will lose money, not to mention that you will lose your own fee. But what can happen is that if you sing poorly, even if you save the concert, they remember that you did not do well and will be reluctant to hire you back. But if you cancel, they may not hire you back anyway, because you've let them down. It's a lose-lose situation. The best you can hope for is, if you think you can sing the concert, to give it your best shot and hope that your experience and expertise will bring it off and make it a success.

There are very few hard-and-fast rules in cancellations. In general, I say very little about an illness or discomfort, except perhaps to the conductor, who can help me in the performance. At the same time, there are so many exceptions to this advice. Sometimes telling everyone that you are sick elicits more sympathy. It's almost more about human relations than illness, and you have to decide on the best path to take.

After any concert, graciously accept all compliments without any provisos or excuses that you weren't up to par. I have seen some of my colleagues embarrass their fans by refusing to accept a compliment, saying, "No, no it was not a good performance; I was not feeling well," and so forth. Then the fan feels foolish for thinking it was good and goes away unsatisfied and frustrated. Always accept compliments in the way they were intended, with graciousness and appreciation, even if the compliment doesn't come out well.

Of the various times I have been ill before a concert, there were two times that I remember well. In hindsight, I realize I probably should have canceled beforehand, but the recitals were out of town and there was no possibility of a replacement. In addition, I thought my voice would last long enough to give the audience their money's worth. I was wrong. After singing a few pieces, I realized that the laryngitis was getting worse. So before I sang some of the harder music, where the voice would have failed totally, I stopped and made an announcement. It was very clear that I was hoarse and the audience was sympathetic. I said first that I would come back as soon as we could find a place in the schedule. Then I pulled up a chair and with a microphone proceeded to tell opera stories and, in general, entertained the audience for another half hour or so. I hope those people felt they got their money's worth. One is not ordinarily paid for an unfinished concert, so when I returned to sing these replacement recitals, the auspices really received two programs for the price of one. One can do this only in a solo recital situation, of course, and when there is some free time afterward, in which you can recover. I was always proud of my efforts. I never felt I was cheating anyone and knew that I had taken my responsibility as an artist seriously.

Words are the bane of a singer's existence. You don't usually forget the melody, but words you can forget, especially in recital when you are singing in several different languages. We all make little mistakes or slips in concert or opera. This is not unusual. Generally the rule is not to stop, so it is necessary to improvise or make up words or sometimes even nonsense syllables, until you're back on track. Usually it's only a moment or two, and most often the audience doesn't notice. They will notice if you show panic or shock, so we must look as though everything's fine and that's the way it's supposed to go. Audiences, by and large, go with the flow of a piece and the general sweep of sound and emotion, not paying so much attention to specific words or syllables. Therefore, above all, you must continue to keep the mood, even if at that moment you are floating and unsure exactly where you are.

Sometimes when I have momentarily lost the first line, I have turned to Jon while he is playing the intro and said under my breath, "Words?" Usually he can fire them at me, and then without missing a beat, I come in on cue as though nothing had happened. That's the best fix or correction: when no one is aware. It's OK to ask your accompanist to give you a line if you're really blank. You do, however, need someone who is very cool under fire. That is another reason why I want my accompanist to use the music and not play from memory.

One of my worst memory slips was in the summer of 1971 at the Temple University Ambler Music Festival. Our program that evening was scheduled for seven o'clock, while it was still light outside, in order to accommodate a performance of *Jesus Christ, Superstar* later that night. In the outdoor festival at Ambler, they had very little concert lighting equipment, and since the concert was to begin before sundown, it was quite bright in the tent/auditorium. We came out onstage, and I could plainly see the audience, which I knew would make big trouble for my concentration and memory.

The program began with Handel's "See the Raging Flames Arise" from the oratorio *Joshua*. I sang the opening theme, but instead of repeating it, which is the norm for this style of aria, I took a wrong turn and went right to the B section in the minor key. What I was singing and what the piano was playing had nothing to do with each other. I thought I could get out of this mistake with some made-up words and a little faking of the melody and some extra scales. But that didn't work, and it was just awful.

Finally I decided I couldn't keep going with the terrible dissonance I was making with the piano. So I stopped with a big flourish and waited for the music to hit the minor key section, which for some reason was still very clear in my mind. I waited and waited. Perhaps it was only five or ten seconds, but it seemed like an eternity, standing there in front of the audience with my mouth closed and big-time egg on my face. When I stopped singing, Jon realized I didn't know where I was and leaned hard into the piano, doubling the octaves and improvising like crazy. (That's one time that Jon's improvisational skill paid big dividends.)

Finally the minor section arrived and I attacked with renewed vigor and extra intensity.

We were both so unnerved that I have no idea how we finished. During the bow, I muttered under my breath, "Can you believe how I fouled that up; never have I made such a terrible mistake."

When we went offstage after the first group, I said, "Tell me we didn't do that to Handel." Jon just shook his head in disbelief and said "Handel? That was Schoenberg!" I can't say I remember much about the rest of the recital, but it taught me something about lighting and its importance for my memory.

In the dressing room after the concert, I said, "The Philadelphia critics will kill us tonight." The next day both Daniel Webster in the *Philadelphia Inquirer* and George K. Diehl in the now defunct *Philadelphia Evening Bulletin* most graciously overlooked it and reviewed the recital as though everything had gone beautifully. (Is it possible they didn't notice that anything was awry?) In any case, gentlemen, thank you.

Several seasons later, I was performing a Bach aria in Severance Hall in Cleveland, Ohio. I made exactly the same mistake in this Bach aria that I made in the Handel aria. I sang the first theme, took a wrong turn, and went directly to the B section. I improvised for a bit, but had to stop and wait until I could pick it up melodically. I somehow got through the remainder of the aria, but I couldn't stop thinking "My God, this is the Severance Hall, the home of the world-famous Cleveland Orchestra, and I have just made a horrible musical mistake." I was sure I would be crucified in the reviews, but again the critics missed it entirely, or else they were being kind.

Switching languages midstream sometimes is a problem. Twenty years or so ago I sang a concert performance of *Carmen* with the Miami Philharmonic, led by its conductor, Maestro Fabian Sevitzski, and starring Jean Madeira and Nicholas di Virgilio. Although I'd done the role in French, the maestro wanted it in English. In the rehearsals I remembered all the words, but at the first performance during the famous "Toreador Song," my mind just went blank. I had sung the aria in French much more often than I had sung it in English, in various concerts and contests, so French was dominant in my memory. As a result, during the aria the English words went right out the window, and I started making up line after line, including nonsense syllables, vainly trying to pull the English words back; but they just wouldn't come. The only option that occurred to me was to finish the aria in French, and so, shrugging my shoulders at the audience, I did just that, and they seemed to accept it. I must have carried it off with enough aplomb and style, because I received a big ovation at the end. It was the only time in my career I finished an aria in a different language from the one in which I started.

Once in a while, as a guest in an opera house, you are subjected to singing in a cast where more than one language is being sung. That is, the chorus is singing in their native language and the principals are singing in the original language. The first time for me was *Otello* in Mannheim, Germany, when the chorus and the small roles were sung in German and the three principals sang in Italian. It was a bit strange. In the original language, you become used to hearing certain nuances in the phrases, and of course they are all very different when translated into the other language. If you're not careful, it can throw off your memory and your timing.

Later in my career, I sang *Macbeth* in Copenhagen, Denmark, where all of the principals except me sang in Danish. And at another performance of *Macbeth* in Prague, I sang in Italian and everyone else sang in Czech. Danish and Czech to my American ear were strange-sounding languages, indeed. Especially in *Macbeth*, where there is much interplay and reaction between singers, it was very weird.

I actually rehearsed myself for these dates by singing my lines in Italian and singing the others' lines in nonsense syllables. I apologize to those who speak these languages, but to me during the performances they sounded like nonsense syllables! I found that I had to practice not listening to my colleagues. If I listened to them sing in their language, I couldn't remember my own words. I don't think I could sing an opera like *Don Giovanni* with recitatives in different languages.

Sometimes the different accents of prompters in opera houses around the world can cause a problem. Usually I will hear my line appropriately in time to sing it, but the accent will be so heavy that it actually sounds like other words and I can become confused, even in roles that I know well. During those times, I have to learn to shut the prompter out of my mind.

The whole issue of mistakes is how you fix them, not that you made them. Unfortunately there are no hard-and-fast rules on covering screwups. The better the musician you are, the more adjustments occur to you. The better you know a language, the easier it is to cover a muff. The most important thing is to not show that something is amiss.

It goes without saying that the better you speak a language, the quicker you can learn a song or a role, not to mention interpret them. I always recommend in my master classes that all singers take as many language courses as they can and when possible spend time in those countries.

Because I'd always planned on teaching in public school or at the university level instead of being a professional singer, I didn't take all the language courses that the applied-degree people (those with a career in mind) had to take. And so I came out of college without a good background in them. I ended up learning passable Italian from Berlitz and passable German with private study. With the subsequent career and mandatory usage of the languages, naturally they improved, but I'm not a great linguist. Oddly enough, my flavor in singing these languages is good. I don't know if it's a matter of talent, having an ear, or lots of hard work—probably a combination of all three.

George Burns once said, somewhat jokingly, "Once you can fake sincerity, you've got it made." Silly as that may sound, that is exactly what we do in singing. We fake sincerity, not by really faking, but by imitating real emotions that we know from other life experiences. Those experiences have given us various joys and pains, and we must allow ourselves to tap into those memories and reproduce the results. I suppose that, in that sense, one could say that we are faking. If internally we feel the real emotion of the moment, we can't possibly meet the vocal demands of the whole opera. For example, in *Madama Butterfly*, if the singer singing the part of Cio-cio-san really feels and lives the pain and sadness of her life, the voice would be unable to function for the whole opera. She would rip out her throat. Real emotions affect our voice immediately.

How many times in movies have we seen someone singing gloriously at a funeral with tears streaming down his or her face? Or singing beautifully while crying because a loved one is leaving? In movies, of course, we have lip-synching, but in real life it is all but impossible. There is something about emotions that all but shut off the vocal mechanism.

CHAPTER TWELVE

The Glamour of Travel

SOMETIMES TRAVELING TO SELDOM-VISITED PLACES can result in some bizarre hotel situations. Xalapa City in Mexico is a difficult place to get to. You have to fly to Mexico City, change planes, and fly to Veracruz on the east coast, and then drive north for two hours to Xalapa City. I had a contract to sing an operatic concert on Mexican television and then make a recording of these arias with the University of Xalapa orchestra, conducted by a fine veteran musician from Mexico City, Luis Herrera de la Fuente. Finally, after many hours of traveling, I arrived in Xalapa City and was deposited at the hotel, where no English was spoken. With my decent Italian, I was able to communicate a little. When I was shown to a rather small room, I said to the bellman that I was supposed to have a suite. I went back to the front desk and tried again.

They then showed me a suite with a king-size bed. I thought that this was more like it. I noticed that there was an odor, something like mold or rotting wood, but I didn't think too much about it, as I was grateful to settle in after more than ten hours of traveling. I unpacked and got ready for bed. When I pulled back the covers on the bed, I saw pale green streaks on the sheets. I smelled it and realized it was mold. It turned out that the room had not been rented for several weeks and therefore had not been cleaned, nor had the sheets been laundered. This, in an intensely hot and humid climate, had allowed bacteria to grow. Ugh! I had to move everything again, and I was livid and a little sick to my stomach. But it is hard to complain when you don't speak the language and are a little nauseated. Perhaps they had tried to tell me about the room before—I don't know. They finally found a decent suite, and ultimately the whole trip and concert and recording went very well, but mold on the sheets in the hotel was a first and I hope a last experience.

In 1995 I went to Prague to sing with orchestra a concert of arias and duets with a Czech soprano. At the same time I was singing *La fanciulla del West* in Bonn, Germany, and it was between performances that I flew to Prague for this concert. I was met at the airport by a new sponsor I didn't know. I had received a fax some weeks prior about staying in a beautiful old castle called Nelahozeves, outside of Prague, with the assurance that I would love it. I had responded by saying I would prefer one of the downtown hotels that I knew, as much for the beauty of the city as for proximity to rehearsals. There wasn't much time to rehearse, and I knew that I could not waste any of the valuable rehearsal time riding in a car.

The new auspices were very polite and helpful, but in their broken English they said something about the old castle outside of Prague. Apparently they had not understood my last fax. Once in the car, I could tell we were bypassing the city. It was a beautiful drive, with fresh snow on the ground, so during the trip I decided not to make a problem and to try to enjoy their choice of dwellings. We drove for more than an hour, and as we ascended a big hill, a fifteenth-century castle with turrets, built around a huge courtyard, came into view. In its time, the castle must have protected the whole area around it. It was still the part-time home of a descendant of the original Lobkowicz family, and I could feel its history. I was shown around and finally taken to the slightly more modern three-room apartment on the second floor. It was a long walk-up.

The bathroom was out in the hall and unheated. The outside temperature was about twenty degrees Fahrenheit, and the inside temperature was only a little warmer. The small apartment was heated with one inefficient electric heater per room and lit by a few dim twenty-watt bulbs. I could order food by using the telephone. There was supposed to be someone who spoke English on the other end in some lower room in the castle. Between some German (there was very little German spoken either) and some English, I could partly communicate with the caretaker when she was there. Most of the time, I felt quite alone. The only entertainment was a stereo with CDs of Broadway music sung by Czech singers in Czech. I began to feel a little bit like I was visiting the Twilight

Zone. When I finally did turn on the stereo, I blew a fuse. Trying to find the phone in the dark, dial the right numbers by feel (because nothing was visible), and talk to the nice caretaker with our lack of a common language was tough. I was grateful she understood the word "electricity." After the fuse blew twice more, I decided I had had my fill of the sound track of the Czech version of Andrew Lloyd Webber's *Phantom of the Opera*.

Here were all these rare and beautiful antiques from past monarchies, museum-ready furniture that was numbered and catalogued in which I was to place my clothes, and no sign of modern living except for this stereo! The bed was not comfortable, the rooms a little dirty, and the whole ambience, while impressive, was a little scary. However, the view from the apartment windows was spectacular, and if I had been on vacation, it would have been charming and beautiful. The rest of the castle had rooms that stretched on and on, with little or no light, many paintings, old-fashioned furniture, high ceilings, and stone steps everywhere.

Somehow, I managed to sleep enough that first night. The next morning, I tiptoed across the freezing hall to use the bathroom and after waiting a few minutes for the water to heat up in a small water heater, I showered in that less-than-warm room. I then got ready to be picked up at eleven in the morning for a rehearsal at noon. It was starting to snow heavily, with those big, fat, sticky flakes that, while beautiful, make for very difficult travel. The car was an hour late, which meant that all the rehearsals for the rest of the day would run late. There was a long program to prepare with a new conductor, a new soprano with whom I had not sung, and a nonoperatic orchestra. I then started to think again about moving into town if there was a hotel available. I could see an impossible schedule developing. There was a rehearsal the morning of the concert, with the program that evening. They had planned for me to return to the castle after the morning rehearsal and come back again in the evening for the concert. The one-way trip was taking an hour to an hour and a half, and this with a driver who did not speak English and only a few words of German. And so, at the rehearsal, I said that I thought we were in for trouble if I stayed at the castle.

Fortunately, they agreed and found a hotel on the Wenceslas Square. This unfortunately meant that after the second rehearsal that day I had to return to the castle, pack all my things, carry them down from the upper floor to the car, and drive back to the center of Prague, check in, and unpack again. I think that I finally was settled in about ten o'clock that night. I was very tired, more from traveling, packing, unpacking, and carrying bags than from rehearsing. The snow continued to fall, and I was glad that I had moved into the city, not least on account of the heated bathroom and all the other amenities a hotel offers. The castle would have been wonderful on a vacation, but on a working trip it was a different animal.

To Russia, and Dr. Hammer, with Love

Many times a performer's travel plans are unavoidably insane. I always tried to schedule wisely to allow for appropriate rest. Unlike an instrumentalist's, a singer's instrument is made up of body tissue and muscle, and it's dangerous to perform when you're totally exhausted. Obviously, a lot of this depends on the particular program or role you're doing. But far too frequently, the more famous you become, the more you are called on to do parts for which you are best known. And they are often the most difficult. Therefore, unwise scheduling sometimes can't be helped. Of course, big fees can be a major factor in the decision to really jam up the schedule.

In May 1989 I was to be in Vienna for some *Tosca*s, fly home to New York for a week's rest, and then make my first trip to Russia. I was to perform an aria concert with orchestra at the Tchaikovsky Conservatory, do a performance of *Tosca* at the Bolshoi Theater, and give a master class and general discussion with the conservatory students. The last turned out to be the most exciting event of the trip because of their great passion for music and their desire to hear what a "Western opera star" had to say about music.

That was the plan: hard work, but, travel-wise, about the norm. While in Vienna, however, I received a call from Armand Hammer's secretary, who asked if it was possible for me to sing at his ninetieth birthday party. Dr. Hammer was at the time the CEO of Occidental Petroleum. Ordinarily I would have declined the invitation, because the birthday celebration was scheduled for the day before the first rehearsal of the aria concert in Russia. In addition, it would involve flying from Los Angeles to Moscow without enough time for the body or voice to adjust (between Los Angeles and Russia there is a ten-hour time difference).

On the plus side, though, Dr. Hammer was a well-known citizen of the world—a man who had helped open Russia to the West—and a philanthropist and cancer fighter. The birthday was to be a huge affair, taking over the majority of the Beverly Hills Hotel. The performers would include Isaac Stern, Mstislav Rostropovich, the Los Angeles Philharmonic, emcee Danny Thomas, the McGuire Sisters, and others.

Now that's a birthday! I was torn between my good sense and my desire to be part of this big event. I said yes and arranged the travel with Dr. Hammer's secretary. They would fly me from Vienna to Los Angeles, I would stay one night at the Beverly Hills Hotel for the birthday, then, immediately after the party, fly to JFK Airport to catch the 9:00 A.M. Concorde to London, staying overnight at a Heathrow hotel. Then I would go on to Moscow first thing the next day, arriving in time to have a meeting with the conductor before that day's rehearsals with the orchestra. In order to make the JFK connection, I would have to take Occidental Petroleum's private jet from Los Angeles to JFK and then catch British Airway's van from Occi's hangar to the Concorde. Dr. Hammer agreed to everything—at a transportation and hotel cost of over $12,000, not including the private jet.

It was an incredible party. I sang the Champagne Aria from Mozart's *Don Giovanni*; "Nemico della patria" from Giordano's *Andrea Chénier*; and "Welcome Home" from Harold Rome's *Fanny*, a piece first sung in 1954 by Ezio Pinza on Broadway after his great success in *South Pacific*. "Welcome Home" has beautiful words and a heartbreaking melody— there wasn't a dry eye in the house. Isaac Stern played one movement of a concerto with orchestra. Rostropovich played an unaccompanied piece for cello. He'd conducted a concert in Paris the night before, flown on the Concorde to New York, and then private-jetted to Los Angeles, so he must have been very tired, but he played beautifully. The McGuire Sisters performed some of their greatest hits, and the L.A. Philharmonic played a number of well-known works as well as accompanying me.

The party was filled with other notables such as Maestro and Mrs. Zubin Mehta, Dr. and Mrs. Robert Schuller, the legendary actor James

Stewart and his wife, Gloria, and a number of CEOs of major corporations. Most of us performers regretfully had to leave early, with Rostropovich off to Washington (where he was music director of the National Symphony) on one Occi jet and Isaac and his wife and me on another private Occi jet to New York. The plane was fully stocked with food and drinks, although we had been completely feted at the birthday party. During the flight, Isaac briefed me about what you could and couldn't find in Russia—especially in the way of toiletries, foodstuffs, and other simple items we take for granted.

I'm generally bad about sleeping on airplanes, but I was able to get an hour or two of rest on the way to JFK. The Sterns and I parted in New York. I took the Concorde to Heathrow and stayed overnight at an airport hotel. The first thing the following morning I took Aeroflot to Moscow. The very long trip gave me lots of time to think. I was really glad I'd squeezed in the party and since then have sung at many Hammer charitable events, mostly occasions to raise money to fight cancer. And very successful at this cause he was!

Over a period of time Dr. Hammer took a lot of criticism for allegedly spending Occidental's money on some of his private and philanthropic endeavors. I don't know anything about the legal or corporate overtones of this; I only know that Dr. Hammer worked tirelessly to solve many worldwide problems.

I felt uneasy when I landed in Moscow because at this time the Iron Curtain was still very much in place and I really didn't know what I was getting into. An artist traveling to the USSR at that time didn't know about the advance hotel reservations. You were totally at the mercy of your host, even though you were supposed to be met at the airport by an interpreter and taken to a hotel.

I got my bags, went through customs, went out into the terminal, and waited—and waited. I tried to look as conspicuous as possible so I could be seen. That is a rule for a performer waiting to be picked up; stand tall, appear as though you are looking for someone, move around slightly, and stand away from the crowd. I felt a bit like a little kid in a strange place waiting for some adults to fetch him. Not a comfortable feeling for an artist of my age and stature.

Finally I made out an information sign at the other end of the terminal, lugged all my bags, filled with formal wear, music, orchestrations, and photos, through the vast hall, and showed my guest-artist contract to the official there. After some difficulty in making myself understood, she at last made an announcement on my behalf, and I waited some more. At that time, there seemed to be no signs in any language other than Russian, and while I'm not a great linguist, I can certainly read the normal airport signs in other languages. The whole situation was very depressing, as I had no idea where to go or what to do, and I was about to lose it. I decided if no one came in another half hour or so, already having waited two hours, I'd go to British Airways and ask when was the next flight back to London—or anywhere in Europe.

Finally, a woman came, whose name was Vera, to ask if I was "Meester Meel-ness." She apologized for being late and got us a taxi, and we went to a hotel. It was a dark, dingy place on the very busy and noisy Gorky Street. We went to check me in, and there were two hours of confusion at the desk—some permission form wasn't in place, and without it I didn't exist and certainly could not check in. I tried to stay calm, and they finally found the right piece of paper clipped to the wrong page in the reservation book. However, they made no apology—no one cared. I went up to the room, and my heart fell. It was like a large closet overlooking the street with horrendous traffic noise. The mattress on the bed was filled with straw, and with my farm background, I knew straw.

The next day I went to Gost Konsert, the state agency that booked the engagement and arranged the visit. Gost Konsert told me all the best hotels were filled with a big convention of all the USSR satellite countries. After some arguing and many reasons why I should be in that terrible hotel, they found me better—not good, but better—accommodations at the Budapest Hotel. They were, however, very friendly there, unlike at the first hotel.

After unpacking, I tried to call my family back in New York, but it took two days to get a line through to the States. Needless to say, I was quite depressed over the living conditions and the attitudes in general. But I must say my interpreter, Vera, couldn't have been more helpful and accommodating. The aria concert went very well. Once again, I found that music cut across all political boundaries, and the audience responded with huge enthusiasm. I was lucky, though, that I'd brought several of the orchestrations with me, because it turned out the Russians didn't have much in the way of orchestral parts, so we used all of my music.

Tosca at the Bolshoi was thrilling. I knew I was in one of the world's great opera houses, and I felt a little like the Illinois farm boy when I was on that magnificent stage. I was a star, but at the same time, I felt privileged to be there.

The Russian audiences at the time weren't used to the more believable stage drama that we take for granted. My Scarpia is much more sexually oriented than some Scarpias of the past. The audience and Tosca herself found it believable, and it gave her much more to play off of, and, I hope, enriched her performance as well. At the end there was huge applause, and many, many curtain calls, as well as many photos and hundreds of autographs—a very exciting evening.

I was scheduled to leave in the evening of the following day, after spending the day with the Tchaikovsky Conservatory students. It was perhaps the most rewarding time of the trip. I worked with half a dozen singers on standard operatic repertoire. It was a normal working situation, much like the master classes that I do here in the States, with some very talented singers. Perhaps the one common problem was that they all tended to push too much, and we discussed and worked on that problem and attitude.

The question-and-answer session afterward was extra special: the students' enthusiasm was obvious. Their passion for music was overflowing, and their questions were profound—things I really had to think about. For example: "What is more important, vocal technique or what the music is saying?" And "Singing loudly is important. If you can't be heard well enough you won't make an effect. But you, Mr. Milnes, talked much about softer singing; would you explain this further?" And so forth. It was a tiring but exciting two hours, showing again that music is a common bond among all people, transcending all other differences.

I left in just enough time to make my plane, although the lack of organization at the airport made me think more than once I would miss it. There were no lines, just hundreds of people jamming into one door. We eventually left, and I was glad to go but grateful for the ten-day human and musical experience. I think it made me a more thoughtful person and more of a world citizen without causing me to lose for a second my pride in being an American.

Even more inspiring and profound in a different way was my first visit to Prague. At one time Prague was the cultural capital of Europe; it is still a very beautiful city. In the 1970s I had been asked to sing *Don Giovanni* in the famous Tyl Theatre, where Mozart premiered it in 1787. I was quite excited to sing the Don in this beautiful baroque theater and even more excited when I found out that I was the first American ever to sing it in this historic place. The set was traditional, but good, and the cast were all leading Czech singers.

Interestingly enough, as most of my colleagues know, when you travel around the world and sing in any given production, in the moments of performance, you could be almost anywhere, in any city. You are in the locale of the opera story and the scenery, not in the city of the theater. Sometimes you remember where you are only when you walk out the stage door and see your surroundings.

Just knowing that this was the theater where Mozart had worked, composed, and rehearsed was a thrill. At the rear of the stage, leading up to the dressing rooms on the second floor, was a spiral staircase, which was the original from before Mozart's time. The wooden steps were worn thin and smooth in the center, but they were the same steps Mozart had used in 1787 during rehearsals and performances of the first *Giovanni*. When I realized that Mozart had contributed to the wear and tear on these steps and that I was treading the same path he had trod, I felt great humility. To sing Mozart's music, to taste his inspiration, and walk where he had walked in this theater gave me a feeling I cannot describe. I felt that this was the closest anyone in the 1970s could come to Mozart's presence and genius from the 1780s.

CHAPTER THIRTEEN

A Decade of Panic

Growing up on the farm, we were rich in food but not in dollars. The actor Christopher Lee, a friend and a big opera buff, once told me of the British expression, "Short of the ones." We were *very* "short of the ones"—my father didn't even carry a wallet, and if my mother, who was the primary bill payer, had four or five dollars in her purse, that would've been perfectly normal.

We seldom went to doctors because of the cost. It's very different now, especially for someone who had a job like mine, where so much was riding on the throat: an income, a career, a life. Treatment is absolutely necessary. Acting defensively when it comes to your health is something every singer learns to do. It took me many years to understand this, however. When I was growing up, my family's attitude was if you treat a cold it takes seven days to get better; if you don't, it takes a week.

Partly because of this background, and an old-fashioned, puritan attitude, I felt that if I became sick, it was somehow my fault; I'd done something careless or stupid. So I'd feel guilty about being ill, especially if it meant a cancellation. Even for things as minor as a dinner date or a party, I would almost never cancel. When some singers are sick or hoarse and have to bow out of a performance, it's just fate or Mother Nature. Italians will often say, "Non è colpa mia"—it's not my fault. This attitude makes life somewhat easier, but I couldn't make that work for me until much later in my life.

In the spring of 1981, I was performing the title role in a Carnegie Hall performance of Ambroise Thomas's *Hamlet*. It's a very long, intense part, and I was singing it in French for the first time. It was presented by the Friends of French Opera and conducted by the noted music historian Robert Lawrence. As with most concert performances, the dress rehearsal, which was more than three hours long, took place the same day as the performance. This schedule has always killed me in terms of my vocal and physical energy. Throughout my career I have tried to avoid this, but this time something happened with the Carnegie Hall schedule, and it couldn't be helped.

Since I had performed *Hamlet* in English several times before, I knew the opera better than most of the cast and the conductor. We had rehearsed for many weeks, but it's different rehearsing with piano as opposed to orchestra. *Hamlet* is an unknown opera, and the orchestra was mostly sight-reading in the first rehearsal. So I ended up doing what I call "slugging," or laying on the voice, too much for my own good, giving too much emphasis on the beats, to help the orchestra and the conductor feel and set tempos. These three things—the two performances in one day (the dress rehearsal and the performance), "slugging" the voice, and the role's own normal demands—added up to my being tremendously fatigued vocally. We don't know for sure if all this was the cause of what happened next, but at the time, it was my and my doctor's best guess.

At some point in the last twenty minutes of the performance—and it was no big dramatic moment, nothing like Mario Lanza spitting up blood in *The Great Caruso*—I felt something strange; my sound was getting breathy. I didn't think so much of it then, because it's normal for me to use a great deal of energy to sing, and it's not uncommon for my throat to be quite tired at the end of a difficult performance.

I've never been what I call in the industry an "easy" singer; it takes a lot of energy to get my tone going. Some fine singers like Jessye Norman, Renée Fleming, Frederica von Stade, or Montserrat Caballé don't appear to use a lot of effort to sing, their voices seem to flow like water out of a tap. Of course that is the ideal. However, I always have had to put a lot of juice into my singing, especially since I portray mostly the heavy baritone roles. That night, my adrenaline, which was sky high, pushed me through the performance and made me ignore the odd, breathy sensation—until the next day.

That following morning I woke up and couldn't talk. It was a very bad case of laryngitis, and I couldn't make a sound—just breath came out. This had never happened to me before. I was supposed to appear in a benefit for the YMCA in Downers Grove, now called the Indian Boundary YMCA. My folks had been instrumental in founding this Y in 1966 by donating the proceeds from the sale of our farmland to it, so it was important to give the performance for the family. In those days I was fearless when it came to my throat, and I'd book things back to back without giving the matter a second thought. The next day after a performance, the voice would always be fine. As a result, it didn't occur to me to cancel the benefit. I couldn't sing, of course, but with a microphone, I gave a rather breathy speech that was appropriate for the occasion. Little did I know that this was the beginning of a very frightening ten years for me.

Flying back to New York, I was still quite hoarse the following day. I went to my throat doctor, Leo Reckford, a grand old Viennese gentleman whose experience spanned many, many decades. (His many patients included Christa Ludwig, Walter Berry, Jerome Hines, Mario del Monaco, Franco Corelli, Leonie Rysanek.) He couldn't see anything but the normal redness and mild swelling of a tired throat, but he was puzzled that it hadn't cleared up after a few days, which is what would normally happen. In fact, for months and months, that hoarseness never really cleared up. It would get better, I'd sing, then it would get worse; then it would get better again, I'd sing again, and then it would get worse again. None of the various doctors I tried could see anything other than fatigue, slight redness, and mild swelling. If I could have many days of rest, I could get through an easy performance reasonably well; but always the next morning I was hoarse. And we are not talking about my normal heavy operatic roles.

Things were getting very scary now: no sing, no pay. A singer with throat trouble is like a pianist with bad arthritis in his fingers or a painter gone blind: your whole life is being taken away, not to mention your income. When it was really bad, my voice would start cracking, almost like a teenager's when his voice is changing. I tried canceling a number of performances to get a really long rest. That seemed to help, but after some extended singing my voice would start to misfire again, and the hoarseness would come back.

Every time I opened my mouth I was scared. Would the regular Sherrill Milnes voice function normally for ten minutes, twenty minutes

. . . could I even sing at all? The various rehearsals were especially frustrating, because when staging, you repeat the same material over and over. Even when I was singing half-voice, my voice would get fatigued. During the performance, when everyone is singing full out, I would really be in trouble because of the residual fatigue from rehearsing. I was sweating terribly during rehearsals, sweating terribly during the performances, just wondering what was going to happen next. It was very difficult to keep making excuses and to pretend that I was more or less normal during all these engagements.

During this time, Luciano and Jan Peerce called me on the phone, asking me if there was anything they could do and offering some advice from their throat doctors. They, of course, didn't know what the problem was, but it was very thoughtful and kind of them to try to help.

Other colleagues and teachers were telling me it was my vocal technique, that I wasn't singing right . . . but how could that be? The vocal principles by which I operated I learned from Andrew White and Hermanus Baer, as well as the many other coaches and conductors with whom I had worked. I'd been vocalizing, singing, and performing the same way for over twenty years with no problem, so I couldn't believe it was my technique.

This all just added to my intense fear and confusion: something kept going wrong, no one could figure out why, and it could be the end of my professional life. I received anonymous letters with all kinds of advice, some well intended, some not so well intended, some suggesting foolish and even dangerous remedies.

In the fall of 1981 I was scheduled for a new production of *Simon Boccanegra* at Covent Garden in London. My hoarseness had now been going on for seven or eight months. I couldn't even get through the Boccanegra part practicing at home. I went to London anyway to start rehearsals, and I called to see my London throat doctor, Norman Punt, but he was on holiday. I was desperate, but I remembered the name of another well-known but somewhat eccentric throat man, the Hungarian-born and Viennese-trained Dr. Alexander. I was nervous about seeing a doctor I didn't know and also about having to relate the whole saga yet again, with so much of it making no vocal or physiological sense. I was, however, somewhat reassured when Shirley Verrett walked out of his office, as the patient before me, in time for her performance of *Samson et Dalila* at Covent Garden.

A real throat exam for a singer, at that time, involved sticking your tongue out as far as it would go, to get it out of the way in order to see down the throat and to help defeat the gag reflex. Then the doctor wrapped gauze around the tongue, pulled it further out, and inserted a curved mirror as far as it could be placed in the back of the throat. With the headband light turned on, he examined your vocal folds in the mirror while asking you to phonate various vowel sounds.

Dr. Alexander pulled so hard, I thought my tongue was going to come out in his hand. I sang, he looked, I sang, he looked. After almost a half hour of this phonating and examination, he finally sat down and told me that diagnosing in hindsight was less than ideal or accurate, but that his best guess was that I had broken a capillary in one vocal cord those many months earlier in Carnegie Hall. He said that he thought it had happened on the underside of the right cord, which was why no one had seen it, and that it was halfway between the center of the cord and the "hinge." He also told me that broken capillaries in the throat are far more common among singers than is generally known. They can be more serious (as this one was for me), or less serious, depending on where the leak is.

The vocal cords look something like an old-fashioned change purse (the kind you squeeze to open), with two strips of muscle connected at each end, contracting and expanding the cords to make different sounds. These two small muscles are connected at the front of the voice box (larynx) just behind the Adam's apple. They are attached to cartilages at the back of the voice box that rotate back and forth to bring them together in order to vibrate and produce sound—or to spread them apart in order to breathe. They are covered by soft tissue called the mucosa, which is almost like Jell-O in texture, and which vibrates as air passes between them. This soft tissue contains many blood vessels and capillaries. The term "broken capillary" really means a small rupture in the wall of a microscopic blood vessel. As the blood leaks out from the capillary, it fills the soft tissue and causes swelling and bruising of the cord, which is not really any different from a black-and-blue bruise of the skin. Capillaries can rupture from a sudden strong vocal strain, like a scream, a cough, or a sneeze, or even an excessively powerful note, especially if you have a cold.

It is often difficult or impossible to determine the cause of a broken capillary. When it occurs, the cords look dreadful, engorged with blood, and red or purple. The swollen cords cannot vibrate properly or symmetrically when air passes through them, resulting in hoarseness and an unpredictable lack of clarity in the voice.

After many blood tests, they found that I did have an allergy to aspirin, which thins the blood, causing it to leak more easily. Yet it wasn't that simple, as I was not a regular aspirin taker, so there was still no explanation for the bruise.

However, when Dr. Alexander gave me a logical explanation for the cause of the vocal trouble, it was one of the biggest emotional moments of my life, and I felt a huge weight coming off my shoulders. This vocal difficulty was finally making some sense; there was a real, physical, analyzable defect that accounted for the problems. I felt somehow that everything my music and singing had stood for all these years was vindicated. Even though I wasn't better and it hadn't been fixed, here was a physiological explanation for everything I'd been feeling, and it wasn't a problem with my mind or my technique at all. I remember at the very least giving the very senior Dr. Alexander a big embrace. I never saw him again, but will always remember him with great fondness.

I sang the upcoming performances of *Simon Boccanegra* as well as I could, and certainly in a better frame of mind, but the problem definitely was not solved.

Upon returning to New York, even though Dr. Reckford was my regular laryngologist, the worry was too great not to seek other advice. There was another laryngologist in New York, the well-known American-trained Dr. Wilbur James Gould. (At that time almost all of the professional singers while in New York went to either Reckford or Gould when there was a problem.) Dr. Gould and Dr. Reckford conferred on my behalf and decided that if I alternated singing with resting, the capillary would clear up by itself. (The possibility of surgery had been touched upon, but it certainly frightened me, and both doctors thought this sing-rest plan would work.) After the London *Boccanegra*s, there were some *Tosca*s at the Met. Luckily, Scarpia is a very acting-oriented role, so I could partially compensate for hurting vocally by being extra convincing onstage.

During this time, I desperately hoped their plan would work, because next on my schedule was a series of *Rigolettos*, one of which would be televised. There's no way to hide in *Rigoletto*; you have to sing fantastically, with long lines of high notes. With my height and size, plus the hump making me bend over, it was the most difficult role in the whole Verdi repertoire for me.

During the *Toscas*, I was really watching and monitoring myself, fingers crossed, not knowing what was going to come out of my mouth, just hoping that my tone wouldn't diminish or crack or disappear. In fact, there was a radio broadcast of one of the *Toscas*, where during Carol Neblett's big soprano aria—"Vissi d'arte"—you can hear me making little falsetto notes, doing a sound check to see if my voice was going to continue to function. Of course, I didn't know my sounds were being picked up on the radio.

To be onstage and not trust that the next note will work—that's real panic. I'm not sure how I was able to have enough chutzpah just to be able to stand in front of the audience and continue, and the problems grew worse the longer I sang.

The sing-rest plan was not working, and things were not any better during the last *Tosca*. I knew I would have to cancel the upcoming *Rigolettos*, including the TV performance. How I hated to do that. I realized that I had to come up with something to solve the problem and fix it or end my career.

Canceling a series of performances during a given period of time is one of the worst things that you can do as a professional. Anyone can get sick and let one or two performances go, but if it becomes a series of performances, word goes around that there may be a bigger problem. Most singers will never admit if they have to cancel for a vocal reason. The flu is OK, or some infection that can be cured in a short time. But real vocal problems, or even rumored vocal problems, can kill your reputation and future contracts. In a series of cancellations, especially when it's the Met, Vienna, Covent Garden, Paris, or La Scala—word gets around. Operas are scheduled years in advance, and when rumors circulate that someone is having serious problems, he or she is considered a risk—and the job offers, little by little, vanish.

In my case, almost no one knew the real story except my wife, my agent, Herbert Barrett, and my doctors, and eventually a few close friends. Basically I said very little about the voice, but one of the big non-vocal problems was that I had to remember to maintain and keep straight all the "layers of deceit" for the sake of my career: the different lies and half-truths about my voice and physical condition I would tell friends, or colleagues, or other singers—or, more important, conductors, and theater managers.

The opera world is rife with rumors. The cancer rumor was beginning to make its ugly way around; I had been in and out of a number of hospitals for various tests, people had seen me, and the rumor mills went into high gear that I was dying of cancer. All of the doctors from the start assured me that this problem had nothing to do with cancer, but the industry didn't know that. Besides, cancer makes a more dramatic story than other possibilities.

Every morning following a performance, while still in bed, I'd make a few falsetto tones to see if something besides breath came out—if sound did come it meant I could probably sing. I never even knew when I said hello to someone if my voice would respond in more than a breathy whisper. I'd walk down the street, and when traffic made enough noise, especially when a noisy bus or truck went by, I'd do a little glissando to see if the sound would work, to see if the cords were coming together. When a singer can't sing, it can destroy you; you feel weak, stripped of your strength, impotent, and without any sexual drive. All the inner power you need to be a performer and to deliver to your audience is gone.

Often I'd lie in bed, covered in cold sweat. Throughout this period I was close to throwing in the towel and taking a full-time teaching job. But that would mean never singing in the major leagues again. When you stop singing professionally, you're out of the loop; almost everything shuts down, and the word goes out that you're no longer available or in any kind of vocal shape.

The doctors had mentioned laser surgery, but only in passing, because it was chancy. No guarantees. There was a well-known doctor in Boston at the time, a pioneer in this laser surgery technique: Dr. Stuart Strong. So I went to get his advice, and he agreed that with the singing-and-resting idea not working at all, we had to do something. Laser surgery was the only possibility, and it was scheduled immediately.

I went into Massachusetts General Hospital in January 1982 under a pseudonym; it would be devastating if word got out that I had had an operation on my throat. It was very frightening—I had no idea what the outcome might be—but at the same time, I was at least doing something, and there was a possibility of getting better. A week after the operation, I started vocalizing little by little, going frequently to both Dr. Reckford and Dr. Gould. They thought the surgery had taken and couldn't see any abnormal swelling.

I had a group of recitals coming up that spring, and after a few weeks of careful vocalizing, I sang through them. Everything was pretty good. Because recitals, of course, are with piano instead of orchestra, you can and must use more soft singing. You must find more colors in the tone, more interpretation in the text. Therefore in these recitals I was able to modulate the voice and put less pressure on it in general. It was a good way to work it back to full strength.

It seemed as though the surgery had worked, and all the problems were slowly ending, mentally and emotionally. However, it was impossible to quickly forget the vocal insecurity and insanity of the preceding year.

The panic was ebbing, but still close to the surface. If I even had a little phlegm, the same as you get from being out in the cold air, I'd think: I've done it again, I've broken another one. I was checking my voice constantly; every little thing that seemed in the slightest way odd would make me think it was happening all over again.

I'd had to cancel the Met *Rigoletto*s, which included the telecast, but then after the successful recitals I was planning to join the Met tour to sing *Macbeth* and *La forza del destino*. I sang one *Macbeth* in Washington, but at the end it started to happen again; I got breathy and couldn't get my falsetto to work as it should, and the next day I had terrible laryngitis. I was sure a capillary had leaked again. As soon as I got home, I went to Dr. Reckford. He looked with his mirror, took a step back, shook his head, and I'll never forget the look of sorrow and sadness on his face when he said, "I'm sorry, I'm sorry!"

The panic under the surface exploded once more; I was in a sweat sitting there listening to the diagnosis, completely soaking wet. He said, "This isn't in such a serious place; it's on top near the middle of the same right vocal fold as before, but not as close to the vibrating edge." I asked him what this meant for my singing, and he said, "I think perhaps in ten days you can sing again."

I was also seeing Dr. Gould at the same time; he was using a then new technology called fiber optics. A television camera on the end of a fiber-optic tube is placed up your nose and down your throat to make video-tapes of your vocal folds. The doctor can clearly see the cords vibrate and adjust as the singer uses different vowel sounds. (This technique is different from the old-fashioned method of the curved mirror in that you can come closer to the vocal folds and zoom in, and of course the picture is preserved on videotape. Also, it's not necessary to have your tongue pulled out of your mouth!) Watching those cords on the TV screen—the physical center of a thirty-plus-year professional career—well, they are the ugliest, slimiest, weakest-looking set of things. It's amazing that such beautiful sounds, or in some cases sounds that aren't so beautiful, can come from these ugly-looking creatures.

Partly from the gag reflex, partly from nerves, partly because it was cutting too close to home, partly because it was my throat and vocal cords, I could never watch the TV monitor during the examination. It took all my willpower to ignore the huge discomfort of that tube going up my nose and all the way down my throat and then having to make various sounds with the tube in (*ee* or *ah* vowels in falsetto or little scales). I've been through it thirty or forty times, and each time every fiber of my body was screaming, "Get that thing out of there!" Seeing it on videotape later was possible, but live, no way!

I had to cancel two weeks of the seven-week Met tour because of this latest problem, but the doctors thought I could do the next *Forza* in Dallas. So I sang every note, always wondering, was it going to be OK? I suppose my singing wasn't as bad as it felt internally, but the vocal insecurities of the preceding years were still so vivid. The tension tired me out tremendously, but the next day, I could talk. The vocal cords apparently had healed.

Once, because of all the rumors, a smart-ass colleague misbehaved. In Minneapolis, soon after that Dallas *Forza*, I was checking into the hotel when a fellow baritone came up to me in the lobby, which was filled with Met singers and local opera fans, and said in a loud voice, "Hey, I hear you popped another one!" I'm sure he thought he was being cute, but I should have punched him out. Feeling as insecure and unfit as I did, I wasn't in a punching mood. But I have not forgotten that son-of-a-bitch.

A confusing factor for any singer is that ordinarily there is no pain connected with a capillary break. It's ironic that an average sore throat, totally nonserious in any life sense, hurts far more than this very serious situation. It is difficult to judge the severity by the discomfort or pain.

Subsequently, I sang in performance after performance, just like the old days, without a single problem, and just as I started to get my old self-confidence back, I broke another one. And this one did not go away, just as before. It wouldn't heal, and the doctors reluctantly decided we had to do the surgery again. The throat cancer rumors were going strong again. A university voice teacher and a friend even wrote to me that he'd heard that a dentist who was working on my teeth had dropped an instrument down my throat and it had cut one of my vocal cords! Physically, that's impossible, but that's the crazy level of stories that were swirling around me. There was also a story that in a performance, I had had an injection of a steroid directly into one of my vocal folds. As before, friends (and I suppose some enemies) were writing letters with all kinds of vocal and psychological advice, telling me they knew of the perfect voice teacher or therapist, that all I had to do was study with one of a variety of people and all would be well.

I had a second round of laser surgery in August 1984, again with Dr. Strong in Boston, again with a pseudonym, again with all those fears. Good singing is much like any physical exercise; you have to keep singing or your stamina diminishes. For every week I didn't sing, I'd have to spend three or four days in vocal exercises, getting back to speed. So I rested and slowly went back to singing, always surrounded by rumors that something horrible was wrong with me—that I was dying. No one would ever bring it up directly, so it was never discussed face-to-face. I couldn't even counter the rumors.

Coming up soon was the Metropolitan Opera Centennial, and they wanted me to sing the *Puritani* duet "Suoni la tromba" with Ruggero Raimondi, and following that in the season, a new production of Verdi's *Ernani*. I hadn't sung *Ernani* in many years, so I needed a lot of review. I was practicing one evening in the piano room at home for about thirty minutes, went to bed, and started talking to my wife . . . and couldn't make a sound, not a whisper. Again no discomfort or pain, but the panic was instant—cold sweat all over again. I had had four breaks and two surgeries, for naught. I was going insane, absolutely insane. I lay awake all night.

The next day, Dr. Gould found the leak with his television camera. The Centennial was only ten days away, and I wanted to be a part of that gala in the worst way. Even if I stayed mute all that time, would I have enough vocal strength to rehearse and then do the performance? I spent a week not making a single sound, except for the testing in the doctors' exams. I was going to both doctors almost every day and kept hoping. The 100th birthday of the Met would never happen again.

Alas, it was not to be. I was improving, but two days before the performance, neither doctor thought that the vocal folds would be ready for me to sing. With a heavy heart, I had to cancel singing in this once-in-a-lifetime concert. It was very rough watching it at home on television—all the great singers I'd always worked with, on the stage where I'd had so many wonderful performances and memories—everyone there but me. It was very emotional and very difficult.

A week later the *Ernani* rehearsals began with Luciano Pavarotti and Leona Mitchell, with James Levine conducting. The role of Don Carlo is a big sing, with plenty of high notes, high tessitura, and a very legato line. At first I was almost afraid to open my mouth to sing. Little by little, with a lot of worry, I strengthened back into the part. Fortunately, with several weeks of rehearsals, I had enough time to work slowly. My stamina did return, and ultimately the performances were successful. There is a beautiful videotape of this *Ernani* available.

From that moment on everything was fine, with no mishaps except worry and sweat. (I use the word "sweat" very specifically: water literally drips off your face onto the floor.)

This time the capillaries healed once and for all, and I've never had another break. They never found a reason why I had had no problem whatsoever for twenty years, then had breaks again and again and, after that, no further problems. Finally, but slowly, my emotional and physical confidence came back and I could sing fully and uninhibitedly again. The fear that my voice wouldn't be there, the sweat-soaked panic of not knowing what would happen when I opened my mouth to sing, ebbed.

Emotionally I'm different, and physically I'm different as well, because the surgeries left scars. Laser surgery, which at the time was considered a state-of-the-art treatment, has come under criticism in more recent years. Dr. Scott Kessler, one of our finest laryngologists, spent some concentrated time with me and I am very grateful to him for his insights and knowledge.

At one performance of *La traviata* at the Met in the late 1980s, he came to my dressing room and stayed for the whole performance. He did several complete throat examinations, before the performance, before the big duet, before the aria "Di Provenza," before the last act, and at the end of the performance. All of these were to check the condition of the vocal folds as the opera progressed. All laryngologists have seen throats many, many times, but seldom have they watched the vocal cords react to full-voice singing over the course of a performance and in a major opera house.

I went to his office the following day and he showed me some pictures he had drawn of my throat from the night before. (One needs to understand that all vocal cords go through changes as they are used in singing.)

Using the drawings as a reference, Dr. Kessler took me through the previous evening. As I warmed up before the performance, he saw the normal "filling up" quality of the vocal folds; a little like going from Jell-O to a pale hot dog. During the early singing, the scar was not very evident. Then after the long duet with Violetta, it was a bit more visible. Vocally as yet, I did not sense anything different.

The "Di Provenza" went well, but after that the scar was much more visible, though vocally I still felt normal. In the third act I could start to feel a little difficulty in maintaining my normal focus, and the turn into top voice (*passaggio*) was no longer automatic. I had to work at it to get the voice to go over. The last act is not so hard, and while I could feel some difficulty, it went well.

After the opera Kessler could see the normal, slightly swollen, slightly pink color of the vocal cords. But the scar tissue was not swollen in the same proportion as the rest of the cords. This meant that, after a certain amount of full-voice singing, I was then using vocal folds of unequal mass. I began to have a bit of difficulty getting "purchase" on the sound—purchase meaning having an appropriate beginning, a healthy initial phonation. Ideally, sounds should begin like water out of a tap, and I could usually do that. But after I had been singing for a while, my voice would not want to phonate immediately and would sometimes stall at the beginning of the pitch.

Dr. Kessler described this phenomenon of what I was feeling in this excerpt from a letter he wrote to me following this exam.

> Although I cannot be sure from your test [the exams from the performance], I surmise that you had developed a "hemorrhagic polyp"—a blood blister at the vibrating edge of your cord. At that time, the laser was exemplary of the 1970s technology and, unfortunately, many surgeons embraced this modality as the ultimate tool in vocal cord surgery. Time has now revealed the laser, in fact, leaves larger amounts of scar tissue, results in slower healing, and actually has no advantage over traditional "cold steel" removal of such lesions. The laser is a concentrated focus beam of light and heat, which actually evaporates and destroys the tissue it is aimed at, and is useful in removing vocal cord lesions that are highly vascular (filled with blood vessels) in order to coagulate, or clot excessive bleeding that may occur as the edge of the tissue is destroyed. As the laser beam hits the tissue, the intense heat evaporates and destroys it. But it leaves a surrounding zone of inflammation and swelling that does not occur with other techniques. It is therefore useful in coagulating or sealing off the ends of blood vessels so that further bleeding is avoided.
>
> I can only presume that the laser was employed in your case with the idea that recurrent oozing from any ruptured capillaries would be prevented. Another analogy is putting a small piece of tape on a balloon and gently inflating the balloon. The tape doesn't expand, doesn't "give," while the surrounding elastic rubber swells evenly and smoothly. Another analogy: think of a leaf floating on a pond. If you make a splash, the ripples smoothly and evenly pass over the surface, except for the area around the leaf, where the ripples are interrupted. Similarly, the vibratory wave of the vocal cord becomes irregular when it passes over and through the area of thickened scar tissue. Furthermore, after prolonged vibration—irritation—inflammation—the entire cord will gradually swell with fluid, except for the scarred region. This was clearly demonstrated during sequential exams backstage, as you know. . . .
>
> Bear in mind that if your particular situation had developed ten years later than it had, laser surgery would probably *not* have been the modality of choice. . . . At the time, your decision to proceed with laser surgery was certainly to be considered "state of the art," as it

were. However—it is interesting to ponder the eventual outcome, had more traditional methods, which are currently regaining popularity, been employed.

The point is that the laser created a peripheral area of scar tissue surrounding the original "lesions" that is less elastic, less supple, less "gelatinous," and less conducive to transmitting vibrations than the area immediately surrounding it—not unlike the "skin" that forms on top of pudding. It is unfortunate and frustrating that no reason was ever found for why you had no problem for twenty years, then suffered repeated hematomas, and have had no problem since. Yet this is the accepted and usual course of events in such cases. Perhaps the scar tissue, with its microscopically condensed, thickened and consolidated nature, prevents capillary rupture in that particular area most susceptible to vocal strain. This is only theory. In fact, you are at this time, as susceptible to bruising that cord as ever, and perhaps you are technically preventing such strain, which is certainly to your credit.*

What Dr. Kessler's experiment and our subsequent conclusions taught me was that I could sing as well as ever for close to an hour before the different coefficient of expansions started to have an effect.

As a result of what I learned about my voice, I sadly had to give up a few long Verdi roles, because I could no longer sing them to my own acceptable level of excellence. Fortunately, however, certain roles were still in my voice.

I learned to ration my normal stamina to apply it to the most difficult parts of a role or a concert. That sometimes meant vocalizing less before and starting a bit colder. It all depended on the ebb and flow of the music. But understanding the physiology of my voice after the surgery made a big difference in my emotions and in my vocal reliability. And it meant that I have continued to sing and perform well for many more years than I might have been able to, with no diminution of audience communication and response.

---

* Dr. Kessler was speaking of the second surgery. The first operation took place on the underside of the right vocal fold, and the scar is not visible from the top.

CHAPTER FOURTEEN

Life after the Met

I'M NOT SURE EXACTLY WHEN my relationship with James Levine and the Met started to deteriorate. For the first twenty years or so, the management would discuss with me all the possible operas I could sing and which ones made sense for the upcoming seasons. After Jim became the music director, he would sometimes come into my dressing room, curl up on the couch, and talk about performances and future repertoire. It was always quite affectionate and friendly and seemed mutually respectful. Certainly I was very comfortable singing with him and have always learned from him. His body energy and facial expressions while you are singing are always inspiring. It's an accepted fact that Jim is one of the major musical forces of our time.

Slowly, however, all this diminished. It happened over so many seasons, I almost didn't notice it. In the 1980s I had those periods of vocal problems that I've already discussed. During that time, however, I performed with Jim and other conductors all over the world. I don't think that my performing quality over the long haul had anything to do with the deterioration of my relationship with Jim and the Met. Any performer has some less-than-ideal evenings. But in the 1990s, I had a series of successes in *Aida*, *La fanciulla del West*, *Tosca*, *Andrea Chénier*, and *Pagliacci*, plus *Falstaff* at the New York City Opera as well as many performances in other major European theaters.

The Met publicly praised me in my twenty-fifth year, 1990–91, with a radio broadcast ceremony onstage during *Andrea Chénier*. It was nicely done and I appreciated it greatly. Ironically, that season I sang only the *Chénier*s; I had the fewest performances of my career to date at the Met.

Two years before my thirtieth year, when that contract normally would have been made, I had heard nothing from the Met except that "they were behind in scheduling, but not to worry." For the better part of a year my management tried to get some information, but to no avail. As we approached ten months from the beginning of a season for which I had no contract, I was beginning to panic. (The major theaters of the world plan two and sometimes three years ahead with their contracts.)

I called Jim's office and finally had a private meeting with him. He said he knew nothing of my scheduling but would look into it. In a short time, they offered me two *Aida*s for the 1995–96 season. I was terribly embarrassed that in my thirtieth-first year I had only two performances. Ironically, within a few months, they offered for the following season (96–97) six *Aida*s and two covers. I was grateful for the performances, and it allayed some of my fear that the Met did not want me there anymore.

During these seasons of uncertainty about future contracts, I was understandably depressed and sometimes a bit angry. After a performance, for instance, when some member of the management would say "good job" or "fine singing," I couldn't resist saying, "But it's not good enough, is it?" I couldn't help revealing some of my frustrations and inner feelings.

The only negative moments with Jim were in the mid-1990s. I had been verbally promised a new *Don Giovanni*, when it came along. However, I heard through the grapevine that there was a new production to be sung by Sam Ramey. He is a great singer and a great guy and deserves all there is. But from my point of view, the Met was not living up to its promise.

About the time the following year's schedule was announced in the papers, I received a letter from the Met telling me that they felt it was Sam's turn. I was very upset by what I perceived to be the impersonal way they handled it, and by not getting the *Giovanni* production. I certainly had no problem with the principle that management has the right to cast. That was not an issue. My whole point in wanting to meet with Jim was to talk candidly and find out where I was vis-à-vis the Met. At that point in my career, I thought that my relationship with Jim had not deteriorated, so I felt comfortable and free to communicate.

We had lunch and it was a normal conversation between performers; only the *Don Giovanni* issue was a sore point. I asked why a formal and impersonal letter saying only that they felt it was Sam's turn had been sent. Jim responded that he and Bruce Crawford, who at the time was the acting general manager, had decided that a letter was the best choice. I was upset about this and said that given my track record at the Met, a personal meeting would have been more appropriate, and that I thought the letter was a "chicken-shit" way of informing me. I don't know if that phrase was a slap in the face or not, but I said what I felt. After some more conversation, I left the lunch feeling somewhat better, partly because face to face Jim is always friendly, polite, and, at least on the surface, understanding when it comes to problems.

Then once again, during the spring and summer of 1996, there was no talk of contracts. My management tried repeatedly to get a response to their frequent inquiries. Once again they were always put off by one excuse or another. Finally the fall of 1996 came. The season started and still no word from the Met management. (This was the season of the six *Aida*s.) I resented terribly having no idea of my future. Even knowing that there was nothing for me would have been much fairer, so that I could have made plans accordingly.

Without any Met contract, there would be a big difference. I was in the middle of a divorce, so my finances were a mess. Still the Met remained silent. Again I thought that perhaps by talking to Jim I would get some kind of answer. We came together in his office. I shared with him my recent *Falstaff* successes at the New York City Opera and expressed my interest in singing it at the Met, as well as the possibility of Puccini's *Gianni Schicchi*, which was new to me that year. He was very cordial and again claimed ignorance of my contractual situation. I asked if he would please look into it and he promised to do so, but I left feeling less than confident.

Within two weeks, Mr. Barrett received a fax stating that they had nothing for me the next season or any future seasons. There was never any explanation except some vague reference to "performance problems," which had never been mentioned before or since. I still believe that management has the right to cast whomever they see fit, but one would hope that the casting would be based on some kind of reality of performance level.

During those last two years, I suppose I should have read the handwriting on the wall. In the business world, when one starts being honored, that generally means you are being retired. I was honored together with Beverly Sills for the twentieth anniversary of her Met debut and my thirtieth year there. In April 1996 I was invited to sing at Jim Levine's twenty-fifth-anniversary concert. It was a marathon of great singers. There was a lovely affair afterward at which I introduced my wife-to-be, Maria, to Jim. He couldn't have been nicer or more complimentary of my singing and certainly made Maria and me feel quite good about my performing that night and our future marriage.

Jim and the management were friendly to my face, but it seemed that they wanted simply to let my contract run out and never say anything: silence, with no explanations or communication.

The only other minor confrontation was at the Tucker Gala in October of 1996, where I had sung the aria from *Il tabarro*, a scene from *Il trovatore*, and the fugue from *Falstaff*. At that point, Mr. Barrett had just received the fax stating that there would be nothing for me in the future. You can imagine how difficult it was to sing that concert in front of many of the Met management and many of the same audience that goes to the Met, knowing that I would never sing there again.

After the concert, there was a dinner that I attended with Maria. It was a real operatic Who's Who affair. While seated at dinner, Joe Volpe, the Met's general manager, with whom I had always had a good relationship, came over to greet the table. He said something complimentary to me, but I felt compelled to say, "You don't have to say that, Joe; your words ring hollow." I'm sure that angered him, but at that point any words of praise from the Met seemed an insult and completely two-faced.

The next day I felt guilty about the possibility that I had embarrassed him. I don't know if my comment was heard by others or not, but I called Joe's office. He was not in, but to his credit, he returned my call. On the phone I apologized if I had embarrassed him in front of others at the table. It was not my intention. But I had said exactly what I felt given the Met's treatment of me. *I said that I saw no reason why I should be grateful for the opportunity to never sing at the Met again after thirty-two years.*

We discussed briefly that there had never been any explanation or communication about why I was finished there. We agreed to come together in a few weeks, but it never happened. The Met's silence and lack of communication was the most frustrating and angering aspect of those last years. It seemed a most ignoble way to leave.

The last performance of my career at the Met was *Aida* on March 22, 1997. Mr. Barrett had received a fax from the Met management asking if there was something they should do to acknowledge it, although what that might have been was unclear. I instructed my management to say I did not want any public announcement or private affair, as that would indicate that this was a mutually agreeable parting and that would have been a lie.

However, at the performance I did expect some personal or individual expression of some kind from someone in management after some six hundred evenings at the Met. But I was disappointed yet again. A few singers who knew that it was my last performance came back and were very loving and appropriate. In fact, I started to tear up several times. My solo bow that night was a very emotional moment. The audience was particularly warm and enthusiastic, and oddly enough it was the best applause of the evening. I'm sure almost no one knew that it was my last performance, but the wave of sound that ensued did move me to tears. And so I left the theater that night in quiet, surrounded by close friends, thinking of it as the beginning of new possibilities. Though I was armed with a better attitude about the rest of my life, it would only be accurate to say that the manner in which the Met let me go was terribly hurtful and depressing.

CHAPTER FIFTEEN

I've Just Met a Girl
Named Maria

THERE IS NO DOUBT that the "decade of panic" and the Met's behavior over those last several years were part of the reason that my life was being turned upside down. I was feeling more and more internal pressure to maintain a career.

It was 1989 when I met Maria Zouves. She was a voice student of a friend and colleague, William Woodruff, for whom I would do an occasional master class. Maria would always be in attendance and sing in the classes. It was interesting to see her from year to year, and I watched her grow as a singer and performer almost before my eyes. People around us seemed to feel the energy we had together, and she somehow etched a little notch in my heart, being very Greek, bubbly, and beautiful.

Despite rumors to the contrary, nothing in the form of a relationship ensued until later in our lives, when she was already ending a marriage and I was deep in the middle of marital troubles with Nancy. Unfortunately for our families, and us, our slow but unrelenting evolution of love hurt those around us. Maria and I tried to be apart, and Nancy and I tried to keep building on a twenty-five-year marriage. During that time I know I made mistakes trying to do the right thing, but it just didn't work. It took a long time for Maria and me to make the commitment to come together, and our efforts led to pain for everyone—and to lying, something of which I am the least proud. I know all those involved went through their own private hell. But our desire to be together overshadowed everything in the end, and we finally married.

During the time that Maria and I had left our other marriages, the rumor factor again went wild about the details of how we came together.

Some of them bordered on the ridiculous, others just annoying. We both had to endure the May-December factor: she was accused of trying to find her career through me, and I, of chasing after my youth.

Because Maria was building a promising career and Nancy continued her voice studio in New York, it often put many of the same people in our musical circles together, creating uncomfortable situations. Not knowing how they would react, we had to guard ourselves against what they would say or what crazy things they had heard. I know that it was very hard on my children, Eric, Erin, and Shawn, and on Nancy and her studio. But we still had to face the world head-on. Every time Maria's name appeared on a cast list, whether it was with me or not, people assumed that *it's because she's the wife*. But Maria has found her own way in a professional career as singer and now executive director of V.O.I.C.Experience, endearing herself to the world in which we exist and helping a lot of other singers find their own career paths.

During all of this personal turmoil, the Met situation only exacerbated our fears and financial worries, and we clung to our friends and sometimes hid behind them, their support and love being precious to us. It wasn't until December 19, 1996, the day we walked into Mayor Giuliani's office to say our vows, that we felt calmer about the world's perception of our true feelings. It all seems like ancient history now, but at the time it was a difficult period in our lives.

Maria and me with Mayor Giuliani on our wedding day at New York City Hall, 1996.

CHAPTER SIXTEEN

Amadeus

MARIA AND I WANTED A BABY. We did all the normal things that people do to get pregnant, but it was not happening. One day Maria's mother excitedly called from her home in Florida and said she had located a relative with whom the family had lost touch. They had not known where Christos Zouves, a nephew of Maria's dad, Nico, was or what he did for a living. Angie, Maria's mom, was watching TV one day and saw a program about in vitro pregnancies and other such techniques. One of the experts in this field, according to the TV program, was Dr. Christos Zouves of San Francisco. Angie was ecstatic. Not only had she rediscovered a long-lost relative, but also he was a well-known fertility doctor. She called the number on the TV screen and asked for Dr. Zouves. He called her back and was equally thrilled to rediscover part of his family. He also mentioned that he had searched for the Zouves name on the Web and had seen Maria's name as an opera singer but had no idea that they were related. Angie told him that this Maria was married to the opera singer Sherrill Milnes, whom Christos knew by reputation. She also told him that we were trying to have a child. Maria called Christos immediately, caught up on all family matters, and then explained our dilemma. He had all kinds of ideas, and we decided quickly to go ahead with one of the procedures. Many tests are necessary before any eggs are harvested and sperm is injected, so we did them all and made plans to go to San Francisco in a few months to complete the process with the doctor.

In the meantime, in May 1999, Maria and I had an all-Verdi program to sing in Stuttgart, Germany, with the Stuttgart Philharmonic. We had

Photo courtesy of Erik Ryding

With my wife,
Maria, 2006.

been asked by the American conductor Arthur Fagan to sing this pair
of concerts with him. We went to Stuttgart and had a fine time in that
beautiful city. Besides singing some great arias and duets, I talked Arthur
into letting me conduct the *Vespri siciliani* overture of Verdi, which I had
conducted many times in the United States. It was exciting to lead this
fine orchestra, and both concerts went well. As one of the encores, Maria
and I sang the comic "Cat Duet" by Rossini, announcing it as a recently
discovered, serious composition by this famous bel canto composer.

Some weeks later Maria was singing Zerlina in the Natchez,
Mississippi, opera's production of *Don Giovanni*. She was complaining
that she didn't feel well. Another week after that we were singing in a
gala concert for the Ocean State Opera in Providence, Rhode Island, at
the request of our soprano friend Maria Spacagna. Again she felt a little
weak and unsteady. It was there in Providence that Maria thought to do
the pregnancy test. She left a rehearsal early, and I stayed to finish my
music. When I arrived back at the hotel, Maria had written on the mirror
in lipstick, "We're pregnant." For some reason my immediate comment
was, "Oh, my heaven's sakes." In hindsight it seems a pretty silly and
old-fashioned phrase, something my parents—born in 1901—would have
said. I guess it shows how their influence on me still holds in moments
of seriousness.

Now every symptom Maria had had for the last month made sense. We were thrilled, and after backdating on the calendar, we realized that she had become pregnant in Stuttgart. Almost immediately, we called Christos Zouves in San Francisco to tell him the good news. After he heard, he quipped, "Wow, I'm so good, I can do it long distance!"

Then on January 21, 2000, Theophilos (Theo) Zouves Milnes was born. A darling baby boy, a huge joy, and a big change for me, with three children ranging from thirty-four to forty-seven years old. Diapers, baby-sitting, baby food, milk, formula, car seats, and all the other equipment necessary for a baby became the norm again. I had some aches and pains and took longer to get up and down on the floor to play with Theo, but I remembered everything it takes to raise a child. He is a beautiful boy with a good set of lungs, and he grows every day.

He doesn't remember any of this, of course, but we played Mozart tapes on Maria's tummy his whole prenatal time. Experts claim that there is a Mozart effect that is said to stimulate the mind, and we wanted it in case it was true. Mozart was christened Joannes Chrysostomus Wolfgangus Theophilus Mozart. He himself latinized Theophilus to Amadeus. They have the same meaning: lover or friend of God. Mozart generally signed his letters and compositions either "W. A. Mozart" or "Wolfgang Amadé Mozart." However, Theo's first name did not come from Mozart. His maternal grandmother's, Maria's mother's, maiden name was Theophilou, with the accent on the next to the last syllable. We used her last name as Theo's first name, with the accent on the second syllable. He loves Mozart, Beethoven, and Bach, and sings the Hallelujah Chorus from *Messiah* and the Beethoven Ninth Symphony choral theme, as well as the sound tracks from *Bear in the Big Blue House*, *Shrek*, *A Bug's Life*, *Monsters, Inc.*, *Bob the Builder*, and other such "classical" compositions. People often ask if he will be a singer or conductor. Who knows?

Theo's informal musical instruction continued in November 2000 when Maria was singing the Humperdinck fairy-tale opera *Hansel and Gretel* with the Baltimore Opera. It was the magical Maurice Sendak production staged by Frank Corsaro. Theo had seen and loved the videotape from the Met, in which he especially loved the witch, sung and acted by Rosalind Elias. He attended many rehearsals in Baltimore and was enraptured by the whole process. At the performances he watched from backstage on the teleprompters.

This was a very demanding and precise production with lots of movement from the Hansel and the Gretel. When Maria, as Gretel, was running around in front of the gingerbread house with Hansel, their actions
were very animated and precise. On one of their fast crosses, Maria's
nose crashed into the Hansel's forehead. The forehead won, and all of us
in the audience heard a loud crack. Fortunately this was a performance
that Theo did not see. I saw Maria grab her nose but continue singing.
She finished the evening in pain; her nose was swelling, and it was clear
she had broken it. Later when our doctor, Scott Kessler, saw her, without
any X-ray, he said, "Ow, you have broken your nose right here, I can see
the break." Maria had to fill out the workman's compensation forms,
and when asked to name any witnesses, she wrote, "Thirty-five hundred
witnesses in the audience all heard and saw the accident." Workman's
compensation didn't argue. Her biggest problem in the ensuing weeks
was how to keep her nose away from Theo's hands. Any one-year-old

As Falstaff at the Florida Grand Opera, 1991.

wants to play with mommy's face. More than once she was unsuccessful, much to her chagrin and pain.

Theo also grew to love *Falstaff*. Maria and I had sung it together with the Orlando Opera before Theo was born. Then we sang it together in Pittsburgh as Tito Capobianco's last scheduled opera as the boss of the Pittsburgh Opera. Theo came to many rehearsals, and the Spanish conductor, Theo Alcantara, gave him a small baton to wave around. Little Theo loved that and again watched many parts of the performances on the teleprompters backstage.

One *Falstaff* story not related to Theo concerns a production in Baltimore when the cast was invited to meet a group of the opera board and contributors after a matinee performance. I had said that I thought that it would be better to greet the patrons before we got out of costume, as it would take me a good hour or more to be ready once I started to undress and take off my rather extensive makeup. We all agreed and went right from the stage. As you all know, Falstaff is a very fat man and I wear a fat suit, which makes me about a size 65 portly, if there is such a thing. So I greeted people in costume over my fat suit. I was told afterward that one of the older ladies had commented, "My, Mr. Milnes has really let himself go. What a shame he has been so careless." This also affects Maria when she is in the audience and I am singing Falstaff: she has to say that she is married to the fat guy. That phrase is usually greeted with a stunned silence! The magic of costume and makeup.

CHAPTER SEVENTEEN

Off the Beaten Path

GRADUALLY, AS THE BIGGER BARITONE ROLES became more difficult, I chose not to sing them. However, certain offbeat parts came my way that very much related to my famous bad-guy roles. In all cases they turned out to be interesting and satisfying. In 1996, while I was still singing at the Met, the Teatro Colón in Buenos Aires asked me to sing the two baritone roles in the trio of operas called *Il trittico* by Puccini: the brooding, emotional Michele in *Il tabarro* and the comic part of Gianni Schicchi in the opera of that name. My characters are a great pair of roles because of their contrast. It was also the first time that I had seen banners with my name on them, hanging over various streets in Buenos Aires advertising the operas. I had had a long history with the Colón, starting around 1970, with operas such as *Rigoletto, Un ballo in maschera, I vespri siciliani,* and *Tosca* (three seasons). During the performances of the Puccini operas in 1998, the music director, the late Michelangelo Veltri, asked me if I knew the opera *Fedora* by Umberto Giordano. I only knew the famous tenor aria, "Amor ti vieta," nothing more. He said that the following year the Colón was presenting it with Plácido and, in her Colón debut, Mirella Freni. Veltri went on to say that because the baritone role was smaller, they could only pay about a third less than what they had paid me in the past. Of course, I didn't like the idea of earning less money, but the offer deserved consideration, for the Colón always did many performances of a single opera. So I looked at a score of *Fedora* and saw immediately that this part, that of the French ambassador to Russia, was a big smaller role and clearly the only important baritone part. It looked like Sharpless in

Butterfly, except with a big aria. I also knew that with a cast of Plácido and Mirella (especially in her debut), the production would receive huge publicity. And that, even with a smaller role for me, would mean that I would be included in that trio of stars. I said yes and proceeded to begin my study even while I was still in Buenos Aires.

I have always believed that taking as much time as one can to study a role is best. You can chip away at the part and then leave it when you have to review other music for other performances. It also gives you time to study related background material and to really get the part in your throat, your body, and your emotions.

Often we Americans think that having a role (or a song, for that matter) memorized is the final refinement and do not take time to really digest it and make it our own. It takes time to work music into our throats and our psyches and to develop some "muscle memory" for the words and a deeper understanding of the poetry. That shortchanging or "hurry-up" mentality really shows in performance and can easily make the difference between a reengagement and a "don't call us." The older American and European singers in my experience tended to take more time to study their music.

I worked on *Fedora* on and off for that whole year, and I listened to all the recordings I could find. I am a believer in recordings; there is so much to learn as long as the singer does not simply imitate and memorize it from the recording. The printed score must still be the dominant source and guide. But recordings are a great way to speed up memorization.

I arrived for rehearsals well before Plácido and Mirella. The opera was double cast, and I worked with the other singers for about ten days. The wonderful Romanian singer Nelly Miricioiu, with whom I had sung several times before, was the other soprano. When I have never sung a part before, I want all the rehearsal I can get. In addition, I knew that Plácido and Mirella, having done the opera often, would bring their own characterizations and musicality with them. As it turned out, Plácido only arrived in Buenos Aires the morning of the evening dress rehearsal and I thought he, of course, would mark the whole opera that evening. Well, that son of a gun came to the dress with just a short nap after his European flight and sang the role full voice with a couple of exceptions. I still don't know how he does that, as often as we have sung together.

On the opening night, when Mirella made her first entrance, the audience went absolutely berserk. The orchestra had to stop and wait while the public screamed and yelled. And this was before she had opened her mouth. (The Argentine audiences have always been very vocal, but far more so than usual this time.) After about two minutes, she was finally able to continue, and it was a huge success. All the evenings with our cast sold out instantly. At some point that week, I was asked if I could stick around two more days to sing an extra performance. Any singer knows if you can spend only two extra days of hotel costs for another whole fee—you do the math. Perhaps non-singers don't realize that we are not paid for the rehearsal time, nor do we normally receive a per diem, unlike movies or Actors' Equity theater. You only start earning money when you perform. I was quite happy to stay; they just wanted to start the performance two and a half hours earlier. Sometimes it pays to eavesdrop. I heard one of the secretaries in the opera office asking an airline about schedules and confirming a flight for Plácido on the night of that extra performance leaving at eleven-thirty for Miami. Then I realized why the performance was starting at six-thirty. Plácido had said he could sing the extra night, but only if they started at the earlier hour, so he could make that flight. The next flights were all twenty-four hours later. I asked if they would get two more reservations, because Maria and I also wanted to get home as quickly as possible. The reservations were made, and the morning of the extra performance my then-agent in Buenos Aires, Alex Szterenfeld, came to the hotel with all the money in cash. The Colón always paid at the end of the run, so one left with pockets full. In the meantime I also heard that Plácido had hired a limo with police escort after the performance to get to the airport on time. I asked if there was a problem with me "piggy-backing" in his car, because even with the early starting hour, the schedule would be tight. He was happy to do it, so Maria came to the first act and then left with a driver to collect the bags at the hotel and go to the airport, where she and I would meet later. Plácido and I had planned to rush out after the performance as quickly as possible. As it turned out, even with this extra performance, the audience was still going bananas: tearing up programs and throwing them on the stage, screaming and hollering, whistling, and breaking every fire code that existed. (In every performance, there were people standing or sitting in every aisle.) Then I was told that there was a little ceremony out in the lobby after the performance. The management had made a bronze plaque commemorating these performances, Mirella's debut, the huge success of this production, and Plácido's singing. (In Buenos Aires he's a god.) They called us the "Tres Mostres," after a phrase that the local media had coined. I was thrilled to be one-third of these "mostres" and of this plaque. (The word "mostre" or "mostro" in Spanish or Italian means monster, but in the opera world the phrase is often used as a compliment to mean a big talent, a great voice, and/or one who is powerful onstage.)

Time was slipping away, but finally everything was finished, and we raced out to the waiting limo, a big black Mercedes, with two motorcycle cops on either side. They were wearing those Star Wars–type helmets that reflect like a mirror, and they had their sirens on and revolving lights flashing. The fans were all over the place, yelling and pounding on the top of the car. If I had not known that they loved us, I might have been scared. (It was a little like the scene in *The Godfather* when Al Pacino and the family are in Cuba at the time of the revolution and Batista. All the Cubans are pounding on the roofs of cars, chanting for the revolution, and firing weapons.)

Our Mercedes took off slowly at first, as we were on a heavily trafficked street and, in addition, in the middle of a bus strike. One of the cops would race ahead to the next intersection and stop all traffic, including moving all the striking buses, while we drove through. Then the other cop would race ahead to the next intersection and repeat the process, while the first cop would catch up with us, alternating back and forth, through the downtown area. All the time the lights were flashing and the sirens wailing. Once we reached the highway the driver opened up this sedan to about 220 kilometers an hour (about 130 miles an hour or more). It was all very surreal; it seemed as if we were flying. We reached the airport in about twenty minutes, a trip that ordinarily takes forty-five to fifty minutes. We thanked the driver and the motorcycle cops and ran for the plane. Maria had done all the preliminary check-in procedures. Thank goodness this was before 9/11. We made it with no time to spare, although they actually held the plane a half-hour for Plácido, claiming engine trouble. In my experience only tenors have that kind of clout, and I was glad to benefit from it.

CHAPTER EIGHTEEN

Sly

THE GRAN TEATRE DEL LICEU in Barcelona is one of the best-known opera houses in the world. I first sang there in 1971 in *The Barber of Seville* and subsequently in several productions of *Tosca*. In 1999 they asked me if I would sing the part of Count Westmoreland in *Sly*, by Ermanno Wolf-Ferrari. It was a little-known opera until José Carreras gave it new life with productions all around the world. The title role, Sly, fits him like a glove, but is very difficult to act and sing. My part, Westmoreland, is a mini-Scarpia (the usual baritone bad guy) who completely destroys Sly's life. At that point in my life, I really didn't want to learn a new role, but because of the theater, with which I had some history, and because Carreras was in the cast, I decided that, like the *Fedora* situation, it would be well worth my time. Musically the opera is a bit spotty and lacks some continuity, but it is interesting as a story, and the production in Barcelona was good. I tried to bring my own brand of realism and energy to the part. The whole run of seven performances was very successful, especially because of José. Koch Records made a CD recording live from the theater, which is available.

Possibly because of this success, the famous Gewandhaus in Leipzig, Germany, asked me to sing *Sly* again in concert form in March of 2002. Maestro Fabio Luisi, with whom I had sung many times, was the conductor. Carreras was not available this time, and they had hired an Italian tenor, Alberto Cupido, to sing the title role. I had sung with him before and knew him to be solid. In my mind, however, I wondered if he knew how hard and how long the part was. But I figured, because they had said we could use the music in the performance, there would be no problem. Also, it was none of my business, except. . . .

I was almost on my way to the airport when the telephone rang. It was my Viennese agent, Erich Arthold, who said that Cupido had just canceled. They had tried everywhere for another tenor who knew the part, but no one was available. Would I be able to sing *Tosca* in a semi-staged version instead? I knew that Scarpia was still well in my memory, after maybe two hundred performances. But I was not happy because I had not sung it for several years. And as any older singer knows, without regular singing, the voice loses elasticity and stamina. However, I did not want to lose the date, and I realized the Gewandhaus management wanted to use as many of the *Sly* singers as possible in the *Tosca* cast to avoid paying off contracts without singing. Nelly Miricioiu was again the soprano in *Sly* as she was in *Fedora* in Buenos Aires, and I knew her to be a great Tosca. I was also excited to visit Leipzig, which was the musical home of Johann Sebastian Bach (at St. Thomas's Church); the home of the composer Felix Mendelssohn (who was an early conductor of the Gewandhaus Orchestra); and the longtime residence of Robert Schumann. Obviously a city with a huge musical history and not often visited or appreciated, as it was behind the Iron Curtain for much of my life. So we went.

As I have said, the conductor and the soprano were good friends and I knew several of the other singers from the Hamburg State Opera, so the rehearsals were very friendly and fun. Then as fate would decree, two days before the performance, I got the flu and was hoarse. I was quite angry and frustrated, but there it was. With the flu and the inherent body aches, when your throat is OK, it is sometimes possible to bull your way through, especially with Scarpia, which is a big acting part. But if you are hoarse, it's a different ball game. I couldn't imagine not singing; it would wreck the performance, in this case, twice wrecked. I called Scott Kessler, my friend and laryngologist in New York, and told him the problem. Obviously early and appropriate treatment can sometimes mean the difference between singing and canceling. Dr Kessler gave me a plan, fortunately using some of the medicines I usually carry with me. When I arrived for the performance, I told the management that I was still sick, but I would sing. They knew that I had not been feeling well, so we made an announcement to that effect. All things considered, the performance went well, and while the audience groaned out loud with the announcement, they were soon thrilled with the energy and the intensity of the evening from the whole cast. And I received one the best reviews of my life from the *Leipziger Volkszeitung*. To show you the irony, here is the review in its entirety.

> Sometimes things go wrong. And sometimes that does not matter at all. In this case, it turned from Wolf-Ferrari's *Sly* into Puccini's *Tosca*. And it happened like this: tenor Alberto Cupido got cold feet about one week before the concert performance in the Gewandhaus and he canceled. Too difficult, that *Sly* title role. This swiped Fabio Luisi's wish to "break a lance" for the underestimated Wolf-Ferrari right off the table [foiled his attempt to present this opera]. But postponed is not canceled. An alternative was found quickly: *Tosca*, because Luisi is a phenomenal Puccini interpreter. In the person of the great Sherrill Milnes, he had one guy in his boat anyway who, as Tosca's satanic opponent, Scarpia, had delivered epoch-making stuff on major stages as well as on record labels. And the MDR [Mitteldeutscher Rundfunk] chorus is always good enough to learn such an oeuvre within just a few days. But, as we said—sometimes things go wrong. And so Milnes had it announced yesterday that the flu had gotten him. He would sing, but [he was] "under the weather."
>
> However, what the 67-year-old baritone icon still has to offer even when he is under the weather is an example that many other colleagues in excellent health should seriously take to heart! Sometimes the lascivious legato suffers just a little bit from intensified use of technique. But this technique puts it far beyond any doubt that this Roman police chief still makes the blood freeze in your veins. And Milnes's majestic appearance does its own bit. This man enters the stage, and at once the house is filled with his personality.
>
> To stand next to a legend is not a very gratifying task. But tenor Ki-Chun Park tackles it with supple shine, and in the course of the three acts he continuously improves as the painter Cavaradossi. He does not quite lose his slight inclination toward sharpness. But his power, his dramatic emphasis, his tremendous legato easily make up for this. Nelly Miricioiu completes the first-class trio as Floria Tosca. She is a soprano of the old school, with wonderful legato [and a] remarkable ability to make herself heard with many theatrical effects. But backing her up is Fabio Luisi, accompanying in virtuoso fashion.

Milnes or no Milnes—the principal part is played by the MDR orchestra around concertmaster Waltraud Waechter. Luisi approaches *Tosca* in a symphonic way and helps the piece's own principles to their rights in a way that would be difficult to realize in an opera house. This makes it sometimes difficult for the soloists to make themselves heard, but is on the other hand good for ecstatic beauty. The leaping flames and the uncompromising musical logic with which Luisi prepares Cavaradossi's moving farewell "E lucevan le stelle" at the beginning of the third act are in their emotional immediacy not offered by any recording on the market!

Go figure! You certainly could not have counted on any kind of good review, let alone this rave.

Sly continued to play a part in my operatic life. Plácido was able to sell the Met on the idea of producing this opera with him in the title role. He also convinced them that his wife, Marta, should be the stage director. This was a different physical production from mine in Barcelona. I didn't sing in this production, because by this time my history at the Met was over, but by and large it was a success for them. However, Plácido's company, the Washington Opera, with José in the title role of Sly, decided to tour Japan with three different operas in the summer of 2002. They asked me to sing Westmoreland on this tour. I'm quite sure it was Carreras who asked them to engage me, because he had liked what we did in Barcelona.

Besides another opportunity to visit Japan, I knew it would feel good to be back in the loop, even for just a short time. It was very interesting to work with Marta on a professional level. I had always known her as Plácido's knowledgeable and supportive wife, but never in a working environment. We rehearsed in Washington for ten days and then flew to Japan. Everything went well. I tried to bring some of my ideas from the Barcelona production and work them in with Marta's ideas. Basically everything fit, and we sang three evenings in Tokyo to huge successes. The Japanese seemed to love the opera and the production, and José and I signed autographs and gave away pictures for two hours after each performance. It was obviously a good choice to learn this part, as it was to learn *Fedora* for the Teatro Colón in Buenos Aires.

The traditional Metropolitan Opera tour, about seventeen of which I sang, finally stopped in about 1990. The Met had been touring the country since the turn of the century with singers such as Caruso and others, so the tour had a long, long history. In the early years the Met would present operas in many different cities for a night or two, as in Des Moines, Iowa, when I saw the performances I have described earlier in this book. The tour gradually settled down to seven major cities, a week of performances in each place. My first two tours, 1966 and 1967, were still in the time of trains, so one spent a lot of time with other members of the company because of the travel time together. I heard many stories of the old giants of the Met, especially of all-night poker games with Caruso, Scotti, Gigli, Tibbett, Pinza, even Ponselle, and many others over the years. There was a family feeling. When everyone started flying, because of the shorter travel time and less freedom moving around on planes, and the principal singers flying in and out, the family feeling diminished.

As much as the Met was loved and for all the musical and operatic value it brought to these cities, the tour was rather a two-edged sword. While it was still functioning, many smaller regional companies in those tour cities existed in some form or size. But because of the obvious prestige of the Met, most of the fund-raising went toward bringing it to that city, thereby making it difficult to raise money for the small company. I must say most of the performances on tour were pretty darn good. I sang about thirty of them and enjoyed the excitement, the parties, the first-class hotels, the fans, pictures, and autographs, and the general atmosphere of that week in those major cities. But year after year, the cost of this gargantuan effort mounted; transporting the whole orchestra, chorus, sets, costumes, makeup, and principals finally became just too expensive. In addition, the logistics of an operation that size became a nightmare, and many in the opera company had already begun to dislike touring and being away from their home and families for those many weeks.

When the Met finally stopped touring, the local fund-raising took a different turn, and the existing smaller companies could then tap into a larger source of support. Over the years many of these companies have grown into major organizations, and the Minnesota Opera is one of these.

In 1997 the management of that company asked me if I would be interested in singing the part of Ajax in the American premiere of *Transatlantic*, by George Antheil. This opera had its world premiere in Frankfurt, Germany, on May 25, 1930. And by all reports it was a big success, even though a small group of German nationalistic agitators didn't want American opera at all in German opera houses. They tried to boo the performance but were completely shouted down by the crowd. Antheil's opera is about an American presidential election that is rigged by my character, Ajax, a wealthy oil baron. The opera also looks at the absurd extravagance of America in the 1920s. Even though the opera is critical of our American system of elections, Hitler and his National Socialist Party, which were coming into power at the time, determined that this American opera should not play again. In addition, the depression in Germany at the time caused subsidies of opera houses to be greatly reduced. So it sat rather unperformed until this major production in Minneapolis.

George Antheil (1900–1959) was born in Trenton, New Jersey, and sailed for Europe in 1922, intent on making a career as a pianist. His specialty was new music, including his own, and soon he was hailed as America's first true avant-gardist. Parts of Europe, however, were not ready for his often bizarre behavior and music. Some of his recitals ended in stormy, booing protests, so he kept a gun on the piano, just to remind the audience who was boss. (How weird was that?) He turned to this opera subject about America and rigged elections in hopes that he could redeem himself in the eyes of the music public in Europe. It is ironic that the politics of the time cut short the life of this opera about the politics of the time, albeit in different countries.

Antheil wrote in a very eclectic style—some very dissonant music, some jazz, and some blues. I think it is clear that Antheil wanted to shock his audience. During these performances in the Ordway Hall in

As Nabucco, in the
half mask, in the
ill-fated 1978 Paris
production. *Left
to right:* Viorica
Cortez, me, Grace
Bumbry. You can
see the shield that
nearly caused me a
serious injury!

With Luciano Pavarotti in *Un Ballo in Maschera*, Hamburg, c. 1974.

As Don Giovanni at the Salzburg Festival, Kleines Festspielhaus, 1978.

Singing a recital for President Ford in the East Room of the White House, 1976.

With Tony Randall on the set of Tony's television show *Love, Sidney*, 1981.

As Amonasro at the Metropolitan Opera, 1990.

With Joan Sutherland in *I Puritani* at the Metropolitan Opera, 1976.

As Iago in *Otello* at the Metropolitan Opera, 1972.

At the Metropolitan Opera opening, 1988, *left to right*, Fiorenza Cossotto, me, Nancy Reagan, Luciano Pavarotti, and Éva Marton.

"Is this a dagger I see before me?" *Macbeth*, Vienna State Opera, 1972.

In the title role of *Rigoletto*, San Francisco Opera, 1973.

With Jon Spong, my lifelong accompanist and friend, 1989.

As Simon Boccanegra with Kiri Te
Kanawa in London's Royal Opera House,
Covent Garden, 1985.

With my brother, Roe, at the dedication of
the Milnes Family Memorial Park, Downers
Grove, Illinois, early 1980s.

With Beverly Sills in *Thaïs* at San Francisco Opera, 1977.

With famed movie bad guy Christopher Lee, one of my dearest friends, at a UNICEF fund-raiser in Munich, February 1996.

Recording *The Barber of Seville*, c. 1976, with Nicolai Gedda.

As Scarpia in the first act of *Tosca* at the Metropolitan Opera, c. 1980.

With Zefferelli on the set of Verdi's *Otello,*
Metropolitan Opera, 1972.

With conductor Karl Böhm at Salzburg, 1978, with baritone Dale
Duesing in the background.

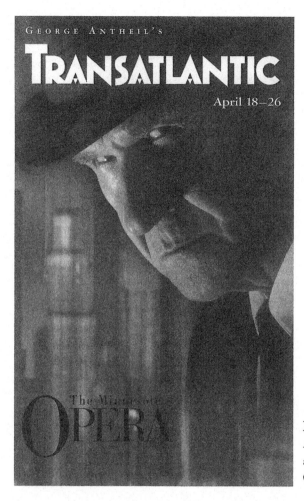

Poster for George
Antheil's *Transatlantic*
at the Minnesota
Opera, 1997.

St. Paul, some of the audience was clearly shocked: I saw them leaving in
the middle of certain scenes where the dissonance was quite upsetting.
Musically I was not thrilled by it, but as a production it was stunning.
As my wife put it, "It was a wild ride." Every modern stage device used
on Broadway today was employed to the maximum. My evil, ruthless,
cigar-smoking character was great fun to play. And in what I called my
cigar choreography (I used several in an evening)—lighting up, smoking,
chewing, pointing, snuffing out, and so on—I did everything a modern
boss can do with a cigar. It made playing my part quite easy, as long as
I could find the right notes. This production was a big success for the
Minnesota Opera, if you ignore the few people who left.

CHAPTER NINETEEN

The Judge

IN THE SUMMER OF 2001 WELZ KAUFMAN, the boss of the Ravinia Festival in Chicago, asked me to sing the part of the Judge in Stephen Sondheim's *Sweeney Todd*, with George Hearn and Patti LuPone. The same cast, including all the other principals, had done the production with the New York Philharmonic the year before, except for the part of the Judge. I really did not know *Sweeney Todd* very well and certainly not the part of the Judge. I borrowed a score and saw that the part was rather difficult for a Broadway piece. I then was told that the aria originally written for the Judge, which had been deleted from the Broadway run because it was too ribald, was to be included. The aria made the part bigger and more impressive, but it was very wordy and I didn't realize how hard it was going to be to memorize. However, with that cast and the prestige of the Ravinia Festival, I said yes. As I studied the previously cut aria, I realized why it had been deleted for Broadway.

The Judge is an old, rather decrepit curmudgeon who spies on his young ward, Johanna, watching her through the keyhole when she dresses and undresses in her bedroom. During the aria he actually comes to orgasm while watching her undress. How one shows that in front of an audience escaped me at first and I suppose scared me as well. But I eventually found that with certain vocal effects and certain body movements, I could convey the idea clearly enough. But I must say that it was more than a little embarrassing for me and took complete suspension of my normal inhibitions to carry it off. There was one other dynamic going on as well. I hadn't been the freshman in a cast for a long time. I was normally the old-timer. Now, because most of the cast had performed it before, I had to fit into an already existing staging. There was no time for new ideas, and the rehearsal time was short. I realized that as the newcomer, I had to know the piece twice as well as the others to fit in quickly and smoothly. They were all very nice to me, but all knew exactly what to do and expected me to do the same with some rather tricky staging and dialogue, which I was not used to.

You know the story. Sweeney Todd, "the Demon Barber of Fleet Street," murders his shaving customers by slitting their throats and dumping their corpses down a chute to the basement. There they are ground up to make fillings for meat pies. This strange and bizarre story does make a great show. Lyric Opera of Chicago included it in their season of 2002 with Bryn Terfel in the title role. It was a big success.

However, I don't think I want to do the part again, partly for orgasmic reasons and partly because of the possibility of a major screwup with memory. There was only one scheduled performance, but because the demand for tickets was so great, they sold seats for the dress rehearsal, which made it a performance as well. And that sold out too. That evening I remembered everything well, which may have given me unwarranted confidence in the real performance. Because the next night (I thought I was concentrating), I "went up" in the middle of the aria. As I said, the words were tricky and rapid-fire and didn't always follow logically. So just before the "orgasm" moment, my memory jumped a page. It took a few seconds before I realized that I was way off. The piece was just too angular to fall into place easily, and the conductor was in back of me, so he really couldn't help or cue. So there I was having an orgasm in front of three thousand people, with no idea where I was musically. Now *that* is embarrassing! The only saving grace was that the audience didn't know the piece, so perhaps they thought that was the way it went. After what seemed like an eternity, I finally found my way back to the right spot and finished the aria. It took all my experience to disguise my humiliation and keep going with the dialogue that ensued. (Remember I was considered the big opera star doing an important character part.) Fortunately, the duets with George Hearn and the rest of the evening went very well. I apologized to Stephen Sondheim after, saying that I owed him several bars of music, but I didn't owe him another climax.

Then, the day after *Sweeney Todd*, I left for Ireland to give one week of master classes and a concert at Limerick University in Ireland. At first (now I'm showing my ignorance), I thought the name was a joke. We Americans think of a limerick as a funny rhyme. But it was bona fide, and Limerick is, in fact, a fine and large university, about one hour south of Shannon by car. The concert at the end of the week was with the singers doing half the program and me doing the other half. I was looking forward to this, especially because my maternal third great-grandfather was Irish. I'd been in Ireland only once before, in Dublin to sing a recital, and I'd enjoyed it immensely. (It was then I was introduced to Guinness. It does taste better in Ireland!) The singers I worked with were from all over the United Kingdom, quite good and very cooperative. We worked hard for six days and then presented the concert. The singers did well and then it was my turn. It is always difficult to sing when you've been teaching six hours a day. A teacher uses his or her voice unselfishly, and it is always fatigued at the end of the day. However, I had managed to save enough voice.

In those years I was presenting a program called "Memories and Music." I would tell some operatic stories and highlight them with music. Naturally I told the Irish audience that my ancestor, Matthew Lyon, was born in Ireland in 1747. (This is described in detail earlier in the book.) I mentioned to the audience that I was sorry that I would not have enough time to visit my ancestor's hometown of Wicklow and that I was very curious to see what it looked like now. The audience laughed out loud and yelled back at me almost in unison: "It looks the same now as it did in 1747." I still have not seen my ancestral town.

CHAPTER TWENTY

Master Classes

ALL THROUGH MY CAREER, starting in about 1960, anytime I sang an opera, recital, or concert I suggested a class or at least an informal meeting with the local singers. For years I just offered them for no cost, but gradually, as I became more famous, I was able to charge for them. Most of all I loved teaching, but I also knew that the teaching was an investment in the future. As I grew older, various schools talked of jobs on their faculty. But while I was still in a full world career, it was too soon.

I know that the following list is long, but I want to give a sense of the breadth of my experience. By the year 2000, I had already taught master classes at the Juilliard School; the Manhattan School of Music; the Mannes School of Music, Yale University; the University of Michigan; the University of Illinois; Peabody Conservatory; Oberlin College; the University of Southern California; Northwestern University; the University of Texas at Austin; the College Conservatory of Music in Cincinnati, Ohio; Drake University in Des Moines, Iowa; the Conservatory of Music at the University of Missouri at Kansas City; the University of Kansas; Florida State University; the University of South Florida; the University of Kentucky; Brigham Young University; the University of North Carolina; the University of South Carolina; the University of Maryland, Westminster Choir College; Portland State University; and many smaller schools and private classes in the United States.

Outside of the United States, I had taught in Seoul, Korea; Tokyo, Japan; Taiwan; Beijing and Shanghai, China; the Tchaikovsky

Conservatory in Moscow; Turin, Italy; Vienna; Prague and Brno, Czech Republic; the Royal Opera House, Covent Garden, London; Teatro Colón, Buenos Aires; the Palacio de Bellas Artes, Mexico City; the Royal Northern College of Music in Manchester, England (where they made me a "fellow," an honor much like our honorary doctor's degree); Limerick University in Ireland; and the Mozarteum in Salzburg.

On balance I suppose I have taught more than four hundred master classes over the years. Since 1990 I had also been on the faculty, part-time, at the Yale Opera School, coaching and giving master classes, an involvement that I only recently stopped. I was brought to Yale by the then dean of the School of Music, the well-known American composer Ezra Laderman, whose music I had premiered several times.

Years ago CBS television had two half-hour segments on Sunday morning, which they called sustaining programs. They were "Lamp Unto My Feet" and "Wake Up and Live" and were usually religious in nature. They were unsponsored, so CBS could program what they wanted. CBS even had an orchestral conductor on staff, Alfredo Antonini, an experienced older Italian gentleman, and they hired an orchestra when needed. (Those days are long gone, of course.) Antonini had probably stayed on there from the time of the Toscanini era and the great NBC Orchestra. No one will ever forget the wonderful symphonic concerts and the concert opera performances in Studio H at NBC and in Carnegie Hall with Toscanini conducting. Another reason for this musical awareness was the influence of the then boss of NBC, David Sarnoff. This period was a phenomenon in American television, when orchestra concerts were a normal part of broadcasting. It was to the credit of CBS that they continued part of this tradition long after the NBC Orchestra was canceled.

Maestro Antonini conducted many, many programs on Sunday morning, and I had seen some of them while I was still on the farm in Chicago. In 1966 my agent, Joe Lippman, arranged an audition for Maestro Antonini, who asked me to sing the part of Joseph in Berlioz's oratorio *L'enfance du Christ* (*The Birth of Christ*). Giorgio Tozzi, Charles Anthony, and Helen Vanni completed the cast. It was all done with ballet beautifully staged and danced by the well-known Carmen de Lavallade and Glen Tetley. In subsequent seasons CBS presented two oratorios by Ezra Laderman: *The Questions of Abraham* and *And David Wept*, with words by Joe Darian of *Man of La Mancha* fame. The words and music of both of these pieces were a perfect blend and a tour de force for the baritone. Ezra also wrote a short cantata for me about Abraham Lincoln for a special Lincoln anniversary broadcast.

One experience taught me a valuable lesson in communication. It's what I call the "moonlight on the water" image. The director for both Ezra's pieces was Jerry Schure, a veteran director. The beginning of *And David Wept* was a long intro with the camera slowly dollying in on me. I had just barely memorized the part and was understandably nervous. As we started the first take, the camera was moving in and my heart was beating faster as I silently counted the measures before my entrance. From the control booth, Jerry called out "Stop!" He told me to relax, that I look nervous. So I shook my arms and hands and thought, Relax, relax. We started again. At about the same spot, Jerry called out again, "Stop, I'm coming in." He came up to me and said, "OK, Sherrill, just relax, you're looking nervous. Think of 'moonlight on the water' or some other such image to free you up." I, of course, tried that image and thought, Relax, relax. I was looking nervous. We tried once more and I thought of everything I could to look relaxed. Finally we just ran out of time, and Jerry couldn't stop. I was hoping that "moonlight on the water" had done something, but when it was broadcast, the opening of my scene showed me with my arms extending away from my body. When we are nervous that extra energy normally feeds through the extremities, in this case making my arms stick out. If Jerry had just said my arms were sticking out, I could have fixed it in an instant. Jerry was an image director, so he was not telling me exactly what was happening, I ended up in that opening scene looking foolish. "Moonlight on the water" did not tell me anything, nor did it help in any way. What I am saying is that being specific and calling it as it is is the way to go.

CHAPTER TWENTY-ONE

Conducting

A BIG THRILL FOR ME WAS MY CARNEGIE HALL conducting debut of Mendelssohn's *Elijah* in 1998, with Mid America Productions. The long musical history with that towering masterpiece and the emotional history with my mother over the years made that night in Carnegie very special. The orchestra was the Brooklyn Philharmonic, and we had a group of fine soloists, including Mark Delevan, one of America's best baritones singing today.

In 1999 I returned to my mother's organization, the Downers Grove Choral Society, and led the Brahms *Requiem* on the fortieth anniversary of the founding of the society. Maria was the soprano soloist. In 2004 we returned there for *Messiah*. Maria and I teamed up again for the Brahms *Requiem* with perhaps the finest amateur choir I know, the Annapolis Chorale in Maryland, prepared by their music director, Ernest Greene. Soon after I conducted another *Elijah*, this time with a group of combined choirs in Greensboro, North Carolina.

A singing of *Elijah* that I remember with great affection was in Oklahoma City in June 2001. John Dexter (not to be confused with the British stage director) had been a choir director at the Plymouth Congregational Church in Des Moines. I had sung with him on several occasions, and we had become very friendly during my college years. He was a fine organist and choral conductor who performed many interesting and challenging works in Des Moines. He was turning eighty in 2001 and wanted to conduct the *Elijah* as his farewell to his church in Oklahoma City. Coincidentally, it turned out to be the last sung *Elijah* of my life, so it was a farewell for me too.

Conducting a concert in Prague, 1988.

In 1999 Michael Chang, the boss of the Memphis Opera, invited me to conduct *Aida* for that company the following season. I was excited but somewhat reluctant. As I have mentioned before, I had conducted several oratorios and sacred works such as *Messiah*, *Elijah*, *Judas Maccabeus*, the Brahms Requiem, and various short orchestral works and had conducted various orchestras in my life such as the Met Orchestra, the Boston Symphony, the Milwaukee Symphony, the Miami Philharmonic, and a host of regional orchestras. I had led the New Philharmonia Orchestra in London, where Plácido Domingo and I conducted arias for each other on an RCA recording. None of these, of course, were complete operas. I knew that *Aida* was a handful, but on balance I felt confident enough of my conducting skills to accept.

I knew that the legendary Komische Opera boss, Walter Felsenstein, believed that the conductor must participate in all rehearsals and become an important partner of the stage director. At some point in the final

One of my mentors and good friends, maestro Erich Leinsdorf, c. 1975.

rehearsals the stage director has to give up the production to the cast. Felsenstein also understood that during the performances the conductor is the only active stage director, the defender of the validity and intelligibility of the concept, and the friend of the singing actor. I made sure that I would be in Memphis for every moment of the rehearsals.

I had about a year to prepare, so I used Erich Leinsdorf's recording on RCA with Leontyne, Plácido, Grace Bumbry, Ruggero Raimondi, and myself, as well as several other versions, to put all the orchestral sounds completely in my ear. I had sung *Aida* often, so most of the sonorities were already part of me. I also spent some hours with Arthur Fagan, of whom I have spoken earlier. Arthur had conducted *Aida* many times in major houses and gave me insights as well as conducting tips. I knew that this engagement would be an ultimate test, because although the Memphis Symphony is a fine regional orchestra, they don't play *Aida* as a regular part of their repertoire. This meant that I really had to teach them the opera, testing my rehearsal skills. I was lucky to have a good cast for my first *Aida*—that made my life easier.

There is a dynamic in opera rehearsals that conductors sometimes miss. It only happens when the conductor is not there for the initial staging period. The stage director and the cast work together for days putting the opera on its feet, and they become a cohesive team. The cast feels comfortable and even affectionate toward the stage director and vice versa. Then the conductor arrives, and he or she must try to become an integral part of the already existing team. The conductor is sometimes resented or at least resisted, often without the singers even realizing it. In addition, tempos without the conductor present are not always performance tempos, which changes the timing of actions and reactions. It takes time for the singers and stage director to make the necessary adjustments and more time for the conductor to become an integral part of the team. Often these dynamics are not spoken or even thought about, but they do exist in the minds of the cast. All this is my way of saying that the conductor should be there from day one.

Conducting the New Philharmonia Orchestra in a recording session, c. 1975.

CHAPTER TWENTY-TWO

Marking

ANOTHER SKILL IN A CAREER that is often talked about, used, and needed, but seldom analyzed or explained, is marking (singing half-voice, or saving the voice where necessary). It is a difficult subject to write about, partly because one cannot easily give vocal examples in the written word, and partly because every singer has different musical and vocal skills, so what works for one singer may not be valid for another. Marking is really a matter of degree, and sometimes just dropping a few high notes is all that is necessary. The singers themselves must decide how much marking, if any, serves their purpose. When singers are ill, marking is almost mandatory, naturally depending on what kind of illness it is and what a laryngologist says. Often in this case the singer should not be singing at all and should therefore cancel those rehearsals. But assuming that he or she feels able to gain some benefit from, and needs, the rehearsal, the following thoughts may be helpful.

The ideal situation is to have enough rehearsal time to be able to sing full voice most of the time. Then you can really put the music in your throat and in your body and explore the poetry and deeper meanings with the full energy of singing out. This, unfortunately, does not happen often. Normally an opera will rehearse for ten days to two and a half weeks from arrival to first performance. (It is assumed that the singer has done all his or her homework ahead of time, translating, making sure rhythms and notes are correct, memorizing well, reading all related materials, doing other study of the period of the work and composer, etc.)

Generally the stage director does not mind and even expects the singer to mark in early blocking rehearsals. Often the conductor, pianist, and singers will run through the scene or aria to be staged and find out just how thoroughly prepared it is. If all is well, they will start to stage. If memories are shaky, or if there are wrong notes or rhythms or pronunciation problems in that language, the staging moves much more slowly.

There is no automatic right way to save the voice; a few of the techniques are taking some focus out of the sound, singing with a smaller core of sound, singing some passages down the octave, and certainly dropping some or all of the high notes. Be very, very careful, however, to keep the rhythmic accuracy and pitch sense on the money, even when you are singing down the octave. What often happens is that we singers give up intensity and accuracy when we mark. The stage director will resent it if we give no emotional intensity, and the conductor will resent it if we give no rhythmic intensity. We do ourselves a disservice by under-energizing and losing the vocal sweep. We also lose that opportunity to strengthen our own musical and vocal systems.

As soon as a scene is on its feet and running, sing it out. This gives the director, the conductor, and the other singers an insight into what you can do. It's no secret that our reactions, energies, and timings are different when we are singing full voice. Too much marking defeats that necessary input for the conductor and director.

Much marking after that point is common sense. A general rule is that you should sing full at the orchestra rehearsals. The conductor and the orchestra need to hear you, just as you need to hear them. However, sometimes, when the orchestra repeats certain passages for their own purposes, it is perfectly fine to mark the repeats.

Singing in voice mandates vocalizing before, which usually means getting up earlier in the morning. Greater discipline is needed, less partying, more sleep, less casual talking, less drinking, and so on. The closer you get to orchestra rehearsals and performances, the more disciplined you must become.

A normal pattern of final rehearsals for opera companies is a *Sitzprobe*, a seated rehearsal, with orchestra, about a week before the opening, in which you should sing. I personally prefer the kind of rehearsal the Germans call a *Wandelprobe*, where you are onstage and do the movements while singing with the orchestra. Then you are rehearsing the music and the staging at the same time, so you can find out where there may be problems. Usually the next rehearsal is the first time onstage in the set, with piano, where marking is recommended; then the following rehearsal is often with the orchestra in the set, where you should sing. Then a piano tech rehearsal follows, where some marking is fine, even necessary. When there is an orchestra rehearsal the day before the final dress, you should probably mark some during it, so that in the dress you feel like singing as in a performance. Normally you have a day of rest between the dress rehearsal and the opening. Don't party, always be disciplined, and rest! On the rare occasion when the dress rehearsal is the day before the opening, you may have to mark some to be in your best voice for the performance. The opera company wants you in your best voice.

A few other thoughts: there is no reason to mark the smaller roles; when every other singer is marking, don't be the only one to sing full; and when every other singer is singing out, don't be the only one to mark.

A story about marking, admittedly exaggerated but true, took place in a production I sang in Barcelona. An Italian bass-baritone was singing a short but important role with some big singing in it. We had about three weeks for rehearsals, and most of us sang out enough for the musical and stage forces to know what we could do. This Italian singer, however, marked all the time. Every high note was dropped, and although his dramatic energy was OK, no one ever heard him sing it in voice. He was quite simpatico and I liked him, but I could see that the forces at the opera house were unhappy, not knowing if he could really sing the role. I knew that he was worried about the part, and even though he did sing a little more at the *Sitzprobe*, it was not sufficient to satisfy the conductor. In the last week the opera house brought in an American singer who had sung the role elsewhere to replace the Italian or at least scare him into singing. Finally they did let him sing the performances, but I don't think he had any idea how close he was to being fired.

He almost lost his job because he never showed what he could do. But the more important point is that he threw away the opportunity to grow and strengthen in the part. With three weeks of rehearsal, one can grow a lot. He obviously did not know this.

In saving your voice, some conductors and stage directors are more understanding than others. Then it really becomes a matter of human relations. Don't be afraid to talk to them about what you intend to do, how you feel that particular day, and what they need from you. Fatigue is, I suppose, the most common ailment. (If that's an ailment.) But we singers sometimes use fatigue as a constant excuse for being lazy or not taking enough time to vocalize to be ready to sing out. As long as you give enough energy and voice for your own growth and show your colleagues and the director and conductor what you can and will do with a role, you will accomplish all that is necessary.

CHAPTER TWENTY-THREE

V.O.I.C.Experience

MARIA AND I HAD ALWAYS THOUGHT ABOUT starting an opera program to help young singers bridge the gap between university training and a successful career. In 2000, with the help of a few others, we came up with the name V.O.I.C.Experience, which stands for "vocal and operatic intensive creative experience." It is rather grand sounding, but "V.O.I.C.Experience" rolls nicely off the tongue. After coining the name and logo V.O.I.C.Experience and obtaining a not-for-profit status, we established programming in New York at the famed Players Club, in Chicago, and the main summer event at Disney World in Orlando, Florida. One of our rationales for holding our summer event there was that "nobody doesn't like Disney World," and besides, my wife, as a Floridian, was a "Disney kid." To the beautiful ambience at the Coronado Springs Resort we invite sixty or so singers to study and interact with some of the best voice teachers and coaches in the country, as well as stars from both the operatic and theatrical worlds, such as Martina Arroyo, Joan Dornemann, Jennifer Larmore, Tony Randall (before his death), Sam Ramey, Renata Scotto, Maria Spacagna, and Fritz Weaver. Master classes and intensive private coachings are offered every day. We emphasize opera as drama, concentrating on acting while still retaining a focus on the more traditional musical values. As I write this, we are in our sixth year. It has been a big success. It takes a huge amount of time on Maria's part, as she is really the workhorse and the brains behind the program. I work hard teaching and coaching in the summer, but she works hard year round. It was difficult at the beginning to convince the

Disney people that this was something they wanted to deal with. Opera and the other fine arts are not priorities at Disney World. But Maria persevered and found some receptive ears. Now they are happy with our presence there, and we present concerts of opera and Broadway to "the mouse" with great success. We are proud of our work in helping singers

At the Players Club, mid 1990s with, *left to right*, Gregory Peck, Lauren Bacall, Celeste Holm, and others.

The V.O.I.C.Experience at the Players Club in New York City, 2006.

to look at their singing in a realistic manner—a reality check, if you will. Because most contests in the world have an age cutoff, some singers are deprived of career advancement when they reach thirty years of age or so. So we decided to include older singers as well, whose careers may be off track or whose plans might have been derailed by family matters. Whatever the dilemma is, we try to help.

CHAPTER TWENTY-FOUR

Northwestern University

As I REDUCED MY SINGING and added more teaching and conducting to my activities, I was looking to gradually add one or two more schools to my master class schedule. Northwestern University was one of those schools where I had presented mini-residencies over the years, and there had been conversations about faculty status. Finally in 2000, the dean of the School of Music, Bernard Dobroski, began to talk seriously to me about joining the staff. To quote *The Godfather*, "He made me an offer I couldn't refuse." I had always had an affectionate spot in my heart for Northwestern because I had matriculated there in 1960–61, studying voice and opera workshop. I sang performances of *Dialogues of the Carmelites* by Poulenc and *Don Pasquale* by Donizetti. My then voice teacher, Hermanus Baer, was the head of the voice department, Robert Gay was the new head of the opera department, and Thor Johnson was the orchestral conductor. So Northwestern had the edge for me in academia. The timing was just right for my life: forty-two years of singing professionally, a new family, moving back to my home territory of northern Illinois, and tenure at the school from day one. (Anyone in academia knows the value of tenure.) I also loved my title: the John Evans Distinguished Professor of Music. John Evans was one of the founders of Northwestern University 150 years ago and the man for whom the town of Evanston was named. I agreed to begin a new phase of my life and commuted from New York to Chicago for one year. That was tough—hotels, airports, taxis, and suitcases. After that year the three of us moved to Illinois. The Chicago area is beautiful in the late spring and summer, but the winters are brutal, and all the memories of winters on the farm early in my life came back.

Notwithstanding the cold, Northwestern is a great university, especially the School of Music. There has been a long list of distinguished deans: George Howerton, the dean in my time (1959–61); Tom Miller, under whom I did many mini-residencies; and the master of fund raising, the musically passionate Bernie Dobroski. He stepped down as dean in July 2003 but is still part of the Northwestern family as an emeritus professor and our friend. I know that all the faculty is enjoying working with the new dean, Toni-Marie Montgomery. She comes here with a fine record and is a lovely person as well as a fine pianist. She is very focused, organized, and intent on making Northwestern an even greater music school than it is now.

Halfway through my third year at Northwestern, in January 2003, I was asked if I would narrate a collection of poems by Dame Edith Sitwell, called *Façade*, set to music by Sir William Walton in the 1920s. I have narrated a few pieces in my career, notably *The Survivor from Warsaw* by Arnold Schoenberg, and I was happy to expand my Sprechstimme repertory. This request was from the professional chamber music series at Pick-Staiger Auditorium at Northwestern with mostly Chicago Symphony faculty instrumentalists. I had heard Tony Randall narrate *Façade* before and had his recording with Arthur Fiedler. There are other recordings out there that use a male and a female voice. I liked the idea of two voices, which automatically produce a wider palette of colors. *Façade* has twenty-one poems, each with a narrator. Some of them are very difficult and very fast, and all of them are very precise rhythmically. I asked Maria if she would be interested in looking at the work and dividing it up. She has always been very expressive with her voice and was very interested. With your permission again, here is a review from a *Chicago Tribune* critic for this non-singing performance.

> Chamber music concerts that draw packed houses on eyeball-freezing January nights? It may seem unlikely, but Northwestern University's Winter Chamber Music Festival keeps doing it. It offered two works, William Walton's *Façade* and Mozart's "Gran Partita" Serenade in B-flat (K. 361), an imaginative pairing of two wildly different styles. The performers were top-level musicians from the Northwestern faculty and the Chicago Symphony Orchestra, mostly woodwind players, but

including cello, string bass, percussion and—in the case of *Façade*—two impeccable reciters of Edith Sitwell's off-the-wall poetry, baritone Sherrill Milnes and soprano Maria Zouves.

If the meanings aren't clear, the moods are, and Walton's settings fit them exactly. His parodies of musical styles—folk, jazz, waltz, hornpipe—are witty and admirably crafted. For musical substance *Façade* is close to the vanishing point, but for cleverness and charm it is a classic. Milnes and Zouves were virtuoso reciters. They put on a verbal ballet, making their voices swoop, croon, growl, simper, or go on tiptoe, always in faithful service to the text.

Would that one could always receive such praise.

I am happy teaching, coaching, conducting, judging vocal competitions the world over, singing much less, and being a father to our six-year-old. I feel as Christa Ludwig must have felt when she said upon her retirement, "I like my time in life when I can welcome a cold and

With Maria and our dear friend Barry Tucker, founder of the Richard Tucker Music Foundation, 1996.

not worry." Although it is clear that I still sing a bit, I always make sure that I have a realistic assessment of my vocal possibilities and program accordingly. But partial retirement from singing makes life easier. One can teach with a cold.

Nor do I miss my time in New York, probably because we go back with some regularity, visiting friends, and attending the Richard Tucker Music Foundation meetings (I am still one of the vice presidents) and annual gala, our foundation V.O.I.C.Experience programs at the Player Club, the George London Foundation events, and other musical affairs.

We moved to Chicago in June 2001. On that fateful day, September 11, 2001, I happened to be sitting in a Chrysler dealership in Skokie, Illinois, waiting for my car to be serviced. They had a small lounge with a TV for customers and I was watching the *Today* show on NBC. As many millions in the United States watched live, we saw the Twin Towers attacked and fall to the ground. It was the first such organized terrorist activity on our soil ever, and as you all well know, it has changed the attitude in New York, the country, and the whole world forever. I was glad that we lived in Chicago at that moment, but we all felt horror and anger at the event. I don't have to mention the extreme change in travel security, which I'm certain is in place forever. These changes have been written about extensively, so I won't spend more time on it here, but we all feel the difference every time we visit New York or check into any airport in the world.

At the Richard Tucker Memorial,
Lincoln Center, mid-1980s.

CHAPTER TWENTY-FIVE

BBC Cardiff Singer of the World Competition

I WANT TO MENTION THIS COMPETITION in Cardiff, Wales, because of its extremely high quality of talent and its extremely high level of organization. For some strange reason this competition is not as well-known in the United States as it is in Europe, but it should be. It is the competition where in 1989 Dmitri Hvorostovsky took the first prize and Bryn Terfel took the lieder award. Quite a pair of winners!

The event is held every two years, and I was asked to be one of the judges in June 1999. The other judges were Joan Sutherland, Carlo Bergonzi, Anthony Freud (head of the Welsh National Opera), Brian McMaster (head of the Edinburgh Festival), and others, seven in all. All music is sung with orchestra if it has been orchestrated. Two orchestras are used, the Welsh National Opera Orchestra and the BBC Wales Orchestra, and two different conductors, Carlo Rizzi as the former music director of the WNO and various other veteran conductors. One singer from each country represented, twenty-five in total, is picked. We hear five singers each night and pick a winner. Then at the finals we hear those five singers and choose from them the Cardiff Singer of the World. Sometimes a singer who did not win his or her evening can end up in the finals if we deem that singer better than another evening's winner.

We judges were treated with the utmost care and respect. The BBC televises the whole affair, and people all over the United Kingdom watch it with tremendous interest. The BBC is to be commended wholeheartedly for its support, enthusiasm, and sponsorship. This year it was on the Internet as well, and fans all over the world viewed it. People are adamant about their choice of singers. People approached us judges on the street sometimes and told us who their favorite was, and who we should vote for, and so on.

I was asked to judge again in June 2003, when the judges were Gundula Janowitz, Galina Vishnevskaya, Dennis O'Neill, Luigi Ferrara (the head of the Wexford Festival), Anthony Freud, and Brian McMaster again. Once more it was wonderfully sorted out, with every detail organized thanks to an extraordinary individual in Cardiff named Anna Williams. To her goes huge appreciation and thanks for making the event so successful. The singers on the panel are generally asked to give master classes to the participants who do not finish in the finals. Those I especially enjoy. An audience-favorite award was added to the event, which everyone loved, and the final presentation was again televised live. Would that that could happen in the United States!

When I judge this Cardiff competition and many others around the world, I am always thrilled when a great voice comes along. I don't believe that I am jealous when I hear someone good, even a baritone; I rejoice in their talent. I hope that my attitude remains. Some of it has to be the satisfaction of forty-two years of active singing and thousands of performances. I am happy with what I've done and with my place in operatic history. I remember what Bob Merrill said to me when we first met in the old Met: "Welcome, there's always room at the top." I hope I can always say that when the talent warrants it.

CHAPTER TWENTY-SIX

Honors

OVER THE YEARS I have been one of the myriad of voters to decide on the Kennedy Center Honorees. Since the inception of the Kennedy Center Honors in 1978, I attended a few of the ceremonies in the 1980s, notably when Beverly Sills was honored and Carol Burnett and I sang some duets for her. Then, in the last few years, quite a few friends of my friends have been honored: Van Cliburn, Victor Borge, Plácido Domingo, Luciano Pavarotti, Joan Sutherland, Beverly Sills, Itzhak Perlman, and James Levine. So naturally Maria and I went, in some cases performing onstage or giving the toast at the Secretary of State's dinner the night before the big show. The performance, which is filmed by CBS and shown in late December, is always a smash, and we thoroughly enjoy it. There are some upsides besides the obvious stargazing. In the 2001 honors, after singing for Luciano's segment, we went to our hotel after the dinner. We had agreed to meet Robert Goulet and his wife for a drink. In the lounge was a group of *famosi*, namely Ron Silver, Jeremy Irons, Lorne Michaels, Jack Nicholson, Michael Douglas, Warren Beatty, and Annette Bening. The Goulets and the Milneses, of course, joined the group, especially because I had sung that night and they all recognized me. Now that was fun, with Jack Nicholson and Michael Douglas buying me drinks and chatting away!

At the Kennedy Center Honors in 2004, *clockwise from upper left*, Samuel Ramey, me, Marilyn Horne, and Joan Sutherland (the honoree of the evening).

It seems that when you reach a certain age (generally at retirement time, whether you retire or not), some people want to honor you. I was made a commendatore of the Italian Republic and a chevalier of the French Republic, honors I love. I was recently inducted into the Lincoln Academy, the highest honor the state of Illinois can bestow, since I was already in the DuPage County Heritage Gallery right next to Billy Graham. I was also honored by Opera Index, a large, well-known opera club in New York, and was voted an outstanding alumnus of my high school alma mater in Downers Grove. In October 2003 I was inducted into the American Academy of Arts and Sciences in Boston, which was started by John Adams, our second president. To see my name side by side with the names of many of the giants of American history is very thrilling and humbling at the same time. But it does reaffirm one's faith in a greater being and confirms that you have been doing something right.

CHAPTER TWENTY-SEVEN

Labors
of Love

I HAVE MADE THREE VIDEOS OVER THE YEARS of which I am very proud: a master-class video from the Juilliard School of Music; *Sherrill Milnes: An All-Star Gala*; and *Homage to Verdi*. I call them labors of love because they were all made on a shoestring budget and I was paid basically nothing for them. But I own them and am proud of them. Some are available commercially.

The one-and-a-half-hour master-class tape from Juilliard was condensed from the filming of five hours of teaching over two days. Master classes are uneven in their interest for a video public, so we reduced this tape to the most exciting moments from these nine of the best singers at the time at Juilliard.

The *Homage to Verdi* was made on location in Italy in 1975. It takes the viewer through Verdi's Italy, with me as the guide. I wrote most of the scripts each morning and memorized them, and then filmed the rest of the day. It features six arias sung by me in different locations meaningful in Verdi's life: Le Roncole (Verdi's birthplace), Bussetto, Villa Verdi, Parma, and others. The family that lives now in Villa Verdi is named Carrara-Verdi. The wife and mother of the family is the granddaughter of Verdi's adopted daughter. She and her husband are both lawyers, and they live there full time and care for this historical property and Verdi's memorabilia. It was through their kind cooperation that we were allowed to shoot some of the only footage ever taken inside his home. Then we shot more footage in Parma and the Parma chorale, and finally live portions of *Rigoletto* performed in Macerata in their outdoor amphitheater. (I was singing *Rigoletto* there that season.)

The *All-Star Gala* was filmed in East Berlin in an outdoor park with an antique carousel and in TV studios there. As a opera lover and a friend, Burt Lancaster appears in the opening and gives the film a real Hollywood feel. He and I have a bit of byplay, and then I sing several well-known arias, the *Traviata* duet with Mirella Freni, the *Don Carlo* duet with Plácido, and a pop duet with Julia Migenes-Johnson. I conduct the *Così* aria "Un aria amorosa" for Peter Schreier (all with the Staatsoper Orchestra, and complete with costumes and sets) and finish with a Strauss song, with Jon Spong at the piano. This is a very rich video, and I derived great satisfaction from the making of it.

CHAPTER TWENTY-EIGHT

Tributes

MANY PEOPLE WHO HAVE HAD AN IMPACT on my life have passed away during the last few decades. I want to pay special tribute to them:

Burt Lancaster, whose death was well covered by the media and whose love of opera was not so widely known; José Ferrer, another one whose love of opera was not so well-known; Gregory Peck, the movie icon of whom I have spoken earlier in the book; the seemingly indestructible Boris Goldovsky (the Goldovsky Foundation carries on his work and his legacy); George London; William Warfield; Jerome Hines; Leonie Rysanek; Renata Tebaldi; Walter Berry; Herman Prey; Marcel Prawy; Chester Ludgin; Norman Treigle, of whom I wrote much in this book; Fausto Cleva; Anton Guadagno, with whom I sang many of my big roles for the first time and for whom I had the greatest respect and love; James McCracken; Anna Moffo; Anselmo Colzani; Franco Corelli; Franco Bonisolli; Nicolai Ghiaurov, my favorite bass; Rudolf Bing; Leonard Bernstein; Herbert von Karajan; Karl Böhm; Erich Leinsdorf; Wolfgang Stoll, my European agent and good friend; William (Bill) Bunge, a life-long school friend; and Werner Klemperer. (Maria and I became very friendly with Werner and his wife, Kim Hamilton, in his last years. Most people think of Werner as Colonel Klink in the TV series *Hogan's Heroes*. Clearly that is his most recognizable image, but he was also well-known in movies and theater. He was the son of the famous conductor Otto Klemperer and was very knowledgeable about music and art. Werner was a wonderful friend, and we miss him.)

My two voice teachers, Andrew White and Hermanus Baer, have also passed away. Their pictures as well as those of many of the above look down at me every day from the walls of my studio at Northwestern University. We have recently lost the icon of American baritones, Robert Merrill. He will be greatly missed, and given our warm and loving relationship, I especially lament his passing and the end of that era of great singing. Of even greater fame in the world at large, my close friend Tony Randall has left us. The film, stage, and television star died in May 2004. His family and the world miss him terribly. Maria and I were devastated. When some of your friends pass away, it makes you realize your own human frailty and vulnerability.

To have sung for more than forty years of my life is a blessing and a responsibility. I look at my career and am very grateful. As I write this latest chapter of my life, I realize that on balance I'm a lucky man. When I look upon my life, my past and my future, I am reminded that peace of mind is possible, and unlike most of my very familiar Verdi operas, life can have a happy ending.

Performance Chronology

This chronology is an overview of debuts and most opera dates in Milnes's career and a complete list of his performances at the Metropolitan Opera. This list does not include Milnes's 500 or so recitals and orchestral concerts around the world in places such as the Ambler Festival; Arena di Verona, Italy; the Barbican, London; Blossom Music Festival; Grant Park in Chicago; the Herkulessaal, Munich; the Hollywood Bowl; the Konzerthaus and Musikverein, Vienna; the Ravinia Festival; Robin Hood Dell; the Saratoga Festival; the Tanglewood Music Festival; the Théâtre du Châtelet, Paris; the Tivoli Gardens in Copenhagen Denmark; the Wolf Trap Festival; and almost every university recital venue in the United States. A specific single date is given for debuts and one-time performances; where a specific date is not given, the engagement consisted of a run of several performances.

1960–65
BORIS GOLDOVSKY
OPERA THEATRE
(PROFESSIONAL OPERA DEBUT)

Masetto in *Don Giovanni* with Holgate and Malas. Later seasons included Escamillo in *Carmen* with Wahl in the title role and Shirley as Don José, *La Bohème, Don Giovanni, Tosca, Rigoletto, Il turco in Italia, King Theodore in Venice, Il tabarro, La traviata,* and *Il barbiere di Siviglia.*

1961–96
BALTIMORE OPERA (DEBUT)

Gerard in *Andrea Chénier* with Baklanova, King, Hankin, Druary, Freeman, Malas, and Vecchione, cond. Grossmann, dir. Stone. Later seasons included *Rigoletto, Carmen,* and *Falstaff.*

1963
MEXICO CITY OPERA (DEBUT),
TEATRO BELLAS ARTES

August 31: Iago in *Otello* with Gonzales as Desdemona and Vickers, cond. Cillario. Figaro in *Il barbiere di Siviglia,* cond. Guadagno.

1964–98
PITTSBURGH OPERA (DEBUT)

February 20: Tonio in *Pagliacci* (Leoncavallo) with Consiglio as Tonio, dir. Capobianco. Later seasons included *Rigoletto, Traviata, Hamlet, Otello,* and *Aida* (Verdi–Ghislanzoni).

1964–74
CINCINNATI SUMMER OPERA AT THE ZOO (DEBUT)

Il trovatore with Ross and Consiglio, cond. Guadagno, dir. Capobianco. Later seasons included *La traviata*, *La forza del destino*, *Carmen*, *Madama Butterfly*, *Pagliacci* (Leoncavallo), *Rigoletto*, and later, at the Music Hall, *Macbeth* and *Il trovatore*.

1964–88
HOUSTON GRAND OPERA (DEBUT)

Pagliacci. Later seasons included *Otello*, *Manon Lescaut*, and *Il barbiere di Siviglia*.

1964–96
NEW YORK CITY OPERA (DEBUT)

October 18: Valentin in *Faust* with Treigle, Molese, Wolff, and Tosini, cond. Patane. Later that season and following seasons included *Carmina Burana* , *La traviata*, Ruprecht in *Flaming Angel* (Prokofiev; American premiere), *Il barbiere di Siviglia*, *Pagliacci*, Dapertutto in *Tales of Hoffmann*, *Tosca*, and John Sorel in *The Consul* with Patricia Neway, dir. Menotti.

1964
TEATRO DELLA PERGOLA, FLORENCE, ITALY (DEBUT)

Figaro in *Il barbiere di Siviglia* with Morris as Almaviva, Love as Rosina, and Tyl as Basilio.

1965
METROPOLITAN OPERA (DEBUT)

December 22: Valentin in *Faust*. See below for a complete performance listing.

1965–80
SEATTLE OPERA (DEBUT)

Il trovatore with Farrell, cond. Katims. Later seasons included *Don Giovanni*.

1966–98
FLORENTINE OPERA, MILWAUKEE

Figaro in *Il barbiere di Siviglia*. Later seasons included *Il trovatore*, *Tosca*, and *La traviata*.

1967–68
TEATRO MUNICIPAL, SANTIAGO, CHILE

Macbeth , cond. Guadagno, stage dir. Capobianco. Later seasons included *Andrea Chénier*, *Un ballo in maschera*, and *Aida*.

1969–73
SAN ANTONIO SYMPHONY
OPERA SEASON

Valentin in *Faust* with Treigle. Later seasons included the Herald in *Lohengrin*; *La traviata* with Moffo; Marco in *Gianni Schicchi* with Baccaloni; and Tonio in *Pagliacci*, cond. Alessandro.

1970
LONDON OPERA SOCIETY

Andrea Chénier with Gulin and Bergonzi, cond. Guadagno. The following season, *La Gioconda* with Suliotis, cond. Cillario.

1970–91
VIENNA STAATSOPER

March 23: European debut in the title role of *Macbeth* with Ludwig as Lady Macbeth, Ridderbusch, Cossutta, and Aichberger, cond. Böhm, dir. Schenk. **April 23**: Valentin in *Faust*. **May 4**: Count di Luna in *Il trovatore*. Later seasons included *Otello, La traviata, Un ballo in maschera, Tosca, Faust, Il trovatore, La forza del destino*, and *Pagliacci*.

1970–2000
GRAN TEATRE DE LICEU, BARCELONA, SPAIN

Il barbiere di Siviglia. Later seasons included *Pagliacci* (Leoncavallo), several productions of *Tosca*, and, in 2000, *Sly* with Carreras.

1971–92
ROYAL OPERA HOUSE, COVENT GARDEN, LONDON (DEBUT)

April 22: Renato in *Un ballo in maschera*. Later seasons included *Il trovatore, Macbeth, Otello*, and *Rigoletto*.

1971–99
TEATRO COLÓN, BUENOS AIRES, ARGENTINA (DEBUT)

Un ballo in maschera. Later seasons included *Rigoletto, I vespri siciliani, Tosca, Il tabarro, Gianni Schicchi*, and, in 1999, *Fedora* with Freni and Domingo.

1971–90
LYRIC OPERA OF CHICAGO

November 10: Posa in *Don Carlos* with Lorengar as Elisabeth, Cossotto as Eboli, and Cosutta in title role, cond. Bartoletti. Later seasons included *Un ballo in maschera, Otello, Tosca, Hamlet*, and *Simon Boccanegra*.

1972
METROPOLITAN OPERA

April 22: Rudolf Bing Gala and Farewell. Sang "Dunque io son" from *Il barbiere di Siviglia* with Roberta Peters.

1972–94
HAMBURG STATE OPERA (DEBUT)

Renato in *Un ballo in maschera* with Pavarotti as Riccardo and Santunione as Amelia, cond. Santi, dir. Dexter. Later seasons included Iago in *Otello* with Domingo; title role in *Otello* (1975) with Riccarelli, cond. Levine, dir. Everding; *Tosca; Rigoletto; Don Carlo; La traviata*; and *Il trovatore*.

1972–87
SAN FRANCISCO OPERA (DEBUT)

Title role in *Rigoletto* with Nawe as Gilda, dir. Ponnelle, cond. Kord. Later seasons included *Ernani* with Caballé and *Thaïs* with Sills.

1972–78
NEW ORLEANS OPERA

Rigoletto with Alexander and Russell, cond. Suppe. Later seasons included *Macbeth* with Tinsley, cond. Andersen.

1972–96
DEUTSCHE OPER, BERLIN (DEBUT)

Don Giovanni with Van Dam as Leporello, cond. Maazel. Later seasons included *Tosca, Andrea Chénier*, and *La traviata*.

1975–90
PARIS OPÉRA (DEBUT)

Count di Luna in *Il trovatore*. Later seasons included *Otello* with Vickers, cond. Santi; *Tosca*, cond. Conlin; and *Nabucco* with Bumbry, Cossutta, Cortez, and R. Raimondi, cond. Santi (videotape available).

1975
MACERATA FESTIVAL, ITALY

Rigoletto with Pavarotti, cond. Franci.

1977–89
MUNICH OPERA, GERMANY

Scarpia in *Tosca* with Domingo and Kubiak, cond. López-Cobos, dir. Friedrich. Later seasons included *Don Giovanni, Pagliacci, La forza del destino*, and *Un ballo in maschera*.

1977–90
TEATRO REGGIO, TORINO, ITALY

Count di Luna in *Il trovatore* with Riccarelli, Cossotto, and Giacomini, cond. Maag. Later seasons included *Tosca* with Guleghina and Olsen, as well as recitals.

1977–90
GREATER MIAMI OPERA (DEBUT)

Title role in *Macbeth*. Later seasons included *Nabucco, Rigoletto, Hamlet, La forza del destino, Ernani*, and *Falstaff*.

1978
METROPOLITAN OPERA

October 15: title role in premiere of *Eugene Onegin*. First performance in Russian at the Met.

1978
TEATRO ALLA SCALA, MILAN, ITALY

Il trovatore with Mauro, Marton, and Cossotto, cond. Mehta.

1978–86
CARACAS, VENEZUELA

Rigoletto, cond. Guadagno, Later seasons included *Don Giovanni*, cond. Alcantara.

1978
TULSA OPERA, OKLAHOMA

Don Giovanni.

1978–85
SAN DIEGO OPERA (DEBUT)

October 7: title role in *Hamlet*, dir. Capobianco. Later seasons included *Simon Boccanegra* and the title role in *Henry VIII.*

1980–88
VERONA FESTIVAL

Rigoletto. Later seasons included *La traviata* and several gala performances.

1980
SAN JUAN FESTIVAL, PUERTO RICO

Rigoletto with Shicoff, Rolandi, and Díaz, cond. Silipigni.

1980–81
BILBAO AND OVIEDO, SPAIN

Ernani with Todisco; *Il trovatore* with Zajick.

1982
PRINCESS THEATRE, MELBOURNE, AUSTRALIA

May 17: title role in *Macbeth* with Hunter as Lady *Macbeth* and Shanks as Banquo, cond. Cillario, dir. Copley.

1982
OPERA HOUSE, SYDNEY, AUSTRALIA

June 9: title role in *Hamlet* with McGregor, cond. Bonynge, dir. Mansouri.

1982
NEW YORK CITY OPERA

Special guest performances of the title role in *Hamlet*.

1983
METROPOLITAN OPERA

January 30: Television concert with Domingo in a varied program of solos and duets, cond. Levine.

1985–94
STAATSOPER, EAST BERLIN, GERMANY

Scarpia in *Tosca*. Later seasons included more *Tosca*s with Murphy, Fabriccini, and Lerin.

1988
METROPOLITAN OPERA TOUR IN JAPAN

Count di Luna in *Il trovatore* with Millo, Bonisolli, and Cossotto, cond. Rudel.

1989
FESTIVAL INTERNATIONAL D'OPÉRA AU CHÂTEAU DE VERSAILLES

La traviata with Aragall and Longhi, cond. Rudel.

1989
OPERA COLORADO, DENVER

La traviata with Soviero and W. MacNeil, cond. Acs, stage dir. Merrill.

1989
THE BOLSHOI, MOSCOW, RUSSIA

June 4: Scarpia in *Tosca*, and an aria concert and a master class at the Tchaikovsky Conservatory.

1990
CLEVELAND OPERA

April 4: Count di Luna in *Il trovatore*.

1991–96
PALM BEACH OPERA, FLORIDA

January 25: Title role in *Don Giovanni*. Later seasons included *Tosca* with Soviero, cond. Guadagno.

1992
TEATRO BELLINI, CATANIA, ITALY

June 2: Title role in *Simon Boccanegra*, dir. del Monaco.

1992–97
BONN OPERA HOUSE, GERMANY

La fanciulla del West with Daniels and Domingo, dir. del Monaco. Later seasons included *Otello* with Domingo, *Pagliacci*, and *La traviata*.

1994
NEW YORK CITY OPERA

Guest performances of *Falstaff.*

1994

Tours in Japan of an "All Verdi Concert" with Sato and Dvorsky, cond. Lenard; and an "All Puccini Concert" with Guleghina and Dvorsky, cond. Luisi, in 1996.

1995
TORRE DEL LAGO*
Tosca with Cura, cond. Guadagno.

1996
METROPOLITAN OPERA
April 27: James Levine, televised gala; sang "Nemico della Patria" from *Andrea Chénier*.

1997
METROPOLITAN OPERA
March 22: *Aida*. Final appearance as a member of the Metropolitan Opera Company after 652 performances in 32 years.

---

* Home of Giacomo Puccini.

1998
SLOVAKIAN NATIONAL THEATER, BRATISLAVA
Scarpia in *Tosca*, with subsequent performances on tour in Japan with Sato and Dvorsky, cond. Lenard.

1998
BUDAPEST OPERA
Scarpia in *Tosca*; in 2000, *Otello* and a concert performance of *Aida* with Marc, Obrazova, et al., cond. Lenard.

1999
MONTREAL OPERA
Germont in *La traviata*.

Metropolitan Opera Company Performances

The numbers in brackets represent three different chronologies. Where the bracketed number follows the date, it represents how many times Milnes has performed that opera. Where the bracketed number follows the opera title, it represents the number of times Met has performed the work. And where the bracketed number comes after Milnes's name, it represents how many times Milnes has performed the role. Thus, the performance of *Pikovaya dama* on December 28, 1965, was Milnes's second appearance with the Met, the Met's twelfth performance of the opera, and Milnes's first performance of the role.

1965–66
METROPOLITAN OPERA HOUSE

December 22, 1965 [1]
Faust (Gounod–Barbier/Carré) [594]
Conducted by Prêtre
Faust: Alexander
Marguerite: Caballé
Méphistophélès: Díaz
Valentin: Milnes [1]
Siebel: Baldwin

December 28, 1965 [2]
Pikovaya dama (P. I. Tchaikovsky–M. Tchaikovsky; in English) [12]
Conducted by Schippers
Lisa: Stratas
Gherman: McCracken
Countess: Thebom
Yeletsky: Milnes [1]
Tomsky: Meredith
Chekalinsky: Franke
Surin: Alvary
Paulina: Grillo
Masha: Ordassy
Master of Ceremonies: Boucher
Chloë: Di Franco

January 6, 1966 [3]
Pikovaya dama (P. I. Tchaikovsky–M. Tchaikovsky; in English) [13]
Conducted by Schippers
Lisa: Weathers
Gherman: McCracken
Countess: Madeira
Yeletsky: Milnes [2]
Tomsky: Meredith
Chekalinsky: Franke
Surin: Alvary
Paulina: Grillo
Masha: Ordassy
Master of Ceremonies: Boucher
Chloë: Di Franco

January 8, 1966 [4]
Fidelio (Beethoven–Sonnleithner/ Breuning/Treitschke) [92]
Conducted by Böhm
Leonore: Nilsson
Florestan: King
Pizarro: Evans
Rocco: Edelmann
Marzelline: Pracht
Jaquino: Anthony
Fernando: Milnes [1]
First Prisoner: Shirley

Directed by Graf
Staged by Merrill
Designed by Armistead

January 12, 1966 [5]
Fidelio (Beethoven–Sonnleithner/
    Breuning/Treitschke) [93]
Conducted by Böhm
Leonore: Dvoráková
Florestan: King
Pizarro: Evans
Rocco: Edelmann
Marzelline: Pracht
Jaquino: Anthony
Fernando: Milnes [2]
First Prisoner: Shirley

January 22, 1966, matinee (broadcast) [6]
Fidelio (Beethoven–Sonnleithner/
    Breuning/Treitschke) [94]
Conducted by Böhm
Leonore: Nilsson
Florestan: King
Pizarro: Evans
Rocco: Edelmann
Marzelline: Pracht
Jaquino: Anthony
Fernando: Milnes [3]
First Prisoner: Shirley

January 22, 1966 [7]
Aida (Verdi–Ghislanzoni) [724]
Conducted by Mehta
Aida: Arroyo
Radames: Corelli
Amneris: Dalis
Amonasro: Milnes [1]
Ramfis: Macurdy
King: Michalski

January 31, 1966 [8]
Fidelio (Beethoven–Sonnleithner/
    Breuning/Treitschke) [96]
Conducted by Böhm
Leonore: Nilsson
Florestan: King
Pizarro: Dooley
Rocco: Edelmann
Marzelline: Pracht
Jaquino: Anthony
Fernando: Milnes [4]
First Prisoner: Shirley

February 8, 1966, matinee (student performance) [9]
La fanciulla del West (Puccini–Civinini/
    Zangarini) [60]
Conducted by Behr
Minnie: Owen
Ramerrez: Bardini
Rance: Milnes [1]
Joe: Marek
Handsome: Sliker
Harry: Zakariasen
Happy: Strang
Sid: De Paola
Sonora: Boucher
Trin: Marcella
Jim: Dunlap
Nick: Anthony
Jake: Sgarro
Ashby: Scott
Post Rider: D'Elia
Castro: Michalski

February 9, 1966 [10]
Fidelio (Beethoven–Sonnleithner/
    Breuning/Treitschke) [97]
Conducted by Rosenstock
Leonore: Dvoráková
Florestan: Thomas
Pizarro: Cassel
Rocco: Edelmann
Marzelline: Clements
Jaquino: Anthony
Fernando: Milnes [5]
First Prisoner: Shirley

February 15, 1966 [11]
Andrea Chénier (Giordano–Illica) [115]
Conducted by Gardelli
Chénier: Bergonzi
Maddalena: Tebaldi
Gérard: Milnes [1]
Bersi: Casei
Countess di Coigny: Kriese
Abbé: Carelli
Fléville: Boucher
Incroyable: Velis
Roucher: Walker
Mathieu: Esparza
Madelon: Madeira
Dumas: Christopher
Fouquier Tinville: Scott

February 24, 1966, matinee (student performance) [12]
La fanciulla del West (Puccini–Civinini/
   Zangarini) [61]
Conducted by Behr
Minnie: Owen
Ramerrez: Bardini
Rance: Milnes [2]
Joe: Marek
Handsome: Sliker
Harry: Zakariasen
Happy: Strang
Sid: De Paola
Sonora: Boucher
Trin: Marcella
Jim: Dunlap
Nick: Anthony
Jake: Sgarro
Ashby: Scott
Post Rider: D'Elia
Castro: Michalski

March 13, 1966 [13]
Aida (Verdi–Ghislanzoni) [728]
Conducted by Mehta
Aida: L. Price
Radames Corelli
Amneris: Cernei
Amonasro: Milnes [2]
Ramfis: Hines
King: Michalski

March 21, 1966, matinee (student performance) [14]
La fanciulla del West (Puccini–Civinini/
   Zangarini) [66]
Conducted by Behr
Minnie: Owen
Ramerrez: Bardini
Rance: Milnes [3]
Joe: Marek
Handsome: Sliker
Harry: Zakariasen
Happy: Strang
Sid: De Paola
Sonora: Boucher
Trin: Marcella
Jim: Dunlap
Nick: Anthony
Jake: Díaz
Ashby: Scott

Post Rider: D'Elia
Castro: Sgarro

March 25, 1966 [15]
Un ballo in maschera (Verdi–Somma) [96]
Conducted by Molinari-Pradelli
Amelia: Crespin
Riccardo: Bergonzi
Renato: Milnes [1]
Ulrica: Baldani
Oscar: Scovotti
Samuel: Alvary
Tom: Sgarro
Silvano: Goodloe

April 6, 1966 [16]
Un ballo in maschera (Verdi–Somma) [97]
Conducted by Molinari-Pradelli
Amelia: Crespin
Riccardo: Tucker
Renato: Milnes [2]
Ulrica: Baldani
Oscar: Scovotti
Samuel: Alvary
Tom: Sgarro
Silvano: Goodloe

April 7, 1966 [17]
Fidelio (Beethoven–Sonnleithner/
   Breuning/Treitschke) [99]
Conducted by Rosenstock
Leonore: Nilsson
Florestan: Vickers
Pizarro: Meredith
Rocco: Wiemann
Marzelline: Pracht
Jaquino: Schmorr
Fernando: Milnes [6]
First Prisoner: Shirley

NEWPORT, RHODE ISLAND

July 15, 1966 (concert performance) [18]
Lucia di Lammermoor (Donizetti–
   Cammarano) [353]
Conducted by Varviso
Lucia: Peters
Edgardo: Peerce
Enrico: Milnes [1]
Raimondo: Michalski
Normanno: Marek

LEWISOHN STADIUM, MANHATTAN

July 21, 1966 (concert performance) [19]
Samson et Dalila (Saint-Saëns–Lemaire)
[129]
Conducted by K. Adler
Samson: McCracken
Dalila: Warfield
High Priest: Milnes [1]
Abimélech: Sgarro
Old Hebrew: Macurdy

July 22, 1966 (concert performance) [20]
Carmen (Bizet–Meilhac/Halévy) [604]
Carmen: Resnik
José: McCracken
Micaela: Pracht
Escamillo: Milnes [1]
Frasquita: Ordassy
Mercedes: Miller
Remendado: Schmorr
Dancaïro: Boucher

1966–67
METROPOLITAN OPERA HOUSE

October 20, 1966 [21]
Faust (Gounod–Barbier/Carré) [604]
Conducted by Prêtre
Faust: G. Raimondi
Marguerite: Freni
Méphistophélès: Tozzi
Valentin: Milnes [2]
Siebel: Baldwin
Directed by Barrault
Staged by Igesz
Designed by Dupont
Choreography by Flindt

October 26, 1966 [22]
Faust (Gounod–Barbier/Carré) [605]
Conducted by Prêtre
Faust: G. Raimondi
Marguerite: Freni
Méphistophélès: Tozzi
Valentin: Milnes [3]
Siebel: Baldwin

October 29, 1966, matinee [23]
Faust (Gounod–Barbier/Carré) [606]
Conducted by Prêtre

Faust: G. Raimondi
Marguerite: Freni
Méphistophélès: Tozzi
Valentin: Milnes [4]
Siebel: Baldwin

November 4, 1966 [24]
Faust (Gounod–Barbier/Carré) [607]
Conducted by Prêtre
Faust: G. Raimondi
Marguerite: Freni
Méphistophélès: Ghiaurov
Valentin: Milnes [5]
Siebel: Baldwin

November 8, 1966 [25]
Faust (Gounod–Barbier/Carré) [608]
Conducted by Prêtre
Faust: G. Raimondi
Marguerite: Freni
Méphistophélès: Ghiaurov
Valentin: Milnes [6]
Siebel: Baldwin

November 15, 1966 [26]
Faust (Gounod–Barbier/Carré) [609]
Conducted by Prêtre
Faust: Alexander
Marguerite: Freni
Méphistophélès: Ghiaurov
Valentin: Milnes [7]
Siebel: Baldwin

**December 8, 1966, benefit sponsored by
the Metropolitan Opera Guild for the
production funds [27]**
Lohengrin (R. Wagner; new production)
[526]
Conducted by Böhm
Lohengrin: Kónya
Elsa: Bjoner
Ortrud: Ludwig
Friedrich: Berry
Heinrich: Macurdy
Herald: Milnes [1]
Directed by W. Wagner and P. Lehmann
Designed by W. Wagner
[Wieland Wagner died October 16, 1966.
  Peter Lehmann took over the produc-
  tion, drawing on Wieland's notes
  and similar stagings by Wieland in
  Hamburg and Bayreuth.]

December 13, 1966 [28]
Lohengrin (R. Wagner) [527]
Conducted by Böhm
Lohengrin: Kónya
Elsa: Bjoner
Ortrud: Ludwig
Friedrich: Berry
Heinrich: Macurdy
Herald: Milnes [2]

December 19, 1966 [29]
Lohengrin (R. Wagner) [528]
Conducted by Böhm
Lohengrin: King
Elsa: Bjoner
Ortrud: Rankin
Friedrich: Berry
Heinrich: Macurdy
Herald: Milnes [3]

December 29, 1966 [30]
Lohengrin (R. Wagner) [529]
Conducted by Böhm
Lohengrin: Kónya
Elsa: Bjoner
Ortrud: Ludwig
Friedrich: Cassel
Heinrich: Macurdy
Herald: Milnes [4]

January 2, 1967 [31]

Aida **(Verdi–Ghislanzoni) [739]**
Conducted by Schippers
Aida: Tucci
Radames: Labò
Amneris: Cernei
Amonasro: Milnes [3]
Ramfis: Hines
King: Sgarro

January 7, 1967 [32]
Lohengrin (R. Wagner) [530]
Conducted by Böhm
Lohengrin: Kónya
Elsa: Bjoner
Ortrud: Ludwig
Friedrich: Cassel
Heinrich: Macurdy
Herald: Milnes [5]

January 11, 1967 [33]
Lohengrin (R. Wagner) [531]

Conducted by Böhm
Lohengrin: Kónya
Elsa: Bjoner
Ortrud: Ludwig
Friedrich: Berry
Heinrich: Macurdy
Herald: Milnes [6]

January 21, 1967, matinee (broadcast) [34]
Lohengrin (R. Wagner) [532]
Conducted by Böhm
Lohengrin: Kónya
Elsa: Bjoner
Ortrud: Ludwig
Friedrich: Berry
Heinrich: Macurdy
Herald: Milnes [7]

March 17, 1967 [35]
Mourning Becomes Electra (M. D. Levy–
   H. Butler; world premiere) [1]
Conducted by Mehta
Lavinia: Lear
Orin: Reardon
Christine: Collier
Adam: Milnes [1]
Ezra: Macurdy
Peter: Bottcher
Directed by Cacoyannis
Designed by Aronson

March 20, 1967 [36]
Mourning Becomes Electra (M. D. Levy–
   H. Butler) [2]
Conducted by Mehta
Lavinia: Lear
Orin: Reardon
Christine: Collier
Adam: Milnes [2]
Ezra: Macurdy
Peter: Bottcher

March 29, 1967 [37]
Mourning Becomes Electra (M. D. Levy–
   H. Butler) [3]
Conducted by Mehta
Lavinia: Lear
Orin: Reardon
Christine: Collier
Adam: Milnes [3]
Ezra: Macurdy
Peter: Bottcher

April 1, 1967, matinee (broadcast) [38]
Mourning Becomes Electra (M. D. Levy–
  H. Butler) [4]
Conducted by Mehta
Lavinia: Lear
Orin: Reardon
Christine: Collier
Adam: Milnes [4]
Ezra: Macurdy
Peter: Bottcher

April 8, 1967 [39]
Mourning Becomes Electra (M. D. Levy–
  H. Butler) [5]
Conducted by Mehta
Lavinia: Lear
Orin: Reardon
Christine: Collier
Adam: Milnes [5]
Ezra: Macurdy
Peter: Bottcher

April 13, 1967 [40]
Mourning Becomes Electra (M. D. Levy–
  H. Butler) [6]
Conducted by Mehta
Lavinia: Lear
Orin: Reardon
Christine: Collier
Adam: Milnes [6]
Ezra: Macurdy
Peter: Bottcher

BOSTON, MASSACHUSETTS

April 17, 1967 [41]
Un ballo in maschera (Verdi–Somma) [98]
Conducted by Schick
Amelia: L. Price
Riccardo: Prevedi
Renato: Milnes [3]
Ulrica: Baldani
Oscar: Clements
Samuel: Alvary
Tom: Sgarro
Silvano: Christopher
Directed by Rennert
Staged by Merrill
Designed by Maximowna
Choreography by Andrew

April 20, 1967 [42]
Lohengrin (R. Wagner) [535]
Conducted by Rosenstock
Lohengrin: Kónya
Elsa: Grümmer
Ortrud: Dalis
Friedrich: Cassel
Heinrich: Giaiotti
Herald: Milnes [8]

CLEVELAND, OHIO

April 25, 1967 [43]
Un ballo in maschera (Verdi–Somma) [99]
Conducted by Schippers
Amelia: L. Price
Riccardo: Prevedi
Renato: Milnes [4]
Ulrica: Baldani
Oscar: Clements
Samuel: Alvary
Tom: Sgarro
Silvano: Christopher

April 26, 1967 [44]
Lohengrin (R. Wagner) [536]
Conducted by Rosenstock
Lohengrin: Kónya
Elsa: Grümmer
Ortrud: Dalis
Friedrich: Cassel
Heinrich: Macurdy
Herald: Milnes [9]

ATLANTA, GEORGIA

May 2, 1967 [45]
Un ballo in maschera (Verdi–Somma)
  [100]
Conducted by Schippers
Amelia: L. Price
Riccardo: Prevedi
Renato: Milnes [5]
Ulrica: Rankin
Oscar: Clements
Samuel: Alvary
Tom: Sgarro
Silvano: Christopher

May 5, 1967 [46]
Lohengrin (R. Wagner) [537]

Conducted by Rosenstock
Lohengrin: Kónya
Elsa: Grümmer
Ortrud: Dalis
Friedrich: Cassel
Heinrich: Macurdy
Herald: Milnes [10]

DALLAS, TEXAS

May 11, 1967 [47]
Lohengrin (R. Wagner) [538]
Conducted by Rosenstock
Lohengrin: Kónya
Elsa: Grümmer
Ortrud: Dalis
Friedrich: Cassel
Heinrich: Macurdy
Herald: Milnes [11]

MINNEAPOLIS, MINNESOTA

May 15, 1967 [48]
Un ballo in maschera (Verdi–Somma)
[101]
Conducted by Schippers
Amelia: L. Price
Riccardo: Prevedi
Renato: Milnes [6]
Ulrica: Baldani
Oscar: Clements
Samuel: Alvary
Tom: Sgarro
Silvano: Goodloe

DETROIT, MICHIGAN

May 22, 1967 [49]
Un ballo in maschera (Verdi–Somma)
[102]
Conducted by Schippers
Amelia: L. Price
Riccardo: Prevedi
Renato: Milnes [7]
Ulrica: Rankin
Oscar: Clements
Samuel: Alvary
Tom: Sgarro
Silvano: Christopher

PHILADELPHIA, PENNSYLVANIA

May 30, 1967 [50]
Un ballo in maschera (Verdi–Somma)
[103]
Conducted by Schippers
Amelia: L. Price
Riccardo: Prevedi
Renato: Milnes [8]
Ulrica: Rankin
Oscar: Welting
Samuel: Alvary
Tom: Sgarro
Silvano: Goodloe

June 2, 1967 [51]
La traviata (Verdi–Piave) [523]
Conducted by Gardelli
Violetta: Moffo
Alfredo: Morell
Germont: Milnes [1]
Flora: Baldwin
Gastone: Anthony
Douphol: Bottcher
D'Obigny: Boucher
Grenvil: Sgarro
Annina: Di Franco

METROPOLITAN OPERA HOUSE

June 12, 1967 [52]
Un ballo in maschera (Verdi–Somma)
[104]
Conducted by Schippers
Amelia: L. Price
Riccardo: Tucker
Renato: Milnes [9]
Ulrica: Rankin
Oscar: Peters
Samuel: Alvary
Tom: Sgarro
Silvano: Goodloe
[The performances of June 12–22 were
    presented as part of the Lincoln Center
    Festival.]

June 21, 1967 [53]
Un ballo in maschera (Verdi–Somma)
[105]
Conducted by Schick
Amelia: L. Price

Riccardo: Prevedi
Renato: Milnes [10]
Ulrica: Baldani
Oscar: Clements
Samuel: Alvary
Tom: Sgarro
Silvano: Goodloe

1967–68
METROPOLITAN OPERA HOUSE

September 21, 1967 [54]
La Gioconda (Ponchielli–Boito) [219]
Conducted by Cleva
Gioconda: Tebaldi
Enzo: Labò
Laura: Cvejic
Barnaba: Milnes [1]
Alvise: Giaiotti
Blind Woman: Elias
Zuàne: Christopher
Isèpo: Schmorr
Monk: Plishka
Directed by Wallmann
Staged by Tavernia
Designed by Montresor
Choreography by Solov

September 25, 1967 [55]
La Gioconda (Ponchielli–Boito) [220]
Conducted by Cleva
Gioconda: Tebaldi
Enzo: Labò
Laura: Cvejic
Barnaba: Milnes [2]
Alvise: Giaiotti
Blind Woman: Elias
Zuàne: Christopher
Isèpo: Schmorr
Monk: Plishka

September 30, 1967, matinee [56]
La Gioconda (Ponchielli–Boito) [221]
Conducted by Cleva
Gioconda: Tebaldi
Enzo: Labò
Laura: Cvejic
Barnaba: Milnes [3]
Alvise: Giaiotti
Blind Woman: Amparán

Zuàne: Christopher
Isèpo: Schmorr
Monk: Plishka

October 6, 1967 [57]
La Gioconda (Ponchielli–Boito) [222]
Conducted by Cleva
Gioconda: Tebaldi
Enzo: Labò
Laura: Cvejic
Barnaba: Milnes [4]
Alvise: Giaiotti
Blind Woman: Amparán
Zuàne: Christopher
Isèpo: Schmorr
Monk: Plishka

October 9, 1967 [58]
La forza del destino (Verdi–Piave) [125]
Conducted by Molinari-Pradelli
Leonora: L. Price
Alvaro: Prevedi
Carlo: Milnes [1]
Father Superior: Flagello
Preziosilla: Williams
Melitone: Corena
Marquis: Sgarro
Curra: Ordassy

October 19, 1967 [59]
La traviata (Verdi–Piave) [534]
Conducted by Cleva
Violetta: Pilou
Alfredo: Shirley
Germont: Milnes [2]
Flora: Williams
Gastone: Anthony
Douphol: Goodloe
D'Obigny: Boucher
Grenvil: Sgarro
Annina: Armstrong

October 21, 1967, matinee [60]
La forza del destino (Verdi–Piave) [126]
Conducted by Rich
Leonora: L. Price
Alvaro: Prevedi
Carlo: Milnes [2]
Father Superior: Ghiaurov
Preziosilla: Williams
Melitone: Corena

Marquis: Sgarro
Curra: Ordassy

October 25, 1967 [61]
La forza del destino (Verdi–Piave) [127]
Conducted by Molinari-Pradelli
Leonora: L. Price
Alvaro: Tucker
Carlo: Milnes [3]
Father Superior: Giaiotti
Preziosilla: Pearl
Melitone: Corena
Marquis: Sgarro
Curra: Ordassy

November 1, 1967 [62]
La traviata (Verdi–Piave) [535]
Conducted by Cleva
Violetta: Lorengar
Alfredo: Alva
Germont: Milnes [3]
Flora: Williams
Gastone: Anthony
Douphol: Goodloe
D'Obigny: Boucher
Grenvil: Sgarro
Annina: Di Franco

November 8, 1967 [63]
La traviata (Verdi–Piave) [536]
Conducted by Cleva
Violetta: Lorengar
Alfredo: Alexander
Germont: Milnes [4]
Flora: Williams
Gastone: Carelli
Douphol: Goodloe
D'Obigny: Boucher
Grenvil: Sgarro
Annina: Di Franco

December 9, 1967 [64]
Mourning Becomes Electra (M. D. Levy–
  H. Butler) [7]
Conducted by Mehta
Lavinia: Lear
Orin: Reardon
Christine: Collier
Adam: Milnes [7]
Ezra: Macurdy
Peter: Bottcher

Directed by Cacoyannis
Designed by B. Aronson

December 14, 1967 [65]
Mourning Becomes Electra (M. D. Levy–
  H. Butler) [8]
Conducted by Mehta
Lavinia: Lear
Orin: Reardon
Christine: Collier
Adam: Milnes [8]
Ezra: Macurdy
Peter: Bottcher

December 19, 1967 [66]
Mourning Becomes Electra (M. D. Levy–
  H. Butler) [9]
Conducted by Mehta
Lavinia: Lear
Orin: Reardon
Christine: Collier
Adam: Milnes [9]
Ezra: Macurdy
Peter: Bottcher

December 22, 1967 [67]
Mourning Becomes Electra (M. D. Levy–
  H. Butler) [10]
Conducted by Mehta
Lavinia: Lear
Orin: Reardon
Christine: Collier
Adam: Milnes [10]
Ezra: Macurdy
Peter: Bottcher

December 28, 1967 [68]
Mourning Becomes Electra (M. D. Levy–
  H. Butler) [11]
Conducted by Mehta
Lavinia: Lear
Orin: Reardon
Christine: Collier
Adam: Milnes [11]
Ezra: Macurdy
Peter: Bottcher

January 1, 1968 [69]
Aida (Verdi–Ghislanzoni) [749]
Conducted by Schippers
Aida: Tucci
Radames: Labò

Amneris: Cernei
Amonasro: Milnes [4]
Ramfis: Giaiotti
King: Plishka

January 20, 1968, matinee (broadcast) [70]
Aida (Verdi–Ghislanzoni) [752]
Conducted by Schippers
Aida: Tucci
Radames: McCracken
Amneris: Dalis
Amonasro: Milnes [5]
Ramfis: Giaiotti
King: Sgarro

February 8, 1968, benefit sponsored by the Metropolitan Opera Guild for the production funds [71]
Luisa Miller (Verdi–Cammarano; new production) [7]
Conducted by Schippers
Luisa: Caballé
Rodolfo: Tucker
Miller: Milnes [1]
Walter: Tozzi
Wurm: Flagello
Federica: Pearl
Directed by Merrill
Designed by Colonnello
Lighting design by Rosenthal
Choreography by Andrew

February 10, 1968, matinee, (broadcast) [72]
Lohengrin (R. Wagner) [546]
Conducted by Klobucar
Lohengrin: Kónya
Elsa: Arroyo
Ortrud: Dvoráková
Friedrich: Cassel
Heinrich: Macurdy
Herald: Milnes [12]

February 14, 1968 [73]
Luisa Miller (Verdi–Cammarano) [8]
Conducted by Schippers
Luisa: Caballé
Rodolfo: Tucker
Miller: Milnes [2]
Walter: Tozzi
Wurm: Flagello

Federica: Pearl

February 17, 1968, matinee (broadcast) [74]
Luisa Miller (Verdi–Cammarano) [9]
Conducted by Schippers
Luisa: Caballé
Rodolfo: Tucker
Miller: Milnes [3]
Walter: Tozzi
Wurm: Flagello
Federica: Pearl

February 22, 1968 [75]
Luisa Miller (Verdi–Cammarano) [10]
Conducted by Schippers
Luisa: Caballé
Rodolfo: Tucker
Miller: Milnes [4]
Walter: Tozzi
Wurm: Flagello
Federica: Pearl

February 26, 1968 [76]
Luisa Miller (Verdi–Cammarano) [11]
Conducted by Schippers
Luisa: Caballé
Rodolfo: Tucker
Miller: Milnes [5]
Walter: Tozzi
Wurm: Flagello
Federica: Pearl

March 2, 1968 [77]
Luisa Miller (Verdi–Cammarano) [12]
Conducted by Schippers
Luisa: Caballé
Rodolfo: Alexander
Miller: Milnes [6]
Walter: Macurdy
Wurm: Flagello
Federica: Pearl

March 16, 1968, benefit sponsored by the Metropolitan Opera Guild for the benevolent and retirement funds [78]
Gala Performance, in which Milnes sang: *Pagliacci* (Leoncavallo), "Si può"; conducted by Cleva

April 1, 1968 [79]
Luisa Miller (Verdi–Cammarano) [13]
Conducted by Schippers

Luisa: Amara
Rodolfo: Tucker
Miller: Milnes [7]
Walter: Hines
Wurm: Flagello
Federica: Pearl

April 4, 1968 [80]
Luisa Miller (Verdi–Cammarano) [14]
Conducted by Schippers
Luisa: Caballé
Rodolfo: Tucker
Miller: Milnes [8]
Walter: Tozzi
Wurm: Flagello
Federica: Pearl

April 9, 1968 [81]
Luisa Miller (Verdi–Cammarano) [15]
Conducted by Schippers
Luisa: Caballé
Rodolfo: Alexander
Miller: Milnes [9]
Walter: Hines
Wurm: Flagello
Federica: Pearl

April 19, 1968 [82]
Luisa Miller (Verdi–Cammarano) [16]
Conducted by Cleva
Luisa: Caballé
Rodolfo: Alexander
Miller: Milnes [10]
Walter: Hines
Wurm: Flagello
Federica: Pearl

BOSTON, MASSACHUSETTS

April 22, 1968 [83]
Luisa Miller (Verdi–Cammarano) [17]
Conducted by Cleva
Luisa: Caballé
Rodolfo: Tucker
Miller: Milnes [11]
Walter: Tozzi
Wurm: Flagello
Federica: Pearl

CLEVELAND, OHIO

April 29, 1968 [84]
Luisa Miller (Verdi–Cammarano) [18]
Conducted by Cleva
Luisa: Caballé
Rodolfo: Tucker
Miller: Milnes [12]
Walter: Tozzi
Wurm: Flagello
Federica: Pearl

ATLANTA, GEORGIA

May 6, 1968 [85]
Luisa Miller (Verdi–Cammarano) [19]
Conducted by Cleva
Luisa: Caballé
Rodolfo: Tucker
Miller: Milnes [13]
Walter: Giaiotti
Wurm: Flagello
Federica: Pearl

MINNEAPOLIS, MINNESOTA

May 17, 1968 [86]
Luisa Miller (Verdi–Cammarano) [20]
Conducted by Cleva
Luisa: Caballé
Rodolfo: Tucker
Miller: Milnes [14]
Walter: Giaiotti
Wurm: Flagello
Federica: Pearl

DETROIT, MICHIGAN

May 20, 1968 [87]
Luisa Miller (Verdi–Cammarano) [21]
Conducted by Cleva
Luisa: Caballé
Rodolfo: Tucker
Miller: Milnes [15]
Walter: Giaiotti
Wurm: Flagello
Federica: Pearl

PHILADELPHIA, PENNSYLVANIA

May 27, 1968 [88]
Carmen (Bizet–Meilhac/Halévy) [632]
Conducted by Lombard
Carmen: Bumbry
José: Gedda
Micaela: Pracht
Escamillo: Milnes [2]
Frasquita: De Paul
Mercedes: Baldwin
Remendado: Anthony
Dancaïro: Boucher

June 1, 1968, matinee [89]
Luisa Miller (Verdi–Cammarano) [22]
Conducted by Cleva
Luisa: Caballé
Rodolfo: Tucker
Miller: Milnes [16]
Walter: Giaiotti
Wurm: Flagello
Federica: Pearl

DALLAS, TEXAS

June 6, 1968 [90]
Luisa Miller (Verdi–Cammarano) [23]
Conducted by Cleva
Luisa: Amara
Rodolfo: Tucker
Miller: Milnes [17]
Walter: Giaiotti
Wurm: Flagello
Federica: Pearl

1968–69
METROPOLITAN OPERA HOUSE

October 17, 1968 [91]
Simon Boccanegra (Verdi–Piave/Boito)
[54]
Conducted by Molinari-Pradelli
Simon: C. MacNeil
Maria: Orlandi-Malaspina
Gabriele: Tucker
Fiesco: Ghiaurov
Paolo: Milnes [1]
Pietro: Plishka

Directed by Webster
Staged by Lehnhoff
Set design by Fox
Costume design by Motley

October 26, 1968, matinee [92]
Simon Boccanegra (Verdi–Piave/Boito)
[55]
Conducted by Molinari-Pradelli
Simon: C. MacNeil
Maria: Orlandi-Malaspina
Gabriele: Tucker
Fiesco: Ghiaurov
Paolo: Milnes [2]
Pietro: Plishka

November 2, 1968 [93]
Simon Boccanegra (Verdi–Piave/Boito)
[56]
Conducted by Molinari-Pradelli
Simon: C. MacNeil
Maria: Orlandi-Malaspina
Gabriele: Prevedi
Fiesco: Ghiaurov
Paolo: Milnes [3]
Pietro: Plishka

November 6, 1968 [94]
Simon Boccanegra (Verdi–Piave/Boito)
[57]
Conducted by Molinari-Pradelli
Simon: C. MacNeil
Maria: Stojanovic
Gabriele: Prevedi
Fiesco: Ghiaurov
Paolo: Milnes [4]
Pietro: Plishka

November 11, 1968 [95]
Simon Boccanegra (Verdi–Piave/Boito)
[58]
Conducted by Molinari-Pradelli
Simon: C. MacNeil
Maria: Stojanovic
Gabriele: Prevedi
Fiesco: Ghiaurov
Paolo: Milnes [5]
Pietro: Sgarro

November 22, 1968, benefit sponsored by the Metropolitan Opera Guild for the production funds [96]
Das Rheingold (R. Wagner; new production) [102]
Conducted by von Karajan
Wotan: Stewart
Fricka: Veasey
Alberich: Kelemen
Loge: Stolze
Erda: Chookasian
Fasolt: Talvela
Fafner: Ridderbusch
Freia: Mangelsdorff
Froh: Grobe
Donner: Milnes [1]
Mime: Velis
Woglinde: Sukis
Directed by Karajan
Set design by Schneider-Siemssen
Costume design by Wakhevitch
Lighting design by Kunmer

November 25, 1968 [97]
Das Rheingold (R. Wagner) [103]
Conducted by von Karajan
Wotan: Stewart
Fricka: Veasey
Alberich: Kelemen
Loge: Stolze
Erda: Chookasian
Fasolt: Talvela
Fafner: Ridderbusch
Freia: Mangelsdorff
Froh: Grobe
Donner: Milnes [2]
Mime: Velis
Woglinde: Sukis

November 29, 1968 [98]
Il barbiere di Siviglia (Rossini–Sterbini) [324]
Conducted by Rich
Figaro: Milnes [1]
Rosina: Berganza
Almaviva: Alva
Bartolo: Corena
Basilio: Hines
Berta: Love
Fiorello: Boucher

November 30, 1968 [99]
Das Rheingold (R. Wagner) [104]
Conducted by von Karajan
Wotan: Stewart
Fricka: Veasey
Alberich: Kelemen
Loge: Stolze
Erda: Chookasian
Fasolt: Talvela
Fafner: Ridderbusch
Freia: Mangelsdorff
Froh: MacWherter
Donner: Milnes [3]
Mime: Velis
Woglinde: Sukis

December 4, 1968 [100]
Il barbiere di Siviglia (Rossini–Sterbini) [325]
Conducted by Bonynge
Figaro: Milnes [2]
Rosina: Berganza
Almaviva: Alva
Bartolo: Corena
Basilio: Hines
Berta: Baldwin
Fiorello: Boucher

December 9, 1968 [101]
Il barbiere di Siviglia (Rossini–Sterbini) [326]
Conducted by Bonynge
Figaro: Milnes [3]
Rosina: Berganza
Almaviva: Shirley
Bartolo: Corena
Basilio: Tozzi
Berta: Love
Fiorello: Boucher

December 14, 1968, matinee (broadcast) [102]
Simon Boccanegra (Verdi–Piave/Boito) [63]
Conducted by Molinari-Pradelli
Simon: C. MacNeil
Maria: Tucci
Gabriele: Shirley
Fiesco: Hines
Paolo: Milnes [6]
Pietro: Sgarro

February 15, 1969, benefit sponsored by the Metropolitan Opera Guild for the Benevolent and Retirement Funds [103]
Gala Performance in which Milnes sang: *Zazà* (Leoncavallo), "Zazà piccola zingara"; conducted by Cleva
Don Carlos (Verdi–Méry/du Locle), act 3, scene 1: Kabaivanska (Elisabeth), Milnes (Rodrigue), Bumbry (Eboli), Siepi (Philippe), Macurdy (Grand Inquisitor), Carelli (Lerme); conducted by Schick; directed by Webster; staged by Igesz; designed by Gérard

February 22, 1969, matinee (broadcast) [104]
Das Rheingold (R. Wagner) [105]
Conducted by von Karajan
Wotan: Adam
Fricka: Reynolds
Alberich: Kelemen
Loge: Stolze
Erda: Chookasian
Fasolt: Talvela
Fafner: Ridderbusch
Freia: Mangelsdorff
Froh: Grobe
Donner: Milnes [4]
Mime: Velis
Woglinde: Rebmann

February 25, 1969 [105]
Das Rheingold (R. Wagner) [106]
Conducted by von Karajan
Wotan: Adam
Fricka: Veasey
Alberich: Kelemen
Loge: Stolze
Erda: Chookasian
Fasolt: Talvela
Fafner: Ridderbusch
Freia: Mangelsdorff
Froh: Grobe
Donner: Milnes [5]
Mime: Velis
Woglinde: Rebmann

March 6, 1969, benefit sponsored by the Metropolitan Opera Guild for the production funds [106]
Il trovatore (Verdi–Cammarano; new production) [373]
Conducted by Mehta
Manrico: Domingo
Leonora: L. Price
di Luna: Milnes [1]
Azucena: Bumbry
Ferrando: Macurdy
Ines: Ordassy
Ruiz: Anthony
Directed by Merrill
Designed by Colonnello

March 10, 1969 [107]
Il trovatore (Verdi–Cammarano) [374]
Conducted by Mehta
Manrico: Domingo
Leonora: L. Price
di Luna: Milnes [2]
Azucena: Bumbry
Ferrando: Macurdy
Ines: Ordassy
Ruiz: Anthony

March 25, 1969 [108]
Il trovatore (Verdi–Cammarano) [376]
Conducted by Mehta
Manrico: McCracken
Leonora: L. Price
di Luna: Milnes [3]
Azucena: Bumbry
Ferrando: Giaiotti
Ines: Ordassy
Ruiz: Anthony

March 29, 1969, matinee (broadcast) [109]
Il trovatore (Verdi–Cammarano) [378]
Conducted by Mehta
Manrico: McCracken
Leonora: L. Price
di Luna: Milnes [4]
Azucena: Bumbry
Ferrando: Macurdy
Ines: Ordassy
Ruiz: Anthony

April 1, 1969 [110]
Il trovatore (Verdi–Cammarano) [379]
Conducted by Mehta
Manrico: McCracken
Leonora: L. Price
di Luna: Milnes [5]
Azucena: Bumbry
Ferrando: Giaiotti
Ines: Ordassy
Ruiz: Anthony

April 5, 1969 [111]
Il trovatore (Verdi–Cammarano) [380]
Conducted by Mehta
Manrico: McCracken
Leonora: L. Price
di Luna: Milnes [6]
Azucena: Bumbry
Ferrando: Macurdy
Ines: Ordassy
Ruiz: Anthony

April 15, 1969 [112]
Il trovatore (Verdi–Cammarano) [382]
Conducted by K. Adler
Manrico: McCracken
Leonora: L. Price
di Luna: Milnes [7]
Azucena: Bumbry
Ferrando: Macurdy
Ines: Ordassy
Ruiz: Anthony

BOSTON, MASSACHUSETTS

April 21, 1969 [113]
Il trovatore (Verdi–Cammarano) [384]
Conducted by Mehta
Manrico: McCracken
Leonora: Arroyo
di Luna: Milnes [8]
Azucena: Dalis
Ferrando: Michalski
Ines: Ordassy
Ruiz: Anthony

CLEVELAND, OHIO

April 28, 1969 [114]
Il trovatore (Verdi–Cammarano) [385]
Conducted by Franci

Manrico: McCracken
Leonora: Tucci
di Luna: Milnes [9]
Azucena: Rankin
Ferrando: Michalski
Ines: Ordassy
Ruiz: Anthony

May 3, 1969, matinee [115]
Il barbiere di Siviglia (Rossini–Sterbini)
[331]
Conducted by Lombard
Figaro: Milnes [4]
Rosina: Moffo
Almaviva: Alva
Bartolo: Corena
Basilio: Tozzi
Berta: Love
Fiorello: Boucher

ATLANTA, GEORGIA

May 9, 1969 [116]
Il barbiere di Siviglia (Rossini–Sterbini)
[332]
Conducted by Lombard
Figaro: Milnes [5]
Rosina: Boky
Almaviva: Alva
Bartolo: Corena
Basilio: Siepi
Berta: Love
Fiorello: Boucher

MEMPHIS, TENNESSEE

May 13, 1969 [117]
Il trovatore (Verdi–Cammarano) [387]
Conducted by Franci
Manrico: McCracken
Leonora: Tucci
di Luna: Milnes [10]
Azucena: Rankin
Ferrando: Macurdy
Ines: Ordassy
Ruiz: Anthony

DALLAS, TEXAS

May 16, 1969 [118]
Il trovatore (Verdi–Cammarano) [388]
Conducted by Franci
Manrico: McCracken
Leonora: Tucci
di Luna: Milnes [11]
Azucena: Rankin
Ferrando: Michalski
Ines: Ordassy
Ruiz: Anthony

MINNEAPOLIS, MINNESOTA

May 24, 1969, matinee [119]
Il barbiere di Siviglia (Rossini–Sterbini)
[333]
Conducted by Lombard
Figaro: Milnes [6]
Rosina: Boky
Almaviva: Alva
Bartolo: Corena
Basilio: Siepi
Berta: Love
Fiorello: Boucher

DETROIT, MICHIGAN

May 29, 1969 [120]
Il trovatore (Verdi–Cammarano) [390]
Conducted by Franci
Manrico: McCracken
Leonora: Tucci
di Luna: Milnes [12]
Azucena: Dalis
Ferrando: Macurdy
Ines: Ordassy
Ruiz: Anthony

METROPOLITAN OPERA HOUSE

June 6, 1969 [121]
Il trovatore (Verdi–Cammarano) [391]
Conducted by Franci
Manrico: McCracken
Leonora: Tucci
di Luna: Milnes [13]
Azucena: Dalis
Ferrando: Macurdy
Ruiz: Anthony

BROOKLYN, NEW YORK

**June 27, 1969 (concert performance)
[122]**
La traviata (Verdi–Piave) [547]
Conducted by Behr
Violetta: Kirsten
Alfredo: Shirley
Germont: Milnes [5]
Flora: Ordassy
Gastone: Anthony
Douphol: Christopher
D'Obigny: Boucher
Grenvil: Harvuot
Annina: Di Franco
Giuseppe: Marcella

1969–70
METROPOLITAN OPERA HOUSE

**January 8, 1970, benefit sponsored by the
Metropolitan Opera Guild for produc-
tion funds [123]**
Cavalleria rusticana (Mascagni–Targioni-
Tozzetti/Menasci; new production)
[443]
Conducted by Bernstein
Santuzza: Bumbry
Turiddu: Corelli
Lola: Casei
Directed by Zeffirelli
Designed by Zeffirelli

Pagliacci **(Leoncavallo; new production)
[481]**
Conducted by Cleva
Nedda: Amara
Canio: Tucker
Tonio: Milnes [1]
Silvio: Walker
Directed by Zeffirelli
Designed by Zeffirelli

January 12, 1970 [124]
Cavalleria rusticana (Mascagni–Targioni-
Tozzetti/Menasci) [444]
Conducted by L. Bernstein
Santuzza: Bumbry
Turiddu: Corelli
Lola: Casei

Pagliacci (Leoncavallo) [482]
Conducted by Cleva
Nedda: Amara
Canto: Tucker
Tonio: Milnes [2]
Silvio: Walker

January 14, 1970 [125]
Aida (Verdi–Ghislanzoni) [765]
Conducted by Molinari-Pradelli
Aida: Amara
Radames: Thomas
Amneris: Dalis
Amonasro: Milnes [6]
Ramfis: Flagello
King: Plishka

January 17, 1970 [126]
Aida (Verdi–Ghislanzoni) [766]
Conducted by Molinari-Pradelli
Aida: Amara
Radames: Corelli
Amneris: Dalis
Amonasro: Milnes [7]
Ramfis: Flagello
King: Plishka

January 20, 1970 [127]
Cavalleria rusticana (Mascagni–Targioni-
  Tozzetti/Menasci) [445]
Conducted by Bernstein
Santuzza: Bumbry
Turiddu: Corelli
Lola: Forst
Pagliacci (Leoncavallo) [483]
Conducted by Cleva
Nedda: Stratas
Canio: Tucker
Tonio: Milnes [3]
Silvio: Walker

**March 21, 1970, matinee (broadcast)
[128]**
La traviata (Verdi–Piave) [551]
Conducted by Rich
Violetta: Pilou
Alfredo: Bergonzi
Germont: Milnes [6]
Flora: Kraft
Gastone: Goeke
Douphol: Goodloe

D'Obigny: Boucher
Grenvil: Sgarro
Annina: Di Franco

March 26, 1970 [129]
La traviata (Verdi–Piave) [553]
Conducted by Rich
Violetta: Curtin
Alfredo: Bergonzi
Germont: Milnes [7]
Flora: Kraft
Gastone: Goeke
Douphol: Goodloe
D'Obigny: Boucher
Grenvil: Sgarro
Annina: Robinson

1970–71
METROPOLITAN OPERA HOUSE

September 14, 1970 [130]
Ernani (Verdi–Piave) [44]
Conducted by Schippers
Ernani: Bergonzi
Elvira: Arroyo
Carlo: Milnes [1]
Silva: R. Raimondi
Giovanna: Myhal
Directed by Butler
Designed by Frances
Choreography by Sparemblek

September 19, 1970, matinee [131]
Ernani (Verdi–Piave) [45]
Conducted by Schippers
Ernani: Bergonzi
Elvira: Arroyo
Carlo: Milnes [2]
Silva: R. Raimondi
Giovanna: Myhal

September 24, 1970 [132]
Ernani (Verdi–Piave) [46]
Conducted by Schippers
Ernani: Bergonzi
Elvira: Arroyo
Carlo: Milnes [3]
Silva: R. Raimondi
Giovanna: Myhal

September 26, 1970 [133]
Cavalleria rusticana (Mascagni–Targioni-
Tozzetti/Menasci) [464]
Conducted by Cleva
Santuzza: Cossotto
Turiddu: Domingo
Lola: Casei
Pagliacci (Leoncavallo) [506]
Conducted by Cleva
Nedda: Stratas
Canio: McCracken
Tonio: Milnes [4]
Silvio: Cossa

October 12, 1970 [134]
La traviata (Verdi–Piave) [569]
Conducted by Bonynge
Violetta: Sutherland
Alfredo: Aragall
Germont: Milnes [8]
Flora: von Stade
Gastone: Goeke
Douphol: Gibbs
D'Obigny: Boucher
Grenvil: Sgarro
Annina: Di Franco

October 22, 1970 [135]
La traviata (Verdi–Piave) [570]
Conducted by Bonynge
Violetta: Sutherland
Alfredo: Pavarotti
Germont: Milnes [9]
Flora: von Stade
Gastone: Goeke
Douphol: Gibbs
D'Obigny: Boucher
Grenvil: Sgarro
Annina: Di Franco

October 27, 1970 [136]
La traviata (Verdi–Piave) [571]
Conducted by Bonynge
Violetta: Sutherland
Alfredo: Bergonzi
Germont: Milnes [10]
Flora: von Stade
Gastone: Anthony
Douphol: Goodloe
D'Obigny: Boucher
Grenvil: Sgarro
Annina: Di Franco

November 4, 1970 [137]
Un ballo in maschera (Verdi–Somma)
[118]
Conducted by Molinari-Pradelli
Amelia: Arroyo
Riccardo: Bergonzi
Renato: Milnes [11]
Ulrica: Chookasian
Oscar: Grist
Samuel: Plishka
Tom: Dobriansky
Silvano: Goodloe

January 8, 1971 [138]
Ernani (Verdi–Piave) [47]
Conducted by Schippers
Ernani: Corelli
Elvira: Arroyo
Carlo: Milnes [4]
Silva: Giaiotti
Giovanna: Myhal

January 16, 1971 [139]
Ernani (Verdi–Piave) [48]
Conducted by Schippers
Ernani: Corelli
Elvira: Arroyo
Carlo: Milnes [5]
Silva: Flagello
Giovanna: Myhal

January 19, 1971 [140]
Ernani (Verdi–Piave) [49]
Conducted by Schippers
Ernani: Domingo
Elvira: Arroyo
Carlo: Milnes [6]
Silva: Flagello
Giovanna: Myhal

January 23, 1971 [141]
Il barbiere di Siviglia (Rossini–Sterbini)
[335]
Conducted by Schippers
Figaro: Milnes [7]
Rosina: Horne
Almaviva: Di Giuseppe
Bartolo: Corena
Basilio: Tozzi
Berta: Kraft
Fiorello: Gibbs
Directed by Ritchard

Staged by Tavemia
Designed by Berman

January 28, 1971 [142]
Il barbiere di Siviglia (Rossini–Sterbini)
[336]
Conducted by Schippers
Figaro: Milnes [8]
Rosina: Horne
Almaviva: Di Giuseppe
Bartolo: Corena
Basilio: Tozzi
Berta: Kraft
Fiorello: Gibbs

February 12, 1971 [143]
Il barbiere di Siviglia (Rossini–Sterbini)
[337]
Conducted by Schippers
Figaro: Milnes [9]
Rosina: Robinson
Almaviva: Di Giuseppe
Bartolo: Corena
Basilio: Gramm
Berta: Love
Fiorello: Boucher

February 16, 1971 [144]
Il barbiere di Siviglia (Rossini–Sterbini)
[338]
Conducted by Schippers
Figaro: Milnes [10]
Rosina: Horne
Almaviva: Di Giuseppe
Bartolo: Corena
Basilio: Gramm
Berta: Kraft
Fiorello: Gibbs

**February 20, 1971, matinee (broadcast)
[145]**
Il barbiere di Siviglia (Rossini–Sterbini)
[339]
Conducted by Schippers
Figaro: Milnes [11]
Rosina: Horne
Almaviva: Di Giuseppe
Bartolo: Corena
Basilio Tozzi
Berta: Kraft
Fiorello: Gibbs

February 24, 1971 [146]
Il barbiere di Siviglia (Rossini–Sterbini)
[340]
Conducted by Schippers
Figaro: Milnes [12]
Rosina: Boky
Almaviva: Bonisolli
Bartolo: Corena
Basilio: Tozzi
Berta: Kraft
Fiorello: Gibbs

March 2, 1971 [147]
Il trovatore (Verdi–Cammarano) [392]
Conducted by Mehta
Manrico: Tucker
Leonora: Arroyo
di Luna: Milnes [14]
Azucena: Chookasian
Ferrando: Michalski
Ines: Myhal
Ruiz: Anthony
Directed by Merrill
Designed by Colonnello

March 5, 1971 [148]
Il trovatore (Verdi–Cammarano) [393]
Conducted by Mehta
Manrico: McCracken
Leonora: Arroyo
di Luna: Milnes [15]
Azucena: Chookasian
Ferrando: Michalski
Ines: Myhal
Ruiz: Anthony

March 17, 1971 [149]
Il trovatore (Verdi–Cammarano) [396]
Conducted by K. Adler
Manrico: Tucker
Leonora: Arroyo
di Luna: Milnes [16]
Azucena: Verrett
Ferrando: Michalski
Ines: Myhal
Ruiz: Anthony

March 20, 1971 [150]
Il trovatore (Verdi–Cammarano) [397]
Conducted by Mehta
Manrico: Tucker

Leonora: Amara
di Luna: Milnes [17]
Azucena: Verrett
Ferrando: Michalski
Ines: Myhal
Ruiz: Anthony

1971–72
METROPOLITAN OPERA HOUSE

September 24, 1971 [151]
Cavalleria rusticana (Mascagni–Targioni-
Tozzetti/Menasci) [474]
Conducted by Keene
Santuzza: Cossotto
Turiddu: Bergonzi
Lola: Casei
Directed by Zeffirelli
Staged by Melano
Designed by Zeffirelli
Pagliacci (Leoncavallo) [512]
Conducted by Keene
Nedda: Stratas
Canio: McCracken
Tonio: Milnes [5]
Silvio: Cossa
Directed by Zeffirelli
Staged by Melano
Designed by Zeffirelli
[The intermezzo from *Manon Lescaut,*
conducted by concertmaster Raymond
Gniewek, was played preceding
Cavalleria rusticana in memory of
Fausto Cleva, who had died on August
6, 1971.]

September 27, 1971 [152]
Cavalleria rusticana (Mascagni–Targioni-
Tozzetti/Menasci) [475]
Conducted by Keene
Santuzza: Cossotto
Turiddu: Bergonzi
Lola: Casei
Pagliacci (Leoncavallo) [513]
Conducted by Keene
Nedda: Stratas
Canio: R. Nagy
Tonio: Milnes [6]
Silvio: Cossa

October 1, 1971 [153]
Cavalleria rusticana (Mascagni–Targioni-
Tozzetti/Menasci) [476]
Conducted by Keene
Santuzza: Dalis
Turiddu: Bergonzi
Lola: Casei
Pagliacci (Leoncavallo) [514]
Conducted by Keene
Nedda: Stratas
Canio: Spiess
Tonio: Milnes [7]
Silvio: Cossa

October 9, 1971, matinee [154]
Cavalleria rusticana (Mascagni–Targioni-
Tozzetti/Menasci) [477]
Conducted by Keene
Santuzza: Dalis
Turiddu: Di Giuseppe
Lola: Casei
Pagliacci (Leoncavallo) [515]
Conducted by Keene
Nedda: Amara
Canio: McCracken
Tonio: Milnes [8]
Silvio: Cossa

October 15, 1971 [155]
Luisa Miller (Verdi–Cammarano) [24]
Conducted by Levine
Luisa: Maliponte
Rodolfo: Tucker
Miller: Milnes [18]
Walter: R. Raimondi
Wurm: Plishka
Federica: Dunn
Directed by Merrill
Designed by Colonnello
Choreography by Andrew

October 20, 1971 [156]
Luisa Miller (Verdi–Cammarano) [25]
Conducted by Levine
Luisa: Maliponte
Rodolfo: Tucker
Miller: Milnes [19]
Walter: R. Raimondi
Wurm: Plishka
Federica: Dunn

December 20, 1971 [157]
Cavalleria rusticana (Mascagni–Targioni-
Tozzetti/Menasci) [481]
Conducted by Keene
Santuzza: Ross
Turiddu: Tagliavini
Lola: Casei
Pagliacci (Leoncavallo) [519]
Conducted by Keene
Nedda: Cruz-Romo
Canio: McCracken
Tonio: Milnes [9]
Silvio: Cossa

December 23, 1971 [158]
Cavalleria rusticana (Mascagni–Targioni-
Tozzetti/Menasci) [482]
Conducted by Keene
Santuzza: Ross
Turiddu: Tagliavini
Lola: Casei
Alfio: Manuguerra
Lucia: Godfrey Ben-David
Pagliacci (Leoncavallo) [520]
Conducted by Keene
Nedda: Amara
Canio: McCracken
Tonio: Milnes [10]
Silvio: Cossa

December 31, 1971 [159]
Cavalleria rusticana (Mascagni–Targioni-
Tozzetti/Menasci) [483]
Conducted by Keene
Santuzza: Arroyo
Turiddu: Tagliavini
Lola: Casei
Pagliacci (Leoncavallo) [521]
Conducted by Keene
Nedda: Cruz-Romo
Canio: McCracken
Tonio: Milnes [11]
Silvio: Uppman

January 5, 1972 [160]
Cavalleria rusticana (Mascagni–Targioni-
Tozzetti/Menasci) [484]
Conducted by K. Adler
Santuzza: Arroyo
Turiddu: Tagliavini
Lola: Casei

Pagliacci (Leoncavallo) [522]
Conducted by K. Adler
Nedda: Cruz-Romo
Canio: McCracken
Tonio: Milnes [12]
Silvio: Cossa

January 12, 1972 [161]
Cavalleria rusticana (Mascagni–Targioni-
Tozzetti/Menasci) [485]
Conducted by K. Adler
Santuzza: Arroyo
Turiddu: Tagliavini
Lola: Forst
Pagliacci (Leoncavallo) [523]
Conducted by K. Adler
Nedda: Sukis
Canio: R. Nagy
Tonio: Milnes [13]
Silvio: Cossa

January 15, 1972 [162]
Cavalleria rusticana (Mascagni–Targioni-
Tozzetti/Menasci) [486]
Conducted by K. Adler
Santuzza: Arroyo
Turiddu: Di Giuseppe
Lola: Forst
Pagliacci (Leoncavallo) [524]
Conducted by K. Adler
Nedda: Sukis
Canio: McCracken
Tonio: Milnes [14]
Silvio: Cossa

January 18, 1972 [163]
Cavalleria rusticana (Mascagni–Targioni-
Tozzetti/Menasci) [487]
Conducted by K. Adler
Santuzza: Arroyo
Turiddu: Di Giuseppe
Lola: Forst
Pagliacci (Leoncavallo) [525]
Conducted by K. Adler
Nedda: Sukis
Canio: McCracken
Tonio: Milnes [15]
Silvio: Uppman

March 25, 1972, benefit sponsored by the Metropolitan Opera Guild for the production funds [164]
Otello (Verdi–Boito; new production) [184]
Conducted by Böhm
Otello: McCracken
Desdemona: Zylis-Gara
Iago: Milnes [1]
Emilia: Love
Cassio: Di Giuseppe
Lodovico: Plishka
Montano: Goodloe
Directed by Zeffirelli
Set design by Zeffirelli
Costume design by Hall

March 29, 1972 [165]
Otello (Verdi–Boito) [185]
Conducted by Böhm
Otello: McCracken
Desdemona: Zylis-Gara
Iago: Milnes [2]
Emilia: Love
Cassio: Di Giuseppe
Lodovico: Plishka
Montano: Goodloe

April 3, 1972 [166]
Otello (Verdi–Boito) [186]
Conducted by Böhm
Otello: McCracken
Desdemona: Zylis-Gara
Iago: Milnes [3]
Emilia: Love
Cassio: Lewis
Lodovico: Plishka
Montano: Goodloe

April 8, 1972, matinee (broadcast) [167]
Otello (Verdi–Boito) [187]
Conducted by Böhm
Otello: McCracken
Desdemona: Zylis-Gara
Iago: Milnes [4]
Emilia: Love
Cassio: Di Giuseppe
Lodovico: Plishka
Montano: Goodloe

April 13, 1972 [168]
Otello (Verdi–Boito) [188]
Conducted by Böhm
Otello: McCracken
Desdemona: Zylis-Gara
Iago: Milnes [5]
Emilia: Love
Cassio: Lewis
Lodovico: Plishka
Montano: Goodloe

April 17, 1972 [169]
Otello (Verdi–Boito) [189]
Conducted by Böhm
Otello: McCracken
Desdemona: Zylis-Gara
Iago: Milnes [6]
Emilia: Love
Cassio: Lewis
Lodovico: Plishka
Montano: Goodloe

April 22, 1972, matinee (broadcast) [170]
Don Carlos (Verdi–Méry/du Locle; in Italian) [93]
Conducted by Molinari-Pradelli
Carlos: Corelli
Elisabeth: Caballé
Rodrigue: Milnes [1]
Eboli: Bumbry
Philippe: Siepi
Grand Inquisitor: Macurdy
Celestial Voice: Amara
Friar: Plishka
Thibault: von Stade
Lerme: Goeke

April 22, 1972, benefit sponsored by the Metropolitan Opera Guild for the benevolent and retirement funds honoring Sir Rudof Bing, who at the end of the season retired after twenty-two years as general manager (telecast) [171]
Gala Performance in which Milnes sang:
Il barbiere di Siviglia (Rossini–Sterbini), "Dunque io son": Peters, Milnes

BOSTON, MASSACHUSETTS

April 26, 1972 [172]
Otello (Verdi–Boito) [191]
Conducted by Molinari-Pradelli
Otello: McCracken
Desdemona: Zylis-Gara
Iago: Milnes [7]
Emilia: Love
Cassio: Lewis
Lodovico: Plishka
Montano: Goodloe

CLEVELAND, OHIO

May 5, 1972 [173]
Otello (Verdi–Boito) [192]
Conducted by Molinari-Pradelli
Otello: McCracken
Desdemona: Zylis-Gara
Iago: Milnes [8]
Emilia: Love
Cassio: Lewis
Lodovico: Plishka
Montano: Goodloe
[McCracken canceled after act 1 and was replaced by Robert Nagy.]

ATLANTA, GEORGIA

May 8, 1972 [174]
Otello (Verdi–Boito) [193]
Conducted by Molinari-Pradelli
Otello: R. Nagy
Desdemona: Zylis-Gara
Iago: Milnes [9]
Emilia: Love
Cassio: Lewis
Lodovico: Plishka
Montano: Goodloe

MEMPHIS, TENNESSEE

May 15, 1972 [175]
Otello (Verdi–Boito) [194]
Conducted by Molinari-Pradelli
Otello: McCracken
Desdemona: Zylis-Gara
Iago: Milnes [10]
Emilia: Love

Cassio: Di Giuseppe
Lodovico: Plishka
Montano: Goodloe

NEW ORLEANS, LOUISIANA

May 18, 1972 [176]
Otello (Verdi–Boito) [195]
Conducted by Molinari-Pradelli
Otello: McCracken
Desdemona: Amara
Iago: Milnes [11]
Emilia: Love
Cassio: Di Giuseppe
Lodovico: Plishka
Montano: Goodloe

MINNEAPOLIS, MINNESOTA

May 22, 1972 [177]
Otello (Verdi–Boito) [196]
Conducted by Molinari-Pradelli
Otello: R. Nagy
Desdemona: Zylis-Gara
Iago: Milnes [12]
Emilia: Love
Cassio: Di Giuseppe
Lodovico: Karlsrud
Montano: Goodloe

May 25, 1972 [178]
Faust (Saint-Saëns–Barbier/Carré) [654]
Conducted by Rich
Faust: Domingo
Marguerite: Tucci
Méphistophélès: R. Raimondi
Valentin: Milnes [8]
Siebel: von Stade

DETROIT, MICHIGAN

May 29, 1972 [179]
Otello (Verdi–Boito) [197]
Conducted by Molinari-Pradelli
Otello: McCracken
Desdemona: Zylis-Gara
Iago: Milnes [13]
Emilia: Love
Cassio: Di Giuseppe
Lodovico: Karlsrud
Montano: Goodloe

METROPOLITAN OPERA HOUSE

June 5, 1972 [180]
Otello (Verdi–Boito) [198]
Conducted by Molinari-Pradelli
Otello: McCracken
Desdemona: Zylis-Gara
Iago: Milnes [14]
Emilia: Love
Cassio: Di Giuseppe
Lodovico: Plishka
Montano: Goodloe
[The performances of June 5–24 were
designated a Verdi Festival.]

June 10, 1972, matinee [181]
Rigoletto (Verdi–Piave) [502]
Conducted by Bonynge
Rigoletto: Milnes [1]
Gilda: Sutherland
Duke: Pavarotti
Maddalena: Godfrey Ben-David
Sparafucile: R. Raimondi
Monterone: Karlsrud
Borsa: Goeke
Marullo: Christopher
Ceprano: Best
Countess Ceprano: Wilcox
Giovanna: Ordassy

June 14, 1972 [182]
Rigoletto (Verdi–Piave) [503]
Conducted by Bonynge
Rigoletto: Milnes [2]
Gilda: Sutherland
Duke: Pavarotti
Maddalena: Godfrey Ben-David
Sparafucile: Vinco
Monterone: Karlsrud
Borsa: Goeke
Marullo: Christopher
Ceprano: Best
Countess Ceprano: Wilcox
Giovanna: Ordassy

1972–73
METROPOLITAN OPERA HOUSE

September 22, 1972 [183]
Un ballo in maschera (Verdi–Somma)
[125]
Conducted by P. H. Adler
Amelia: Arroyo
Riccardo: Domingo
Renato: Milnes [12]
Ulrica: Chookasian
Oscar: Robinson
Samuel: Morris
Tom: Best
Silvano: Goodloe
Directed by Rennert
Designed by Maximowna
Choreography by Andrew

September 28, 1972 [184]
Un ballo in maschera (Verdi–Somma)
[126]
Conducted by P. H. Adler
Amelia: Arroyo
Riccardo: Domingo
Renato: Milnes [13]
Ulrica: Chookasian
Oscar: Robinson
Samuel: Morris
Tom: Best
Silvano: Goodloe

October 2, 1972 [185]
Un ballo in maschera (Verdi–Somma)
[127]
Conducted by P. H. Adler
Amelia: Ross
Riccardo: Domingo
Renato: Milnes [14]
Ulrica: Chookasian
Oscar: Robinson
Samuel: Morris
Tom: Best
Silvano: Goodloe

October 5, 1972 [186]
La traviata (Verdi–Piave) [590]
Conducted by Molinari-Pradelli
Violetta: Tucci
Alfredo: Kraus

Germont: Milnes [11]
Flora: Kraft
Gastone: Anthony
Douphol: Goodloe
D'Obigny: Boucher
Grenvil: Sgarro
Annina: Norden

October 11, 1972 [187]
La traviata (Verdi–Piave) [591]
Conducted by Molinari-Pradelli
Violetta: Tucci
Alfredo: Kraus
Germont: Milnes [12]
Flora: Kraft
Gastone: Anthony
Douphol: Goodloe
D'Obigny: Boucher
Grenvil: Sgarro
Annina: Norden

October 14, 1972 [188]
Un ballo in maschera (Verdi–Somma)
[128]
Conducted by P. H. Adler
Amelia: Ross
Riccardo: Di Giuseppe
Renato: Milnes [15]
Ulrica: Baldani
Oscar: Robinson
Samuel: Morris
Tom: Best
Silvano: Goodloe

December 29, 1972 [189]
Otello (Verdi–Boito) [206]
Conducted by Levine
Otello: McCracken
Desdemona: Zylis-Gara
Iago: Milnes [15]
Emilia: Love
Cassio: Lewis
Lodovico: Morris
Montano: Goodloe

January 2, 1973 [190]
Otello (Verdi–Boito) [207]
Conducted by Levine
Otello: McCracken
Desdemona: Tebaldi
Iago: Milnes [16]

Emilia: Kraft
Cassio: Lewis
Lodovico: Morris
Montano: Goodloe

January 5, 1973 [191]
Otello (Verdi–Boito) [208]
Conducted by Levine
Otello: McCracken
Desdemona: Tebaldi
Iago: Milnes [17]
Emilia: Kraft
Cassio: Lewis
Lodovico: Morris
Montano: Goodloe

January 8, 1973 [192]
Otello (Verdi–Boito) [209]
Conducted by Levine
Otello: McCracken
Desdemona: Tebaldi
Iago: Milnes [18]
Emilia: Kraft
Cassio: Lewis
Lodovico: Morris
Montano: Goodloe

January 25, 1973 [193]
Macbeth (Verdi–Piave/Maffei; revised
production) [26]
Conducted by Molinari-Pradelli
Macbeth: Milnes [1]
Lady Macbeth: Arroyo
Banquo: R. Raimondi
Macduff: Tagliavini
Malcolm: MacWherter
Lady-in-Attendance: Ordassy
Physician: Karlsrud
Manservant: Dater
Murderer: Best
Warrior: Christopher
Directed by Igesz
Designed by Neher, Jampolis

**January 27, 1973, matinee (broadcast)
[194]**
Un ballo in maschera (Verdi–Somma)
[133]
Conducted by P. H. Adler
Amelia: Cruz-Romo
Riccardo: Tucker

Renato: Milnes [16]
Ulrica: Dalis
Oscar: Robinson
Samuel: Morris
Tom: Best
Silvano: Christopher

January 31, 1973 [195]
Macbeth (Verdi–Piave/Maffei) [27]
Conducted by Molinari-Pradelli
Macbeth: Milnes [2]
Lady Macbeth: Arroyo
Banquo: R. Raimondi
Macduff: Tagliavini
Malcolm: MacWherter
Lady-in-Attendance: Ordassy
Physician: Karlsrud
Manservant: Dater
Murderer: Best
Warrior: Christopher

February 3, 1973, matinee (broadcast) [196]
Macbeth (Verdi–Piave/Maffei) [28]
Conducted by Molinari-Pradelli
Macbeth: Milnes [3]
Lady Macbeth: Arroyo
Banquo: R. Raimondi
Macduff: Tagliavini
Malcolm: MacWherter
Lady-in-Attendance: Ordassy
Physician: Karlsrud
Manservant: Dater
Murderer: Best
Warrior: Christopher

February 7, 1973 [197]
Macbeth (Verdi–Piave/Maffei) [29]
Conducted by Molinari-Pradelli
Macbeth: Milnes [4]
Lady Macbeth: Arroyo
Banquo: R. Raimondi
Macduff: Lewis
Malcolm: MacWherter
Lady-in-Attendance: Ordassy
Physician: Karlsrud
Manservant: Dater
Murderer: Best
Warrior: Christopher

February 13, 1973 [198]
Macbeth (Verdi–Piave/Maffei) [30]
Conducted by Molinari-Pradelli
Macbeth: Milnes [5]
Lady Macbeth: Arroyo
Banquo: R. Raimondi
Macduff: Tagliavini
Malcolm: MacWherter
Lady-in-Attendance: Ordassy
Physician: Karlsrud
Manservant: Dater
Murderer: Best
Warrior: Christopher

February 17, 1973 [199]
Macbeth (Verdi–Piave/Maffei) [31]
Conducted by Molinari-Pradelli
Macbeth: Milnes [6]
Lady Macbeth: Arroyo
Banquo: R. Raimondi
Macduff: Tagliavini
Malcolm: MacWherter
Lady-in-Attendance: Ordassy
Physician: Karlsrud
Manservant: Dater
Murderer: Best
Warrior: Christopher

February 23, 1973 [200]
Macbeth (Verdi–Piave/Maffei) [32]
Conducted by Molinari-Pradelli
Macbeth: Milnes [7]
Lady Macbeth: Ross
Banquo: R. Raimondi
Macduff: Tagliavini
Malcolm: MacWherter
Lady-in-Attendance: Ordassy
Physician: Karlsrud
Manservant: Dater
Murderer: Best
Warrior: Christopher

March 3, 1973 [201]
Macbeth (Verdi–Piave/Maffei) [33]
Conducted by Molinari-Pradelli
Macbeth: Milnes [8]
Lady Macbeth: Ross
Banquo: Tozzi
Macduff: Tagliavini
Malcolm: MacWherter
Lady-in-Attendance: Ordassy

Physician: Karlsrud
Manservant: Dater
Murderer: Best
Warrior: Christopher

March 12, 1973 [202]
Macbeth (Verdi–Piave/Maffei) [34]
Conducted by Cillario
Macbeth: Milnes [9]
Lady Macbeth: Ross
Banquo: Tozzi
Macduff: Lewis
Malcolm: MacWherter
Lady-in-Attendance: Ordassy
Physician: Karlsrud
Manservant: Dater
Murderer: Best
Warrior: Christopher

BOSTON, MASSACHUSETTS

April 27, 1973 [203]
Macbeth (Verdi–Piave/Maffei) [35]
Conducted by Molinari-Pradelli
Macbeth: Milnes [10]
Lady Macbeth: Arroyo
Banquo: R. Raimondi
Macduff: Lewis
Malcolm: Anthony
Lady-in-Attendance: Ordassy
Physician: Karlsrud
Manservant: Simeone
Murderer: Best
Warrior: Christopher

CLEVELAND, OHIO

May 4, 1973 [204]
Macbeth (Verdi–Piave/Maffei) [36]
Conducted by Molinari-Pradelli
Macbeth: Milnes [11]
Lady Macbeth: Arroyo
Banquo: R. Raimondi
Macduff: Gibbs
Malcolm: Anthony
Lady-in-Attendance: Ordassy
Physician: Karlsrud
Manservant: Simeone
Murderer: Best
Warrior: Christopher

ATLANTA, GEORGIA

May 11, 1973 [205]
Macbeth (Verdi–Piave/Maffei) [37]
Conducted by Molinari-Pradelli
Macbeth: Milnes [12]
Lady Macbeth: Bumbry
Banquo: R. Raimondi
Macduff: Gibbs
Malcolm: Anthony
Lady-in-Attendance: Ordassy
Physician: Karlsrud
Manservant: Simeone
Murderer: Best
Warrior: Goodloe

MEMPHIS, TENNESSEE

May 15, 1973 [206]
Macbeth (Verdi–Piave/Maffei) [38]
Conducted by Molinari-Pradelli
Macbeth: Milnes [13]
Lady Macbeth: Bumbry
Banquo: R. Raimondi
Macduff: Corelli
Malcolm: MacWherter
Lady-in-Attendance: Ordassy
Physician: Karlsrud
Manservant: Simeone
Murderer: Best
Warrior: Christopher

DALLAS, TEXAS

May 18, 1973 [207]
Macbeth (Verdi–Piave/Maffei) [39]
Conducted by Molinari-Pradelli
Macbeth: Milnes [14]
Lady Macbeth: Bumbry
Banquo: R. Raimondi
Macduff: Corelli
Malcolm: MacWherter
Lady-in-Attendance: Ordassy
Physician: Karlsrud
Manservant: Simeone
Murderer: Best
Warrior: Goodloe

MINNEAPOLIS, MINNESOTA

May 21, 1973 [208]
Macbeth (Verdi–Piave/Maffei) [40]
Conducted by Molinari-Pradelli
Macbeth: Milnes [15]
Lady Macbeth: Bumbry
Banquo: Tozzi
Macduff: Corelli
Malcolm: MacWherter
Lady-in-Attendance: Ordassy
Physician: Karlsrud
Manservant: Simeone
Murderer: Best
Warrior: Christopher

DETROIT, MICHIGAN

May 31, 1973 [209]
Macbeth (Verdi–Piave/Maffei) [41]
Conducted by Molinari-Pradelli
Macbeth: Milnes [16]
Lady Macbeth: Bumbry
Banquo: Tozzi
Macduff: Lewis
Malcolm: Anthony
Lady-in-Attendance: Ordassy
Physician: Karlsrud
Manservant: Simeone
Murderer: Best
Warrior: Christopher

METROPOLITAN OPERA HOUSE

June 4, 1973 [210]
Macbeth (Verdi–Piave/Maffei) [42]
Conducted by Molinari-Pradelli
Macbeth: Milnes [17]
Lady Macbeth: Bumbry
Banquo: R. Raimondi
Macduff: Lewis
Malcolm: Anthony
Lady-in-Attendance: Ordassy
Physician: Karlsrud
Manservant: Simeone
Murderer: Best
Warrior: Goodloe

June 8, 1973 [211]
Otello (Verdi–Boito) [210]

Conducted by Levine
Otello: Vickers
Desdemona: Lorengar
Iago: Milnes [19]
Emilia: Kraft
Cassio: Goeke
Lodovico: Morris
Montano: Goodloe

1973–74
METROPOLITAN OPERA HOUSE

January 31, 1974, benefit sponsored by the Metropolitan Opera Guild for the production funds [212]
Les vêpres siciliennes (Verdi–Scribe/
Duveyrier; in Italian; new production;
Metropolitan Opera stage premiere)
[2]
Conducted by Levine
Hélène: Caballé
Henri: Gedda
Monfort: Milnes [1]
Procida: Díaz
Ninetta: Munzer
Daniéli: Ahlstedt
Mainfroid: Franke
Thibaud: Castel
Béthune: Goodloe
Directed by Dexter
Set design by Svoboda
Costume design by Skalicky
Choreography by Badolato
Translation by Caimi

February 6, 1974 [213]
Les vêpres siciliennes (Verdi–Scribe/
Duveyrier; in Italian) [3]
Conducted by Levine
Hélène: Caballé
Henri: Gedda
Monfort: Milnes [2]
Procida: Díaz
Ninetta: Munzer
Daniéli: Ahlstedt
Mainfroid: Franke
Thibaud: Castel
Béthune: Goodloe

February 11, 1974 [214]
Les vêpres siciliennes (Verdi–Scribe/
Duveyrier; in Italian) [4]
Conducted by Levine
Hélène: Caballé
Henri: Gedda
Monfort: Milnes [3]
Procida: Díaz
Ninetta: Munzer
Daniéli: Ahlstedt
Mainfroid: Franke
Thibaud: Castel
Béthune: Goodloe

February 23, 1974 [215]
Les vêpres siciliennes (Verdi–Scribe/
Duveyrier; in Italian) [5]
Conducted by Levine
Hélène: Caballé
Henri: Gedda
Monfort: Milnes [4]
Procida: Díaz
Ninetta: Munzer
Daniéli: Ahlstedt
Mainfroid: Franke
Thibaud: Schmorr
Béthune: Goodloe

February 26, 1974 [216]
Les vêpres siciliennes (Verdi–Scribe/
Duveyrier; in Italian) [6]
Conducted by Levine
Hélène: Caballé
Henri: Gedda
Monfort: Milnes [5]
Procida: Díaz
Ninetta: Munzer
Daniéli: Ahlstedt
Mainfroid: Franke
Thibaud: Castel
Béthune: Goodloe

March 1, 1974 [217]
Les vêpres siciliennes (Verdi–Scribe/
Duveyrier; in Italian) [7]
Conducted by Levine
Hélène: Caballé
Henri: Gedda
Monfort: Milnes [6]
Procida: Díaz
Ninetta: Munzer

Daniéli: Ahlstedt
Mainfroid: Franke
Thibaud: Castel
Béthune: Goodloe

March 9, 1974, matinee (broadcast) [218]
Les vêpres siciliennes (Verdi–Scribe/
Duveyrier; in Italian) [8]
Conducted by Levine
Hélène: Caballé
Henri: Gedda
Monfort: Milnes [7]
Procida: Díaz
Ninetta: Munzer
Daniéli: Ahlstedt
Mainfroid: Franke
Thibaud: Castel
Béthune: Goodloe

March 12, 1974 [219]
Les vêpres siciliennes (Verdi–Scribe/
Duveyrier; in Italian) [9]
Conducted by Levine
Hélène: Caballé
Henri: Gedda
Monfort: Milnes [8]
Procida: Díaz
Ninetta: Munzer
Daniéli: Ahlstedt
Mainfroid: Franke
Thibaud: Castel
Béthune: Goodloe

**March 28, 1974, benefit sponsored by the
Metropolitan Opera Guild for the pro-
duction funds [220]**
Don Giovanni (Mozart–Da Ponte) [317]
Conducted by Levine
Giovanni: Milnes [1]
Anna: L. Price
Ottavio: Burrows
Elvira: Zylis-Gara
Leporello: Berry
Zerlina: Stratas
Directed by Graf
Staged by Tavernia
Designed by Berman
Choreography by Solov

April 1, 1974 [221]
Don Giovanni (Mozart–Da Ponte) [318]

Conducted by Levine
Giovanni: Milnes [2]
Anna: L. Price
Ottavio: Burrows
Elvira: Zylis-Gara
Leporello: Berry
Zerlina: Stratas

April 5, 1974 [222]
Don Giovanni (Mozart–Da Ponte) [319]
Conducted by Rudolf
Giovanni: Milnes [3]
Anna: L. Price
Ottavio: Burrows
Elvira: Zylis-Gara
Leporello: Berry
Zerlina: Stratas

April 10, 1974 [223]
Don Giovanni (Mozart–Da Ponte) [320]
Conducted by Levine
Giovanni: Milnes [4]
Anna: L. Price
Ottavio: Burrows
Elvira: Zylis-Gara
Leporello: Berry
Zerlina: Stratas

April 13, 1974, matinee (broadcast) [224]
Don Giovanni (Mozart–Da Ponte) [321]
Conducted by Levine
Giovanni: Milnes [5]
Anna: L. Price
Ottavio: Burrows
Elvira: Zylis-Gara
Leporello: Berry
Zerlina: Stratas

April 16, 1974 [225]
Don Giovanni (Mozart–Da Ponte) [322]
Conducted by Rudolf
Giovanni: Milnes [6]
Anna: Moser
Ottavio: Burrows
Elvira: Zylis-Gara
Leporello: Berry
Zerlina: Stratas

April 19, 1974 [226]
Don Giovanni (Mozart–Da Ponte) [323]
Conducted by Rudolf
Giovanni: Milnes [7]
Anna: Moser

Ottavio: Burrows
Elvira: Zylis-Gara
Leporello: Berry
Zerlina: von Stade

BOSTON, MASSACHUSETTS

April 24, 1974 [227]
Don Giovanni (Mozart–Da Ponte) [324]
Conducted by Rudolf
Giovanni: Milnes [8]
Anna: Moser
Ottavio: Goeke
Elvira: Lear
Leporello: Corena
Zerlina: von Stade

DETROIT, MICHIGAN

April 29, 1974 [228]
Don Giovanni (Mozart–Da Ponte) [325]
Conducted by Rudolf
Giovanni: Milnes [9]
Anna: Moser
Ottavio: Goeke
Elvira: Lear
Leporello: Corena
Zerlina: von Stade
[*L'Italiana in Algeri* had been scheduled
for this date but was replaced by *Don
Giovanni* because several of the singers
were ill.]

April 30, 1974 [229]
Don Giovanni (Mozart–Da Ponte) [326]
Conducted by Rudolf
Giovanni: Milnes [10]
Anna: Moser
Ottavio: Goeke
Elvira: Lear
Leporello: Berry
Zerlina: von Stade

ATLANTA, GEORGIA

May 8, 1974 [230]
Don Giovanni (Mozart–Da Ponte) [327]
Conducted by Rudolf
Giovanni: Milnes [11]
Anna: Moser
Ottavio: Gocke

Elvira: Lear
Leporello: Corena
Zerlina: von Stade

MEMPHIS, TENNESSEE

May 15, 1974 [231]
Don Giovanni (Mozart–Da Ponte) [328]
Conducted by Rudolf
Giovanni: Milnes [12]
Anna: Moser
Ottavio: Livings
Elvira: Lear
Leporello: Berry
Zerlina: von Stade

DALLAS, TEXAS

May 18, 1974 [232]
Don Giovanni (Mozart–Da Ponte) [329]
Conducted by Rudolf
Giovanni: Milnes [13]
Anna: Moser
Ottavio: Livings
Elvira: Lear
Leporello: Berry
Zerlina: von Stade

MINNEAPOLIS, MINNESOTA

May 23, 1974 [233]
Don Giovanni (Mozart–Da Ponte) [330]
Conducted by Rudolf
Giovanni: Milnes [14]
Anna: Moser
Ottavio: Livings
Elvira: Lear
Leporello: Corena
Zerlina: von Stade

METROPOLITAN OPERA HOUSE

May 29, 1974 [234]
Don Giovanni (Mozart–Da Ponte) [331]
Conducted by Rudolf
Giovanni: Milnes [15]
Anna: Moser
Ottavio: Goeke
Elvira: Lear
Leporello: Berry
Zerlina: von Stade

1974–75
CLEVELAND, OHIO

September 17, 1974 [235]
Les vêpres siciliennes (Verdi–Scribe/
  Duveyrier; in Italian) [17]
Conducted by Levine
Hélène: Deutekom
Henri: Lewis
Monfort: Milnes [9]
Procida: Plishka
Ninetta: Munzer
Daniéli: Ahlstedt
Mainfroid: Franke
Thibaud: Castel
Béthune: Goodloe
Directed by Dexter
Staged by Melano
Set design by Svoboda
Costume design by Skalicky
Choreography by Badolato
Translation by Caimi

September 19, 1974 [236]
Don Giovanni (Mozart–Da Ponte) [336]
Conducted by Rudolf
Giovanni: Milnes [16]
Anna: Deutekom
Ottavio: Goeke
Elvira: Zylis-Gara
Leporello: Plishka
Zerlina: Peters
Directed by Graf
Staged by Tavernia
Designed by Berman
Choreography by Solov

METROPOLITAN OPERA HOUSE

September 23, 1974 [237]
Les vêpres siciliennes (Verdi–Scribe/
  Duveyrier; in Italian) [18]
Conducted by Levine
Hélène: Deutekom
Henri: Domingo
Monfort: Milnes [10]
Procida: Plishka
Ninetta: Munzer
Daniéli: Ahlstedt
Mainfroid: Franke

Thibaud: Castel
Béthune: Goodloe

September 28, 1974 [238]
Don Giovanni (Mozart–Da Ponte) [337]
Conducted by Rudolf
Giovanni: Milnes [17]
Anna: Deutekom
Ottavio: Goeke
Elvira: Zylis-Gara
Leporello: Plishka
Zerlina: Peters

October 2, 1974 [239]
Les vêpres siciliennes (Verdi–Scribe/
    Duveyrier; in Italian) [19]
Conducted by Levine
Hélène: Deutekom
Henri: Domingo
Monfort: Milnes [11]
Procida: Plishka
Ninetta: Munzer
Daniéli: Ahlstedt
Mainfroid: Franke
Thibaud: Castel
Béthune: Goodloe

**October 5, 1974, matinee (broadcast)
[240]**
Don Giovanni (Mozart–Da Ponte) [338]
Conducted by Rudolf
Giovanni: Milnes [18]
Anna: Deutekom
Ottavio: Goeke
Elvira: Zylis-Gara
Leporello: Plishka
Zerlina: Peters

October 11, 1974 [241]
Don Giovanni (Mozart–Da Ponte) [339]
Conducted by Rudolf
Giovanni: Milnes [19]
Anna: Deutekom
Ottavio: Goeke
Elvira: Zylis-Gara
Leporello: Plishka
Zerlina: Peters

October 21, 1974 [242]
Don Giovanni (Mozart–Da Ponte) [340]
Conducted by Rudolf
Giovanni: Milnes [20]

Anna: Mathes
Ottavio: Goeke
Elvira: Zylis-Gara
Leporello: Plishka
Zerlina: Peters

October 26, 1974 [243]
Les vêpres siciliennes (Verdi–Scribe/
    Duveyrier; in Italian) [21]
Conducted by Levine
Hélène: Scotto
Henri: Domingo
Monfort: Milnes [12]
Procida: Plishka
Ninetta: Munzer
Daniéli: Ahlstedt
Mainfroid: Franke
Thibaud: Castel
Béthune: Goodloe

October 29, 1974 [244]
Don Giovanni (Mozart–Da Ponte) [341]
Conducted by Rudolf
Giovanni: Milnes [21]
Anna: Mathes
Ottavio: Goeke
Elvira: Zylis-Gara
Leporello: Plishka
Zerlina: Peters

November 4, 1974 [245]
Les vêpres siciliennes (Verdi–Scribe/
    Duveyrier; in Italian) [23]
Conducted by Levine
Hélène: Scotto
Henri: Domingo
Monfort: Milnes [13]
Procida: Plishka
Ninetta: Munzer
Daniéli: Ahlstedt
Mainfroid: Franke
Thibaud: Castel
Béthune: Goodloe

November 7, 1974 [246]
Don Giovanni (Mozart–Da Ponte) [342]
Conducted by Rudolf
Giovanni: Milnes [22]
Anna: Mathes
Ottavio: Goeke
Elvira: Zylis-Gara

Leporello: Plishka
Zerlina: Peters

January 1, 1975 [247]
Cavalleria rusticana (Mascagni–Targioni-
   Tozzetti/Menasci) [502]
Conducted by Nelson
Santuzza: Ross
Turiddu: Lewis
Lola: Casei
Pagliacci (Leoncavallo) [540]
Conducted by Nelson
Nedda: Moffo
Canio: McCracken
Tonio: Milnes [16]
Silvio: Carlson

January 10, 1975 [248]
Cavalleria rusticana (Mascagni–Targioni-
   Tozzetti/Menasci) [503]
Conducted by Nelson
Santuzza: Grillo
Turiddu: Theyard
Lola: Baldwin
Pagliacci (Leoncavallo) [541]
Conducted by Nelson
Nedda: Moffo
Canio: McCracken
Tonio: Milnes [17]
Silvio: Carlson
[This performance was dedicated to the
   memory of Richard Tucker, who had
   died on January 8, 1975.]

**January 18, 1975, matinee (broadcast)
[249]**
Cavalleria rusticana (Mascagni–Targioni-
   Tozzetti/Menasci) [504]
Conducted by Nelson
Santuzza: Bumbry
Turiddu: Theyard
Lola: Grillo
Pagliacci (Leoncavallo) [542]
Conducted by Nelson
Nedda: Moffo
Canio: McCracken
Tonio: Milnes [18]
Silvio: Carlson

March 6, 1975 [250]
Les vêpres siciliennes (Verdi–Scribe/
   Duveyrier; in Italian) [24]

Conducted by Levine
Helene: Deutekom
Henri: Lewis
Monfort: Milnes [14]
Procida: Plishka
Ninetta: Munzer
Daniéli: Ahlstedt
Mainfroid: Franke
Thibaud: Castel
Bethune: Goodloe

March 12, 1975 [251]
Les vêpres siciliennes (Verdi–Scribe/
   Duveyrier; in Italian) [25]
Conducted by Levine
Helene: Deutekom
Henri: Ochman
Monfort: Milnes [15]
Procida: Morris
Ninetta: Munzer
Daniéli: Ahlstedt
Mainfroid: Franke
Thibaud: Castel
Bethune: Goodloe

March 22, 1975 [252]
Les vêpres siciliennes (Verdi–Scribe/
   Duveyrier; in Italian) [26]
Conducted by Levine
Helene: Deutekom
Henri: Ochman
Monfort: Milnes [16]
Procida: Morris
Ninetta: Munzer
Daniéli: Ahlstedt
Mainfroid: Franke
Thibaud: Castel
Bethune: Goodloe

March 28, 1975 [253]
Les vêpres siciliennes (Verdi–Scribe/
   Duveyrier; in Italian) [27]
Conducted by Levine
Helene: Niska
Henri: Ochman
Monfort: Milnes [17]
Procida: Plishka
Ninetta: Munzer
Daniéli: Ahlstedt
Mainfroid: Franke
Thibaud: Castel
Bethune: Goodloe

March 31, 1975 [254]
Les vêpres siciliennes (Verdi–Scribe/
	Duveyrier; in Italian) [28]
Conducted by Levine
Helene: Niska
Henri: Lewis
Monfort: Milnes [18]
Procida: Plishka
Ninetta: Munzer
Daniéli: Anthony
Mainfroid: Franke
Thibaud: Castel
Bethune: Goodloe

April 12, 1975, matinee (broadcast) [255]
Les vêpres siciliennes (Verdi–Scribe/
	Duveyrier; in Italian) [29]
Conducted by Levine
Helene: Niska
Henri: Lewis
Monfort: Milnes [19]
Procida: Plishka
Ninetta: Munzer
Daniéli: Ahlstedt
Mainfroid: Franke
Thibaud: Castel
Bethune: Goodloe

VIENNA, VIRGINIA (WOLF TRAP
FARM PARK)

June 25, 1975 [256]
La traviata (Verdi–Piave) [619]
Conducted by Maag
Violetta: Maliponte
Alfredo: Alexander
Germont: Milnes [13]
Flora: Munzer
Gastone: Ahlstedt
Douphol: Goodloe
D'Obigny: Boucher
Grenvil: Karlsrud
Annina: Webber

June 28, 1975 [257]
Cavalleria rusticana (Mascagni–Targioni-
	Tozzetti/Menasci) [512]
Conducted by Nelson
Santuzza: Ross
Turiddu: Theyard

Lola: Baldwin
Pagliacci (Leoncavallo) [550]
Conducted by Nelson
Nedda: Azuma
Canio: R. Nagy
Tonio: Milnes [19]
Silvio: Carlson

1975–76
METROPOLITAN OPERA HOUSE

December 9, 1975 [258]
Un ballo in maschera (Verdi–Somma)
	[144]
Conducted by Lewis
Amelia: Ross
Riccardo: Morell
Renato: Milnes [17]
Ulrica: Forrester
Oscar: Shane
Samuel: Best
Tom: Booth
Silvano: Goodloe

December 17, 1975 [259]
Un ballo in maschera (Verdi–Somma)
	[145]
Conducted by Lewis
Amelia: Ross
Riccardo: Morell
Renato: Milnes [18]
Ulrica: Forrester
Oscar: Shane
Samuel: Michalski
Tom: Booth
Silvano: Goodloe

December 26, 1975 [260]
Un ballo in maschera (Verdi–Somma)
	[146]
Conducted by Lewis
Amelia: Ross
Riccardo: Raitzin
Renato: Milnes [19]
Ulrica: Forrester
Oscar: Shane
Samuel: Michalski
Tom: Booth
Silvano: Goodloe

January 3, 1976 [261]
Un ballo in maschera (Verdi–Somma)
[147]
Conducted by Lewis
Amelia: Ross
Riccardo: Morell
Renato: Milnes [20]
Ulrica: Kraft
Oscar: Shane
Samuel: Michalski
Tom: Booth
Silvano: Goodloe

January 8, 1976 [262]
Un ballo in maschera (Verdi–Somma)
[148]
Conducted by Lewis
Amelia: Barlow
Riccardo: Raitzin
Renato: Milnes [21]
Ulrica: Kraft
Oscar: Shane
Samuel: Best
Tom: Booth
Silvano: Goodloe

February 25, 1976, benefit sponsored by the Metropolitan Opera Guild for the production funds [263]
I Puritani (Bellini–Pepoli; new production) [9]
Conducted by Bonynge
Elvira: Sutherland
Arturo: Pavarotti
Riccardo: Milnes [1]
Giorgio: Morris
Enrichetta: Munzer
Directed by Sequi
Set design by M. C. Lee
Costume design by Hall

February 28, 1976 [264]
I Puritani (Bellini–Pepoli) [10]
Conducted by Bonynge
Elvira: Sutherland
Arturo: Pavarotti
Riccardo: Milnes [2]
Giorgio: Morris
Enrichetta: Munzer

March 2, 1976 [265]
I Puritani (Bellini–Pepoli) [11]
Conducted by Bonynge
Elvira: Sutherland
Arturo: Pavarotti
Riccardo: Milnes [3]
Giorgio: Morris
Enrichetta: Munzer

March 5, 1976 [266]
I Puritani (Bellini–Pepoli) [12]
Conducted by Bonynge
Elvira: Sutherland
Arturo: Pavarotti
Riccardo: Milnes [4]
Giorgio: Morris
Enrichetta: Munzer

March 9, 1976 [267]
I Puritani (Bellini–Pepoli) [13]
Conducted by Bonynge
Elvira: Sutherland
Arturo: Pavarotti
Riccardo: Milnes [5]
Giorgio: Morris
Enrichetta: Munzer

March 13, 1976, matinee (broadcast) [268]
I Puritani (Bellini–Pepoli) [14]
Conducted by Bonynge
Elvira: Sutherland
Arturo: Pavarotti
Riccardo: Milnes [6]
Giorgio: Morris
Enrichetta: Munzer

March 17, 1976 [269]
I Puritani (Bellini–Pepoli) [15]
Conducted by Bonynge
Elvira: Sutherland
Arturo: Pavarotti
Riccardo: Milnes [7]
Giorgio: Morris
Enrichetta: Munzer

1976–77
METROPOLITAN OPERA HOUSE

November 27, 1976 [270]
La forza del destino (Verdi–Piave) [175]
Conducted by Levine
Leonora: Arroyo
Alvaro: Giacomini
Carlo: Milnes [4]
Father Superior: Giaiotti
Preziosilla: Elias
Melitone: Flagello
Marquis: Booth
Curra: Ordassy
Mayor: Dobriansky
Directed by Dexter
Set design by Berman
Costume design by Hall
Choreography by Vesak

December 2, 1976 [271]
La forza del destino (Verdi–Piave) [176]
Conducted by Levine
Leonora: Arroyo
Alvaro: Giacomini
Carlo: Milnes [5]
Father Superior: Giaiotti
Preziosilla: Elias
Melitone: Flagello
Marquis: Booth
Curra: Ordassy
Mayor: Dobriansky

December 18, 1976 [272]
Tosca (Puccini–Illica/Giacosa) [590]
Conducted by Santi
Tosca: Bumbry
Cavaradossi: Giacomini
Scarpia: Milnes [1]
Sacristan: Capecchi
Spoletta: Velis
Angelotti: Monk
Sciarrone: Christopher
Directed by Schenk
Staged by Melano
Designed by Heinrich

December 21, 1976 [273]
Tosca (Puccini–Illica/Giacosa) [591]
Conducted by Santi

Tosca: Bumbry
Cavaradossi: Giacomini
Scarpia: Milnes [2]
Sacristan: Capecchi
Spoletta: Velis
Angelotti: Monk
Sciarrone: Christopher

December 25, 1976 [274]
Tosca (Puccini–Illica/Giacosa) [592]
Conducted by Santi
Tosca: Bumbry
Cavaradossi: Giacomini
Scarpia: Milnes [3]
Sacristan: Capecchi
Spoletta: Velis
Sacristan: Capecchi
Spoletta: Velis
Angelotti: Monk
Sciarrone: Christopher

January 1, 1977, matinee (broadcast) [275]
Tosca (Puccini–Illica/Giacosa) [593]
Conducted by Santi
Tosca: Bumbry
Cavaradossi: Giacomini
Scarpia: Milnes [4]
Sacristano: Capecchi
Spoletta: Velis
Angelotti: Monk
Sciarrone: Christopher

January 7, 1977 [276]
Tosca (Puccini–Illica/Giacosa) [594]
Conducted by Santi
Tosca: Bumbry
Cavaradossi: Giacomini
Scarpia: Milnes [5]
Sacristano: Capecchi
Spoletta: Velis
Angelotti: Monk
Sciarrone: Christopher

January 12, 1977 [277]
Tosca (Puccini–Illica/Giacosa) [595]
Conducted by Santi
Tosca: Bumbry
Cavaradossi: Giacomini
Scarpia: Milnes [6]
Sacristano: Capecchi

Spoletta: Velis
Angelotti: Monk
Sciarrone: Christopher

January 21, 1977 [278]
Tosca (Puccini–Illica/Giacosa) [596]
Conducted by Woitach
Tosca: Kubiak
Cavaradossi: Morell
Scarpia: Milnes [7]
Sacristano: Capecchi
Spoletta: Velis
Angelotti: Monk
Sciarrone: Christopher

January 24, 1977 [279]
Tosca (Puccini–Illica/Giacosa) [597]
Conducted by Woitach
Tosca: Zylis-Gara
Cavaradossi: Morell
Scarpia: Milnes [8]
Sacristano: Capecchi
Spoletta: Velis
Angelotti: Monk
Sciarrone: Christopher

January 31, 1977 [280]
Tosca (Puccini–Illica/Giacosa) [598]
Conducted by Woitach
Tosca: Zylis-Gara
Cavaradossi: Morell
Scarpia: Milnes [9]
Sacristan: Capecchi
Spoletta: Velis
Angelotti: Monk
Sciarrone: Christopher

February 10, 1977 [281]
Tosca (Puccini–Illica/Giacosa) [599]
Conducted by Woitach
Tosca: Zylis-Gara
Cavaradossi: Morell
Scarpia: Milnes [10]
Sacristan: Capecchi
Spoletta: Velis
Angelotti: Monk
Sciarrone: Christopher

February 25, 1977 [282]
La forza del destino (Verdi–Piave) [177]
Conducted by Levine
Leonora: L. Price

Alvaro: Domingo
Carlo: Milnes [6]
Father Superior: Talvela
Preziosilla: Elias
Melitone: Capecchi
Marquis: Booth
Curra: Ordassy
Mayor: Dobriansky

1977–78
METROPOLITAN OPERA HOUSE

October 6, 1977 (broadcast) [283]
Met Marathon (master of ceremonies: R.
   Sherman), in which Milnes sang:
Otello (Verdi–Boito), "Credo"
[This concert was a fund-raising event
   performed before an audience of
   contributors and patrons of the
   Metropolitan Opera. It was broadcast
   nationally, and donations from listen-
   ers were pledged by phone.]

October 15, 1977 [284]
Eugene Onegin (Tchaikovsky–
   Tchaikovsky/Shilovsky) [39]
Conducted by Levine
Onegin: Milnes [1]
Tatiana: Zylis-Gara
Lensky: Gedda
Olga: I. Jones
Gremin: Talvela
Larina: Kraft
Filipievna: Godfrey Ben-David
Triquet: Velis
Directed by Igesz
Set design by Gerard
Costume design by Diffen
Lighting design by Wechsler
Choreography by Vesak

October 20, 1977 [285]
Eugene Onegin (Tchaikovsky–
   Tchaikovsky/Shilovsky) [40]
Conducted by Levine
Onegin: Milnes [2]
Tatiana: Zylis-Gara
Lensky: Gedda
Olga: I. Jones
Gremin: Talvela

Larina: Kraft
Filipievna: Godfrey Ben-David
Triquet: Velis

October 24, 1977 [286]
Eugene Onegin (Tchaikovsky–
Tchaikovsky/Shilovsky) [41]
Conducted by Levine
Onegin: Milnes [3]
Tatiana: Zylis-Gara
Lensky: Gedda
Olga: I. Jones
Gremin: Plishka
Larina: Kraft
Filipievna: Godfrey Ben-David
Triquet: Velis

**October 31, 1977, benefit sponsored by
the Metropolitan Opera Guild for the
production funds [287]**
Rigoletto (Verdi–Piave; new production)
[528]
Conducted by Levine
Rigoletto: Milnes [3]
Gilda: Cotrubas
Duke: Domingo
Maddalena: I. Jones
Sparafucile: Díaz
Monterone: Shinall
Borsa: Atherton
Marullo: Goodloe
Ceprano: Booth
Countess Ceprano: Di Franco
Giovanna: Bybee
Directed by Dexter
Designed by Moiseiwitsch
Lighting design by Wechsler
Choreography by Vesak

November 3, 1977 [288]
Eugene Onegin (Tchaikovsky–
Tchaikovsky/Shilovsky) [43]
Conducted by Levine
Onegin: Milnes [4]
Tatiana: Zylis-Gara
Lensky: Gedda
Olga: I. Jones
Gremin: Talvela
Larina: Kraft
Filipievna: Godfrey Ben-David
Triquet: Velis

**January 18, 1978, benefit sponsored by
the Metropolitan Opera Guild for the
production funds [289]**
Thaïs (Massenet–Gallet; new production)
[47]
Conducted by Pritchard
Thaïs: Sills
Athanaël: Milnes [1]
Nicias: Gibbs
Palemon: Morris
Crobyle: Norden
Myrtale: I. Jones
Charmeuse: Wohlafka
Directed by Capobianco
Designed by Toms
Lighting design by Wechsler
Choreography by Seetoo, Denda
[This production was borrowed from the
San Francisco Opera. Denda choreo-
graphed the "Meditation," which was
performed by Sills.]

January 21, 1978 [290]
Thaïs (Massenet–Gallet) [48]
Conducted by Pritchard
Thaïs: Sills
Athanaël: Milnes [2]
Nicias: Gibbs
Palemon: Morris
Crobyle: Norden
Myrtale: I. Jones
Charmeuse: Wohlafka

January 25, 1978 [291]
Thaïs (Massenet–Gallet) [49]
Conducted by Pritchard
Thaïs: Sills
Athanaël: Milnes [3]
Nicias: Gibbs
Palemon: Morris
Crobyle: Norden
Myrtale: I. Jones
Charmeuse: Wohlafka

**January 28, 1978, matinee (broadcast)
[292]**
Thaïs (Massenet–Gallet) [50]
Conducted by Pritchard
Thaïs: Sills
Athanaël: Milnes [4]
Nicias: Gibbs

Palemon: Morris
Crobyle: Norden
Myrtale: I. Jones
Charmeuse: Wohlafka

January 31, 1978 [293]
Thaïs (Massenet–Gallet) [51]
Conducted by Pritchard
Thaïs: Sills
Athanaël: Milnes [5]
Nicias: Gibbs
Palemon: Morris
Crobyle: Norden
Myrtale: I. Jones
Charmeuse: Wohlafka

February 3, 1978 [294]
Cavalleria rusticana (Mascagni–Targioni-
Tozzetti/Menasci) [521]
Conducted by Patane
Santuzza: Arroyo
Turiddu: Ochman
Lola: I. Jones
Pagliacci (Leoncavallo) [559]
Conducted by Patane
Nedda: Mauti-Nunziata
Canio: Giacomini
Tonio: Milnes [20]
Silvio: Monk

February 6, 1978 [295]
Thaïs (Massenet–Gallet) [52]
Conducted by Pritchard
Thaïs: Sills
Athanaël: Milnes [6]
Nicias: Van Ree
Palemon: Morris
Crobyle: Di Franco
Myrtale: I. Jones
Charmeuse: Wohlafka

February 9, 1978 [296]
Thaïs (Massenet–Gallet) [53]
Conducted by Pritchard
Thaïs: Sills
Athanaël: Milnes [7]
Nicias: Van Ree
Palemon: Morris
Crobyle: Norden
Myrtale: I. Jones
Charmeuse: Wohlafka.

February 13, 1978 [297]
Eugene Onegin (Tchaikovsky–
Tchaikovsky/Shilovsky) [44]
Conducted by Levine
Onegin: Milnes [5]
Tatiana: Zylis-Gara
Lensky: Gedda
Olga: I. Jones
Gremin: Talvela
Larina: Kraft
Filipievna: Godfrey Ben-David
Triquet: Velis

February 18, 1978, matinee (broadcast) [298]
Eugene Onegin (Tchaikovsky–
Tchaikovsky/Shilovsky) [45]
Conducted by Levine
Onegin: Milnes [6]
Tatiana: Zylis-Gara
Lensky: Gedda
Olga: I. Jones
Gremin: Plishka
Larina: Kraft
Filipievna: Godfrey Ben-David
Triquet: Atherton

February 21, 1978, benefit sponsored by the Metropolitan Opera Guild for the production funds [299]
La favorite (Donizetti–Scribe/Royer/
Vaez; in Italian; new production) [11]
Conducted by López-Cobos
Leonor: Verrett
Fernand: Pavarotti
Alphonse: Milnes [1]
Balthazar: Giaiotti
Directed by Tavenua
Set design by M. C. Lee
Costume design by Greenwood
Lighting design by Wechsler
Choreography by Pazik
Translator unknown
[This production was borrowed from the
San Francisco Opera.]

February 23, 1978 [300]
Thaïs (Massenet–Gallet) [56]
Conducted by Pritchard
Thaïs: Sills
Athanaël: Milnes [8]

Nicias: Van Ree
Palemon: Morris
Crobyle: Norden
Myrtale: I. Jones
Charmeuse: Wohlafka

February 24, 1978 [301]
Otello (Verdi–Boito) [227]
Conducted by Levine
Otello: McCracken
Desdemona: Ricciarelli
Iago: Milnes [20]
Emilia: Kraft
Cassio: Little
Lodovico: Morris
Montano: Goodloe
[MacNeil canceled after act 1 and was
    replaced by Milnes.]

February 25, 1978 [302]
La favorite (Donizetti–Scribe/Royer/
    Vaez; in Italian) [12]
Conducted by López-Cobos
Leonor: Verrett
Fernand: Pavarotti
Alphonse: Milnes [2]
Balthazar: Giaiotti

March 1, 1978 [303]
La favorite (Donizetti–Scribe/Royer/
    Vaez; in Italian) [13]
Conducted by López-Cobos
Leonor: Verrett
Fernand: Pavarotti
Alphonse: Milnes [3]
Balthazar: Giaiotti

March 3, 1978 [304]
Thaïs (Massenet–Gallet) [57]
Conducted by Pritchard
Thaïs: Sills
Athanaël: Milnes [9]
Nicias: Van Ree
Palemon: Morris
Crobyle: Norden
Myrtale: I. Jones
Charmeuse: Wohlafka

March 7, 1978 [305]
La favorite (Donizetti–Scribe/Royer/
    Vaez; in Italian) [14]
Conducted by López-Cobos

Leonor: Verrett
Fernand: Pavarotti
Alphonse: Milnes [4]
Balthazar: Giaiotti

**March 11, 1978, matinee (broadcast)
[306]**
La favorite (Donizetti–Scribe/Royer/
    Vaez; in Italian) [15]
Conducted by López-Cobos
Leonor: Verrett
Fernand: Pavarotti
Alphonse: Milnes [5]
Balthazar: Giaiotti

March 15, 1978 [307]
La favorite (Donizetti–Scribe/Royer/
    Vaez; in Italian) [16]
Conducted by López-Cobos
Leonor: Verrett
Fernand: Pavarotti
Alphonse: Milnes [6]
Balthazar: Giaiotti

March 20, 1978 [308]
La favorite (Donizetti–Scribe/Royer/
    Vaez; in Italian) [17]
Conducted by López-Cobos
Leonor: Verrett
Fernand: Alexander
Alphonse: Milnes [7]
Balthazar: Giaiotti

March 23, 1978 [309]
La favorite (Donizetti–Scribe/Royer/
    Vaez; in Italian) [18]
Conducted by López-Cobos
Leonor: Casei
Fernand: Alexander
Alphonse: Milnes [8]
Balthazar: Giaiotti

March 31, 1978 [310]
Cavalleria rusticana (Mascagni–Targioni-
    Tozzetti/Menasci) [522]
Conducted by Levine
Santuzza: Troyanos
Turiddu: Solovianenko
Lola: I. Jones
Pagliacci (Leoncavallo) [560]
Conducted by Levine
Nedda: Stratas

Canio: Giacomini
Tonio: Milnes [21]
Silvio: Monk

April 3, 1978 [311]
Don Giovanni (Mozart–Da Ponte) [355]
Conducted by Pritchard
Giovanni: Milnes [23]
Anna: Tomowa-Sintow
Ottavio: Burrows
Elvira: Harwood
Leporello: Gramm
Zerlina: Peters

April 5, 1978 (simulcast) [312]
Cavalleria rusticana (Mascagni–Targioni-
Tozzetti/Menasci) [523]
Conducted by Levine
Santuzza: Troyanos
Turiddu: Domingo
Lola: I. Jones
Pagliacci (Leoncavallo) [561]
Conducted by Levine
Nedda: Stratas
Canio: Domingo
Tonio: Milnes [22]
Silvio: Monk

April 7, 1978 [313]
Don Giovanni (Mozart–Da Ponte) [356]
Conducted by Pritchard
Giovanni: Milnes [24]
Anna: Tomowa-Sintow
Ottavio: Burrows
Elvira: Harwood
Leporello: Gramm
Zerlina: Peters

April 12, 1978 [314]
Don Giovanni (Mozart–Da Ponte) [357]
Conducted by Pritchard
Giovanni: Milnes [25]
Anna: Tomowa-Sintow
Ottavio: Burrows
Elvira: Harwood
Leporello: Gramm
Zerlina: Peters

April 15, 1978, matinee (broadcast) [315]
Cavalleria rusticana (Mascagni–Targioni-
Tozzetti/Menasci) [525]
Conducted by Levine

Santuzza: Troyanos
Turiddu: Solovianenko
Lola: I. Jones
Pagliacci (Leoncavallo) [563]
Conducted by Levine
Nedda: Stratas
Canio: Giacomini
Tonio: Milnes [23]
Silvio: Monk

CLEVELAND, OHIO

April 17, 1978 [316]
Thaïs (Massenet–Gallet) [58]
Conducted by Pritchard
Thaïs: Sills
Athanaël: Milnes [10]
Nicias: Van Ree
Palemon: Díaz
Crobyle: Norden
Myrtale: I. Jones
Charmeuse: Wohlafka

April 22, 1978 [317]
Don Giovanni (Mozart–Da Ponte) [358]
Conducted by Pritchard
Giovanni: Milnes [26]
Anna: Carden
Ottavio: Burrows
Elvira: Shade
Leporello: Gramm
Zerlina: Peters

BOSTON, MASSACHUSETTS

April 24, 1978 [318]
Thaïs (Massenet–Gallet) [59]
Conducted by Pritchard
Thaïs: Sills
Athanaël: Milnes [11]
Nicias: Van Ree
Palemon: Díaz
Crobyle: Norden
Myrtale: I. Jones
Charmeuse: Wohlafka

April 29, 1978, matinee [319]
Don Giovanni (Mozart–Da Ponte) [359]
Conducted by Pritchard
Giovanni: Milnes [27]
Anna: Carden

Ottavio: Burrows
Elvira: Harwood
Leporello: Gramm
Zerlina: Peters

ATLANTA, GEORGIA

May 1, 1978 [320]
Thaïs (Massenet–Gallet) [60]
Conducted by Pritchard
Thaïs: Sills
Athanaël: Milnes [12]
Nicias: Van Ree
Palemon: Díaz
Crobyle: Norden
Myrtale: I. Jones
Charmeuse: Wohlafka

May 6, 1978, matinee [321]
Don Giovanni (Mozart–Da Ponte) [360]
Conducted by Pritchard
Giovanni: Milnes [28]
Anna: Carden
Ottavio: Burrows
Elvira: Harwood
Leporello: Gramm
Zerlina: Peters

MEMPHIS, TENNESSEE

May 8, 1978 [322]
Thaïs (Massenet–Gallet) [61]
Conducted by Pritchard
Thaïs: Sills
Athanaël: Milnes [13]
Nicias: Gibbs
Palemon: Díaz
Crobyle: Norden
Myrtale: I. Jones
Charmeuse: Wohlafka

DALLAS, TEXAS

May 13, 1978 [323]
Don Giovanni (Mozart–Da Ponte) [361]
Conducted by Pritchard
Giovanni: Milnes [29]
Anna: Carden
Ottavio: Burrows
Elvira: Harwood

Leporello: Gramm
Zerlina: Peters

MINNEAPOLIS, MINNESOTA

May 15, 1978 [324]
Thaïs (Massenet–Gallet) [62]
Conducted by Pritchard
Thaïs: Sills
Athanaël: Milnes [14]
Nicias: Gibbs
Palemon: Díaz
Crobyle: Norden
Myrtale: I. Jones
Charmeuse: Wohlafka

May 20, 1978, matinee (broadcast) [325]
Don Giovanni (Mozart–Da Ponte) [362]
Conducted by Pritchard
Giovanni: Milnes [30]
Anna: Carden
Ottavio: Blake
Elvira: Harwood
Leporello: Gramm
Zerlina: Mandac

DETROIT, MICHIGAN

May 22, 1978 [326]
Thaïs (Massenet–Gallet) [63]
Conducted by Pritchard
Thaïs: Sills
Athanaël: Milnes [15]
Nicias: Gibbs
Palemon: Díaz
Crobyle: Norden
Myrtale: I. Jones
Charmeuse: Wohlafka

May 27, 1978, matinee [327]
Don Giovanni (Mozart–Da Ponte) [363]
Conducted by Alcantara
Giovanni: Milnes [31]
Anna: Carden
Ottavio: Blake
Elvira: Harwood
Leporello: Gramm
Zerlina: Peters

1978-79
METROPOLITAN OPERA HOUSE

January 13, 1979 [328]
Luisa Miller (Verdi–Cammarano) [39]
Conducted by Levine
Luisa: Scotto
Rodolfo: Domingo
Miller: Milnes [20]
Walter: Giaiotti
Wurm: Morris
Federica: Kraft

January 17, 1979 [329]
Luisa Miller (Verdi–Cammarano) [40]
Conducted by Levine
Luisa: Scotto
Rodolfo: Domingo
Miller: Milnes [21]
Walter: Giaiotti
Wurm: Morris
Federica: Kraft

January 20, 1979 (simulcast) [330]
Luisa Miller (Verdi–Cammarano) [41]
Conducted by Levine
Luisa: Scotto
Rodolfo: Domingo
Miller: Milnes [22]
Walter: Giaiotti
Wurm: Morris
Federica: Kraft

January 24, 1979 [331]
Luisa Miller (Verdi–Cammarano) [42]
Conducted by Levine
Luisa: Scotto
Rodolfo: Domingo
Miller: Milnes [23]
Walter: Giaiotti
Wurm: Morris
Federica: Kraft

January 27, 1979, matinee (broadcast) [332]
Luisa Miller (Verdi–Cammarano) [43]
Conducted by Levine
Luisa: Scotto
Rodolfo: Domingo
Miller: Milnes [24]
Walter: Giaiotti

Wurm: Morris
Federica: Kraft

February 5, 1979, benefit sponsored by the Metropolitan Opera Guild for the production funds [333]
Don Carlos (Verdi–Méry/du Locle; in Italian; new production) [97]
Conducted by Levine
Carlos: Giacomini
Elisabeth: Scotto
Rodrigue: Milnes [2]
Eboli: Horne
Philippe: Ghiaurov
Grand Inquisitor: Morris
Celestial Voice: Mitchell
Friar: Cheek
Thibault: Norden
Forester: Manno
Lerme: Talley
Directed by Dexter
Set design by Reppa
Costume design by Diffen
Lighting design by Wechsler
Translation by Lauzieres, Zanardini
[The original act 1, "The woods at Fontainebleau," not performed by the company since March 12, 1921, was reinstated with this production. "La Peregrina," the classic ballet intended for act 3, scene 1, "A grotto in the queen's garden," however, was not included.]

February 8, 1979 [334]
Don Carlos (Verdi–Méry/du Locle; in Italian) [98]
Conducted by Levine
Carlos: Giacomini
Elisabeth: Scotto
Rodrigue: Milnes [3]
Eboli: Horne
Philippe: Ghiaurov
Grand Inquisitor: Morris
Celestial Voice: Mitchell
Friar: Cheek
Thibault: Norden
Forester: Manno
Lerme: Talley

February 12, 1979 [335]
Don Carlos (Verdi–Méry/du Locle; in
 Italian) [99]
Conducted by Levine
Carlos: Giacomini
Elisabeth: Scotto
Rodrigue: Milnes [4]
Eboli: Horne
Philippe: Ghiaurov
Grand Inquisitor: Morris
Celestial Voice: Mitchell
Friar: Cheek
Thibault: Norden
Forester: Manno
Lerme: Talley

February 16, 1979 [336]
Don Carlos (Verdi–Méry/du Locle; in
 Italian) [101]
Conducted by Levine
Carlos: Giacomini
Elisabeth: Scotto
Rodrigue: Milnes [5]
Eboli: Horne
Philippe: Ghiaurov
Grand Inquisitor: Morris
Celestial Voice: Mitchell
Friar: Cheek
Thibault: Norden
Forester: Manno
Lerme: Talley

February 20, 1979 [337]
Don Carlos (Verdi–Méry/du Locle; in
 Italian) [102]
Conducted by Levine
Carlos: Giacomini
Elisabeth: Scotto
Rodrigue: Milnes [6]
Eboli: Horne
Philippe: Ghiaurov
Grand Inquisitor: Morris
Celestial Voice: Mitchell
Friar: Cheek
Thibault: Norden
Forester: Manno
Lerme: Talley

**February 24, 1979, matinee (broadcast)
[338]**
Don Carlos (Verdi–Méry/du Locle; in
 Italian) [103]
Conducted by Levine
Carlos: Giacomini
Elisabeth: Scotto
Rodrigue: Milnes [7]
Eboli: Horne
Philippe: Ghiaurov
Grand Inquisitor: Morris
Celestial Voice: Mitchell
Friar: Cheek
Thibault: Norden
Forester: Sliker
Lerme: Talley

February 28, 1979 [339]
Don Carlos (Verdi–Méry/du Locle; in
 Italian) [104]
Conducted by Levine
Carlos: Giacomini
Elisabeth: Scotto
Rodrigue: Milnes [8]
Eboli: Horne
Philippe: Plishka
Grand Inquisitor: Morris
Celestial Voice: Mitchell
Friar: Cheek
Thibault: Smith
Forester: Sliker
Lerme: Talley

March 3, 1979 [340]
Don Carlos (Verdi–Méry/du Locle; in
 Italian) [105]
Conducted by Levine
Carlos: Giacomini
Elisabeth: Scotto
Rodrigue: Milnes [9]
Eboli: M, Horne
Philippe: Plishka
Grand Inquisitor: Morris
Celestial Voice: Mitchell
Friar: Cheek
Thibault: Smith
Forester: Sliker
Lerme: Talley

March 4, 1979 (broadcast) [341]
Met Marathon (announcer, P. Allen; master of ceremonies, R. Sherman), in which Milnes sang:
I Puritani (Bellini–Pepoli), "Suoni la tromba": Milnes, Morris
[This concert was a fund-raising event performed before an audience of contributors and patrons of the Metropolitan Opera. It was broadcast nationally, and donations from listeners were pledged by phone.]

March 7, 1979 [342]
Don Carlos (Verdi–Méry/du Locle; in Italian) [106]
Conducted by Levine
Carlos: Giacomini
Elisabeth: Scotto
Rodrigue: Milnes [10]
Eboli: Horne
Philippe: Plishka
Grand Inquisitor: Kavrakos
Celestial Voice: Mitchell
Friar: Cheek
Thibault: Smith
Forester: Sliker
Lerme: Talley

March 10, 1979 [343]
Don Carlos (Verdi–Méry/du Locle; in Italian) [107]
Conducted by Levine
Carlos: Giacommi
Elisabeth: Scotto
Rodrigue: Milnes [11]
Eboli: Horne
Philippe: Plishka
Grand Inquisitor: Kavrakos
Celestial Voice: Mitchell
Friar: Cheek
Thibault: Smith
Forester: Manno
Lerme: Talley

CLEVELAND, OHIO

April 17, 1979 [344]
Otello (Verdi–Boito) [233]
Conducted by Levine

Otello: Vickers
Desdemona: Cruz-Romo
Iago: Milnes [21]
Emilia: Kraft
Cassio: Little
Lodovico: Morris
Montano: Goodloe

April 20, 1979 [345]
Don Carlos (Verdi–Méry/du Locle; in Italian) [108]
Conducted by Levine
Carlos: Moldoveanu
Elisabeth: Cruz-Romo
Rodrigue: Milnes [12]
Eboli: Denize
Philippe: Plishka
Grand Inquisitor: Morris
Celestial Voice: Brandson
Friar: Cheek
Thibault: Norden
Forester: Sliker
Lerme: Talley

BOSTON, MASSACHUSETTS

April 24, 1979 [346]
Otello (Verdi–Boito) [234]
Conducted by Levine
Otello: Cassilly
Desdemona: Cruz-Romo
Iago: Milnes [22]
Emilia: Kraft
Cassio: Little
Lodovico: Morris
Montano: Goodloe

April 27, 1979 [347]
Don Carlos (Verdi–Méry/du Locle; in Italian) [109]
Conducted by Levine
Carlos: Moldoveanu
Elisabeth: Cruz-Romo
Rodrigue: Milnes [13]
Eboli: Denize
Philippe: Plishka
Grand Inquisitor: Morris
Celestial Voice: Brandson
Friar: Cheek
Thibault: Norden

Forester: Sliker
Lerme: Talley

ATLANTA, GEORGIA

May 1, 1979 [348]
Otello (Verdi–Boito) [235]
Conducted by Levine
Otello: Cassilly
Desdemona: Cruz-Romo
Iago: Milnes [23]
Emilia: Kraft
Cassio: Little
Lodovico: Morris
Montano: Goodloe

May 4, 1979 [349]
Don Carlos (Verdi–Méry/du Locle; in
    Italian) [110]
Conducted by Levine
Carlos: Moldoveanu
Elisabeth: Cruz-Romo
Rodrigue: Milnes [14]
Eboli: Denize
Philippe: Plishka
Grand Inquisitor: Morris
Celestial Voice: Brandson
Friar: Cheek
Thibault: Norden
Forester: Sliker
Lerme: Talley

MINNEAPOLIS, MINNESOTA

May 15, 1979 [350]
Otello (Verdi–Boito) [236]
Conducted by Levine
Otello: Vickers
Desdemona: Cruz-Romo
Iago: Milnes [24]
Emilia: Kraft
Cassio: Little
Lodovico: Morris
Montano: Goodloe

May 18, 1979 [351]
Don Carlos (Verdi–Méry/du Locle; in
    Italian) [111]
Conducted by Levine
Carlos: Moldoveanu
Elisabeth: Cruz-Romo

Rodrigue: Milnes [15]
Eboli: Denize
Philippe: Plishka
Grand Inquisitor: Morris
Celestial Voice: Brandson
Friar: Cheek
Thibault: Smith
Forester: Manno
Lerme: Talley

DETROIT, MICHIGAN

May 23, 1979 [352]
Otello (Verdi–Boito) [237]
Conducted by Levine
Otello: Vickers
Desdemona: Cruz-Romo
Iago: Milnes [25]
Emilia: Kraft
Cassio: Little
Lodovico: Morris
Montano: Goodloe

May 26, 1979 [353]
Don Carlos (Verdi–Méry/du Locle; in
    Italian) [112]
Conducted by Levine
Carlos: Moldoveanu
Elisabeth: Cruz-Romo
Rodrigue: Milnes [16]
Eboli: Denize
Philippe: Hines
Grand Inquisitor: Morris
Celestial Voice: Brandson
Friar: Cheek
Thibault: Smith
Forester: Manno
Lerme: Talley

1979–80
METROPOLITAN OPERA HOUSE

September 24, 1979 (simulcast)
Otello (Verdi–Boito) [240]
Conducted by Levine
Otello: Domingo
Desdemona: Cruz-Romo
Iago: Milnes [26]
Emilia: Love

Cassio: Ciannella
Lodovico: Moll
Montano: Darrenkamp
Directed by Zeffirelli
Staged by Melano
Set design by Zeffirelli
Costume design by Hall
Lighting design by Wechsler

September 28, 1979 [355]
Otello (Verdi–Boito) [241]
Conducted by Levine
Otello: Domingo
Desdemona: Cruz-Romo
Iago: Milnes [27]
Emilia: Love
Cassio: Gibbs
Lodovico: Moll
Montano: Darrenkamp

October 2, 1979 [356]
Otello (Verdi–Boito) [242]
Conducted by Levine
Otello: Domingo
Desdemona: Cruz-Romo
Iago: Milnes [28]
Emilia: Love
Cassio: Gibbs
Lodovico: Moll
Montano: Darrenkamp

October 6, 1979, matinee [357]
Otello (Verdi–Boito) [243]
Conducted by Levine
Otello: Domingo
Desdemona: Cruz-Romo
Iago: Milnes [29]
Emilia: Love
Cassio: Gibbs
Lodovico: Moll
Montano: Darrenkamp

October 10, 1979 [358]
Otello (Verdi–Boito) [244]
Conducted by Levine
Otello: Domingo
Desdemona: Cruz-Romo
Iago: Milnes [30]
Emilia: Love
Cassio: Gibbs
Lodovico: Booth

Montano: Darrenkamp

December 18, 1979 [359]
Rigoletto (Verdi–Piave) [569]
Conducted by Veltri
Rigoletto: Milnes [4]
Gilda: Devia
Duke: Shicoff
Maddalena: I. Jones
Sparafucile: Hines
Monterone: Robbins
Borsa: Anthony
Marullo: Goodloe
Ceprano: Booth
Countess Ceprano: Di Franco
Giovanna: Bybee
Directed by Dexter
Designed by Moiseiwitsch
Lighting design by Wechsler
Choreography by Vesak

December 21, 1979 [360]
Rigoletto (Verdi–Piave) [570]
Conducted by Veltri
Rigoletto: Milnes [5]
Gilda: Devia
Duke: Shicoff
Maddalena: I. Jones
Sparafucile: Hines
Monterone: Robbins
Borsa: Anthony
Marullo: Goodloe
Ceprano: Booth
Countess Ceprano: Di Franco
Giovanna: Bybee

December 31, 1979 [361]
Rigoletto (Verdi–Piave) [571]
Conducted by Veltri
Rigoletto: Milnes [6]
Gilda: Devia
Duke: Shicoff
Maddalena: I. Jones
Sparafucile: Hines
Monterone: Shinall
Borsa: Anthony
Marullo: Goodloe
Ceprano: Booth
Countess Ceprano: Di Franco
Giovanna: Bybee

January 4, 1980 [362]
Rigoletto (Verdi–Piave) [572]
Conducted by Veltri
Rigoletto: Milnes [7]
Gilda: Devia
Duke: Shicoff
Maddalena: Grillo
Sparafucile: Booth
Monterone: Shinall
Borsa: Anthony
Marullo: Goodloe
Ceprano: Dobriansky
Countess Ceprano: Di Franco
Giovanna: Bybee

January 7, 1980 [363]
Rigoletto (Verdi–Piave) [573]
Conducted by Veltri
Rigoletto: Milnes [8]
Gilda: Devia
Duke: Shicoff
Maddalena: Grillo
Sparafucile: Booth
Monterone: Shinall
Borsa: Anthony
Marullo: Goodloe
Ceprano: Dobriansky
Countess Ceprano: Di Franco
Giovanna: Bybee

January 12, 1980 [364]
Rigoletto (Verdi–Piave) [574]
Conducted by Veltri
Rigoletto: Milnes [9]
Gilda: Devia
Duke: Bini
Maddalena: I. Jones
Sparafucile: Booth
Monterone: Robbins
Borsa: Talley
Marullo: Goodloe
Ceprano: Dobriansky
Countess Ceprano: Di Franco
Giovanna: Bybee

January 16, 1980 [365]
Rigoletto (Verdi–Piave) [575]
Conducted by Veltri
Rigoletto: Milnes [10]
Gilda: Robinson
Duke: Bini

Maddalena: I. Jones
Sparafucile: Hines
Monterone: Robbins
Borsa: Talley
Marullo: Goodloe
Ceprano: Booth
Countess Ceprano: Di Franco
Giovanna: Bybee

January 19, 1980, matinee (broadcast) [366]
Rigoletto (Verdi–Piave) [576]
Conducted by Stivender
Rigoletto: Milnes [11]
Gilda: Robinson
Duke: Bini
Maddalena: I. Jones
Sparafucile: Hines
Monterone: Robbins
Borsa: Talley
Marullo: Goodloe
Ceprano: Booth
Countess Ceprano: Di Franco
Giovanna: Bybee

January 23, 1980 [367]
Rigoletto (Verdi–Piave) [577]
Conducted by Stivender
Rigoletto: Milnes [12]
Gilda: Robinson
Duke: Bini
Maddalena: I. Jones
Sparafucile: Hines
Monterone: Robbins
Borsa: Talley
Marullo: Goodloe
Ceprano: Booth
Countess Ceprano: Di Franco
Giovanna: Bybee

January 26, 1980 [368]
Rigoletto (Verdi–Piave) [578]
Conducted by Stivender
Rigoletto: Milnes [13]
Gilda: Devia
Duke: Bini
Maddalena: I. Jones
Sparafucile: Wildermann
Monterone: Robbins
Borsa: Talley
Marullo: Goodloe

Ceprano: Booth
Countess Ceprano: Di Franco
Giovanna: Bybee

January 31, 1980 [369]
Otello (Verdi–Boito) [245]
Conducted by Levine
Otello: Cassilly
Desdemona: Zylis-Gara
Iago: Milnes [31]
Emilia: Kraft
Cassio: Little
Lodovico: Morris
Montano: Darrenkamp

February 5, 1980 [370]
Otello (Verdi–Boito) [246]
Conducted by Levine
Otello: Cassilly
Desdemona: Zylis-Gara
Iago: Milnes [32]
Emilia: Kraft
Cassio: Little
Lodovico: Morris
Montano: Darrenkamp

February 9, 1980, matinee (broadcast) [371]
Otello (Verdi–Boito) [247]
Conducted by Levine
Otello: Cassilly
Desdemona: Zylis-Gara
Iago: Milnes [33]
Emilia: Kraft
Cassio: Little
Lodovico: Morris
Montano: Darrenkamp
[Cassilly canceled after act 1 and was re-placed by Edward Sooter.]

February 14, 1980 [372]
Don Carlos (Verdi–Méry/du Locle; in Italian) [114]
Conducted by Levine
Carlos: Moldoveanu
Elisabeth: Scotto
Rodrigue: Milnes [17]
Eboli: Troyanos
Philippe: Plishka
Grand Inquisitor: Hines
Celestial Voice: Brandson

Friar: Cheek
Thibault: Norden
Forester: Sliker
Lerme: Talley
Directed by Dexter
Set design by Reppa
Costume design by Diffen
Lighting design by Wechsler
Translation by Lauzieres, Zanardini

February 18, 1980 [373]
Don Carlos (Verdi–Méry/du Locle; in Italian) [115]
Conducted by Levine
Carlos: Moldoveanu
Elisabeth: Scotto
Rodrigue: Milnes [18]
Eboli: Troyanos
Philippe: Plishka
Grand Inquisitor: Hines
Celestial Voice: Brandson
Friar: Cheek
Thibault: Norden
Forester: Sliker
Lerme: Talley

February 21, 1980 (simulcast) [374]
Don Carlos (Verdi–Méry/du Locle; in Italian) [116]
Conducted by Levine
Carlos: Moldoveanu
Elisabeth: Scotto
Rodrigue: Milnes [19]
Eboli: Troyanos
Philippe: Plishka
Grand Inquisitor: Hines
Celestial Voice: Brandson.
Friar: Cheek
Thibault: Norden
Forester: Sliker
Lerme: Talley
[This performance was videotaped for the *Live from the Met* series and first televised over PBS on April 12, 1980.]

February 26, 1980 [375]
Don Carlos (Verdi–Méry/du Locle; in Italian) [117]
Conducted by Levine
Carlos: Moldoveanu
Elisabeth: Scotto

Rodrigue: Milnes [20]
Eboli: Troyanos
Philippe: Hines
Grand Inquisitor: Furlanetto
Celestial Voice: Brandson
Friar: Cheek
Thibault: Norden
Forester: Sliker
Lerme: Talley

February 29, 1980 [376]
Don Carlos (Verdi–Méry/du Locle; in
   Italian) [118]
Conducted by Levine
Carlos: Giacomini
Elisabeth: Scotto
Rodrigue: Milnes [21]
Eboli: Troyanos
Philippe: Hines
Grand Inquisitor: Furlanetto
Celestial Voice: Brandson
Friar: Cheek
Thibault: Norden
Forester: Sliker
Lerme: Talley

March 7, 1980 [377]
Don Carlos (Verdi–Méry/du Locle; in
   Italian) [119]
Conducted by Levine
Carlos: Giacomini
Elisabeth: Cruz-Romo
Rodrigue: Milnes [22]
Eboli: Troyanos
Philippe: Plishka
Grand Inquisitor: Hines
Celestial Voice: Brandson
Friar: Robbins
Thibault: Norden
Forester: Sliker
Lerme: Talley

March 10, 1980 [378]
Don Carlos (Verdi–Méry/du Locle) [120]
Conducted by Levine
Carlos: Giacomini
Elisabeth: Cruz-Romo
Rodrigue: Milnes [23]
Philippe: Ghiaurov
Grand Inquisitor: Hines
Celestial Voice: Brandson

Friar: Cheek
Thibault: Smith
Forester: Sliker
Lerme: Talley

**March 15, 1980, matinee (broadcast)
[379]**
Don Carlos (Verdi–Méry/du Locle; in
   Italian) [121]
Conducted by Levine
Carlos: Giacomini
Elisabeth: Cruz-Romo
Rodrigue: Milnes [24]
Eboli: Troyanos
Philippe: Plishka
Grand Inquisitor: Hines
Celestial Voice: Brandson
Friar: Cheek
Thibault: A. J. Smith
Forester: Sliker
Lerme: Talley

March 20, 1980 [380]
Don Carlos (Verdi–Méry/du Locle; in
   Italian) [122]
Conducted by Levine
Carlos: Giacomini
Elisabeth: Cruz-Romo
Rodrigue: Milnes [25]
Eboli: Baglioni
Philippe: Ghiaurov
Grand Inquisitor: Hines
Celestial Voice: Brandson
Friar: Robbins
Thibault: Norden
Forester: Sliker
Lerme: Talley

WASHINGTON, D.C.

April 22, 1980 [381]
Otello (Verdi–Boito) [248]
Conducted by Levine
Otello: Cassilly
Desdemona: Cruz-Romo
Iago: Milnes [34]
Emilia: Kraft
Cassio: Little
Lodovico: Plishka
Montano: Darrenkamp

April 25, 1980 [382]
Otello (Verdi–Boito) [249]
Conducted by Levine
Otello: Cassilly
Desdemona: Hazzan
Iago: Milnes [35]
Emilia: Kraft
Cassio: Little
Lodovico: Morris
Montano: Darrenkamp

1980–81
METROPOLITAN OPERA HOUSE

February 7, 1981 [383]
Un ballo in maschera (Verdi–Somma)
 [176]
Conducted by Veltri
Amelia: Zylis-Gara
Riccardo: Bergonzi
Renato: Milnes [22]
Ulrica: Berini
Oscar: Peters
Samuel: Robbins
Tom: Fleck
Silvano: Darrenkamp

February 14, 1981, matinee (broadcast) [384]
Un ballo in maschera (Verdi–Somma)
 [178]
Conducted by Veltri
Amelia: Cruz-Romo
Riccardo: Bergonzi
Renato: Milnes [23]
Ulrica: Berini
Oscar: Peters
Samuel: Robbins
Tom: Fleck
Silvano: Thompson

February 23, 1981 [385]
Un ballo in maschera (Verdi–Somma)
 [180]
Conducted by Veltri
Amelia: Zylis-Gara
Riccardo: Domingo
Renato: Milnes [24]
Ulrica: Berini
Oscar: Blegen

Samuel: Robbins
Tom: Fleck
Silvano: Thompson

February 27, 1981 [386]
Un ballo in maschera (Verdi–Somma)
 [181]
Conducted by Veltri
Amelia: Zylis-Gara
Riccardo: Bergonzi
Renato: Milnes [25]
Ulrica: Berini
Oscar: Robinson
Samuel: Robbins
Tom: Fleck
Silvano: Thompson

April 14, 1981 [387]
La traviata (Verdi–Piave) [668]
Conducted by Levine
Violetta: Malfitano
Alfredo: Ciannella
Germont: Milnes [14]
Flora: Casei
Gastone: Talley
Douphol: Darrenkamp
D'Obigny: Robbins
Grenvil: Fleck
Annina: Godfrey Ben-David
Giuseppe: Marcella

WASHINGTON, D.C.

April 21, 1981 [388]
La traviata (Verdi–Piave) [670]
Conducted by Fulton
Violetta: Malfitano
Alfredo: Rendall
Germont: Milnes [15]
Flora: Casei
Gastone: Talley
Douphol: Darrenkamp
D'Obigny: Robbins
Grenvil: Fleck
Annina: Decker

April 25, 1981, matinee [389]
Don Giovanni (Mozart–Da Ponte) [365]
Conducted by Levine
Giovanni: Milnes [32]
Anna: Meier

Ottavio: Rendall
Elvira: Neblett
Leporello: Gramm
Zerlina: Battle
Directed by Graf
Staged by Donnell
Designed by Berman
Lighting design by Wechsler
Choreography by Solov

ATLANTA, GEORGIA

May 4, 1981 [390]
La traviata (Verdi–Piave) [672]
Conducted by Fulton
Violetta: Malfitano
Alfredo: Ciannella
Germont: Milnes [16]
Flora: Bybee
Gastone: Talley
Douphol: Darrenkamp
D'Obigny: Robbins
Grenvil: Fleck
Annina: Godfrey Ben-David

May 9, 1981, matinee [391]
Cavalleria rusticana (Mascagni–Targioni-
   Tozzetti/Menasci) [559]
Conducted by Stivender
Santuzza: Dunn
Turiddu: Malamood
Lola: Grillo
Pagliacci (Leoncavallo) [597]
Conducted by Stivender
Nedda: Malfitano
Canio: Mauro
Tonio: Milnes [24]
Silvio: Carlson

DALLAS, TEXAS

May 14, 1981 [392]
La traviata (Verdi–Piave) [673]
Conducted by Fulton
Violetta: Malfitano
Alfredo: Ciannella
Germont: Milnes [17]
Flora: Casei
Gastone: Talley
Douphol: Darrenkamp

D'Obigny: Robbins
Grenvil: Fleck
Annina: Decker

MINNEAPOLIS, MINNESOTA

May 18, 1981 [393]
La traviata (Verdi–Piave) [674]
Conducted by Fulton
Violetta: Malfitano
Alfredo: Ciannella
Germont: Milnes [18]
Flora: Casei
Gastone: Talley
Douphol: Darrenkamp
D'Obigny: Robbins
Grenvil: Fleck
Annina: Godfrey Ben-David

DETROIT, MICHIGAN

May 30, 1981 [394]
La traviata (Verdi–Piave) [675]
Conducted by Fulton
Violetta: Malfitano
Alfredo: Ciannella
Germont: Milnes [19]
Flora: Casei
Gastone: Talley
Douphol: Darrenkamp
D'Obigny: Robbins
Grenvil: Fleck
Annina: Decker

CLEVELAND, OHIO

June 4, 1981 [395]
La traviata (Verdi–Piave) [676]
Conducted by Fulton
Violetta: Malfitano
Alfredo: Ciannella
Germont: Milnes [20]
Flora: Bybee
Gastone: Talley
Douphol: Darrenkamp
D'Obigny: Robbins
Grenvil: Fleck
Annina: Decker

BOSTON, MASSACHUSETTS

June 11, 1981 [396]
La traviata (Verdi–Piave) [677]
Conducted by Fulton
Violetta: Malfitano
Alfredo: Rendall
Germont: Milnes [21]
Flora: Casei
Gastone: Talley
Douphol: Darrenkamp
D'Obigny: Robbins
Grenvil: Fleck
Annina: Decker

June 13, 1981, matinee [397]
Cavalleria rusticana (Mascagni–Targioni-
  Tozzetti/Menasci) [563]
Conducted by Stivender
Santuzza: Dunn
Turiddu: Malamood
Lola: I. Jones
Pagliacci (Leoncavallo) [601]
Conducted by Stivender
Nedda: Craig
Canio: Mauro
Tonio: Milnes [25]
Silvio: Carlson

CENTRAL PARK, MANHATTAN, NEW YORK

June 16, 1981 (concert performance) [398]
Tosca (Puccini–Illica/Giacosa) [656]
Conducted by Levine
Tosca: Scotto
Cavaradossi: Domingo
Scarpia: Milnes [11]
Sacristan: Fleck
Spoletta: Anthony
Angelotti: Courtney
Sciarrone: Christopher
[The performances of June 16–27 were
  presented as part of the free Public
  Parks Series.]

1981–82

METROPOLITAN OPERA HOUSE

November 14, 1981, matinee (broadcast) [399]
Tosca (Puccini–Illica/Giacosa) [663]
Conducted by Patane
Tosca: Zylis-Gara
Cavaradossi: Giacomini
Scarpia: Milnes [12]
Sacristan: Fleck
Spoletta: Velis
Angelotti: Courtney
Sciarrone: Christopher

November 21, 1981 (concert performance) [400]
Tosca (Puccini–Illica/Giacosa) [665]
Conducted by Patane
Tosca: Neblett
Cavaradossi: Carreras
Scarpia: Milnes [13]
Sacristan: Capecchi
Spoletta: Castel
Angelotti: Courtney
Sciarrone: Christopher

November 26, 1981 [401]
Tosca (Puccini–Illica/Giacosa) [666]
Conducted by Patane
Tosca: Neblett
Cavaradossi: Carreras
Scarpia: Milnes [14]
Sacristan: Capecchi
Spoletta: Castel
Angelotti: Courtney
Sciarrone: Christopher

November 30, 1981 [402]
Tosca (Puccini–Illica/Giacosa) [667]
Conducted by Patane
Tosca: Neblett
Cavaradossi: Carreras
Scarpia: Milnes [15]
Sacristan: Capecchi
Spoletta: Castel
Angelotti: Courtney
Sciarrone: Christopher

December 5, 1981, matinee (broadcast) [403]
Tosca (Puccini–Illica/Giacosa) [668]
Conducted by Patane
Tosca: Neblett
Cavaradossi: Carreras
Scarpia: Milnes [16]
Sacristan: Capecchi
Spoletta: Castel
Angelotti: Courtney
Sciarrone: Christopher

1982–83
METROPOLITAN OPERA HOUSE

September 22, 1982 [404]
La forza del destino (Verdi–Piave) [183]
Conducted by Levine
Leonora: Mitchell
Alvaro: Giacomini
Carlo: Milnes [7]
Father Superior: Giaiotti
Preziosilla: I. Jones
Melitone: Bacquier
Marquis: Vernon
Curra: Kraft
Mayor: Courtney
Directed by Dexter
Staged by Sell
Set design by Berman
Costume design by Hall
Choreography by D. Mahler

September 25, 1982, matinee [405]
La forza del destino (Verdi–Piave) [184]
Conducted by Levine
Leonora: Mitchell
Alvaro: Giacomini
Carlo: Milnes [8]
Father Superior: Giaiotti
Preziosilla: I. Jones
Melitone: Bacquier
Marquis: Vernon
Curra: Kraft
Mayor: Courtney

September 30, 1982 [406]
La forza del destino (Verdi–Piave) [185]
Conducted by Levine
Leonora: Mitchell

Alvaro: Giacommi
Carlo: Milnes [9]
Father Superior: Giaiotti
Preziosilla: I. Jones
Melitone: Bacquier
Marquis: Vernon
Curra: Kraft
Mayor: Courtney

October 4, 1982 [407]
La forza del destino (Verdi–Piave) [186]
Conducted by Levine
Leonora: Mitchell
Alvaro: Giacomini
Carlo: Milnes [10]
Father Superior: Giaiotti
Preziosilla: I. Jones
Melitone: Bacquier
Marquis: Vernon
Curra: Kraft
Mayor: Courtney

October 8, 1982 [408]
La forza del destino (Verdi–Piave) [187]
Conducted by Levine
Leonora: Mitchell
Alvaro: Giacomini
Carlo: Milnes [11]
Father Superior: Morris
Preziosilla: I. Jones
Melitone: Bacquier
Marquis: Vernon
Curra: Kraft
Mayor: Courtney

October 11, 1982 [409]
La forza del destino (Verdi–Piave) [188]
Conducted by Levine
Leonora: Mitchell
Alvaro: Bergonzi
Carlo: Milnes [12]
Father Superior: Morris
Preziosilla: Conrad
Melitone: Bacquier
Marquis: Vernon
Curra: Kraft
Mayor: Courtney

October 16, 1982 [410]
La forza del destino (Verdi–Piave) [189]
Conducted by Levine

Leonora: Mitchell
Alvaro: Bergonzi
Carlo: Milnes [13]
Father Superior: Morris
Preziosilla: Conrad
Melitone: Bacquier
Marquis: Vernon
Curra: Kraft
Mayor: Courtney

November 18, 1982 [411]
Macbeth (Verdi–Piave/Maffei; new production) [43]
Conducted by Levine
Macbeth: Milnes [18]
Lady Macbeth: Scotto
Banquo: R. Raimondi
Macduff: Giacomini
Malcolm: Gilmore
Lady-in-Attendance: Bureau
Physician: Robbins
Manservant: Harper
Duncan: Murphy
Fleance: McCallum
Murderer: Courtney
Herald: Brewer
Hecate: Kimball
Warrior: Christopher
Directed by Hall
Designed by Bury
Lighting design by Wechsler
Choreography by Hopps

November 22, 1982 [412]
Macbeth (Verdi–Piave/Maffei) [44]
Conducted by Levine
Macbeth: Milnes [19]
Lady Macbeth: Scotto
Banquo: R. Raimondi
Macduff: Giacomini
Malcolm: Gilmore
Lady-in-Attendance: Bureau
Physician: Robbins
Manservant: Harper
Duncan: Murphy
Fleance: McCallum
Murderer: Courtney
Herald: Brewer
Hecate: Kimball
Warrior: Christopher

November 27, 1982 [413]
Macbeth (Verdi–Piave/Maffei) [45]
Conducted by Levine
Macbeth: Milnes [20]
Lady Macbeth: Scotto
Banquo: R. Raimondi
Macduff: Giacomini
Malcolm: Gilmore
Lady-in-Attendance: Bureau
Physician: Robbins
Manservant: Harper
Duncan: Murphy
Fleance: McCallum
Murderer: Courtney
Herald: Brewer
Hecate: Kimball
Warrior: Christopher

December 1, 1982 [414]
Macbeth (Verdi–Piave/Maffei) [46]
Conducted by Levine
Macbeth: Milnes [21]
Lady Macbeth: Scotto
Banquo: R. Raimondi
Macduff: Giacomini
Malcolm: Gilmore
Lady-in-Attendance: Bureau
Physician: Robbins
Manservant: Harper
Duncan: Murphy
Fleance: McCallum
Murderer: Courtney
Herald: Brewer
Hecate: Kimball
Warrior: Christopher

December 4, 1982 [415]
Macbeth (Verdi–Piave/Maffei) [47]
Conducted by Levine
Macbeth: Milnes [22]
Lady Macbeth: Scotto
Banquo: R. Raimondi
Macduff: Giacomini
Malcolm: Gilmore
Lady-in-Attendance: Bureau
Physician: Robbins
Manservant: Harper
Duncan: Murphy
Fleance: McCallum
Murderer: Courtney

Herald: Brewer
Hecate: Kimball
Warrior: Christopher

December 10, 1982 [416]
Macbeth (Verdi–Piave/Maffei) [49]
Conducted by Levine
Macbeth: Milnes [23]
Lady Macbeth: Stapp
Banquo: Plishka
Macduff: Stamm
Malcolm: Gilmore
Lady-in-Attendance: Bureau
Physician: Vernon
Manservant: Harper
Duncan: Murphy
Fleance: McCallum
Murderer: Courtney
Herald: Brewer
Hecate: Kimball
Warrior: Christopher

December 15, 1982 [417]
Macbeth (Verdi–Piave/Maffei) [50]
Conducted by Levine
Macbeth: Milnes [24]
Lady Macbeth: Scotto
Banquo: Plishka
Macduff: Jenkins
Malcolm: Gilmore
Lady-in-Attendance: Bureau
Physician: Vernon
Manservant: Harper
Duncan: Murphy
Fleance: McCallum
Murderer: Courtney
Herald: Brewer
Hecate: Kimball
Warrior: Christopher

December 18, 1982, matinee (broadcast) [418]
Macbeth (Verdi–Piave/Maffei) [51]
Conducted by Levine
Macbeth: Milnes [25]
Lady Macbeth: Scotto
Banquo: Plishka
Macduff: Jenkins
Malcolm: Gilmore
Lady-in-Attendance: Bureau
Physician: Vernon

Manservant: Harper
Duncan: Murphy
Fleance: McCallum
Murderer: Courtney
Herald: Brewer
Hecate: Kimball
Warrior: Christopher

December 21, 1982 [419]
Macbeth (Verdi–Piave/Maffei) [52]
Conducted by Levine
Macbeth: Milnes [26]
Lady Macbeth: Scotto
Banquo: Morris
Macduff: Jenkins
Malcolm: Gilmore
Lady-in-Attendance: Bureau
Physician: Vernon
Manservant: Harper
Duncan: Murphy
Fleance: McCallum
Murderer: N. Andersson
Herald: Brewer
Hecate: Kimball
Warrior: Christopher

December 24, 1982 [420]
Macbeth (Verdi–Piave/Maffei) [53]
Conducted by Levine
Macbeth: Milnes [27]
Lady Macbeth: Scotto
Banquo: Morris
Macduff: Jenkins
Malcolm: Gilmore
Lady-in-Attendance: Bureau
Physician: Vernon
Manservant: Courtney
Duncan: Murphy
Fleance: McCallum
Murderer: Andersson
Herald: Brewer
Hecate: Kimball
Warrior: Christopher

January 30, 1983, concert (simulcast) [421]
Conducted by Levine
Les pêcheurs de perles (Bizet–Carré/ Cormon), "Au fond du temple saint": Domingo, Milnes

Hamlet (Thomas–Carré/Barbier), "O vin dissipe la tristesse": Milnes
Andrea Chénier (Giordano–Illica), "Un di all'azzurro spazio": Domingo
La Bohème (Puccini–Giacosa/Illica), "O Mimì, tu più non torni": Domingo, Milnes
Manon Lescaut (Puccini), Intermezzo
La Gioconda (Ponchielli–Boito), "Enzo Grimaldo": Domingo, Milnes
La forza del destino (Verdi–Piave), "O tu che in seno agli angeli": Domingo; "Solenne in quest'ora": Domingo, Milnes, Christopher; "Urna fatale": Milnes; Overture; "Invano Alvaro": Domingo, Milnes
Otello (Verdi–Boito), "Era la notte," "Si pel ciel": Domingo, Milnes
[This program was videotaped for the *In Concert at the Met* series and first televised over PBS on May 11, 1983.]

WASHINGTON, D.C.

April 23, 1983 [422]
Macbeth (Verdi–Piave/Maffei) [54]
Conducted by Levine
Macbeth: Milnes [28]
Lady Macbeth: Scotto
Banquo: Plishka
Macduff: Jenkins
Malcolm: Gilmore
Lady-in-Attendance: Bureau
Physician: Robbins
Manservant: Brewer
Duncan: Mellow
Fleance: Peloso
Murderer: Courtney
Herald: Brewer
Hecate: Ross
Warrior: Christopher

DALLAS, TEXAS

May 13, 1983 [423]
La forza del destino (Verdi–Piave) [194]
Conducted by Levine
Leonora: Mitchell
Alvaro: Mauro
Carlo: Milnes [14]

Father Superior: Morris
Preziosilla: Conrad
Melitone: Capecchi
Marquis: Vernon
Curra: Kraft
Mayor: Courtney

MINNEAPOLIS, MINNESOTA

May 17, 1983 [424]
Macbeth (Verdi–Piave/Maffei) [58]
Conducted by Levine
Macbeth: Milnes [29]
Lady Macbeth: Scotto
Banquo: Plishka
Macduff: Jenkins
Malcolm: Gilmore
Lady-in-Attendance: Bureau
Physician: Robbins
Manservant: Brewer
Duncan: Mellow
Fleance: Peloso
Murderer: Courtney
Herald: Brewer
Hecate:. Ross
Warrior: Christopher

May 21, 1983 [425]
La forza del destino (Verdi–Piave) [195]
Conducted by Levine
Leonora: Mitchell
Alvaro: Mauro
Carlo: Milnes [15]
Father Superior: Morris
Preziosilla: I. Jones
Melitone: Capecchi
Marquis: Vernon
Curra: Love
Mayor: Courtney

DETROIT, MICHIGAN

May 24, 1983 [426]
Macbeth (Verdi–Piave/Maffei) [59]
Conducted by Levine
Macbeth: Milnes [30]
Lady Macbeth: Scotto
Banquo: Plishka
Macduff: Jenkins
Malcolm: Gilmore

Lady-in-Attendance: Bureau
Physician: Robbins
Manservant: Brewer
Duncan: Mellow
Fleance: Peloso
Murderer: Courtney
Herald: Brewer
Hecate: Ross
Warrior: Christopher

CLEVELAND, OHIO

June 4, 1983 [427]
La forza del destino (Verdi–Piave) [197]
Conducted by Levine
Leonora: Mitchell
Alvaro: Mauro
Carlo: Milnes [16]
Father Superior: Morris
Preziosilla: Conrad
Melitone: Capecchi
Marquis: Vernon
Curra: Kraft
Mayor: Courtney

BOSTON, MASSACHUSETTS

June 7, 1983 [428]
Macbeth (Verdi–Piave/Maffei) [61]
Conducted by Levine
Macbeth: Milnes [31]
Lady Macbeth: Scotto
Banquo: Plishka
Macduff: Mauro
Malcolm: Gilmore
Lady-in-Attendance: Bureau
Physician: Robbins
Manservant: Brewer
Duncan: Mellow
Fleance: Peloso
Murderer: Courtney
Herald: Brewer
Hecate:. Ross
Warrior: Christopher

June 11, 1983 [429]
La forza del destino (Verdi–Piave) [198]
Conducted by Levine
Leonora: Mitchell
Alvaro: Mauro

Carlo: Milnes [17]
Father Superior: Morris
Preziosilla: Conrad
Melitone: Capecchi
Marquis: Vernon
Curra: Kraft
Mayor: Courtney

1983–84
METROPOLITAN OPERA HOUSE

November 18, 1983, benefit sponsored by the Metropolitan Opera Guild for the production funds [430]
Ernani (Verdi–Piave; new production) [50]
Conducted by Levine
Ernani: Pavarotti
Elvira: Mitchell
Carlo: Milnes [7]
Silva: R. Raimondi
Giovanna: Kraft
Directed by Samaritani
Set design by Samaritani
Costume design by Hall
Lighting design by Wechsler

November 21, 1983 [431]
Ernani (Verdi–Piave) [51]
Conducted by Levine
Ernani: Pavarotti
Elvira: Mitchell
Carlo: Milnes [8]
Silva: R. Raimondi
Giovanna: Kraft

November 24, 1983 [432]
Ernani (Verdi–Piave) [52]
Conducted by Levine
Ernani: Pavarotti
Elvira: Mitchell
Carlo: Milnes [9]
Silva: R. Raimondi
Giovanna: Kraft

November 30, 1983 [433]
Ernani (Verdi–Piave) [53]
Conducted by Levine
Ernani: Pavarotti
Elvira: Mitchell

Carlo: Milnes [10]
Silva: R. Raimondi
Giovanna: Kraft

December 3, 1983 [434]
Ernani (Verdi–Piave) [54]
Conducted by Levine
Ernani: Pavarotti
Elvira: Negri
Carlo: Milnes [11]
Silva: R. Raimondi
Giovanna: Kraft

December 6, 1983 [435]
Ernani (Verdi–Piave) [55]
Conducted by Levine
Ernani: Pavarotti
Elvira: Mitchell
Carlo: Milnes [12]
Silva: R. Raimondi
Giovanna: Kraft

December 12, 1983 [436]
Ernani (Verdi–Piave) [57]
Conducted by Levine
Ernani: Pavarotti
Elvira: Mitchell
Carlo: Milnes [13]
Silva: R. Raimondi
Giovanna: Kraft

December 17, 1983, matinee (simulcast) [437]
Ernani (Verdi–Piave) [58]
Conducted by Levine
Ernani: Pavarotti
Elvira: Mitchell
Carlo: Milnes [14]
Silva: R. Raimondi
Giovanna: Kraft
[This performance was broadcast as part of the regular Saturday radio series and telecast directly to Europe. Additionally, it was videotaped for the *Live from the Met* series and first televised over PBS on December 21, 1983.]

December 23, 1983 [438]
Ernani (Verdi–Piave) [60]
Conducted by Levine
Ernani: Mauro
Elvira: Mitchell

Carlo: Milnes [15]
Silva: R. Raimondi
Giovanna: Kraft

December 28, 1983 [439]
Ernani (Verdi–Piave) [61]
Conducted by Levine
Ernani: Mauro
Elvira: Mitchell
Carlo: Milnes [16]
Silva: R. Raimondi
Giovanna: Kraft

January 12, 1984 [440]
Macbeth (Verdi–Piave/Maffei) [62]
Conducted by Levine
Macbeth: Milnes [32]
Lady Macbeth: Scotto
Banquo: Morris
Macduff: Ciannella
Malcolm: Gilmore
Lady-in-Attendance: Bureau
Physician: Vernon
Manservant: Brewer
Duncan: Murphy
Fleance: McCallum
Murderer: Courtney
Herald: Harper
Hecate: Ross
Warrior: Christopher
Directed by Hall
Staged by Mills
Designed by Bury
Lighting design by Wechsler
Choreography by Hopps

January 16, 1984 [441]
Macbeth (Verdi–Piave/Maffei) [63]
Conducted by Levine
Macbeth: Milnes [33]
Lady Macbeth: Scotto
Banquo: Plishka
Macduff: Ciannella
Malcolm: Gilmore
Lady-in-Attendance: Bureau
Physician: Vernon
Manservant: Brewer
Duncan: Murphy
Fleance: McCallum
Murderer: Courtney
Herald: Harper

Hecate: Ross
Warrior: Christopher

January 20, 1984 [442]
Macbeth (Verdi–Piave/Maffei) [64]
Conducted by Levine
Macbeth: Milnes [34]
Lady Macbeth: Scotto
Banquo: Plishka
Macduff: Jenkins
Malcolm: Gilmore
Lady-in-Attendance: Bureau
Physician: Vernon
Manservant: Brewer
Duncan: Murphy
Fleance: McCallum
Murderer: Courtney
Herald: Harper
Hecate: Ross
Warrior: Christopher

January 25, 1984 [443]
Macbeth (Verdi–Piave/Maffei) [65]
Conducted by Levine
Macbeth: Milnes [35]
Lady Macbeth: Scotto
Banquo: Plishka
Macduff: Shicoff
Malcolm: Gilmore
Lady-in-Attendance: Bureau
Physician: Vernon
Manservant: Brewer
Duncan: Murphy
Fleance: McCallum
Murderer: Courtney
Herald: Harper
Hecate: Ross
Warrior: Christopher

January 28, 1984, matinee (broadcast) [444]
Macbeth (Verdi–Piave/Maffei) [66]
Conducted by Levine
Macbeth: Milnes [36]
Lady Macbeth: Scotto
Banquo: Plishka
Macduff: Shicoff
Malcolm: Gilmore
Lady-in-Attendance: Bureau
Physician: Vernon
Manservant: Brewer

Duncan: Murphy
Fleance: McCallum
Murderer: Courtney
Herald: Harper
Hecate: Ross
Warrior: Christopher

January 31, 1984 [445]
Macbeth (Verdi–Piave/Maffei) [67]
Conducted by Levine
Macbeth: Milnes [37]
Lady Macbeth: Scotto
Banquo: Plishka
Macduff: Shicoff
Malcolm: Gilmore
Lady-in-Attendance: Bureau
Physician: Robbins
Manservant: Brewer
Duncan: Murphy
Fleance: McCallum
Murderer: Courtney
Herald: Harper
Hecate: Ross
Warrior: Christopher

February 16, 1984 [446]
Macbeth (Verdi–Piave/Maffei) [70]
Conducted by Fulton
Macbeth: Milnes [38]
Lady Macbeth: Negri
Banquo: Plishka
Macduff: Shicoff
Malcolm: Gilmore
Lady-in-Attendance: Bureau
Physician: Robbins
Manservant: Brewer
Duncan: Murphy
Fleance: McCallum
Murderer: Courtney
Herald: Harper
Hecate: Ross
Warrior: Christopher

WASHINGTON, D.C.

April 25, 1984 [447]
Ernani (Verdi–Piave) [62]
Conducted by Fulton
Ernani: Mauro
Elvira: Mitchell

Carlo: Milnes [17]
Silva: Plishka
Giovanna: Beer

May 1, 1984 [448]
Ernani (Verdi–Piave) [63]
Conducted by Fulton
Ernani: Mauro
Elvira: Mitchell
Carlo: Milnes [18]
Silva: Plishka
Giovanna: Beer

May 5, 1984 [449]
Tosca (Puccini–Illica/Giacosa) [670]
Conducted by Levine
Tosca: Scotto
Cavaradossi: Mauro
Scarpia: Milnes [17]
Sacristan: Tajo
Spoletta: Laciura
Angelotti: Darrenkamp
Sciarrone: Nimnicht

ATLANTA, GEORGIA

May 9, 1984 [450]
Ernani (Verdi–Piave) [64]
Conducted by Fulton
Ernani: Mauro
Elvira: Mitchell
Carlo: Milnes [19]
Silva: Plishka
Giovanna: Beer

MEMPHIS, TENNESSEE

May 15, 1994 [451]
Tosca (Puccini–Illica/Giacosa) [672]
Conducted by Fulton
Tosca: Cruz-Romo
Cavaradossi: Mauro
Scarpia: Milnes [18]
Sacristan: Tajo
Spoletta: Laciura
Angelotti: Darrenkamp
Sciarrone: Nimnicht

MINNEAPOLIS, MINNESOTA

May 23, 1984 [452]
Ernani (Verdi–Piave) [65]
Conducted by Fulton
Ernani: Mauro
Elvira: Mitchell
Carlo: Milnes [20]
Silva: Plishka
Giovanna: Beer

May 26, 1984, matinee [453]
Tosca (Puccini–Illica/Giacosa) [674]
Conducted by Levine
Tosca: Scotto
Cavaradossi: Mauro
Scarpia: Milnes [19]
Sacristan: Tajo
Spoletta: Laciura
Angelotti: Courtney
Sciarrone: Nimnicht

DETROIT, MICHIGAN

May 30, 1984 [454]
Ernani (Verdi–Piave) [66]
Conducted by Fulton
Ernani: Mauro
Elvira: Mitchell
Carlo: Milnes [21]
Silva: Plishka
Giovanna: Beer

TORONTO, CANADA

June 6, 1984 [455]
Ernani (Verdi–Piave) [67]
Conducted by Fulton
Ernani: Mauro
Elvira: Mitchell
Carlo: Milnes [22]
Silva: Plishka
Giovanna: Beer

June 9, 1984, matinee [456]
Tosca (Puccini–Illica/Giacosa) [676]
Conducted by Levine
Tosca: Scotto
Cavaradossi: Mauro
Scarpia: Milnes [20]
Sacristan: Tajo

Spoletta: Laciura
Angelotti: Courtney
Sciarrone: Nimnicht

CLEVELAND, OHIO

June 13, 1984 [457]
Ernani (Verdi–Piave) [68]
Conducted by Fulton
Ernani: Mauro
Elvira: Mitchell
Carlo: Milnes [23]
Silva: Plishka
Giovanna: Beer

1984–85
METROPOLITAN OPERA HOUSE

November 23, 1984 [458]
Simon Boccanegra (Verdi–Piave/Boito; new production) [76]
Conducted by Levine
Simon: Milnes [1]
Maria: Tomowa-Sintow
Gabriele: Moldoveanu
Fiesco: Plishka
Paolo: Glossop
Pietro: Courtney
Directed by Capobianco
Designed by Pizzi
Lighting design by Wechsler
[The production was originally designed and directed for Lyric Opera of Chicago by Pier Luigi Pizzi, with several innovative improvements by Capobianco.]

November 26, 1984 [459]
Simon Boccanegra (Verdi–Piave/Boito) [77]
Conducted by Levine
Simon: Milnes [2]
Maria: Tomowa-Sintow
Gabriele: Moldoveanu
Fiesco: Plishka
Paolo: Glossop
Pietro: Courtney

November 29, 1984 [460]
Simon Boccanegra (Verdi–Piave/Boito) [78]
Conducted by Levine
Simon: Milnes [3]
Maria: Tomowa-Sintow
Gabriele: Moldoveanu
Fiesco: Plishka
Paolo: Glossop
Pietro: Courtney

December 3, 1984 [461]
Simon Boccanegra (Verdi–Piave/Boito) [79]
Conducted by Levine
Simon: Milnes [4]
Maria: Millo
Gabriele: Moldoveanu
Fiesco: Plishka
Paolo: Glossop
Pietro: Courtney

December 7, 1984 [462]
Simon Boccanegra (Verdi–Piave/Boito) [80]
Conducted by Levine
Simon: Milnes [5]
Maria: Tomowa-Sintow
Gabriele: Moldoveanu
Fiesco: Plishka
Paolo: Glossop
Pietro: Courtney

December 12, 1984 [463]
Simon Boccanegra (Verdi–Piave/Boito) [81]
Conducted by Levine
Simon: Milnes [6]
Maria: Tomowa-Sintow
Gabriele: Moldoveanu
Fiesco: Plishka
Paolo: Glossop
Pietro: Courtney

December 18, 1984 [464]
Simon Boccanegra (Verdi–Piave/Boito) [83]
Conducted by Levine
Simon: Milnes [7]
Maria: Tomowa-Sintow
Gabriele: Popov

Fiesco: Plishka
Paolo: Clark
Pietro: Cook

December 22, 1984 [465]
Simon Boccanegra (Verdi–Piave/Boito)
[84]
Conducted by Levine
Simon: Milnes [8]
Maria: Millo
Gabriele: Moldoveanu
Fiesco: Plishka
Paolo: Clark
Pietro: Courtney

December 26, 1984 [466]
Simon Boccanegra (Verdi–Piave/Boito)
[85]
Conducted by Levine
Simon: Milnes [9]
Maria: Tomowa-Sintow
Gabriele: Moldoveanu
Fiesco: Plishka
Paolo: Clark
Pietro: Courtney

December 29, 1984, matinee (simulcast) [467]
Simon Boccanegra (Verdi–Piave/Boito)
[86]
Conducted by Levine
Simon: Milnes [10]
Maria: Tomowa-Sintow
Gabriele: Moldoveanu
Fiesco: Plishka
Paolo: Clark
Pietro: Courtney
[This performance was broadcast as part
of the regular Saturday radio series
and telecast directly to Europe. A vid-
eotape was first televised in the United
States over PBS on April 17, 1985, as
part of the *Live from the Met* series.]

January 4, 1985 [468]
Simon Boccanegra (Verdi–Piave/Boito)
[88]
Conducted by Levine
Simon: Milnes [11]
Maria: Tomowa-Sintow
Gabriele: Moldoveanu

Fiesco: Furlanetto
Paolo: Clark
Pietro: Cook

January 21, 1985 [469]
Otello (Verdi–Boito) [250]
Conducted by Levine
Otello: Domingo
Desdemona: M. Price
Iago: Milnes [36]
Emilia: Kraft
Cassio: Lewis
Lodovico: Howell
Montano: Darrenkamp
Directed by Zeffirelli
Staged by Melano
Set design by Zeffirelli
Costume design by Hall
Lighting design by Wechsler

January 25, 1985 [470]
Otello (Verdi–Boito) [251]
Conducted by Levine
Otello: Domingo
Desdemona: M. Price
Iago: Milnes [37]
Emilia: Kraft
Cassio: Lewis
Lodovico: Howell
Montano: Darrenkamp

January 29, 1985 [471]
Otello (Verdi–Boito) [252]
Conducted by Levine
Otello: Domingo
Desdemona: M. Price
Iago: Milnes [38]
Emilia: Kraft
Cassio: Lewis
Lodovico: Howell
Montano: Darrenkamp

February 2, 1985, matinee (broadcast) [472]
Otello (Verdi–Boito) [253]
Conducted by Levine
Otello: Domingo
Desdemona: M. Price
Iago: Milnes [39]
Emilia: Kraft
Cassio: Lewis

Lodovico: Howell
Montano: Darrenkamp

February 7, 1985 [473]
Otello (Verdi–Boito) [254]
Conducted by Levine
Otello: Domingo
Desdemona: M. Price
Iago: Milnes [40]
Emilia: Kraft
Cassio: Lewis
Lodovico: Cook
Montano: Darrenkamp

BOSTON, MASSACHUSETTS

April 26, 1985 [474]
Simon Boccanegra (Verdi–Piave/Boito)
[89]
Conducted by Santi
Simon: Milnes [12]
Maria: Millo
Gabriele: Moldoveanu
Fiesco: Plishka
Paolo: Clark
Pietro: Courtney

CLEVELAND, OHIO

May 2, 1985 [475]
Simon Boccanegra (Verdi–Piave/Boito)
[90]
Conducted by Santi
Simon: Milnes [13]
Maria: Millo
Gabriele: Moldoveanu
Fiesco: Plishka
Paolo: Clark
Pietro: Courtney

ATLANTA, GEORGIA

May 9, 1985 [476]
Simon Boccanegra (Verdi–Piave/Boito)
[91]
Conducted by Santi
Simon: Milnes [14]
Maria: Millo
Gabriele: Moldoveanu
Fiesco: Plishka

Paolo: Glossop
Pietro: Courtney

MINNEAPOLIS, MINNESOTA

May 16, 1985 [477]
Simon Boccanegra (Verdi–Piave/Boito)
[92]
Conducted by Sand
Simon: Milnes [15]
Maria: Millo
Gabriele: Moldoveanu
Fiesco: Plishka
Paolo: Glossop
Pietro: Courtney

DETROIT, MICHIGAN

May 23, 1985 [478]
Simon Boccanegra (Verdi–Piave/Boito)
[93]
Conducted by Santi
Simon: Milnes [16]
Maria: Millo
Gabriele: Moldoveanu
Fiesco: Plishka
Paolo: Glossop
Pietro: Courtney

WASHINGTON, D.C.

May 31, 1985 [479]
Simon Boccanegra (Verdi–Piave/Boito)
[94]
Conducted by Santi
Simon: Milnes [17]
Maria: Millo
Gabriele: Moldoveanu
Fiesco: Plishka
Paolo: Clark
Pietro: Courtney

1985–86
METROPOLITAN OPERA HOUSE

November 4, 1985 [480]
Cavalleria rusticana (Mascagni–Targioni-
Tozzetti/Menasci) [564]
Conducted by Navarro

Santuzza: Behrens
Turiddu: Moldoveanu
Lola: I. Jones
Directed by Zeffirelli
Staged by Melano
Designed by Zeffirelli
Lighting design by Wechsler
Pagliacci (Leoncavallo) [602]
Conducted by Navarro
Nedda: Pilou
Canio: Veronelli
Tonio: Milnes [26]
Silvio: Schexnayder
Directed by Zeffirelli
Staged by Melano
Designed by Zeffirelli
Lighting design by Wechsler

November 8, 1985 [481]
Cavalleria rusticana (Mascagni–Targioni-
Tozzetti/Menasci) [565]
Conducted by Navarro
Santuzza: Behrens
Turiddu: Moldoveanu
Lola: I. Jones
Pagliacci (Leoncavallo) [603]
Conducted by Navarro
Nedda: Pilou
Canio: Veronelli
Tonio: Milnes [27]
Silvio: Schexnayder

November 13, 1985 [482]
Cavalleria rusticana (Mascagni–Targioni-
Tozzetti/Menasci) [566]
Conducted by Navarro
Santuzza:. Behrens
Turiddu: Moldoveanu
Lola: I. Jones
Pagliacci (Leoncavallo) [604]
Conducted by Navarro
Nedda: Pilou
Canio: Veronelli
Tonio: Milnes [28]
Silvio: Schexnayder

November 23, 1985 [483]
Cavalleria rusticana (Mascagni–Targioni-
Tozzetti/Menasci) [569]
Conducted by Navarro
Santuzza: Dunn

Turiddu: Moldoveanu
Lola: I. Jones
Pagliacci (Leoncavallo) [607]
Conducted by Navarro
Nedda: Nicolesco
Canio: Vickers
Tonio: Milnes [29]
Silvio: Hartman

November 27, 1985 [484]
Cavalleria rusticana (Mascagni–Targioni-
Tozzetti/Menasci) [570]
Conducted by Navarro
Santuzza: Behrens
Turiddu: Popov
Lola: I. Jones
Pagliacci (Leoncavallo) [608]
Conducted by Navarro
Nedda: Nicolesco
Canio: Vickers
Tonio: Milnes [30]
Silvio: Schexnayder

November 30, 1985 [485]
Cavalleria rusticana (Mascagni–Targioni-
Tozzetti/Menasci) [571]
Conducted by Navarro
Santuzza: Behrens
Turiddu: Popov
Lola: I. Jones
Pagliacci (Leoncavallo) [609]
Conducted by Navarro
Nedda: Nicolesco
Canio: Vickers
Tonio: Milnes [31]
Silvio: Hartman

December 3, 1985 [486]
Cavalleria rusticana (Mascagni–Targioni-
Tozzetti/Menasci) [572]
Conducted by Navarro
Santuzza: Behrens
Turiddu: Moldoveanu
Lola: I. Jones
Pagliacci (Leoncavallo) [610]
Conducted by Navarro
Nedda: Pilou
Canio: Vickers
Tonio: Milnes [32]
Silvio: Schexnayder

December 7, 1985, matinee (broadcast) [487]
Cavalleria rusticana (Mascagni–Targioni-
   Tozzetti/Menasci) [573]
Conducted by Navarro
Santuzza: Behrens
Turiddu: Moldoveanu
Lola: I. Jones
Alfio: Clark
Lucia: Godfrey Ben-David
Pagliacci (Leoncavallo) [611]
Conducted by Navarro
Nedda: Pilou
Canio: Vickers
Tonio: Milnes [33]
Silvio: Schexnayder

February 21, 1986 [488]
Simon Boccanegra (Verdi–Piave/Boito)
   [95]
Conducted by Chung
Simon: Milnes [18]
Maria: Tomowa-Sintow
Gabriele: Moldoveanu
Fiesco: Plishka
Paolo: Clark
Pietro: Cook
Directed by Capobianco
Staged by Kneuss
Designed by Pizzi
Lighting design by Wechsler

February 24, 1986 [489]
Simon Boccanegra (Verdi–Piave/Boito)
   [96]
Conducted by Chung
Simon: Milnes [19]
Maria: Tomowa-Sintow
Gabriele: Moldoveanu
Fiesco: Plishka
Paolo: Clark
Pietro: Cook

February 27, 1986 [490]
Simon Boccanegra (Verdi–Piave/Boito)
   [97]
Conducted by Chung
Simon: Milnes [20]
Maria: Tomowa-Sintow
Gabriele: Moldoveanu
Fiesco: Plishka

Paolo: Clark
Pietro: Cook

March 4, 1986 [491]
Simon Boccanegra (Verdi–Piave/Boito)
   [98]
Conducted by Chung
Simon: Milnes [21]
Maria: Tomowa-Sintow
Gabriele: Moldoveanu
Fiesco: Plishka.
Paolo: Courtney
Pietro: Cook

March 7, 1986 [492]
Simon Boccanegra (Verdi–Piave/Boito)
   [99]
Conducted by Chung
Simon: Milnes [22]
Maria: Tomowa-Sintow
Gabriele: Moldoveanu
Fiesco: Morris
Paolo: Courtney
Pietro: Cook

March 12, 1986 [493]
Simon Boccanegra (Verdi–Piave/Boito)
   [100]
Conducted by Chung
Simon: Milnes [23]
Maria: Te Kanawa
Gabriele: Moldoveanu
Fiesco: Plishka
Paolo: Clark
Pietro: Cook

March 15, 1986, matinee (broadcast) [494]
Simon Boccanegra (Verdi–Piave/Boito)
   [101]
Conducted by Chung
Simon: Milnes [24]
Maria: Te Kanawa
Gabriele: Moldoveanu
Fiesco: Plishka
Paolo: Clark
Pietro: Cook

March 19, 1986 [495]
Simon Boccanegra (Verdi–Piave/Boito)
   [102]
Conducted by Chung

Simon: Milnes [25]
Maria: Te Kanawa
Gabriele: Moldoveanu
Fiesco: Plishka
Paolo: Clark
Pietro: Cook

March 22, 1986 [496]
Simon Boccanegra (Verdi–Piave/Boito)
[103]
Conducted by Chung
Simon: Milnes [26]
Maria: Te Kanawa
Gabriele: Moldoveanu
Fiesco: Morris
Paolo: Clark
Pietro: Cook

March 27, 1986 [497]
Simon Boccanegra (Verdi–Piave/Boito)
[104]
Conducted by Chung
Simon: Milnes [27]
Maria: Te Kanawa
Gabriele: Moldoveanu
Fiesco: Plishka
Paolo: Clark
Pietro: Cook

1986–87
METROPOLITAN OPERA HOUSE

**November 14, 1986, benefit sponsored by
the Metropolitan Opera Guild in celebra-
tion of Joan Sutherland's twenty-fifth an-
niversary with the company [498]**
I Puritani (Bellini–Pepoli) [19]
Conducted by Bonynge
Elvira: Sutherland
Arturo: Fisichella
Riccardo: Milnes [8]
Giorgio: Ramey
Enrichetta: Hillhouse
Directed by Sequi
Set design by M. C. Lee
Costume design by Hall
Lighting design by Wechsler

November 18, 1986 [499]
I Puritani (Bellini–Pepoli) [20]

Conducted by Bonynge
Elvira: Sutherland
Arturo: Fisichella
Riccardo: Milnes [9]
Giorgio: Ramey
Enrichetta: Hillhouse

November 22, 1986 [500]
I Puritani (Bellini–Pepoli) [21]
Conducted by Bonynge
Elvira: Sutherland
Arturo: Fisichella
Riccardo: Milnes [10]
Giorgio: Ramey
Enrichetta: Hillhouse

November 26, 1986 [501]
I Puritani (Bellini–Pepoli) [22]
Conducted by Bonynge
Elvira: Sutherland
Arturo: Fisichella
Riccardo: Milnes [11]
Giorgio: Ramey
Enrichetta: Hillhouse

November 29, 1986, matinee [502]
I Puritani (Bellini–Pepoli) [23]
Conducted by Bonynge
Elvira: Garner
Arturo: Fisichella
Riccardo: Milnes [12]
Giorgio: Ramey
Enrichetta: Deng

December 6, 1986 [503]
I Puritani (Bellini–Pepoli) [25]
Conducted by Bonynge
Elvira: Sutherland
Arturo: Blake
Riccardo: Milnes [13]
Giorgio: Robbins
Enrichetta: Hillhouse

December 9, 1986 [504]
I Puritani (Bellini–Pepoli) [26]
Conducted by Bonynge
Elvira: Sutherland
Arturo: Blake
Riccardo: Milnes [14]
Giorgio: Ramey
Enrichetta: Hillhouse

December 13, 1986, matinee (broadcast) [505]
I Puritani (Bellini–Pepoli) [27]
Conducted by Bonynge
Elvira: Sutherland
Arturo: Blake
Riccardo: Milnes [15]
Giorgio: Ramey
Enrichetta: Hillhouse

December 22, 1986 [506]
Rigoletto (Verdi–Piave) [629]
Conducted by Fulton
Rigoletto: Milnes [14]
Gilda: Devia
Duke: Di Giuseppe
Maddalena: I. Jones
Sparafucile: Kavrakos
Monterone: Clark
Borsa: Olsen
Marullo: Hamilton
Ceprano: Vernon
Countess Ceprano: Wohlafka
Giovanna: Green
Directed by Dexter
Staged by Sell
Designed by Moiseiwitsch
Lighting design by Wechsler
Choreography by Vesak

December 25, 1986 [507]
Rigoletto (Verdi–Piave) [630]
Conducted by Fulton
Rigoletto: Milnes [15]
Gilda: Devia
Duke: Raffanti
Maddalena: I. Jones
Sparafucile: Kavrakos
Monterone: Clark
Borsa: Olsen
Marullo: Hamilton
Ceprano: Vernon
Countess Ceprano: Wohlafka
Giovanna: Green

December 30, 1986 [508]
Rigoletto (Verdi–Piave) [631]
Conducted by Fulton
Rigoletto: Milnes [16]
Gilda: Devia
Duke: Raffanti

Maddalena: I. Jones
Sparafucile: Kavrakos
Monterone: Clark
Borsa: Olsen
Marullo: Hamilton
Ceprano: Vernon
Countess Ceprano: Wohlafka
Giovanna: Green

January 2, 1987 [509]
Rigoletto (Verdi–Piave) [632]
Conducted by Fulton
Rigoletto: Milnes [17]
Gilda: Devia
Duke: Raffanti
Maddalena: I. Jones
Sparafucile: Macurdy
Monterone: Clark
Borsa: Olsen
Marullo: Hamilton
Ceprano: Wentzel
Countess Ceprano: Wohlafka
Giovanna: Johnsson

January 5, 1987 [510]
Rigoletto (Verdi–Piave) [633]
Conducted by Fulton
Rigoletto: Milnes [18]
Gilda: Devia
Duke: Gulyas
Maddalena: I. Jones
Sparafucile: Kavrakos
Monterone: Clark
Borsa: Olsen
Marullo: Hamilton
Ceprano: Wentzel
Countess Ceprano: Wohlafka
Giovanna: Deng

January 10, 1987, matinee (broadcast) [511]
Rigoletto (Verdi–Piave) [634]
Conducted by Fulton
Rigoletto: Milnes [19]
Gilda: Devia
Duke: Gulyas
Maddalena: I. Jones
Sparafucile: Kavrakos
Monterone: Clark
Borsa: Olsen
Marullo: Hamilton

Ceprano: Wentzel
Countess Ceprano: Wohlafka
Giovanna: Deng

January 13, 1987 [512]
Rigoletto (Verdi–Piave) [635]
Conducted by Fulton
Rigoletto: Milnes [20]
Gilda: Bradley
Duke: Gulyas
Maddalena: I. Jones
Sparafucile: Kavrakos
Monterone: Smartt
Borsa: Olsen
Marullo: Hamilton
Ceprano: Vernon
Countess Ceprano: Di Franco
Giovanna: Deng

January 16, 1987 [513]
Rigoletto (Verdi–Piave) [636]
Conducted by Fulton
Rigoletto: Milnes [21]
Gilda: Bradley
Duke: Gulyas
Maddalena: I. Jones
Sparafucile: Kavrakos
Monterone: Smartt
Borsa: Olsen
Marullo: Hamilton
Ceprano: Vernon
Countess Ceprano: Di Franco
Giovanna: Deng

CENTRAL PARK, MANHATTAN,
NEW YORK

**June 16, 1987 (concert performance)
[514]**
Tosca (Puccini–Illica/Giacosa) [716]
Conducted by Navarro
Tosca: Zschau
Cavaradossi: Domingo
Scarpia: Milnes [21]
Sacristan: Tajo
Spoletta: Velis
Angelotti: Smartt
Sciarrone: Christopher

1987–88
METROPOLITAN OPERA HOUSE

October 16, 1987 [515]
Tosca (Puccini–Illica/Giacosa) [722]
Conducted by Badea
Tosca: Marton
Cavaradossi: Giacomini
Scarpia: Milnes [22]
Sacristan: Capecchi
Spoletta: Velis
Angelotti: Courtney
Sciarrone: Christopher
Directed by Zeffirelli
Staged by Kneuss
Set design by Zeffirelli
Costume design by Hall
Lighting design by Wechsler

October 21, 1987 [516]
Tosca (Puccini–Illica/Giacosa) [723]
Conducted by Badea
Tosca: Zschau
Cavaradossi: Giacomini
Scarpia: Milnes [23]
Sacristan: Capecchi
Spoletta: Velis
Angelotti: Courtney
Sciarrone: Christopher

October 27, 1987 [517]
Tosca (Puccini–Illica/Giacosa) [724]
Conducted by Badea
Tosca: Marton
Cavaradossi: Giacomini
Scarpia: Milnes [24]
Sacristan: Tajo
Spoletta: Velis
Angelotti: Courtney
Sciarrone: Christopher

October 31, 1987, matinee [518]
Tosca (Puccini–Illica/Giacosa) [725]
Conducted by Badea
Tosca: Marton
Cavaradossi: Giacomini
Scarpia: Milnes [25]
Sacristan: Tajo
Spoletta: Velis
Angelotti: Courtney
Sciarrone: Christopher

November 4, 1987 [519]
Tosca (Puccini–Illica/Giacosa) [726]
Conducted by Badea
Tosca: Marton
Cavaradossi: Popov
Scarpia: Milnes [26]
Sacristan: Tajo
Spoletta: Velis
Angelotti: Courtney
Sciarrone: Christopher

November 7, 1987 [520]
Tosca (Puccini–Illica/Giacosa) [727]
Conducted by Badea
Tosca: Marton
Cavaradossi: Popov
Scarpia: Milnes [27]
Sacristan: Tajo
Spoletta: Velis
Angelotti: Courtney
Sciarrone: Christopher

November 14, 1987, matinee [521]
Tosca (Puccini–Illica/Giacosa) [728]
Conducted by Badea
Tosca: Marton
Cavaradossi: Popov
Scarpia: Milnes [28]
Sacristan: Tajo
Spoletta: Velis
Angelotti: Courtney
Sciarrone: Christopher

November 19, 1987 [522]
La traviata (Verdi–Piave) [721]
Conducted by Fulton
Violetta: Soviero
Alfredo: Rosenshein
Germont: Milnes [22]
Flora: Bybee
Gastone: Olsen
Douphol: Eckhoff
D'Obigny: Courtney
Grenvil: Cook
Annina: Wray
Directed by Graham
Staged by Kneuss
Designed by Moiseiwitsch
Lighting design by Wechsler
Choreography by Solov

November 25, 1987 [523]
La traviata (Verdi–Piave) [722]
Conducted by Fulton
Violetta: Soviero
Alfredo: Rosenshein
Germont: Milnes [23]
Flora: Bybee
Gastone: Olsen
Douphol: Darrenkamp
D'Obigny: Courtney
Grenvil: Cook
Annina: Wray

November 28, 1987 [524]
La traviata (Verdi–Piave) [723]
Conducted by Fulton
Violetta: Tomowa-Sintow
Alfredo: Rosenshein
Germont: Milnes [24]
Flora: Bybee
Gastone: Olsen
Douphol: Eckhoff
D'Obigny: Courtney
Grenvil: Cook
Annina: Wray

December 2, 1987 [525]
La traviata (Verdi–Piave) [724]
Conducted by Fulton
Violetta: Tomowa-Sintow
Alfredo: Rosenshein
Germont: Milnes [25]
Flora: Bybee
Gastone: Olsen
Douphol: Eckhoff
D'Obigny: Courtney
Grenvil: Cook
Annina: Wray

December 9, 1987 [526]
La traviata (Verdi–Piave) [725]
Conducted by Fulton
Violetta: Soviero
Alfredo: Raffanti
Germont: Milnes [26]
Flora: Bybee
Gastone: Olsen
Douphol: Eckhoff
D'Obigny: Courtney
Grenvil: Cook
Annina: Wray

December 22, 1987 [527]
La traviata (Verdi–Piave) [728]
Conducted by Fulton
Violetta: Tomowa-Sintow
Alfredo: Rosenshein
Germont: Milnes [27]
Flora: Kesling
Gastone: Olsen
Douphol: Eckhoff
D'Obigny: Courtney
Grenvil: Cook
Annina: Wray

December 26, 1987, matinee (broadcast) [528]
La traviata (Verdi–Piave) [729]
Conducted by Fulton
Violetta: Tomowa-Sintow
Alfredo: Rosenshein
Germont: Milnes [28]
Flora: Kesling
Gastone: Olsen
Douphol: Eckhoff
D'Obigny: Courtney
Grenvil: Cook
Annina: Wray

January 1, 1988 [529]
La traviata (Verdi–Piave) [730]
Conducted by Fulton
Violetta: Soviero
Alfredo: Glassman
Germont: Milnes [29]
Flora: Kesling
Gastone: Olsen
Douphol: Eckhoff
D'Obigny: Courtney
Grenvil: Cook
Annina: Wray

February 2, 1988 [530]
Luisa Miller (Verdi–Cammarano) [53]
Conducted by Santi
Luisa: Millo
Rodolfo: Mauro
Miller: Milnes [25]
Walter: Plishka
Wurm: De Grandis
Federica: Dunn

February 6, 1988, matinee (broadcast) [531]
Luisa Miller (Verdi–Cammarano) [54]
Conducted by Santi
Luisa: Millo
Rodolfo: Mauro
Miller: Milnes [26]
Walter: Plishka
Wurm: De Grandis
Federica: Dunn
[Mauro canceled following act 1 and was replaced by Allan Glassman.]

February 10, 1988 [532]
Luisa Miller (Verdi–Cammarano) [55]
Conducted by Santi
Luisa: Millo
Rodolfo: Mauro
Miller: Milnes [27]
Walter: Plishka
Wurm: De Grandis
Federica: I. Jones

February 13, 1988 [533]
Luisa Miller (Verdi–Cammarano) [56]
Conducted by Santi
Luisa: Mosca
Rodolfo: Mauro
Miller: Milnes [28]
Walter: Plishka
Wurm: Koptchak
Federica: I. Jones

TOKYO, JAPAN

May 29, 1988 [534]
Il trovatore (Verdi–Cammarano) [508]
Conducted by Rudel
Manrico: Bonisolli
Leonora: Millo
di Luna: Milnes [18]
Azucena: Cossotto
Ferrando: De Grandis
Ines: Wray
Ruiz: Baker

June 2, 1988 [535]
Il trovatore (Verdi–Cammarano) [509]
Conducted by Rudel
Manrico: Bonisolli
Leonora: Millo

di Luna: Milnes [19]
Azucena: Cossotto
Ferrando: De Grandis
Ines: Wray
Ruiz: Baker

June 5, 1988 [536]
Il trovatore (Verdi–Cammarano) [510]
Conducted by Rudel
Manrico: Bonisolli
Leonora: Millo
di Luna: Milnes [20]
Azucena: Cossotto
Ferrando: De Grandis
Ines: Wray
Ruiz: Anthony

NAGOYA, JAPAN

June 8, 1988 [537]
Il trovatore (Verdi–Cammarano) [511]
Conducted by Rudel
Manrico: Bonisolli
Leonora: Millo
di Luna: Milnes [21]
Azucena: Cossotto
Ferrando: De Grandis
Ines: Wray
Ruiz: Anthony

1988–89
METROPOLITAN OPERA HOUSE

September 26, 1988 [538]
Il trovatore (Verdi–Cammarano) [512]
Conducted by Levine
Manrico: Pavarotti
Leonora: Marton
di Luna: Milnes [22]
Azucena: Cossotto
Ferrando: Wells
Ines: Di Franco
Ruiz: Baker
Directed by Melano
Set design by Frigerio
Costume design by Squarciapino
Lighting design by Wechsler

September 29, 1988 [539]
Il trovatore (Verdi–Cammarano) [513]

Conducted by Levine
Manrico: Pavarotti
Leonora: Millo
di Luna: Milnes [23]
Azucena: Cossotto
Ferrando: Wells
Ines: Di Franco
Ruiz: Baker

October 3, 1988 [540]
Il trovatore (Verdi–Cammarano) [514]
Conducted by Levine
Manrico: Pavarotti
Leonora: Millo
di Luna: Milnes [24]
Azucena: Cossotto
Ferrando: Wells
Ines: Di Franco
Ruiz: Baker

October 8, 1988 [541]
Il trovatore (Verdi–Cammarano) [515]
Conducted by Levine
Manrico: Pavarotti
Leonora: Marton
di Luna: Milnes [25]
Azucena: Zajick
Ferrando: Wells
Ines: Di Franco
Ruiz: Baker

October 11, 1988 [542]
Il trovatore (Verdi–Cammarano) [516]
Conducted by Levine
Manrico: Pavarotti
Leonora: Marton
di Luna: Milnes [26]
Azucena: Zajick
Ferrando: Wells
Ines: Di Franco
Ruiz: Baker
[The performance was dedicated to the
memory of James McCracken, who had
died on April 30, 1988.]

**October 15, 1988, matinee (simulcast)
[543]**
Il trovatore (Verdi–Cammarano) [517]
Conducted by Levine
Manrico: Pavarotti
Leonora: Marton

di Luna: Milnes [27]
Azucena: Zajick
Ferrando: Wells
Ines: Di Franco
Ruiz: Baker
[This performance was telecast directly
to Europe. A videotape was first tele-
vised in the United States over PBS on
October 21, 1988, as part of the *Live
from the Met* series.]

October 27, 1988 [544]
Il trovatore (Verdi–Cammarano) [520]
Conducted by Fagen
Manrico: Lamberti
Leonora: Millo
di Luna: Milnes [28]
Azucena: Cossotto
Ferrando: Wells
Ines: Kraft
Ruiz: Anthony

October 31, 1988 [545]
Il trovatore (Verdi–Cammarano) [521]
Conducted by Fagen
Manrico: Lamberti
Leonora: Millo
di Luna: Milnes [29]
Azucena: Cossotto
Ferrando: Cook
Ines: Kraft
Ruiz: Anthony

**December 8, 1988, benefit sponsored by
the Metropolitan Opera Guild [546]**
Aida (Verdi–Ghislanzoni; new produc-
tion) [924]
Verdi-Ghislanzoni
Conducted by Levine
Aida: Mitchell
Radames: Domingo
Amneris: Cossotto
Amonasro: Milnes [8]
Ramfis: Plishka
King: Kavrakos
Directed by Frisell
Set design by Quaranta
Costume design by Saligeri
Lighting design by Wechsler
Choreography by Griffin

December 12, 1988 [547]
Aida (Verdi–Ghislanzoni) [925]
Conducted by Levine
Aida: Mitchell
Radames: Domingo
Amneris: Cossotto
Amonasro: Milnes [9]
Ramfis: Plishka
King: Kavrakos

December 16, 1988 [548]
Aida (Verdi–Ghislanzoni) [926]
Conducted by Levine
Aida: Mitchell
Radames: Domingo
Amneris: Cossotto
Amonasro: Milnes [10]
Ramfis: Plishka
King: Kavrakos

December 20, 1988 [549]
Aida (Verdi–Ghislanzoni) [927]
Conducted by Levine
Aida: Mitchell
Radames: Domingo
Amneris: Cossotto
Amonasro: Milnes [11]
Ramfis: Plishka
King: Kavrakos

December 28, 1988 [550]
Aida (Verdi–Ghislanzoni) [929]
Conducted by Badea
Aida: Mitchell
Radames: Bartolini
Amneris: Cossotto
Amonasro: Milnes [12]
Ramfis: Plishka
King: Kavrakos

December 31, 1988 [551]
Aida (Verdi–Ghislanzoni) [930]
Conducted by Levine
Aida: Millo
Radames: Bartolini
Amneris: Toczyska
Amonasro: Milnes [13]
Ramfis: Plishka
King: Kavrakos

January 3, 1989 [552]
Aida (Verdi–Ghislanzoni) [931]
Conducted by Levine
Aida: Millo
Radames: Domingo
Amneris: Toczyska
Amonasro: Milnes [14]
Ramfis: Plishka
King: Kavrakos

**January 7, 1989, matinee (broadcast)
[553]**
Aida (Verdi–Ghislanzoni) [932]
Conducted by Levine
Aida: Millo
Radames: Domingo
Amneris: Toczyska
Amonasro: Milnes [15]
Ramfis: Plishka
King: Kavrakos

January 17, 1989 [554]
Il trovatore (Verdi–Cammarano) [522]
Conducted by Levine
Manrico: Pavarotti
Leonora: Millo
di Luna: Milnes [30]
Azucena: Cossotto
Ferrando: Plishka
Ines: Kraft
Ruiz: Anthony

**January 21, 1989, matinee (broadcast)
[555]**
Il trovatore (Verdi–Cammarano) [523]
Conducted by Levine
Manrico: Pavarotti
Leonora: Millo
di Luna: Milnes [31]
Azucena: Cossotto
Ferrando: Plishka
Ines: Kraft
Ruiz: Anthony

January 24, 1989 [556]
Il trovatore (Verdi–Cammarano) [524]
Conducted by Levine
Manrico: Bartolini
Leonora: Mosca
di Luna: Milnes [32]
Azucena: Dunn

Ferrando: Plishka
Ines: Kraft
Ruiz: Anthony

February 2, 1989 [557]
Aida (Verdi–Ghislanzoni) [937]
Conducted by Badea
Aida: Mitchell
Radames: Popov
Amneris: Toczyska
Amonasro: Milnes [16]
Ramfis: Plishka
King: Dupont

CENTRAL PARK, MANHATTAN, NEW YORK,

**June 19, 1989 (concert performance)
[558]**
Il trovatore (Verdi–Cammarano) [525]
Conducted by Fulton
Manrico: Bartolino
Leonora: Dunn
di Luna: Milnes [33]
Azucena: Toczyska
Ferrando: Plishka
Ines: Wray
Ruiz: Anthony
[The performances of June 19–July 8
were presented as part of the free
Public Parks Series.]

BRONX, NEW YORK

**June 23, 1989 (concert performance)
[559]**
Il trovatore (Verdi–Cammarano) [526]
Conducted by Fulton
Manrico: Bonanome
Leonora: Esperian
di Luna: Milnes [34]
Azucena: Toczyska
Ferrando: Plishka
Ines: Wray
Ruiz: Gilmore

STATEN ISLAND, NEW YORK

June 28, 1989 (concert performance) [560]
Il trovatore (Verdi–Cammarano) [527]
Conducted by Fulton
Manrico: Bonanome
Leonora: Dunn
di Luna: Milnes [35]
Azucena: Dunn
Ferrando: Plishka
Ines: Di Franco
Ruiz: Anthony

WATERLOO VILLAGE, STANHOPE, NEW JERSEY

July 5, 1989 (concert performance) [561]
Il trovatore (Verdi–Cammarano) [529]
Conducted by Fulton
Manrico: Bartolini
Leonora: Dunn
di Luna: Milnes [36]
Azucena: Toczyska
Ferrando: Plishka
Ines: Di Franco
Ruiz: Anthony

PENNSAUKEN, NEW JERSEY

July 8, 1989 (concert performance) [562]
Il trovatore (Verdi–Cammarano) [530]
Conducted by Fulton
Manrico: Bartolino
Leonora: Dunn
di Luna: Milnes [37]
Azucena: Toczyska
Ferrando: Cook
Ines: Di Franco
Ruiz: Anthony

1989–90
METROPOLITAN OPERA HOUSE

September 25, 1989 [563]
Aida (Verdi–Ghislanzoni) [938]
Conducted by Levine
Aida: Millo
Radames: Domingo

Amneris: Zajick
Amonasro: Milnes [17]
Ramfis: Burchuladze
King: De Grandis
Directed by Frisell
Set design by Quaranta
Costume design by Saligeri
Lighting design by Wechsler
Choreography by Griffin

September 28, 1989 [564]
Aida (Verdi–Ghislanzoni) [939]
Conducted by Levine
Aida: Millo
Radames: Domingo
Amneris: Zajick
Amonasro: Milnes [18]
Ramfis: Dupont
King: Kavrakos

October 2, 1989 [565]
Aida (Verdi–Ghislanzoni) [940]
Conducted by Levine
Aida: Millo
Radames: Domingo
Amneris: Zajick
Amonasro: Milnes [19]
Ramfis: Burchuladze
King: Kavrakos
[Zajick canceled after act 2 and was replaced by Barbara Conrad.]

October 7, 1989, matinee (simulcast) [566]
Aida (Verdi–Ghislanzoni) [941]
Conducted by Levine
Aida: Millo
Radames: Domingo
Amneris: Zajick
Amonasro: Milnes [20]
Ramfis: Burchuladze
King: Kavrakos
[This performance was videotaped for the *Metropolitan Opera Presents* series and first televised over PBS on December 27, 1989.]

November 4, 1989, matinee [567]
La traviata (Verdi–Piave) [736]
Conducted by Veltri
Violetta: Huffstodt

Alfredo: Shicoff
Germont: Milnes [30]
Flora: White
Gastone: Fracker
Douphol: Capecchi
D'Obigny: Courtney
Grenvil: Vernon
Annina: Kelly

November 8, 1989 [568]
La traviata (Verdi–Piave) [737]
Conducted by Veltri
Violetta: Huffstodt
Alfredo: Shicoff
Germont: Milnes [31]
Flora: White
Gastone: Fracker
Douphol: Capecchi
D'Obigny: Courtney
Grenvil: Vernon
Annina: Kelly

November 11, 1989 [569]
La traviata (Verdi–Piave) [738]
Conducted by Veltri
Violetta: Gruberova
Alfredo: W. MacNeil
Germont: Milnes [32]
Flora: White
Gastone: Forest
Douphol: Capecchi
D'Obigny: Courtney
Grenvil: Vernon
Annina: Kelly

November 16, 1989 [570]
La traviata (Verdi–Piave) [739]
Conducted by Veltri
Violetta: Huffstodt
Alfredo: Shicoff
Germont: Milnes [33]
Flora: White
Gastone: Forest
Douphol: Capecchi
D'Obigny: Courtney
Grenvil: Vernon
Annina: Kelly

November 30, 1989 [571]
Aida (Verdi–Ghislanzoni) [947]
Conducted by Badea

Aida: Mitchell
Radames: Mauro
Amneris: Zajick
Amonasro: Milnes [21]
Ramfis: Plishka
King: Kavrakos

December 4, 1989 [572]
Aida (Verdi–Ghislanzoni) [948]
Conducted by Badea
Aida: Mitchell
Radames: Mauro
Amneris: Zajick
Amonasro: Milnes [22]
Ramfis: Plishka
King: Kavrakos

December 8, 1989 [573]
Aida (Verdi–Ghislanzoni) [949]
Conducted by Badea
Aida: Marc
Radames: Mauro
Amneris: Zajick
Amonasro: Milnes [23]
Ramfis: Plishka
King: Kavrakos

December 13, 1989 [574]
Aida (Verdi–Ghislanzoni) [950]
Conducted by Badea
Aida: Mitchell
Radames: Mauro
Amneris: Zajick
Amonasro: Milnes [24]
Ramfis: Plishka
King: Kavrakos

December 16, 1989 [575]
Aida (Verdi–Ghislanzoni) [951]
Conducted by Badea
Aida: Mitchell
Radames: Mauro
Amneris: Zajick
Amonasro: Milnes [25]
Ramfis: Plishka
King: Cook

December 23, 1989 [576]
Aida (Verdi–Ghislanzoni) [953]
Conducted by Badea
Aida: Mitchell
Radames: Mauro

Amneris: Zajick
Amonasro: Milnes [26]
Ramfis: Plishka
King: Cook

BROOKLYN, NEW YORK

June 13, 1990 (concert performance) [577]
La traviata (Verdi–Piave) [744]
Conducted by Badea
Violetta: Huffstodt
Alfredo: Kraus
Germont: Milnes [34]
Flora: Guzman
Gastone: Forest
Douphol: Hamilton
D'Obigny: Courtney
Grenvil: Vernon
Annina: Kelly

STATEN ISLAND, NEW YORK

June 16, 1990 (concert performance) [578]
La traviata (Verdi–Piave) [745]
Conducted by Badea
Violetta: Huffstodt
Alfredo: Kraus
Germont: Milnes [35]
Flora: Guzman
Gastone: Forest
Douphol: Hamilton
D'Obigny: Courtney
Grenvil: Vernon
Annina: Kelly

CENTRAL PARK, MANHATTAN, NEW YORK

June 21, 1990 (concert performance) [579]
La traviata (Verdi–Piave) [746]
Conducted by Badea
Violetta: Mims
Alfredo: Kraus
Germont: Milnes [36]
Flora: Bybee
Gastone: Forest
Douphol: Hamilton

D'Obigny: Courtney
Grenvil: Cook
Annina: Kelly

WATERLOO VILLAGE, STANHOPE, NEW JERSEY

June 27, 1990 (concert performance) [580]
La traviata (Verdi–Piave) [748]
Conducted by Badea
Violetta: Mims
Alfredo: Kraus
Germont: Milnes [37]
Flora: Bybee
Gastone: Redmann
Douphol: Hamilton
D'Obigny: Courtney
Grenvil: Cokorinos
Annina: Kelly

PENNSAUKEN, NEW JERSEY

June 30, 1990, concert performance [581]
La traviata (Verdi–Piave) [749]
Conducted by Badea
Violetta: Mims
Alfredo: Kraus
Germont: Milnes [38]
Flora: Bybee
Gastone: Forest
Douphol: Hamilton
D'Obigny: Courtney
Grenvil: Cokorinos
Annina: Kelly

1990–91
METROPOLITAN OPERA HOUSE

December 8, 1990 [582]
Andrea Chénier (Giordano–Illica; new production) [143]
Conducted by Rudel
Chénier: Martinucci
Maddalena: Millo
Gerard: Milnes [2]
Bersi: Kesling
Countess di Coigny: Castle
Abbe: Fitch

Fleville: Sokol
Incroyable: Velis
Roucher: Schexnayder
Mathieu: Capecchi
Madelon: Johnson
Dumas: Wells
Fouquier Tinville: Courtney
Directed by Mansouri, Melano
Set design by Skalicki
Costume design by Greenwood
Lighting design by Wechsler
Choreography by Levy
[This production was borrowed from its co-owners, the San Francisco Opera and the Houston Grand Opera.]

December 11, 1990 [583]
Andrea Chénier (Giordano–Illica) [144]
Conducted by Rudel
Chénier: Martinucci
Maddalena: Millo
Gerard: Milnes [3]
Bersi: Kesling
Countess di Coigny: Castle
Abbe: Fitch
Fleville: Sokol
Incroyable: Velis
Roucher: Schexnayder
Mathieu: Capecchi
Madelon: Johnson
Dumas: Wells
Fouquier Tinville: Courtney
[Millo canceled after act 2 and was replaced by Stefka Evstatieva.]

December 14, 1990 [584]
Andrea Chénier (Giordano–Illica) [145]
Conducted by Rudel
Chénier: Martinucci
Maddalena: Evstatieva
Gerard: Milnes [4]
Bersi: Kesling
Countess di Coigny: Castle
Abbe: Fitch
Fleville: Sokol
Incroyable: Velis
Roucher: Schexnayder
Mathieu: Capecchi
Madelon: Johnson
Dumas: Wells
Fouquier Tinville: Courtney

December 19, 1990 [585]
Andrea Chénier (Giordano–Illica) [146]
Conducted by Rudel
Chénier: Martinucci
Maddalena: Millo
Gerard: Milnes [5]
Bersi: Kesling
Countess di Coigny: Castle
Abbe: Fitch
Fleville: Sokol
Incroyable: Velis
Roucher: Schexnayder
Mathieu: Capecchi
Madelon: Johnson
Dumas: Wells
Fouquier Tinville: Courtney

December 22, 1990, matinee (broadcast), in celebration of Sherrill Milnes's twenty-fifth anniversary with the company [586]
Andrea Chénier (Giordano–Illica) [147]
Conducted by Rudel
Chénier: Martinucci
Maddalena: Millo
Gerard: Milnes [6]
Bersi: Kesling
Countess di Coigny: Castle
Abbe: Fitch
Fleville: Sokol
Incroyable: Velis
Roucher: Schexnayder
Mathieu: Capecchi
Madelon: Johnson
Dumas: Wells
Fouquier Tinville: Courtney
Presentation by Volpe
[The onstage ceremony honoring Milnes followed act 3.]

December 27, 1990 [587]
Andrea Chénier (Giordano–Illica) [148]
Conducted by Rudel
Chénier: Popov
Maddalena: Millo
Gerard: Milnes [7]
Bersi: Kesling
Countess di Coigny: Castle
Abbe: Fracker
Fleville: Kaston
Incroyable: Laciura
Roucher: Schexnayder

Mathieu: Capecchi
Madelon: Johnson
Dumas: Wells
Fouquier Tinville: Courtney

December 31, 1990 [588]
Andrea Chénier (Giordano–Illica) [149]
Conducted by Rudel
Chénier: Popov
Maddalena: Evstatieva
Gerard: Milnes [8]
Bersi: Kesling
Countess di Coigny: Christin
Abbe: Fracker
Fleville: Kaston
Incroyable: Laciura
Roucher: Schexnayder
Mathieu: Capecchi
Madelon: Johnson
Dumas: Wells
Fouquier Tinville: Courtney

January 3, 1991 [589]
Andrea Chénier (Giordano–Illica) [150]
Conducted by Rudel
Chénier: Bartolini
Maddalena: Guleghina
Gerard: Milnes [9]
Bersi: Kesling
Countess di Coigny: Christin
Abbe: Fracker
Fleville: Kaston
Incroyable: Laciura
Roucher: Schexnayder
Mathieu: Capecchi
Madelon: Johnson
Dumas: Wells
Fouquier Tinville: Zeller

January 7, 1991 [590]
Andrea Chénier (Giordano–Illica) [151]
Conducted by Rudel
Chénier: Bartolini
Maddalena: Guleghina
Gerard: Milnes [10]
Bersi: Bybee
Countess di Coigny: Christin
Abbe: Fracker
Fleville: Kaston
Incroyable: Laciura
Roucher: Schexnayder

Mathieu: Capecchi
Madelon: Amara
Dumas: Wells
Fouquier Tinville: Zeller

1991–92
METROPOLITAN OPERA HOUSE

September 23, 1991 (simulcast), in celebration of the twenty-fifth anniversary of the opening of the Metropolitan Opera House at Lincoln Center for the Performing Arts [591]
Gala Performance
Rigoletto (Verdi–Piave), act 3
Rigoletto: Nucci
Gilda: Studer
Duke: Pavarotti
Directed by Schenk
Staged by Thomas
Designed by Brown
Otello (Verdi–Boito), act 3
Otello: Domingo
Desdemona: Freni
Iago: Díaz
Emilia: Kelly
Cassio: Heilmann
Lodovico: Plishka
Directed by Zeffirelli
Staged by Melano
Set design by Zeffirelli
Costume design by Hall
Die Fledermaus (J. Strauss–Haffner/ Genée), act 2
Rosalinde: Daniels
Gabriel: Prey
Adele: Kilduff
Orlofsky: Otter
Falke: Croft
Frank: Hornik
Guest artists: J. Anderson, Battle, Domingo, Freni, Furlanetto, Hampson, Millo, Milnes, Pavarotti, Ramey, von Stade
Directed by Schenk
Staged by Mills
Set design by Schneider-Siemssen
Costume design by Hall
Conducted by Levine

Lighting design by Wechsler
[This performance was transmitted live over cable television systems as the company's first home pay-per-view presentation. A videotape was first televised over PBS on March 9, 1992, as part of the *Metropolitan Opera Presents* series. The guest artists appearing in the second act of Strauss's opera presented an unbilled gala-concert-within-the-gala as a feature of the festivities at Prince Orlofsky's party
West Side Story (Bernstein), "Maria": Milnes [and many others]

September 25, 1991 [592]
Un ballo in maschera (Verdi–Somma) [210]
Conducted by Fulton
Amelia: Mitchell
Riccardo: Dvorsky
Renato: Milnes [26]
Ulrica: Toczyska
Oscar: Jo
Samuel: Cook
Tom: Vernon
Silvano: Croft
Directed by Faggioni
Staged by Kneuss
Designed by Faggioni
Lighting design by Faggioni

September 28, 1991, matinee [593]
Un ballo in maschera (Verdi–Somma) [211]
Conducted by Fulton
Amelia: Mitchell
Riccardo: Dvorsky
Renato: Milnes [27]
Ulrica: Toczyska
Oscar: Jo
Samuel: Cook
Tom: Vernon
Silvano: Croft

October 10, 1991, benefit sponsored by the Metropolitan Opera Guild [594]
La fanciulla del West (Puccini–Civinini/ Zangarini; new production) [76]
Conducted by Slatkin
Minnie: Daniels

Ramerrez: Domingo
Rance: Milnes [4]
Joe: Forest
Handsome: Vernon
Harry: Fitch
Happy: Short
Sid: Ward
Sonora: Pola
Trin: Anthony
Jim: Josephson
Nick: Laciura
Jake: Cook
Ashby: Robbins
Post Rider: Best
Castro: Hartman
Directed by Del Monaco
Designed by Scott
Lighting design by Wechsler

October 14, 1991 [595]
La fanciulla del West (Puccini–Civinini/ Zangarini) [77]
Conducted by Slatkin
Minnie: Daniels
Ramerrez: Domingo
Rance: Milnes [5]
Joe: Forest
Handsome: Vernon
Harry: Fitch
Happy: Short
Sid: Courtney
Sonora: Pola
Trin: Anthony
Jim: Josephson
Nick: Laciura.
Jake: Cook
Ashby: Robbins
Post Rider: Best
Castro: Hartman

October 18, 1991 [596]
La fanciulla del West (Puccini–Civinini/ Zangarini) [78]
Conducted by Slatkin
Minnie: Daniels
Ramerrez: Domingo
Rance: Milnes [6]
Joe: Forest
Handsome: Vernon
Harry: Fitch

Happy: Short
Sid: Courtney
Sonora: Pola
Trin: Anthony
Jim: Josephson
Nick: Laciura
Jake: Cook
Ashby: Robbins
Post Rider: Best
Castro: Hartman

October 21, 1991 [597]
Un ballo in maschera (Verdi–Somma)
[217]
Conducted by Fulton
Amelia: Voigt
Riccardo: Dvorsky
Renato: Milnes [28]
Ulrica: Toczyska
Oscar: Jo
Samuel: Cook
Tom: Vernon
Silvano: Croft

October 23, 1991 [598]
La fanciulla del West (Puccini–Civinini/
Zangarini) [79]
Conducted by Slatkin
Minnie: Daniels
Ramerrez: Domingo
Rance: Milnes [7]
Joe: Forest
Handsome: Vernon
Harry: Fitch
Happy: Short
Sid: Courtney
Sonora: Pola
Trin: Anthony
Jim: Josephson
Nick: Laciura
Jake: Cook
Ashby: Robbins
Post Rider: Best
Castro: Hartman

October 26, 1991, matinee [599]
La fanciulla del West (Puccini–Civinini/
Zangarini) [80]
Conducted by Slatkin
Minnie: Daniels
Ramerrez: Popov

Rance: Milnes [8]
Joe: Forest
Handsome: Vernon
Harry: Fitch
Happy: Short
Sid: Courtney
Sonora: Pola
Trin: Anthony
Jim: Josephson
Nick: Laciura
Jake: Cook
Ashby: Robbins
Post Rider: Best
Castro: Hartman

November 1, 1991 [600]
Un ballo in maschera (Verdi–Somma)
[219]
Conducted by Fulton
Amelia: Mitchell
Riccardo: Ichihara
Renato: Milnes [29]
Ulrica: Toczyska
Oscar: Jo
Samuel: Cook
Tom: Vernon
Silvano: Croft

February 13, 1992 [601]
Un ballo in maschera (Verdi–Somma)
[220]
Conducted by Fulton
Amelia: Mitchell
Riccardo: Ichihara
Renato: Milnes [30]
Ulrica: Quivar
Oscar: Murphy
Samuel: Cook
Tom: Wells
Silvano: Croft

February 18, 1992 [602]
Un ballo in maschera (Verdi–Somma)
[221]
Conducted by Fulton
Amelia: Mitchell
Riccardo: Ichihara
Renato: Milnes [31]
Ulrica: Quivar
Oscar: Murphy
Samuel: Cook

Tom: Wells
Silvano: Croft

February 22, 1992, matinee (broadcast)
[603]
Un ballo in maschera (Verdi–Somma)
[222]
Conducted by Fulton
Amelia: Mitchell
Riccardo: Ichihara
Renato: Milnes [32]
Ulrica: Quivar
Oscar: Murphy
Samuel: Cook
Tom: Wells
Silvano: Croft

April 1, 1992 [604]
La fanciulla del West (Puccini–Civinini/
Zangarini) [82]
Conducted by Slatkin
Minnie: Daniels
Ramerrez: Domingo
Rance: Milnes [9]
Joe: Forest
Handsome: Vernon
Harry: Fitch
Happy: Short
Sid: Courtney
Sonora: Josephson
Trin: Anthony
Jim: Croft
Nick: Laciura
Jake: Yannissis
Ashby: Robbins
Post Rider: Best
Castro: Hartman

April 4, 1992 [605]
La fanciulla del West (Puccini–Civinini/
Zangarini) [83]
Conducted by Slatkin
Minnie: Daniels
Ramerrez: Domingo
Rance: Milnes [10]
Joe: Forest
Handsome: Vernon
Harry: Fitch
Happy: Short
Sid: Courtney
Sonora: Josephson

Trin: Anthony
Jim: Croft
Nick: Laciura
Jake: Yannissis
Ashby: Robbins
Post Rider: Best
Castro: Hartman

April 8, 1992 (simulcast) [606]
La fanciulla del West (Puccini–Civinini/
Zangarini) [85]
Conducted by Slatkin
Minnie: Daniels
Ramerrez: Domingo
Rance: Milnes [11]
Joe: Forest
Handsome: Vernon
Harry: Fitch
Happy: Short
Sid: Courtney
Sonora: Josephson
Trin: Anthony
Jim: Croft
Nick: Laciura
Jake: Yannissis
Ashby: Robbins
Post Rider: Best
Castro: Hartman
[This performance was video for the
Metropolitan Opera series and first tele-
vised over PBS on June 10, 1992.]

April 11, 1992, matinee (broadcast) [607]
La fanciulla del West (Puccini–Civinini/
Zangarini) [86]
Conducted by Slatkin
Minnie: Daniels
Ramerrez: Domingo
Rance: Milnes [12]
Joe: Forest
Handsome: Vernon
Harry: Fitch
Happy: Short
Sid: Courtney
Sonora: Josephson
Trin: Anthony
Jim: Croft
Nick: Laciura
Jake: Yannissis
Ashby: Robbins

Post Rider: Best
Castro: Hartman

April 16, 1992 [608]
La fanciulla del West (Puccini–Civinini/
　Zangarini) [87]
Conducted by Slatkin
Minnie: Daniels
Ramerrez: Popov
Rance: Milnes [13]
Joe: Forest
Handsome: Vernon
Harry: Fitch
Happy: Short
Sid: Courtney
Sonora: Josephson
Trin: Anthony
Jim: Croft
Nick: Laciura
Jake: Yannissis
Ashby: Robbins
Post Rider: Best
Castro: Hartman

1992–93
METROPOLITAN OPERA HOUSE

November 11, 1992 [609]
Tosca (Puccini–Illica/Giacosa) [748]
Conducted by Badea
Tosca: Neblett
Cavaradossi: Ivanov
Scarpia: Milnes [29]
Sacristan: Loup
Spoletta: Anthony
Angelotti: Held
Sciarrone: Short

November 14, 1992 [610]
Tosca (Puccini–Illica/Giacosa) [749]
Conducted by Badea
Tosca: Dimitrova
Cavaradossi: Ivanov
Scarpia: Milnes [30]
Sacristan: Loup
Spoletta: Anthony
Angelotti: Held
Sciarrone: Short

November 17, 1992 [611]
Tosca (Puccini–Illica/Giacosa) [750]
Conducted by Badea
Tosca: Dimitrova
Cavaradossi: Bartolini
Scarpia: Milnes [31]
Sacristan: Loup
Spoletta: Anthony
Angelotti: Held
Sciarrone: Short

November 21, 1992, matinee [612]
Tosca (Puccini–Illica/Giacosa) [751]
Conducted by Badea
Tosca: Dimitrova
Cavaradossi: Bartolini
Scarpia: Milnes [32]
Sacristan: Loup
Spoletta: Anthony
Angelotti: Held
Sciarrone: Short

March 15, 1993 [613]
La fanciulla del West (Puccini–Civinini/
　Zangarini) [94]
Conducted by Badea
Minnie: Neblett
Ramerrez: Martinucci
Rance: Milnes [14]
Joe: Forest
Handsome: Vernon
Harry: Fitch
Happy: Short
Sid: Ward
Sonora: Josephson
Trin: Grossman
Jim: Malis
Nick: Laciura
Jake: Cook
Ashby: Wells
Post Rider: Best
Castro: Hartman

March 19, 1993 [614]
La fanciulla del West (Puccini–Civinini/
　Zangarini) [95]
Conducted by Badea
Minnie: Dimitrova
Ramerrez: Martinucci
Rance: Milnes [15]
Joe: Forest

Handsome: Aceto
Harry: Fitch
Happy: Short
Sid: Courtney
Sonora: Josephson
Trin: Grossman
Jim: Malis
Nick: Laciura
Jake: Cook
Ashby: Wells
Post Rider: Best
Castro: Hartman

March 26, 1993 [615]
La traviata (Verdi–Piave) [777]
Conducted by Domingo
Violetta: Fabbricini
Alfredo: Rosenshein
Germont: Milnes [39]
Flora: Hoffman
Gastone: Fitch
Douphol: Fiorito
D'Obigny: Courtney
Grenvil: Cokorinos
Annina: Shaulis
Giuseppe: Hanriot

March 31, 1993 [616]
La traviata (Verdi–Piave) [778]
Conducted by Domingo
Violetta: Fabbricini
Alfredo: Rosenshein
Germont: Milnes [40]
Flora: Hoffman
Gastone: Fitch
Douphol: Fiorito
D'Obigny: Courtney
Grenvil: Cokorinos
Annina: Shaulis
Giuseppe: Hanriot

April 3, 1993 [617]
La traviata (Verdi–Piave) [779]
Conducted by Domingo
Violetta: Fabbricini
Alfredo: Rosenshein
Germont: Milnes [41]
Flora: Hoffman
Gastone: Fitch
Douphol: Fiorito
D'Obigny: Courtney

Grenvil: Cokorinos
Annina: Shaulis

April 6, 1993 [618]
La traviata (Verdi–Piave) [780]
Conducted by Cristler
Violetta: Fabbricini
Alfredo: Rosenshein
Germont: Milnes [42]
Flora: Hoffman
Gastone: Forest
Douphol: Fiorito
D'Obigny: Courtney
Grenvil: Cokorinos
Annina: Shaulis

April 14, 1993 [619]
La traviata (Verdi–Piave) [781]
Conducted by Domingo
Violetta: Villarroel
Alfredo: Farina
Germont: Milnes [43]
Flora: Bybee
Gastone: Forest
Douphol: Fiorito
D'Obigny: Courtney
Grenvil: Yannissis
Annina: Kelly

April 17, 1993 [620]
La traviata (Verdi–Piave) [782]
Conducted by Domingo
Violetta: Villarroel
Alfredo: Farina
Germont: Milnes [44]
Flora: Bybee
Gastone: Fitch
Douphol: Fiorito
D'Obigny: Courtney
Grenvil: Yannissis
Annina: Kelly

1993–94
METROPOLITAN OPERA HOUSE

September 27, 1993, broadcast in celebration of Plácido Domingo's and Luciano Pavarotti's twenty-fifth anniversaries with the company [621]
Gala Performance

Die Walküre (R. Wagner), act 1
Siegmund: Domingo
Sieglinde: Meier
Hunding: Sotin
Directed by Schenk
Staged by Berkowitz
Set design by Schneider-Siemssen
Costume design by Langenfass
Otello (Verdi–Boito), act 1
Otello: Pavarotti
Desdemona: Esperian
Iago: Milnes
Cassio: Baker
Montano: Josephson
Roderigo: Anthony
Directed by Zeffirelli
Staged by Melano
Set design by Zeffirelli
Costume design by Hall
Il trovatore (Verdi–Cammarano), act 3
Manrico: Domingo, Pavarotti
Leonora: Esperian
di Luna: Chernov
Azucena: Zajick
Ferrando: Plishka
Ruiz: Anthony, Pavarotti
Directed by Melano
Set design by Frigerio
Costume design by Squarciapino
Conducted by Levine
Lighting design by Wechsler
[For act 3 of *Il trovatore*, the role
of Manrico was billed as "To Be
Announced." The part was begun by
Plácido Domingo but after a shuf-
fling of roles was taken up by Luciano
Pavarotti; both tenors joined for the
final note of "Di quella pira."

October 2, 1993, matinee [622]
Tosca (Puccini–Illica/Giacosa) [755]
Conducted by Rudel
Tosca: Guleghina
Cavaradossi: Domingo
Scarpia: Milnes [33]
Sacristan: Loup
Spoletta: Anthony
Angelotti: Perry
Sciarrone: Garvin
Directed by Zeffirelli

Staged by Charruyer
Set design by Zeffirelli
Costume design by Hall
Lighting design by Wechsler

October 6, 1993 [623]
Tosca (Puccini–Illica/Giacosa) [756]
Conducted by Rudel
Tosca: Guleghina
Cavaradossi: Domingo
Scarpia: Milnes [34]
Sacristan: Loup
Spoletta: Anthony
Angelotti: Perry
Sciarrone: Garvin

October 9, 1993, matinee [624]
Tosca (Puccini–Illica/Giacosa) [757]
Conducted by Rudel
Tosca: Guleghina
Cavaradossi: Domingo
Scarpia: Milnes [35]
Sacristan: Loup
Spoletta: Anthony
Angelotti: Perry
Sciarrone: Garvin

October 12, 1993 [625]
Tosca (Puccini–Illica/Giacosa) [758]
Conducted by Rudel
Tosca: Guleghina
Cavaradossi: Ivanov
Scarpia: Milnes [36]
Sacristan: Loup
Spoletta: Anthony
Angelotti: Perry
Sciarrone: Garvin

October 16, 1993 [626]
Tosca (Puccini–Illica/Giacosa) [759]
Conducted by Rudel
Tosca: Guleghina
Cavaradossi: Ivanov
Scarpia: Milnes [37]
Sacristan: Loup
Spoletta: Anthony
Angelotti: Perry
Sciarrone: Garvin

March 3, 1994 [627]
Adriana Lecouvreur (Cilea–Colauti) [60]
Conducted by R. Abbado

Adriana: Freni
Maurizio: Lima
Princess di Bouillon: Toczyska
Michonnet: Milnes [1]
Bouillon: Courtney
Abbe: Fitch
Jouvenot: Gonzales
Dangeville: Shaulis
Poisson: Stevenson
Directed by Merrill
Staged by Koenig
Set design by Parravicini and Cristini
Costume design by Diffen
Lighting design by Wechsler
Choreography by LaFosse

March 7, 1994 [628]
Adriana Lecouvreur (Cilea–Colauti) [61]
Conducted by R. Abbado
Adriana: Freni
Maurizio: Lima
Princess di Bouillon: Toczyska
Michonnet: Milnes [2]
Bouillon: Courtney
Abbe: Fitch
Jouvenot: Gonzales
Dangeville: Shaulis
Poisson: Stevenson

March 11, 1994 [629]
Adriana Lecouvreur (Cilea–Colauti) [62]
Conducted by R. Abbado
Adriana: Freni
Maurizio: Lima
Princess di Bouillon: Toczyska
Michonnet: Milnes [3]
Bouillon: Courtney
Abbe: Fitch
Jouvenot: Gonzales
Dangeville: Shaulis
Poisson: Stevenson

March 14, 1994 [630]
Adriana Lecouvreur (Cilea–Colauti) [63]
Conducted by R. Abbado
Adriana: Freni
Maurizio: Lima
Princess di Bouillon: Toczyska
Michonnet: Milnes [4]
Bouillon: Courtney
Abbe: Fitch

Jouvenot: Gonzales
Dangeville: Shaulis
Poisson: Stevenson

March 19, 1994, matinee (broadcast) [631]
Adriana Lecouvreur (Cilea–Colauti) [64]
Conducted by R. Abbado
Adriana: Freni
Maurizio: Lima
Princess di Bouillon: Toczyska
Michonnet: Milnes [5]
Bouillon: Courtney
Abbe: Fitch
Jouvenot: Gonzales
Dangeville: Shaulis
Poisson: Stevenson

March 26, 1994 [632]
Adriana Lecouvreur (Cilea–Colauti) [66]
Conducted by R. Abbado
Adriana: Freni
Maurizio: Lima
Princess di Bouillon: Toczyska
Michonnet: Milnes [6]
Bouillon: Courtney
Abbe: Anthony
Jouvenot: Gonzales
Dangeville: Shaulis
Poisson: Stevenson

1994–95
METROPOLITAN OPERA HOUSE

October 5, 1994 [633]
Tosca (Puccini–Illica/Giacosa) [771]
Conducted by Levine
Tosca: Vaness
Cavaradossi: Pavarotti
Scarpia: Milnes [38]
Sacristan: Evitts
Spoletta: Anthony
Angelotti: Courtney
Sciarrone: Cokorinos
Directed by Zeffirelli
Staged by Charruyer
Set design by Zeffirelli
Costume design by Hall
Lighting design by Wechsler

October 8, 1994 [634]
Tosca (Puccini–Illica/Giacosa) [772]
Conducted by Levine
Tosca: Vaness
Cavaradossi: Pavarotti
Scarpia: Milnes [39]
Sacristan: Evitts
Spoletta: Anthony
Angelotti: Courtney
Sciarrone: Cokorinos

October 14, 1994 [635]
Tosca (Puccini–Illica/Giacosa) [773]
Conducted by Levine
Tosca: Vaness
Cavaradossi: Pavarotti
Scarpia: Milnes [40]
Sacristan: Evitts
Spoletta: Anthony
Angelotti: Courtney
Sciarrone: Cokorinos

October 18, 1994 [636]
Tosca (Puccini–Illica/Giacosa) [774]
Conducted by Levine
Tosca: Vaness
Cavaradossi: Pavarotti
Scarpia: Milnes [41]
Sacristan: Evitts
Spoletta: Anthony
Angelotti: Courtney
Sciarrone: Cokorinos

October 22, 1994 [637]
Tosca (Puccini–Illica/Giacosa) [775]
Conducted by Levine
Tosca: Vaness
Cavaradossi: Pavarotti
Scarpia: Milnes [42]
Sacristan: Evitts
Spoletta: Anthony
Angelotti: Courtney
Sciarrone: Cokorinos

November 9, 1994 [638]
Cavalleria rusticana (Mascagni–Targioni-
  Tozzetti/Menasci) [610]
Conducted by Badea
Santuzza: Guleghina
Turiddu: Armiliato
Lola: Livengood
Alfio: Noble

Pagliacci (Leoncavallo) [650]
Conducted by Badea
Nedda: Soviero
Canio: Atlantov
Tonio: Milnes [34]
Silvio: Oswald

November 12, 1994, matinee [639]
Cavalleria rusticana (Mascagni–Targioni-
  Tozzetti/Menasci) [611]
Conducted by Badea
Santuzza: Guleghina
Turiddu: Armiliato
Lola: Livengood
Alfio: Pola
Pagliacci (Leoncavallo) [651]
Conducted by Badea
Nedda: Soviero
Canio: Atlantov
Tonio: Milnes [35]
Silvio: Oswald

November 15, 1994 [640]
Cavalleria rusticana (Mascagni–Targioni-
  Tozzetti/Menasci) [612]
Conducted by Badea
Santuzza: Guleghina
Turiddu: Johannsson
Lola: Livengood
Alfio: Pola
Pagliacci (Leoncavallo) [652]
Conducted by Badea
Nedda: Kazarnovskaya
Canio: Atlantov
Tonio: Milnes [36]
Silvio: Oswald

February 7, 1995 [641]
Cavalleria rusticana (Mascagni–Targioni-
  Tozzetti/Menasci) [616]
Conducted by Badea
Santuzza: Guleghina
Turiddu: Johannsson
Lola: White
Alfio: Pola
Pagliacci (Leoncavallo) [656]
Conducted by Badea
Nedda: Geyer
Canio: Barasorda
Tonio: Milnes [37]
Silvio: Croft

February 10, 1995 [642]
Cavalleria rusticana (Mascagni–Targioni-
  Tozzetti/Menasci) [617]
Conducted by Badea
Santuzza: Guleghina
Turiddu: Johannsson
Lola: White
Alfio: Pola
Pagliacci (Leoncavallo) [657]
Conducted by Badea
Nedda: Dessi
Canio: Martinucci
Tonio: Milnes [38]
Silvio: Croft

February 16, 1995 [643]
Cavalleria rusticana (Mascagni–Targioni-
  Tozzetti/Menasci) [618]
Conducted by Badea
Santuzza: Guleghina
Turiddu: Johannsson
Lola: White
Alfio: Pola
Pagliacci (Leoncavallo) [658]
Conducted by Badea
Nedda: Dessi
Canio: Martinucci
Tonio: Milnes [39]
Silvio: Croft

October 31, 1995 [644]
Aida (Verdi–Ghislanzoni) [989]
Conducted by Badea
Aida: Gruber
Radames: Sylvester
Amneris: Dever
Amonasro: Milnes [27]
Ramfis: Lloyd
King: Robbins

November 4, 1995, matinee [645]
Aida (Verdi–Ghislanzoni) [990]
Conducted by Badea
Aida: Rautio
Radames: Sylvester
Amneris: Dever
Amonasro: Milnes [28]
Ramfis: Lloyd
King: Robbins

**April 27, 1996, simulcast in celebration of
James Levine's twenty-fifth anniversary
with the company [646]**
Gala Performance in which Milnes sang:
Andrea Chénier (Giordano–Illica),
  "Nemico della Patria"; conducted by
  Levine
[At the conclusion of the performance,
  invited artists who had not performed
  joined the full company onstage to
  honor James Levine.]

METROPOLITAN OPERA HOUSE

February 17, 1997 [647]
Aida (Verdi–Ghislanzoni) [1002]
Conducted by Fischer
Aida: Sweet
Radames: Sylvester
Amneris: Toczyska
Amonasro: Milnes [29]
Ramfis: Halfvarson
King: Tian
Directed by Frisell
Staged by Hazlehurst
Set design by Quaranta
Costume design by Saligeri
Lighting design by Wechsler
Choreography by Griffin

February 21, 1997 [648]
Aida (Verdi–Ghislanzoni) [1003]
Conducted by Fischer
Aida: Sweet
Radames: Sylvester
Amneris: Toczyska
Amonasro: Milnes [30]
Ramfis: Halfvarson
King: Tian

March 10, 1997 [649]
Aida (Verdi–Ghislanzoni) [1007]
Conducted by Fischer
Aida: Sweet
Radames: Sylvester
Amneris: Zajick
Amonasro: Milnes [31]
Ramfis: Colombara
King: Tian

March 15, 1997 [650]
Aida (Verdi–Ghislanzoni) [1008]
Conducted by Fischer
Aida: Sweet
Radames: Sylvester
Amneris: Zajick
Amonasro: Milnes [32]
Ramfis: Colombara
King: Pape

March 18, 1997 [651]
Aida (Verdi–Ghislanzoni) [1009]
Conducted by Fischer
Aida: Gasteen
Radames: Margison

Amneris: Dever
Amonasro: Milnes [33]
Ramfis: Colombara
King: Pape

March 22, 1997 [652]
Aida (Verdi–Ghislanzoni) [1010]
Conducted by Fischer
Aida: Gasteen
Radames: Margison
Amneris: Zajick
Amonasro: Milnes [34]
Ramfis: Colombara
King: Pape

Index

CPSIA information can be obtained
at www.ICGtesting.com
Printed in the USA
LVOW04s0520300416

486057LV00001B/5/P